Penguin Special S266
Student Power

David Adelstein (21) is a student of sociology at the London School of Economics. He was suspended in February 1967 for his activities as President of the Union, but reinstated after a ten-day student occupation.

Perry Anderson (29) is preparing a thesis on Brazilian politics at Reading University and is editor of *New Left Review*.

Robin Blackburn (28) is assistant lecturer in sociology at the LSE and a member of the editorial committee of *New Left Review*.

Alexander Cockburn (27) has worked for *The Times Literary Supplement* and the *New Statesman*; he is now writing a book on American imperialism in Europe, and is on the editorial committee of *New Left Review*.

Carl Davidson (24) was at Pennsylvania State University and is now a full-time organizer and vice-president of SDS.

Tom Fawthrop (21) tore up his finals papers at Hull University in Summer 1968, then led a student occupation of the university buildings.

Fred Halliday (21) is a student of politics at the School of Oriental and African Studies, London University.

Gareth Stedman Jones (25) is preparing a history thesis at Oxford University and is a member of the *New Left Review* editorial committee.

Tom Nairn (31) lectured in the history of art at Hornsey College until his expulsion in 1968; he is on the editorial committee of *New Left Review*.

Jim Singh-Sandhu (23) is a student at Hornsey and was a member of the sit-in committee during the occupation of Summer 1968.

Linda Tinkham (25) is now a schoolteacher: she was formerly president of the London Institute of Education's Students' Union.

David Triesman (21) studies sociology at Essex University; he was suspended in the summer term of 1968, but reinstated after a student occupation.

David Widgery (20) is a medical student at the Royal Free Hospital and an active student journalist.

Student Power/Problems, Diagnosis, Action

Edited by Alexander Cockburn and
Robin Blackburn

Penguin Books
in association with
New Left Review

Penguin Books Ltd, Harmondsworth, Middlesex, England
Penguin Books Inc., 7110 Ambassador Road, Baltimore,
Maryland 21207, USA
Penguin Books Australia Ltd, Ringwood, Victoria, Australia

First published by Penguin Books 1969
Copyright © New Left Review, 1969

Made and printed in Great Britain by
Hazell Watson & Viney Ltd,
Aylesbury, Bucks
Set in Linotype Plantin

Contents

INTRODUCTION Alexander Cockburn 7

The Gathering Storm
THE MEANING OF THE STUDENT REVOLT Gareth
   Stedman Jones 25

The Condition of Higher Education
ROOTS OF THE BRITISH CRISIS David
   Adelstein 59
LEARNING ONE'S LESSON Linda Tinkham 82
EDUCATION OR EXAMINATION? Tom
   Fawthrop 99
CHAOS IN THE ART COLLEGES Tom Nairn and
   Jim Singh-Sandhu 103

The Failure of Student Institutions
NUS – THE STUDENT'S MUFFLER David
   Widgery 119
THE CIA AND STUDENT POLITICS David
   Triesman 141

The Repressive Culture
A BRIEF GUIDE TO BOURGEOIS IDEOLOGY
   Robin Blackburn 163
COMPONENTS OF THE NATIONAL CULTURE
   Perry Anderson 214

International Experience
STUDENTS OF THE WORLD UNITE Fred
   Halliday 287
CAMPAIGNING ON THE CAMPUS Carl
   Davidson 327

Documents
ON REVOLUTION Herbert Marcuse 367
WHY SOCIOLOGISTS? Nanterre Students 373

Introduction

New Spectres

The emergence of the student movement promises a renewal of revolutionary politics as well as the arrival of a new social force. Student insurgents have rejected established models of political action: they refuse to pin their hopes on the remote manoeuvres of parliamentary assemblies or party conferences. The main student movements are quite aware that their struggle is against the social system as a whole: they refuse to participate in it on its own terms.

In exchange for their political passivity bourgeois democracy offers people ballot papers – every five years. In exchange for this quinquennial 'participation' people surrender control over their everyday existence. The revolutionary student movements have denounced this capitalistic bargain as the graveyard of any hope of transforming society. Their aim is to create an extra-parliamentary opposition which aims to reconquer power from below – power over their everyday life exercised by the people themselves in all the particular institutions which comprise society, as well as in general social control of the economy.

In most of the advanced countries of the capitalist world students have already posed the demand for student power: for control by the students of the organization and content of the education they receive. On the whole this demand has not just taken the form of resolutions or appeals to the authorities. Instead it has been embodied in acts of occupation, during which students elaborate the nature of the counter-institutions they wish to create.

The reaction of the authorities has been notorious. When their attempts at co-optation are rejected, they vigorously deploy the armoury of repression developed for such purposes: special police, para-military units, guard dogs, water cannon, tear gas, shock grenades, etc. The exact balance of force and fraud in each country varies with the strength of the student movement: but nowhere does the mask of repressive tolerance long conceal the true visage of authority, in its determination to defend the authoritarian principle.

Why are the actions of students feared and hated? What is it that has made students act, and what is it that gives a potentially revolutionary character to their actions?

1. Bourgeois Society and the Spectacle

It is now commonplace that the advanced capitalist countries are moving beyond the first stage of industrial mass production. But they are doing this with a property system that remains basically unchanged. This fact furnishes the characteristic contradictions of modern capitalism. The immense productivity of these societies is, for them, their central problem. In economic terms the problem which faces each capitalist society is how to absorb most profitably the surplus productive capacity which the process of capital accumulation throws up without undermining the value of existing capital.*

In political terms the problem is to conceal from the masses the fact that the material preconditions for social liberation already exist. On the one hand, the best energies of modern capitalist societies are devoted to the profitable waste of resources (arms expenditure, advertising, built-in obsolescence, etc.) and on the other, to the distraction of the masses from awareness of the repression of man's historic possibilities which it practises on so vast a scale.

The two prongs of this operation are necessarily complementary. The citizen whose work is robbed of meaning by the capitalist production system is being conditioned for the role of passive consumer and inactive citizen. Of course those who operate this neo-capitalist dreamland know that it has a very precarious existence. Teams of work study engineers, ergonomists, labour relations experts, industrial psychologists and sociologists scurry about, all striving to ensure that the maximum surplus labour is extracted with the minimum of trouble.

* Baran and Sweezy, *Monopoly Capital*, Penguin Books, 1968 and Martin Nicolaus, 'The Unknown Marx', *New Left Review*, March–April 1968.

At the same time similar teams of experts orchestrate the loyalty of the consumer to the goods which the system is prepared to supply him: market researchers, media planners, account executives, copywriters and so forth. The overdeveloped state of the mode of production entails a corresponding change in the mode of consumption.

In the liberal epoch capitalism consisted of a multitude of competing enterprises supplying the individual commodity to the market. In the modern capitalist economy competition is fiercer because it assumes monopolistic and oligopolistic forms, and works itself out on an international scale in the competition of national and international units. In a similar development the isolated, individual commodity is caught up in the general process of the *spectacle* * and of spectacular consumption. Just as monopoly capital fuses together units of production so the spectacle fuses together the items of consumption into a given life style. Traditional bourgeois and proletarian culture is converted into raw material for the fashion industry. Late bourgeois society can offer the underlying population neither security nor adventure. Bourgeois politics with its soporific consensus tries to provide a substitute for the former while the spectacle provides a substitute for the latter. The chronic institutional stagnation of advanced capitalism is veiled by the dizzying succession of spectacles. Britain, the most stagnant capitalist country, has naturally become a centre of spectacular production. Within the electronic space created by the new media the consumer is drenched in the pseudo-dramas and myths of the spectacle: and the ethos and mode of the spectacle penetrates the entire culture. In effect this spectacle supplements the market as the overall regulator of the system. The true source of the value of commodities – namely, human labour – is erased: only the spectacle itself appears to allot values, in the name of fashion.

Our waning imperial system needs its combination of bread and circuses to retain the support of the population. In late capitalist society the fetishized commodity and the spectacle conveniently answer this need. In helping to alleviate the curse of over-production the spectacle brings into existence a motley

* This *ad hoc* term was suggested by Henri Lefebvre in *Critique de la Vie Quotidienne*; however it is still in need of a scientific foundation.

retine of its own: television producers, fashion consultants, show business personalities, gossip columnists, public relations officers, press departments, etc. The very essence of the spectacle is that the spectator should remain passively receptive towards the whole design, however frenzied he is in the pursuit of a particular spectacular myth or fashion. So long as modishness is accepted as a vocation, then energy, even in quite creative ways, can be expended in its service.

How does this rapid evocation of modern capitalism help us to understand the role of higher education in Britain today?

Just as the colonization of Africa and Asia transformed the public schools in the nineteenth century, so the twentieth-century colonization of everyday life requires its appropriate educational institutions. The primary role of higher education is now to train the flood of technicians and manipulators which neo-capitalism and the spectacle demand. An important part of this training is provided simply by the way in which higher education is organized, regardless of the specific content of courses.

Any student who has gone through the mangle of repeated examinations, set text books, accepted authorities and styles of work (classes, lectures, weekly essays, tutorials) has undergone a most formidable conditioning process. The technology or science graduate who enters industry only to discover that everything he has been taught is years out of date thinks that he has learnt nothing. He is wrong. He has been taught to isolate the rationality of his technique and to leave unquestioned the social purposes which that technique serves. This lobotomy is worth time and money to the system and that is why it will pay for the process (education) which performs it – a process, incidentally, diametrically opposite in result to that attributed to it by educational humanists with their reverent obeisances to the 'whole man'. The burgeoning departments of social science, the colleges of art and design, the new universities all help to provide the specific skills which neo-capitalism or the spectacle require. Within this framework the personnel officer can bring to bear his knowledge of micro-social dynamics, the advertising copywriter display his cultured mastery of asyntactic hyperbole.

Before they can perform their allotted tasks the manipulators have to be manipulated. This is a dangerous process. The future manipulator needs to be fairly lucid – even have his own share of subjective cynicism – about how the system operates. The student who might become a political commentator or an industrial relations expert must know a little bit about Marx and the reasons why workers go on strike, qualifications which have not been necessary in the past. Such students must be taught their own role in a particular confidence trick: but not enough to rumble the whole game. Similarly the future fashion designer must be capable of creativity without resenting his subordination to the market and the rules of the spectacle.

2. Student Power

The objective conditions for student revolt exist throughout the institutions of higher education. Everywhere one finds education subordinated to exams, competition and grading: most fields of study are stunted by academic philistinism and hostility towards ideas (especially new ideas); social relations between staff and students are usually infected by paternalism, deference, careerism and, of course, traditional status divisions. However the first students to revolt against such conditions may not necessarily be those who suffer them most acutely. Those students who are required to achieve some insight into the way the system works are likely to be the first to rebel against it. The student of social science is being given the training of a future 'directing' intellectual of the dominant class. He is being taught the techniques of domination which he must first practise willingly *on himself* as a professional preparation for the task of organizing consciousness in the service of capital. The nature of his training also demands that he should be acquainted with some of the major achievements of traditional culture at the same time as he learns the techniques of bourgeois domination.

The system, in this difficult business, has not yet learnt the way of painlessly socializing the new cadres it needs. The lobotomy does not always go well.

Unsurprisingly, those students whose studies invite them to perceive the whole game have been in the van of student revolt. They have begun by rejecting the passivity which the system seeks to impose on them. Direct action – sit-ins, occupations, etc. – is contagious and cumulative among students because it gives them a glimpse of disalienation. During such events the rock-solid structures of the institution seem to dissolve. The mysterious operations of bureaucracy are exposed. Familiar unquestionable routines no longer seem part of the natural order of things. Pretensions of authority seem arrogant and hollow. Before the laughing audience the conjuror has lost his mirrors, his curtain, his false-bottomed hat and his capacious sleeves, and is reduced to simulated jocosity and fervent hopes that the attendants will throw them all out.

Of course if the mass of students are not sustained by a sure knowledge of what they are doing and why, they may be alarmed by their new-found freedom. This is the source of the backlash against student power which has sometimes emerged in the wake of student occupations. Often, of course, it is very difficult for students to have a clear perspective on the uprising in which they have been involved. After weeks, or terms, of mundane political activity in which it had seemed impossible to develop enough momentum for any radical onset, suddenly the situation dramatically alters. The 'revolutionary moment' has arrived. There will not lack those who say it has not arrived, has come too soon – or too late. It arrives under many guises: provocation from the authorities; a vote in the union, which changes the entire situation.

At all events, the militants suddenly find themselves with the initiative, even though the moderates are already agitating for negotiations and concessions; in that sense the backlash already exists. The usual meetings, an hour and a half in length, once a week, term on term, are suddenly contracted into debates that last a day and a night. Under these conditions a term's political work can be done in a day: this is the crucial moment when the waverer, the usually 'apolitical' person, living as he is in a system momentarily transparent, can be shown that system's fundamental premises.

Sometimes the authoritarianism which has been successfully challenged lurks in a covert form, in exaggerated attempts by students to show that they can, once the master has been dislodged, mimic his role themselves. They want to prove their own 'responsibility' as substitute super-egos; their determination to avoid 'undue provocation' to the temporarily absent authorities is constantly made manifest, and with political agitation frowned on, good insurgent energies are wasted on efforts to present an unsullied countenance to the Department of Education or the national press: such manoeuvres represent only the freedom of the lemming, as he goes bounding along with his friends.

But, good or bad, all these impulses are manifestations of the revolution from below, along with the hastily convened action committees; the discussion; the necessity, both in practical and psychological terms to control everything from lectures to telephones, to catering. All the more reason for the militants, in this atmosphere, to keep their heads: total control for a week, or a month, does not equal the capitulation of the enemy. But it does not mean, once the enemy has returned, that control was useless, or that the confrontation of the system on their own ground by students has been a vain thing.

Often both student militants and traditional revolutionaries are blind to the actual charge insurgency contains and what it will react to. The traditional revolutionary, on the one hand, too speedily wishes to witness an uncompromising assault on the capitalist system. He becomes agitated when the struggle, as it develops, seems to be deviating from the well-beaten path of orthodox left politics.

The student radical, on the other hand, perhaps fresh to any kind of militant action, becomes suspicious of any declamations which seem to shove him precipitately into a confrontation with the whole weight of the established order – the capitalist system. Thus his own pugnacity might well become salted with caution. Is he really battling against capitalism – or against the vice-chancellor: are the two synonymous? Where is the link? He is being asked to plunge into an idiom which may be entirely new to him. Or, alternatively, if he is based in a tradition of political activism, he is asking his fellow students to strike out into this unfamiliar terrain.

The consequence may well be a reduction in the force of the student insurrection, since after the initial detonation, which may have caught everyone including the 'revolutionary vanguard' by surprise, the leaders note that the moderates or the apathetic of yesterday are the militants of today and are uncertain of what precisely they may be thinking tomorrow.

In such extremities, when those behind cry 'forward' and those before cry 'back', it is worth remembering that student power, often attacked as a limited and distorting phrase, still means what it says: the power of students to determine the structure and content of their education. Of course the eventual aim is the cementing of a revolutionary bloc with working class forces; but the immediate power of the student lies in his university, his college, where he works as a student.

3. Revolutionary Roles

Any active student movement will concern itself with collective action on its own ground: students can occupy their colleges, they cannot occupy factories. Student power is not primarily a matter of constitutional rights but rather of the students' autonomous capacity for mobilization and struggle. By engaging in struggles with university or college authorities students can make inroads on established power, but these gains will only be lasting where the consciousness of the mass of students has been aroused. In fact student power has only acquired a truly *revolutionary* character where students have rejected the notion that higher education is a world of its own.

The student movements in France, West Germany, Japan and elsewhere have all soon discovered the necessity of breaking the isolation which bourgeois society imposes on students in the form of privilege. These movements have reached out to all the potentially revolutionary forces in society as a whole and in the world as a whole – in particular they have sought real forms of solidarity with the anti-imperialist struggles of the under-developed world and to make real connexions with the anti-capitalist struggles of the working class of their own countries. The former type of solidarity has often provided the initial stimulus for student actions while the latter has usually become an overriding preoccupation after the student revolutionaries have already achieved some success within their own milieu.

In the context of advanced capitalism there is a certain common theme in the struggles of workers and those of students. The great majority of workers' struggles (especially unofficial ones) reflect an urge to wrench control over the factory process from the chosen representatives of capital. Some three-quarters of all strikes do not directly concern demands for wage increases: they are attempts to limit the power of management over such questions as the pace of work, hiring and firing policy, changes in production methods and so on.* Both students and workers are often trying to achieve *power from below*. There are of course great differences in the implications their actions have in a capitalist society. In the long run modern capitalism may need the skills taught to students, but on an everyday basis it is immediately and massively dependent on the exploitation of the working class. However subjectively subversive students may be they cannot by themselves bring the whole social process to a halt, as can the actions of the working class.

Of course there remains a great gap between even the most complete general strike and an actual revolution. Indeed few western revolutionaries have been willing to consider the manifold and cumulative power any revolutionary movement would have to possess if it were really to overthrow an advanced capitalist order. Even in the pre-revolutionary period it will surely be necessary, as Gramsci always maintained, to build a hegemonic movement capable of tapping the energies of all the potentially revolutionary forces in society. The implication of recent student actions is that from them the beginnings of an answer to this problem are emerging. Once the student movement is committed to an alliance with the working class it can begin to explore the specific contribution it can itself make to the general revolutionary cause.

Too many traditional schemas on the Left allot students a purely external role in revolutionary politics – namely that of supplying solidarity to the really revolutionary force. For some the only worth-while confrontation is that between imperialism and the national liberation forces of the Third World. For others the sole revolutionary force is the proletariat of the advanced capitalist countries. As very few students can participate directly

* Tony Topham 'Shop Stewards and Workers Control', *New Left Review*, March–April 1964.

in these conflicts, they are usually asked to cheer on the comba-
tants from the touch-lines. The assumption of such analysis is
that capitalism is riven by one, simple master contradiction
which determines all else, and the revolution is a question of
unlocking its progressive potential.*

Now if the history of this century shows anything it is that
revolutions do not arrive by any such direct route to their
ultimate consummation. The international capitalist order first
broke at its 'weakest link' not in a country where the opposition
between capital and labour was at its purest. Moreover in Russia
itself the revolution was the product of a series of different
contradictions involving peasants, intellectuals and divisions
within the ruling order, as well as the historic actions of the
Russian proletariat. After the experience of the Chinese, Cuban
and Vietnamese revolutions this point should not need labouring.
Just as the liberation movements of the Third World have long
ago decided not to wait for the liberation of their countries as a
consequence of the socialist revolution in the imperial metropolis, so students today refuse to wait for some external deliver-
ance from their condition as victims of the bourgeois education
system and participants in the misery and boredom of the late
capitalist spectacle. Solidarity movements may help a new force to
develop its strength and they will certainly be vital in cementing
a revolutionary alliance but they cannot be its sole form of action.

The student movement must first *be itself* before it can be a
useful ally to anyone. Fortunately the French confrontation of
May 1968 at least made it clear that students acting as an
independent revolutionary force can ignite a much more general
conflagration – thus also disposing of the myth that the modern
working class is irredeemably integrated into contemporary
capitalist society.

4. Revolutionary Culture and the Red Bases

In their own right colleges and universities are clearly important
bastions of power for the bourgeois social order. The older univer-

* Those interested in the theoretical issue raised here should consult
'Contradiction and Overdetermination', Louis Althusser *New Left Review*,
1941.

sities have always been and remain fortresses of wealth and privilege. Other higher educational institutions have the function of providing the secondary elite discussed above.

Both largely exclude the sons and daughters of the working class, so that where class discrimination and sex discrimination combine a working-class girl in Britain has a *six hundred to one* chance against receiving higher education. A significant function of many colleges and universities is to generate the themes of ideology within the social system as a whole. Finally bourgeois power relations are inscribed in the structure of these institutions themselves with their hierarchies, bureaucracies and boards of governors.

Power in a modern capitalist country is not uniquely concentrated in one institution (army or parliament). It is rather embedded in the fabric of all social relations so that every factory, office, church, college, housing estate, hospital, prison, school, trade union or party both partakes of and contributes to the power of the dominant class. Indeed many organizations which were created to advance interests opposed to those of the dominant class have been confiscated from their original function by a social system which specializes in such reversals. The emergent student revolutionaries aim to turn the tables on the system, by using its universities and colleges as base areas from which to undermine other key institutions of the social order. No advanced capitalist state can afford to maintain a permanent police occupation of all colleges or universities, nor can it act like a Latin American military thug and simply close down the universities – which after all are necessary, in the long run, to the productive process. So long as the universities and colleges provide some sort of space which cannot be permanently policed they can become 'red bases' of revolutionary agitation and preparation. The new revolutionaries propose that bourgeois power must be confronted directly – and confronted in all the diverse forms it assumes in the ramified institutional apparatus with which late capitalism protects itself against the perils of popular spontaneity. Actions are engaged which expose the repressive and mystifying structure of the institution in question – expose it above all to the inmates themselves, the alienated and the administered, the exploited and the oppressed. This strategy presupposes a sustained and continuing work of political and theoretical self-formation by the revolutionary militant. If the militant cannot himself produce the concepts and analytic framework with which to interpret his experience then he will succumb to the 'common sense' of our society which is inescapably pressed in the mould of bourgeois ideology.

This is especially true in Britain with its relative weakness of native revolutionary traditions. In fact all the great revolutions have been preceded by cultural renovation with far-reaching revolutionary implications. The French Enlightenment, the Chinese Renaissance of the May 4 Movement and the explosion of Russian revolutionary culture in the nineteenth and early twentieth century were all indispensable preparations for the momentous historic events which were to follow. It is worth while noting the richness and sweep of the cultural premonitions of socialist revolution in Russia as the question of revolution in the advanced capitalist democracies is scarcely likely to be less demanding. In their various ways Belinsky and Herzen, Chernyshevsky and Dobrolyubov, Gogol and Saltikov-Schedrin, Bakunin and Kropotkin, Tolstoy and Dostoyevsky, Chekhov and Gorky, Tugan-Baranovsky and Plekhanov, Lunacharsky and Riazanov, together with a host of others too numerous to mention, all contributed to the cultural background of the Russian revolutionary. In China, the astonishing works of Mao Tse Tung – philosopher and general, poet and statesman – bear witness to the flowering of the May 4 Movement which preceded it, and which has justly been called the Chinese Renaissance. Among Western Marxists, Gramsci always insisted that the revolutionary movement must acquire 'civil hegemony' *before* the seizure of power: he emphasized that revolutionary practice must be wedded to a thorough critique of established ideologies.*

The first wave of the student movement was marked by a tendency to reject not just ruling ideology but the need for revolutionary theory as such. The perils of such self-denial are that student revolutionaries risk being absorbed on its own terms by the spectacle, as just one more pseudo-conflict. Students

* For an excellent introduction to Gramsci's thought see 'The Marxism of Antonio Gramsci' by John Merrington in *Socialist Register: 1968* edited by Ralph Miliband and John Saville.

inescapably play some part in the social production and reproduction of ideology: for student revolutionaries to be unarmed theoretically can ultimately only mean political defeat. There are now definite signs that the student movements do wish to create a revolutionary theory and culture adequate to the prodigious task they have set themselves.*

In Britain the fledgling student movement is confronted with a heavy heritage of traditional British philistinism and reformism, the national hostility to ideas and fetishism of the practical. It will be necessary to reclaim the genuinely critical and iconoclastic intelligences of Harrington and Hobbes, Mandeville and Gibbon, Hazlitt and Byron, Blake and Shelley, Morris and Wilde – to rewrite the history of English culture, which has been thoroughly confiscated and obscured by reactionary or bienpensant commentary. However a sober recovery and revaluation of the past must be complemented by a revolutionary critique of the culture of the dominant class. As yet there is little written by British left-wing writers which has the polemical force of Dmitri Mirsky's *The Intelligentsia of Great Britain* or Leon Trotsky's *Where is Britain Going?*.

The development of a genuinely revolutionary force in Britain would necessarily entail a thorough-going *internationalization* of political culture on the Left. A narrow 'national' approach to revolutionary politics which disdains the major revolutionary thought and experience of our epoch is less than ever viable when the international character of capitalism is more than ever an economic and political reality. Students have special responsibilities in this task of developing a revolutionary culture as the guarantor of revolutionary practice. Indeed in every country where the student movement itself has developed one now finds a common interest in studying the experience of past revolutions (and counter-revolutions) combined with a lively discussion of such writers as Georg Lukacs, Antonio Gramsci, Herbert Marcuse, Louis Althusser and Jean-Paul Sartre.

* Here are just a few such 'signs': 'Where are we Heading?' by Greg Calvert and Carol Nieman; 'Where the Revolution Is At' by Jack Smith; both in the *Guardian* (USA), May/June 1968; Martin Nicolaus 'The Contradiction of Advanced Capitalist Society and its Resolution', Radical Education Project, USA 1968: Rudi Dutschke 'Intervista', *Quaderni Piacentini*, 1968: Vittorio Rieser *Problemi del Socialismo* 26/7.

In different ways the essays in this book explore the issues we have raised above. Gareth Stedman Jones analyses the meaning of the student revolt in historical and sociological terms. He outlines the major demands put forward by student movements and confronts the objections put to them. Finally he offers a general political perspective on future strategy.

The lack of control by students of the educational process they undergo is documented by the contributors to Part Two of the book. Linda Tinkham vividly evokes the authoritarianism which has remained almost unchallenged so far in the teacher training colleges. Tom Fawthrop argues that the examination system is the major means whereby colleges and universities maintain the power of staff and administration over students – in doing so they systematically violate the educational aims they profess. David Widgery and David Triesman recount the ways in which the students' own representative organizations are used to keep them in a state of passivity: a mock liberalism thinly concealing reactionary bureaucratic manipulation and international subscription to the Cold War. Tom Nairn and Jim Singh-Sandhu examine the widespread resistance in the Art Colleges to the clumsy attempt to force art and design education into the accepted examination mould. David Adelstein argues that the contradictory forces of imposed modernization and a recalcitrant traditionalism could create conditions in which British students are provoked into a mass awareness of the necessity for student action.

Robin Blackburn attacks the inherently conservative assumptions of the brand of social science usually inculcated in British universities and colleges. Perry Anderson suggests that the evident bankruptcy of the major British intellectual traditions makes it particularly vulnerable to a revolutionary critique.

The British student movement has already gained some impetus from international example. Fred Halliday reviews the experience of student struggle in Latin America, Japan, China, Spain, Italy, West Germany and France; in a key concluding section he points up the lessons to be drawn from this record.

No survey of student insurgency would be complete without acknowledgement to the students of the United States, confronting from within the most powerful imperialism in the world. Carl Davidson's article is much more than a record of experience. As an organizer for the SDS he provides a critical reflection on that experience whose tactical and strategic insights no British militant can afford to ignore.

ALEXANDER COCKBURN

New Left Review
7 Carlisle St
London, W. 1

The Gathering Storm

The Meaning of the Student Revolt/
Gareth Stedman Jones

The emergence of militant student movements has been one of the most dramatic and novel social phenomena of the present decade throughout the world. From Berlin to Peking, from Tokyo to New York, in Paris and in Prague, the rise of these movements has altered the nature of politics – even in countries like West Germany and the USA where the Cold War had almost obliterated all politics. Virtually every government has some reason to fear its students. With good reason. From Cuba in 1958 to Czechoslovakia and France in 1968 students have played a crucial role in political change, again and again helping to discredit, transform or topple governments. Students were traditionally considered in the West to be an elite group comfortably closeted in an academic playpen on the borderland of the real world. It is not often that an illusion has been so completely shattered. Students have erupted into the world of politics with a suddenness no one could have foretold. They are today a new social force of incalculable significance.

Students have now made their impact in every part of the world – Asia, Africa, Latin America, Europe and the USA. However, it is noticeable that they have played their most striking role in the advanced industrial countries, whether capitalist or socialist. What is the meaning of their revolt? Can it be comprehended within the framework of classical social theory? A concrete historical understanding of their own movement is a priority for student militants today. What is the sociological character of a student movement? What have been the causes of the great international upsurge of the last few years? There are two main theories today which claim to provide an explanation of the nature of students and their unrest. They are diametrically opposed, and it will be well to start by considering them.

Students as the New Proletariat

A number of writers in the USA, France and Germany have advanced the thesis that universities and colleges today are no longer primarily concerned with the transmission of a cultural heritage, but are fast becoming a central element of the 'forces of production' in both the advanced capitalist countries and the USSR. These 'post-industrial societies' are said to be dominated either by vast impersonal private organisations, or else by over-whelming state apparatuses. The French sociologist Alain Touraine argues that,

If it is true that knowledge and technical progress are the motors of the new society, as the accumulation of capital was the motor of the preceding (industrial) society, does not the university then occupy the same place as the great capitalist enterprise formerly did? Thus, is not student movement, in principle at least, of the same importance as the labour movement of the past? [1]

Touraine goes on to make a historical parallel. He compares the first 'primitive' mass actions of students with the reaction of the traditional poor in the nineteenth century to the first devastating impact of industrialization. In both cases, the birth pangs of a new mode of production are accompanied by millenarianism, utopianism, spontaneous and uncontrolled explosions and the proliferation of sects. Changing the comparison somewhat, leaders like Savio in Berkeley or Dutschke in Berlin are seen to be more akin to Brazilian 'messiahs' than to the methodical leaders of the organized trade union movement of today.

For this interpretation, the peculiar features of the student revolt – the contradictory mixtures of apathy and fiery insurgence, of utopianism and the conservative defence of vested interests – consequently bear great resemblance to the social characteristics of the working class in the first phase of industrialization. In both cases the aim of the radical movements is 'expressive' rather than 'instrumental'. But this confusion in no way diminishes its significance. Looked at superficially,

the agitation of socialist or communist sects during the July Monarchy were merely doctrinaire, reactionary or marginal responses to the grand sweep of industrialization. Yet they were the beginning

1. Numbers refer to notes at the end of the chapter.

of an active critique of that society – the acknowledgement of capitalist domination and the formation of the labour movement.[2]

Student activism in advanced industrial countries may similarly presage a qualitatively new form of social conflict engendered by a new form of social domination. For student movements are not simply pressure groups designed to secure the advancement of their sectional interests within an accepted *status quo*. They have identified themselves with the heroic image of Che Guevara; they have everywhere formed movements of solidarity with the National Liberation Front of South Vietnam; and they have put in question the whole accepted framework of advanced industrial society. Therefore, far from being an ephemeral phenomenon, student radicalism may be a new social movement at the core of the new forces of production. It follows that the idea of the university as a community of teachers and taught is now as illusory as the philosophy of the Guild system in the first stages of the industrial revolution. Students and teachers must acknowledge their separate interests and establish new institutions based, not upon the idea of community, but inherent and permanent conflict – just as capital and labour are in structural conflict in the factory.

This interpretation may initially seem to have certain merits. It appears to be an attempt to grapple with the magnitude of student radicalism as a phenomenon, and to provide a comprehensive theory of it. Nevertheless, there is no doubt that its basic thesis is scientifically incorrect and politically reactionary. For the whole argument depends upon the unspoken assumption of some form of 'managerial revolution'. It uses the concept of bourgeois sociology, with the latter's bland synthesis of capitalist and socialist modes of production into 'mass society' or 'industrialism'. In fact there is no evidence to support the notion that the motor of bourgeois society has changed from the 'accumulation of capital' to 'knowledge and technical progress'. Nor is it true to assert that the focal point of decision has shifted from the factory to the university.

The falsity of the thesis is evident in any concrete analysis of the social groups involved. The emergence of industrial capitalism depended on the existence of two groups – a capitalist class and a propertyless proletariat forced to sell its labour power.

The new model seems to imply a managerial technocratic class, permeating university teaching staff and the state, and a student body forced into 'alienated' forms of intellectual production by the exigencies of technical progress. This model involves two major confusions. Firstly, students, unlike workers, do not constitute a class. The situation of the working class is a permanent one – it is a life situation. On the other hand, one of the most important social characteristics of students is that their situation is always transient. Furthermore, their social destination is either into professional groups or else into the managerial, technocratic class itself. It is no accident that those groups of students closest to the forces of production in Touraine's sense – applied scientists and engineers – are usually among the least militant of students.

The second basic error of this model lies in the profound differences of political and economic power enjoyed by the entrepreneur in the nineteenth century and the university staff of the twentieth. In one case, power over factory production was translated into political and economic power over the institutions of the State. In the other, power to make political and economic decisions is dictated from outside the university by the State apparatus which reflects the power of the dominant class – not university professors but the owners of capital.

The political upheavals within the university in the last years are not the product of an imaginary substitution of workers by students. For as Louis Althusser has shown, although the determinant contradiction of a capitalist society in the last instance is always between capital and labour, it is still possible that the dominant contradiction at any given moment of time will lie elsewhere.[3] To maintain, therefore, that the most explosive contradiction of advanced capitalism may at certain specific historical moments reside in the university, by no means entails dismissing the industrial proletariat as the revolutionary class alone capable of overthrowing contemporary capitalism. The encroachment of the scientific and military needs of neo-capitalism upon a largely unreformed system of higher education does not necessitate the invention of a new mode of production to explain it. Nor is it inconsistent that this development should engender a crisis, through the formation of a qualitatively new subaltern group whose needs and aspirations are in contradiction to the dictates of the economy. It is correct to emphasize the spontaneity, inconsistency and millenarianism of many student movements up till now. But this is not surprising since the situation confronted by fhe students is unprecedented. Students and teachers are both being forced into a new form of conflict, in which there are no pre-established rules: responses to this situation are often quite naturally instructured and utopian. There is no need to make an artificial comparison with the nineteenth-century working class to understand this. If students have, for the present, become perhaps the most obvious focus of subversion in the West, it is not because they have stepped into the shoes of an obsolete proletariat.

Students as Traditional Middle Class

The opposing view of the nature and role of students today is that which is officially espoused by bureaucratic orthodoxy in the East, and which lingers on among sectarian currents of the socialist movement of the West. According to this interpretation, students are a traditional elite group, overwhelmingly bourgeois or petit-bourgeois by recruitment and outlook, and therefore ultimately a trivial or reactionary force. In the West, all specifically student militancy becomes a diversion from the true struggle, which is located on the factory floor. The best that can be hoped for is that a minority of radical students might provide manpower for industrial picket lines. Any separate student strategy or movement would merely reflect its petit-bourgeois provenance; socialist students should therefore by and large forget their student status. In the East, the consequences of this doctrine have been much more serious. Its crude counterposition of workers against students was used by Novotny in Czechoslovakia and Gomulka in Poland to suppress democratic demands by students which had fundamental importance for society as a whole. Its reactionary character became evident and it was repudiated by the very workers who had been demagogically set against the students. Such ouvrierism – the belief that the traditional working class has a monopoly of socialist potential – is a mystification wherever it manifests itself. The fact is that students today, whether in the West or the East, are not to be identified with either the capitalist or the working class. They are a *distinct social group*, which has produced distinct forms of struggle. Obstinate persistence in the increasingly unreal and misleading belief that they are merely adolescent members of the ruling class is a nostalgic self-deception. Socialists must make the effort to produce the new theoretical concepts with which to comprehend the contemporary student movement. This demands a genuine respect for its autonomy, and a rejection of all pseudo-explanations which merely reduce it to either a bourgeois or a proletarian basis. Both the two theses discussed here rely on a unilateral economic determinism in order to define students as a group, neglecting their much more complex position within industrial social structures and their politico-cultural systems. Any adequate theory of the student revolt must do justice to this complexity.

Student Revolt: The Overdetermined Contradiction

A scientific explanation of the international student revolt must account for the specific *concatenation* of causes that have combined to produce it. There is no one master explanation of this phenomenon. On the contrary, mass student insurgency is *par excellence* an 'overdetermined' phenomenon. Three major forces have been at work. Together they have produced the contemporary structure of the student movement.

The Sociological Growth of Intellectual Labour

The first and most fundamental fact is that all advanced industrial societies have an imperative need for large numbers of highly trained professional and technical cadres. Industry, government, communications and education now have a rapidly expanding demand for intellectually skilled manpower. The rapid rate of technical and scientific advance in the last two decades has created for the first time in history the beginnings of mass intellectual labour.

This phenomenon has been analysed by Marxists above all as

an index of the tremendous growth in the forces of production that the expansion of capital, despite itself, produces. Ernest Mandel has recently written that:

What the student revolt represents on a much broader and social and historic scale is the colossal transformation of the productive forces which Marx foresaw in his *Grundrisse*: the reintegration of intellectual labour into productive labour, men's intellectual capacities becoming the prime productive force in society.[4]

André Glucksmann has spoken of the volcanic May events in France as a 'revolt of the ensemble of productive forces against the relations of production'.[5] These formulations contain an important moment of truth, but a scientific analysis of the development of intellectual labour in advanced capitalism must be a dialectical one. For, in effect, while this development genuinely represents *a growth of the forces of* production, it also represents *a new involution of the relations of production* of advanced capitalism. This is immediately apparent once the concrete social destiny of students today is considered.

A large number of students are trained for skilled scientific work in industry and technology. Their labour immediately increases social wealth and yields a surplus: it is productive in the classic sense. But, side by side with these traditional engineers, monopoly capitalism needs a new elite of social engineers. A vast wave of market researchers, media planners, entertainment specialists, fashion designers and advertising copywriters has emerged. These are the technicians of *consumption* who form the indispensable complement of the technicians of *production*. For the fundamental contradiction of capitalism remains the disposal of the surplus value which it extracts from its workers: the new middle-elite of mediators, designers and persuaders perform the vital function of ensuring that consumption assumes the forms and dimensions which are necessary for the system – and no others. Their task is to ensure the obedience and conformity of the masses in the supermarket and the living-room as well as the workplace. A third category of intellectual labour is that of the technicians of *consent*. A crucial section of the new social engineers – journalists, editors, television personalities, filmmakers, personnel managers and so on – are concerned, not with strictly economic tasks, but with the political and cultural in-doctrination of the population with the values of the capitalist 'consensus'. The rising educational standards of the working class and the increasingly blatant irrationality of the economic system (its gargantuan waste of resources and its imperialist pathology) make a massive and Byzantine network of mystifica-tion and manipulation an essential condition of contemporary capitalism. Many students will eventually find themselves in these stifling careers, with all the demoralized consciousness that accompanies them. Finally, the university itself, of course, is a crucial mechanism in the maintenance of capitalist relations of production, by its generation and transmission of an academic culture which is profoundly conformist and conservative, func-tioning as the highest and most sophisticated legitimation of the social *status quo*.[6] It is no accident that from the Kennedy Administration onwards, university professors have been co-opted *en masse* into the entourages of professional politicians in the United States. They represent, however, only the summit of a pyramid of collusion.

It is thus incorrect to emphasize the role of higher education within the forces of production, without equally emphasizing its role within the relations of production of capitalist society. It is this dual role which has combined to create the mushroom growth of the student population all over the Western world. The country where this phenomenon is most evident, of course, is the USA – with its four million students, who compose 30 per cent of their age-group of the population. The eventual destina-tions of these students differ widely, as has been seen. But during their training, they are everywhere subjected to the same process of stultification, which constitutes the general institutional framework of the revolt within universities and colleges.

These students are formally trained to develop a creative and critical intelligence: their future occupations often demand specialized and skilled verbal or conceptual performances. But at the same time, the universities and colleges where they study impose deadeningly conformist syllabuses and systematically segregated departments of knowledge. These apprentice intel-lectual workers are thus riven by a constant contradiction: they must be alert and intelligent within their narrowly defined discipline, and yet be numbed and inert outside it. They must not apply the intelligence they are being urged to develop, either to the institutions where they are studying or to the society which produces them. André Gorz has aptly defined their situation.

Monopoly capital dreams of a particular kind of specialized technician, identifiable by the coexistence in one and the same person of zest for his job and indifference to its purpose, professional enterprise and social submission, power and responsibility over technical questions and irresponsibility over questions of economic and social management.[7]

Higher education is the functional system designed to produce this new social category: an 'intelligentsia' without ideas. Students are its trainees. They are massed together in increasingly large and bureaucratized institutions, where they often experience with unprecedented intensity the contradictory demands made upon them by capitalist society.

They are exhorted to think for themselves, yet their colleges are authoritarian complexes run by a small clique of professors, bureaucrats and lay governors (typically an elderly collection of businessmen, retired politicians and military functionaries). The official liberal ideology goes on claiming that the student should acquire knowledge for its own sake, even while the relentless pressure of examinations reminds him that it is the instrumental marks that count. The examination will label him with a quantified assessment of his success in absorbing the accepted syllabus of his subject. The canons of traditional 'humane' education were that the object of higher education was to form the 'whole man'. This was not completely misleading. The total personality of the student, not merely his aptitudes, may be moulded at university. Hence it has often been argued by student militants that the student is engaged in 'producing himself', not some external object. But the student has virtually no control over this process: courses, rules and results are determined by others. Thus, students often experience the educational system as an immediate 'alienation' of themselves – the high incidence of nervous collapses is partly the consequence of this. The meaningful choice before the student will only concern the precise degree of self-subordination he is prepared to undergo in the interests of self-advancement. The student of the 'humanities' is liable to become aware of these contradictions more easily than the student of the natural sciences, since the clash of the former with dominant utilitarian standards is more evident. But the scientist and technologist are also trained to develop a demanding intellectual discipline and yet never examine its social implications. University expansion has doubled and trebled the size of student populations in all advanced countries in the last ten years. Mass higher education means that fewer students will achieve elite positions, and so one important consolation for the suffocated student no longer obtains. The prospect of becoming a helot intellectual is not an inviting one.

How, then, should students today be defined? Any characterization of students as a social group must simultaneously encompass student *origins*, the student *situation* itself, and the social *destination* of students. It is the unilateral insistence upon any one of these factors to the exclusion of the others that has resulted in lopsided or reductionist theories of student consciousness. The complexity of the social destination of students has already been outlined: some will constitute productive labour yielding surplus value; others will constitute unproductive labour and be financed out of the surplus. Plainly, therefore, any interpretation of students as an apprentice intellectual proletariat is much too simplistic.

On the other hand, those who dismiss students as a petit bourgeois group, concentrate almost exclusively upon student origins. It is of course true that the vast majority of the student population (75 per cent or more in Britain) do come from non-working-class backgrounds. But this in no way provides an exclusive definition of students as a social group. Students cannot be simply conflated with other petit-bourgeois strata – peasants or small traders for instance. For the role of a student is not an occupation in the normal sense. Nor can it simply be defined as an apprenticeship to an occupation, since the ultimate occupation is ambiguous and often unknown even to the student himself. It is the very transience of the student situation and the uncertainty of destination which makes students irreducible either to their origins or their destinations.

It is not therefore surprising, as even casual observation reveals, that the particular sub-culture created by students, their spending habits, sexual mores, political activity and cultural values, are those neither of the petit-bourgeoisie nor of the proletariat.

A sociological analysis must provide a systematic account of the origin, situation and destination of students. These three 'moments' are not, however, of interchangeable weight or significance. They form a complex whole, *dominated* by one structure – the student situation. The present here predominates over past or future. This has important strategic consequences for any student movement. From a political perspective, it is neither origin nor destination, but the student situation itself which has overriding priority.[8]

For there is a permanent contradiction within the universities and colleges of advanced capitalist countries today. On the one hand, these societies have an absolute functional need of a mass of intellectual workers. On the other, they cannot tolerate the realization of the critical potential of this mass. Large numbers of alert and culturally equipped individuals grouped together will, in the long run, inevitably become rebellious against a society founded on unreason and repression. (In the socialist countries, intellectuals have shown a persistent tendency to take socialist democracy seriously where it has been suppressed by political bureaucracies.) Isolated, these same individuals are absorbable. When they take up jobs in civil life, they are dispersed throughout the social structure and quite assimilable there – although even then, a minority of them have often tended to become oppositional members of society. But this period of training is the one time in their life when they are assembled together, and so have a chance of developing a *collective* consciousness. Naturally, this produces a wide and deep revolt against the oppressive complex that dominates culture, politics, and economy alike. Critical reason, once multiplied in a large collectivity and made its *raison d'être*, necessarily becomes explosive. The student revolt is an international product of this explosion. Students are not a class, but a temporary occupation: they are apprentice intellectual workers who no sooner become conscious of themselves as a community than they tend to be dispersed – and hence neutralized. But in the brief interlude of their training, they form a compact group which has shown a tremendous political elan in country after country.

The Political Reversal of Values

Such, then, is the basic sociological cause of the student revolt. But what is the explanation of its *forms*? For there is nothing more striking about the international student upsurge than its spontaneous adoption of revolutionary methods, unsanctified by parliamentarist rules or formalistic conventions. Over and over again, students in revolt have used or invented new, radical forms of protest: collective jousts with the police (Japan), public trials of professors (Italy), mock funerals (Germany), sit-ins (USA) or collection of arms (Venezuela). What are the reasons for this untrammelled radicalism, which has so shocked their elders? The answer must be sought in the political context of recent world history. For as future intellectual workers, students provide a particularly sensitive register of changes in the nature of international politics. The initial experiences of a generation are always an indispensable guide to its later consciousness. In the twenties, British students from Oxford and Cambridge were strike breakers against the working-class movement. Later, the threat of Fascism and the Depression in the thirties radicalized a significant number of students even in these same ruling-class bastions. From 1947 onwards, Western students were on the whole apolitical or reactionary in most capitalist countries (though working-class struggles in France and Italy did win some student support).

The Cold War was the decisive political experience of a whole decade of students. It formed their vision of the world, and of the possible means and limits of changing it. The conflict between the USA and the USSR was posed by both sides as a competition between equals. The two blocs were presented as rival social systems backed by equivalent military and industrial might. In fact, the rivals were never equal, and the Soviet Union – a much poorer society with a much more backward social structure – never had the economic resources to make a genuine political challenge to the West. The Eastern camp did not represent a socialist alternative to advanced capitalism, but rather to the backward capitalism of what is today often called the 'Third World'.

The affluent and advanced West was never deeply challenged from within by this social model. Russia was manifestly authoritarian and violent, whereas Western capitalist societies had in most cases a long bourgeois–democratic tradition. But politically, violence and bureaucracy was pitted, without historical mediations, against the bland parliamentarism of the West, in a world where socialism was an encircled enclave within the world imperialist economy. This was the meaning and genesis of the Cold War.[9]

The sombre and threatening aspects Russia assumed for the population of the West produced massive anti-Communism. At the same time, the tremendous fear of thermonuclear war between the two blocs traumatized a whole generation. In this dual situation, even progressive reaction in the West was often to press for peace and negotiation. The generation which grew up then naturally tended to associate violence and radicalism only with international war or 'totalitarian' oppression. It became psychologically addicted to compromise and legality at all costs. It is no accident that students remained passive in the West during the Cold War.

In the 1960s, however, the whole structure of international conflict changed. The classic Cold War between the USA and the USSR was amortized in the era of 'peaceful coexistence'. The storm-centre of international affairs shifted dramatically. The new conflict was between Euro-American imperialism and the poor and coloured peoples of Asia, Africa and Latin America, struggling for national liberation against their metropolitan oppressors. The USA emerged unmistakably in the role of brutalized world gendarme. The new conflict was no longer a competition between false equals, which threatened the world with a nuclear war. It was a struggle between manifestly *unequal* forces – starving and exploited peasants and workers in the underdeveloped world and imperialist military machines. The heroic struggles of the Algerians against France, the Adenis against Britain and the Cubans and Vietnamese against the United States was not a struggle between rival social systems of equivalent power. It could not become a substitute for internal politics in the imperialist homelands. On the contrary, in the United States, the incredible war of national liberation waged by the Vietnamese inspired a black revolt at home, and fostered a new Left within a country where the hysteria of the Cold War had previously smothered all radical politics.

This Left now discovered the truth of its own society. The liberal, 'pluralist' democracy which had been so celebrated by patriotic apologists during the Cold War now revealed itself as the military juggernaut responsible for untold death and destruction in Vietnam. At home, its parliamentary institutions became seen as a screen for manipulation and oppression – its formal freedoms as themselves an instrument for deadening popular consciousness and dissent. 'Repressive tolerance', in Marcuse's words, was the key to the political structure which had stifled all unrest within late capitalism.[10] Thus, for the student generation of the 1960s, it suddenly became clear that violence could have a liberating purpose. Abroad, the ruthless and indiscriminate violence of imperialism – the saturation bombing of B 52s over Vietnam – could only be defeated by popular violence – the people's war. This produced the phenomenon of the extraordinary prestige of Che Guevara and Ho Chi Minh in campuses all over the world. At home, there was a wave of strikes, sit-ins and riots: expressions of a conviction that such forms of protest obliged the authoritarian institutions of advanced capitalism to reveal themselves for what they were, and so to show the true nature of 'repressive tolerance'. The tolerance was exposed as counterfeit; the repression as its truth, when the police invaded the campus at Columbia and occupied Oakland with armoured cars. These students have learnt that it is only through uninhibited struggle that a genuinely free and democratic society – not an authoritarian system posing as one – can be achieved, and coercion truly abolished.

The Cultural Acceleration of Generational Gap

The third decisive cause of world-wide student unrest is the growing gap between generations, triggered off by the tremendous acceleration of scientific and technical change. Intellectual and cultural advance is now in many subjects so rapid that communication between age-groups separated by decades is becoming as difficult as it previously was between epochs. In the last twenty or thirty years, our basic notions of time and space have been revolutionized. The limits of the planet have been transcended. Electronic computers have multiplied the speed of thought-processes a thousand times over. Language laboratories have made possible mass polyglot mastery. Television and teaching machines have transformed the mechanisms of assimilation of all knowledge. The techniques of instructing such a traditional subject as mathematics have been so revolutionized that parents may not be able to follow the lessons learnt by primary school children. The McLuhanite universe is predominantly that of the very young, for whom live transmissions of colour television from Australia will soon be a matter of course. Meanwhile, the concepts, images and symbols of culture have undergone ceaseless, ever quicker transformations. New sciences and disciplines have sprung up, reforming and overthrowing conceptions of man and nature. Today, the parents of a Western student will often have only the haziest ideas of the subjects their child may be taught at universities. Their very names will often mean little to them: semiology, econometrics, psycholinguistics, systems analysis, cryo-physics, topology, information theory or – in Britain – even sociology. Scientific progress finds an inevitable – if uneven – correlation in intellectual and moral changes. The sexual revolution so much bruited about by the media is largely a product of them; for a technical advance such as the pill is both a concomitant and a condition of a new sexual ethic.

This intense, multi-dimensional cultural explosion means that each new generation travels through a different mental universe *en route* to adulthood; and the gap between its cultural shell and that of its predecessors is constantly widening. Such gaps have always existed in the past and have acted as indirect reflections – natural focal points – of much deeper social contradictions that have little to do with age. Today, the faster history moves, the wider the gap becomes and the deeper the socio-political fissures it may reveal. The implosion of communications and their insatiable quest for novelty are radically unmaking and remaking the culture of the advanced capitalist countries. Heracleitus's famous observation that a man cannot step into the same river twice, is more than ever true of this swift torrent. The sociological and political bases of the student revolt are thus complemented and intensified by a cultural base, inherent in the scientific advances of the past two decades.

Britain

The three structural causes – sociological, political and cultural – of the student revolt have been examined in their international context. They form a global complex, which recurs in virtually every important industrial nation today. However, the specific strength of each, and the form it takes, varies greatly from country to country. It is now necessary to consider the particular situation of Britain. Each of the three motive forces of the international student upsurge is visible here, but each has been modified and inflected by national characteristics.

In the first case, there have been important structural changes in the British university system since 1954. The most fundamental of these, of course, has been a rapid increase in the number of students engaged in higher education. Before the Second World War, this number never rose above 70,000. But the pace of expansion began to increase after the war, and by 1954–5, the number had risen to 122,000. This, however, was still insignificant beside the acceleration of expansion in the late 1950s and the 1960s. By 1962–3 the numbers had vaulted to 216,000. Only three years later (1965–6) the number had gone above 300,000, and, according to the annual report of the Ministry of Education for 1966, all targets for student numbers in the Robbins Report had been surpassed.

These dramatic increases can only be seen in their proper perspective when set in counterpoint to a consistently low level of government expenditure on education, which has resulted in a decisive worsening of the material conditions of student existence. Successive governments, while sanctioning university expansion, have not been prepared to allocate proportionate increases in expenditure. The result has been a growing ratio of students to teachers and the physical overcrowding of students in university and college buildings. At the London School of Economics, for instance, a library built to accommodate 900 students is now supposed to house 3,500. The unwillingness of governments to raise student grants in proportion to rises in prices has been equally aggravating. The difference is supposed to be met by parents, but there is no legal means of forcing them to do so. Nor has it ever been made clear whether student grants are intended simply for the term time or for the whole year; thus many parents claim to have fulfilled their obligations simply by providing room and keep for students in vacations. The result is that students who wish to avoid financial blackmail by their parents, even those paid the maximum grant, are often reduced to genuine poverty. Many students live on £6 a week, of which £3 goes on rent. These are no 'pampered products of the welfare state'.

The rise in the number of students reflects a profound change in their social situation. Before the Second World War, students engaged in higher education only constituted 2.7 per cent of their age-group. By 1967, this proportion had risen to 11 per cent. Students in Britain are still a minority group, but their social destination has shifted. The university no longer provides immediate membership of an elite professional class. Now, a much larger and less exclusive sample achieves degree qualification. The pre-war university pre-eminently prepared its members for law, medicine, church or civil service. In the modern university or college the predominant goals of students are divided between industry, teaching and further academic research. This changing social function of higher education has been reflected in the introduction of new subjects – in particular social sciences, which encourage the student to understand and participate in the apparatus of social control needed by contemporary capitalist society. In Britain, as elsewhere, it is often these students who most militantly reject the roles offered to them.

Britain thus has shared the general sociological precondition for the rise of a student movement. But a number of important qualifications must be made. The expansion of higher education in Britain has been rapid by comparison with past performance: but it has been considerably slower than in most other industrial countries. Thus, although there has been a substantial increase in the number of students, there has been nothing like the same process of massification that has occurred in the USA or Japan. There is no Berkeley in England, and there is unlikely to be anything similar, at least in the next ten years. Touraine is able to compare Nanterre to the company towns of the industrial revolution. But such an evocation hardly applies to Sussex or Keele.

This situation has reflected itself in the whole British conception of the student, which is very different from anything found abroad. Traditionally, there have been two complementary images of the student in England. The first, reserved for a small privileged minority, was that of the 'undergraduate' – a debased version of the renaissance polymath, a gentleman taught by gentlemen, freed from prejudice by the tranquil ceremonies of Socratic debate. Comfortably housed, well fed, sometimes even waited on by feudal retainers, the undergraduates developed little or no corporate consciousness. The liberal philosophy of academic freedom and the non-vocational university united both teachers and taught in an abstract and unfettered quest for wisdom. The university was a community of gentlemen well versed in the arts of civilization. This was the ideal of Oxford and Cambridge. Later, provincial universities were often a shabby but sedulous imitation of it.

But the undergraduate was only a small proportion of the student population. The vast majority of students – in art and technical schools, training colleges and institutions – enjoyed neither the privileges, the prestige nor the educational advantages of a liberal education. Neglected or ignored, deprived of social identity, they were condemned to the bleak waste land of a cheap and grindingly utilitarian higher education. The unalloyed input /output model of utilitarian education was concealed by blazers, communal drinking, debating clubs and a predominant atmosphere of philistinism. Linda Tinkham gives a vivid account of the feminine version of these institutions – a college of education. This stultifying apartheid of liberal and utilitarian higher education was strikingly successful in preventing the emergence of any collective student consciousness. The very notion of the 'student' is a recent one in England, where it was for long obscured by the myth of the 'undergraduate'. Student unions meant no more than clubs for nursery training in the skills of parliamentary repartee (locally), or cheap passes to foreign museums and youth hostels in southern Europe (nationally). David Widgery and David Triesman examine different aspects of this retrograde institutional syndrome.

This peculiar national backwardness has buffered the explosive impact of the recent expansion of higher education. Britain is still some considerable distance from the development of a mass student revolt. A central reason for this has been the prior historical absence of any revolutionary culture in Britain. To be truly explosive, the temporary concentration of young intellectual workers needs a vital and creative anti-culture to oppose the otherwise suffocating weight of official academic orthodoxy. In France, Italy, Germany and Japan students can gain this necessary sustenance from a powerful tradition of critical and penetrating Marxist thought. In the United States, a lively populist tradition, whatever its intellectual shortcomings, has provided much of the necessary tinder to set alight the student revolt. In Britain the situation is different. Far from challenging the reactionary values embodied in the university, British intellectuals (or what passes for them) have traditionally shared these beliefs and done their utmost to foster conformity to them. Just as the student is presented with an institutional division between non-vocational humanism versus utilitarian technocracy, so he finds the same sterile couplet incarnate in British thought. The absence of any native revolutionary intellectual tradition has thus been an important brake on the emergence of a militant student movement.

The same traditional liberal stasis largely accounts for the comparatively lethargic reaction of British youth to the dramatic transformation of international political conflict in the sixties. Probably the most striking British reaction to international events after the Second World War was the Campaign for Nuclear Disarmament. This at times achieved an impressive degree of militancy and attracted very large numbers to it. Nevertheless, it remained as it had begun, an expression of the liberal tradition of British political culture, more comparable to the Campaign against the Boer War than to the SDS in Berlin or the Provos in Amsterdam. It encapsulated the hallmarks of radical liberalism – great idealism, intellectual confusion, and a virtual absence of strategy or tactics. True to its ancestry, it relied upon the appeal to men of good will, and praised the enlightened role of such statesmen as President Tito. Its attitude to the Cold War was often reminiscent of Harold Wilson's treatment of Clause Four – it tended to deny the reality of ideological conflict. Such an attitude, however justified it might have appeared in the fifties, left British students perilously unprepared to comprehend the changed political circumstances of the 1960s. They were consequently slower to become aware of the omnipresent brutality of American imperialism, and of the need to fight against it.

A second legacy of CND was an incomprehension of the necessity of violence in certain political circumstances. CND was inspired by the non-violent dissent of Gandhi; it thereby mistook a tactic for a principle. Such tremendously effective campaigns as that launched by the SDS against the Springer Press in Germany, were completely outside the orbit of its conceptions. In France, Germany and the USA, identification with the example of the Vietnamese and Cubans resulted in an early awareness that in certain situations the use of non-violence is tantamount to political passivity. This has been reflected in the increasingly militant nature of student demonstrations in many parts of the advanced world – itself a reaction to the unremitting violence of US imperialism. The heritage of CND undoubtedly retarded such developments in Britain. Recent events, however, have shown that Britain is not immune to the logic of international politics. British students have begun to become aware that CND protests are only likely to be smothered by the 'repressive tolerance' of advanced capitalism. The Grosvenor Square demonstrations have marked the opening of a new phase in British student politics.

The sociological and political forces behind the international student revolt have thus been somewhat filtered and delayed in Britain – although they are now evidently gaining impetus. By contrast, the third main force which has transformed the situation of students in the advanced countries – accelerated generational gap – has played a major and positive role. There has been no great intellectual progress in the last decade in Britain; quite the contrary – stagnation and regression have evidently prevailed. Nor has the technological impact of the new electronic media – the theme of McLuhan's preoccupations – been particularly marked; US or Canadian standards are still some distance away. What has, on the other hand, occurred is a moral and aesthetic upheaval which has transformed the life-styles of youth. Its most prominent characteristics have been the sudden creative liberation of popular music, the diversification of dress, the switch from literary to visual awareness and the decisive rejection of all that was traditionally associated with British sexual puritanism. It is the young working class which has led this transformation – a change which naturally shocked their parents whose life experience was shaped by the exigencies of the Depression, the hardships of the Second World War, and the post-war austerity. Students – who were from predominantly middle-class homes – never formed the vanguard of this movement, but increasing numbers of them have begun to participate in it. This is reflected in the substantial gains in sexual freedom of recent years. This phenomenon has affected the militant student as much as, if not more than, other sections of the student population. The old imprisonment of radical politics within a puritan sexual code can now end. The forces of the neo-capitalist spectacle have, of course, made every effort to confiscate this cultural effervescence among youth.

There is no doubt that the recent changes in mores has forced apart generations in a way that creates the preconditions for an upsurge of properly political radicalism.

Until 1967, British higher education was silently undergoing these changes. Apparently, nothing was moving within it. Students performed their traditional roles uncomplainingly. Then, in 1967, mass demonstrations against the raising of overseas student fees and the explosion at the LSE suddenly signalled the beginnings of change. For the first time, British students showed collective solidarity in their role as students. These events marked the first occasion in Britain when students used their corporate strength against the arbitrary power of the academic staff and the State. The British student belatedly became part of the international movement of militant student action. Throughout the months since, unrest and insurgency have erupted in numerous campuses.

Nevertheless, in comparison with events in the USA, Germany or Japan, the revolt of British students has been limited. In some vital respects, the student movement is still just beginning. It is impossible to predict what its future course will be, and it would be wrong to try and determine it in advance. But it is now clear that any authentic student movement will have to take up a position on five fundamental problems which affect the life of all students.

1. Students and Citizens

The demand that students should enjoy the same legal rights as any other citizens is a preliminary and rudimentary right. No other section of the adult population is subject to a special extra-legal moral code. There is no reason why students should be an exception. They should be responsible for their conduct like anyone else – before the civil courts only. This right involves the complete destruction of the *in loco parentis* system, in all its aspects. It means the total abolition of all special university disciplinary powers over the private lives and conduct of students. Student organizations should have the same freedom to raise and dispose of funds as any other public body.

2. Students and the State

The relationship between students and the State forms the second natural focus for any militant student movement. At present, the standard of living of the whole student population is under attack by the Wilson regime. Grants have been frozen, with the result that the standard of living of students has dropped by 15 per cent in the last five years. It is now proposed in official government circles to sap even this reduced level by introducing loans which would penalize the student's most difficult years of post-college existence. Any genuine student movement will obviously demand a proper and legitimate increase in the size of grants and fight all talk of loans. It will also insist on a fourth year of education at those colleges and universities where this does not now exist, and a substantial increase in the funds available for research students.

Finally, and most fundamentally, it will demand complete *democratization* of access to higher education — abolishing the present discrimination against children from working-class homes. This demand should make it clear that students are not neglecting the much worse material conditions of other sectors of the population, in fighting for improvements in higher education. No militant student movement would suggest for a moment that it was less privileged than the working class; such an idea would be absurd. But university oppression is not cancelled out by industrial exploitation. Resistance by students to the Government's economic policies can become a part of the general resistance to the Government's freezing of wages and cutting of social services. Students are not a luxury in an advanced capitalist country — as we have argued above, these societies now need the services of a large and rapidly growing intellectual labour force, whose skills can only be attained through a complex higher education system. Students are not parasites on the taxpayer; they have become an economic necessity. Contrary to popular belief, the student is forced to make himself work hard. Those who point to the absence of direct punitive sanctions on student idleness forget that capitalist society itself effectively punishes the unsuccessful student by publicly labelling him as such in his degree result: hence the student maxim that from the point of view of employment a bad degree is worse than no degree at all.

A democratization programme for higher education would naturally include the complete abolition of discrimination between the sexes which, as Linda Tinkham shows, is a major feature of the present system. Discrimination against women takes two forms: firstly, at the point of entry there are quite simply many fewer places for women (at Oxbridge there is an eight to one ratio between men and women); secondly, women's institutions within the higher educational system are invariably subject to special rules. Numerical inequality and restrictive interference with women students' lives inevitably distorts the relations between the sexes within the student community, as well as denying most girls (especially working-class girls) the chance of higher education.

3. Students and Staff

There are four, and only four, groups that have a functional role in the institutions of higher education: teachers, researchers, students and technical staff. Elementary democracy demands that there should be complete *social equality* between them. The hierarchy of different facilities and rights, with its cortege of segregated buildings and privileges which exists today, has no justification. All those who work in higher education should share the same plant. The relationship between the four functional groups in higher education is not, however, a naturally harmonious one. It is spontaneously and inherently *conflictual*. Not, as some have suggested, because students are in some manner 'workers' and professors are 'bosses'. Such an analogy is dangerously misleading, and implies a quite false political model of the university. The true point is that there will be an inevitable conflict of interests between these groups over such issues as the allocation of teaching, forms of instruction, hours of work (lectures, seminars, tutorials, use of teaching aids and classes), and finally the use of university and college funds and facilities. Such struggle will not necessarily take an ideological form. There is, for instance, a quite natural polarity between the teacher who is anxious to devote as much of his time as possible to research, and the student who wants to ensure that he will get adequate instruction for the courses that he is pursuing. The search for a lost community of scholars and students, like all myths of a golden past, is doomed. Students must, however, beware of legalistic schemes for 'a share' of university or college government. This is what the Americans denounce as 'co-optation'. Manipulative talk of partial student 'participation' in university or college government must be firmly rejected as a bid to dupe students – as discreet forms of suffocation. Carl Davidson provides an admirable sketch of the correct demands that should be made here. The crucial point is that student power will never be essentially a matter of formal rights or constitutions – *it will be the concrete capacity for mass mobilization of the student movement. It is their capacity for mass struggle which will make students a decisive force on or off campus*, that staff and administration will be obliged to reckon with, whether they like it or not. It is the balance of forces, not the institutional charter, that counts. When such power from below has been built, the student movement can decide on the forms democratic control of higher education should take – learning from the considerable international experience available (particularly ample in Latin America where *cogobierno* has been successfully operated in a number of countries). The strategic priority, however, is to build a mass movement – the basis of all student power in practice.

4. Students and Courses

Fourthly, students must demand democratic control over the content of education. This means conflict with teaching staff over course patterns, reading lists, syllabuses and above all methods of assessment. In the United States and South America students have been able to win control over a number of staff appointments. It should be remembered that the power of the staff derives not so much from any direct authority vested in them by the institution as from their possession of a particular type of knowledge – namely the knowledge necessary to do well in the exams they set and mark. This is one reason why control over content will ultimately be a crucial demand of a student movement. Without it, other educational demands can be turned in safely reformist directions. A primary concern of the combative student on campus must be acquisition of scientific, critical knowledge, uncontaminated by the soporifics of bourgeois ideology. Pitted against this demand is the dominant culture of advanced capitalism, which constantly strives to channel critical intelligence away from the turbulent ocean of reason into safe and specialized rivulets, leading only to the backwaters of academic routine. Control over the means of acquiring uninhibited and synthesizing knowledge will be a focal point of any revolutionary student struggle. It is essential that it be integrated into the British student movement.

These four sectors comprise the essential scope of a specifically student movement within higher education. They provide the terrain on which the realities of student power can be built. It may be useful to consider here the standard objections to the idea of 'student power'. David Adelstein has recently made a powerful reply to these criticisms. He comments that there are three main arguments advanced by reactionary spokesmen of academic establishments.

(1) Students are an ephemeral social group, which has no stable existence. Higher education is merely an interlude through which they will pass to an adult working occupation, which will thereafter be their station in life. The academic staff, by contrast, are the permanent community engaged in higher education, and therefore alone have the right to power of decision within it.

(2) Students are by definition ignorant. They are in higher education to learn what they do not yet know. The staff, by contrast, are by definition those who already possess science and knowledge. They alone are therefore equipped to determine what should be taught, and how it should be taught. Control over courses and content of education is logically the prerogative of the teaching staff.

(3) There must be no confusing talk of democratizing universities and colleges. Parliament is the only possible place for democracy. Cultural institutions are no different from economic organizations in this respect. The only practical way to run a university or a factory is with a firm hierarchical discipline. All such institutions are necessarily autocratic.

These arguments may have seemed plausible in the torpor of the fifties. Today, after the recent upheavals, it is not difficult to counter them. To begin with, the fact that students are transient participants in higher education actually makes their years there *far more* important to them than the same years for any member of the permanent staff. Any given series of years is an indifferent part of the continuing routine of the teaching staff: it is of no special significance to them. But for students, their experience of higher education is an absolutely crucial period in their life. Their whole future careers may be determined there. Not only this: their ideas, attitudes and beliefs – their whole conception of the world – may be decisively formed in this cultural exploration. The students, precisely because higher education is a once-and-for-all and not a routine part of their lives, have a much greater interest in the institutions and its courses than the teaching staff, for whom these vital issues are largely decided. Here it is not the length of time but the depth of involvement in higher education that is the issue. It follows that students have just as much right to power and control in universities and colleges as staff.

The contention that students are debarred from any say in determining the content of courses because of their ignorance is equally dubious. All knowledge is a relative affair. At no specific point does anyone suddenly achieve definitive enlightenment. The assumption of the present system is that the moment a lecturer is appointed, he is admitted to the charmed circle of the knowledgeable. Previously, he was wholly incompetent to make any academic decisions; now he magically becomes able to do so. The division is quite artificial. Everyone knows that some students are often more gifted and imaginative than their often pedestrian instructors. But in any event this is not the main issue. The fact is that the central purpose of higher education is not to instil a predetermined sequence of facts and techniques into the student. This is true not only of the humanities and the social sciences, but of the natural sciences. A doctor will remember very little detail from his student days: what he has learnt is the ability to obtain the fact he needs, when he wants it. The function of higher education is essentially to teach the rules and methods, the principles of a particular discipline. But these are themselves not immutable, given once and for all. The advance of knowledge involves precisely their constant revision and criticism. It is here that relative student 'ignorance' actually has a positive function for higher education. For students are not mentally enclosed within the prevailing intellectual orthodoxy of their disciplines, by years of acceptance and transmission. They have not been so habituated to received notions that they no longer notice them. Their very lack of established knowledge is also dialectically a freedom from convention and dogma. They are thus much more given to question orthodox ideas and doubt standard answers. Such open and critical questioning is an absolute condition of all cultural progress. It is, in fact, essential for the teachers themselves to be challenged in novel and unexpected forms by their students. They only benefit from such stimulation. The learning that occurs in higher education is always and necessarily a two-way process: the teachers learn from the taught, while the taught are learning from the teachers. Academic standards would then not be impaired but promoted by their democratic government. It is no accident that the Cordoba Manifesto ushered in 'the golden age of Argentinian scholarship'.[11]

The claim that democracy is in any case impossible in all institutions other than Parliament is an open confession of the authoritarian nature of modern capitalism. It is not irrelevant that many apologists for the present social system admit that Parliament itself is increasingly devoid of significance. Socialist thought, by contrast, must insist that democracy will only be concrete and authentic when it is extended to all the institutions of society – economic, political and cultural. The revolutionary tradition of workers' councils has embodied this belief in democratic, popular control from below. The movement for 'student power' today is a natural descendant of this lineage. Resistance to it is resistance to the basic principle of democracy – the right of people to govern themselves. This right is only meaningful if it is exercised in the daily activity of each citizen in every place of work. The possibility of voting every five years cannot compensate for the absence of freedom in everyday life. The common demand for participatory democracy in its fullest and most explosive sense provides the possibility for an inner unity in the struggle of students and workers.

5. Students and Society

Lastly, and most crucially of all, what should be the relationship of a revolutionary student movement to society as a whole? Carl Davidson has formulated the correct critique of any idea that students can, on their own, succeed in any total liberation of higher education. The notion of 'socialism in one campus', he points out, 'is an infantile disorder'. Not only this. Students can never become the main social force in any revolutionary bloc capable of overthrowing advanced capitalism. Where they play a vanguard role – under capitalism or socialism – this is an index of the temporarily restricted level of revolutionary development, as Fred Halliday demonstrates. For to succeed, such struggle must mobilize the classical revolutionary class – the proletariat.

When it is temporarily passive or integrated, students may – and if possible should – assume a vanguard role, as 'the petrels of a future general uprising'. But they can never usurp the social class without whose leadership it is impossible to liberate advanced industrial society from the dominion of capital. This means that a student movement must constantly and unflaggingly seek ways of linking itself to the central arena of class struggle, the long effort of the industrial working class to free itself and all others from the exploitation inherent in the private ownership of the means of production. Steadfast support for workers' struggles against capital, whether industrial or political, including all available forms of material assistance, is an imperative for any student movement.

It should at the same time be said that only a student movement which can prove its mettle within the campus will provide a serious contribution outside it. The minimal precondition of genuine participation in revolutionary struggle led by the working class, is the ability to carry the fight into the quiet precincts of higher education. The experience of the last few years has shown the effectiveness of this possibility in the USA, West Germany and France. The presence of a revolutionary student movement would be of much greater value to working-class struggle than the efforts of individual students at the factory gates.

For students have a specific contribution to make to socialist struggles. In Britain, the Labour movement – whatever its organizational allegiances – has traditionally suffered from its lack of socialist theory. Its notorious empiricism, which has so often made it the prisoner of reformist illusions, has partly been the result of the historic absence of revolutionary intellectuals in England – those intellectuals whom Lenin said were essential to bring socialist ideas into the Labour movement. British students today, who are for the first time showing a certain radicalization, could help overcome this long-standing barrier to the emergence of an insurgent working-class movement in England. The converse is equally true, of course: revolutionary ideas will only be born from concrete engagement in mass struggle. Students have another contribution to make here. For material sociological reasons, they are perhaps more spontaneously internationalist in outlook than any other group in the population: they work in institutions with a high proportion of foreigners, they have the time and means to travel, the possibility of learning other languages, and thus the chance to exchange experiences with their counterparts abroad. They are for the same reasons least subject to racism. Recent experience has shown that the internationalism of students – their capacity to respond, swiftly and tumultuously, to struggles in other countries, whether USA, Germany, France or Poland – is a tremendous asset to socialist struggle as a whole. Students were the first to combat the rising tide of racism in England. A student detachment within a wider socialist movement can thus bring to it specific strengths, which are badly needed today.

Of course, these will come to nothing in isolation. The necessary relationships between student militancy and society are well defined by Carl Davidson: 'This transformation, while it *begins* with the demands of the students' and teachers' work situation, cannot take place unless it occurs *within* and is organically connected *to* the practice of a mass radical *political* movement.' The student movement in Britain today will only grow if it constantly and dynamically unites the struggle on the campus to the struggle against capitalist society at large. It will not ultimately succeed in achieving any substantial advances unless it wins its place within a revolutionary bloc much vaster than itself, under the hegemony of the working class. But it can meanwhile use its opportunities to act as a starting-gun for wider social conflict. The slogan of Berlin resounds through Europe: 'Today the Students – Tomorrow the Workers'.

REFERENCES

1. 'Naissance d'un Mouvement Etudiant', Alain Touraine, *Le Monde*, 7 and 8 March 1968. Touraine is a professor of sociology at Nanterre, where the French student revolt which led to the Paris riots of May 1968 began. For a crude version of these themes, see Daniel Bell 'The Post-Industrial Society' *Public Interest* Nos 6 and 7. Bell was a prominent member of the reactionary establishment at Columbia University in New York, where a student strike was repressed with massive police violence in the same month.
2. ibid.

3. 'Contradiction and Overdetermination', *New Left Review* 41, January–February 1967.
4. Ernest Mandel, 'The New Revolutionary Vanguard', *Black Dwarf* no 2.
5. André Glucksmann, *Le Nouvel Observateur*, June 1968.
6. This aspect of the university system raises the complex question as to which of those formed by it should be considered 'intellectuals' in the true meaning of the word. The most important contribution to an understanding of this problem is undoubtedly Antonio Gramsci's distinction between 'organic' and 'traditional' intellectuals – or what might be renamed 'functional' and 'classical' intellectuals. Gramsci pointed out that every social class produces a category of organizers and specialists who possess a certain technical knowledge which answers to a social or economic need of the class. Thus the capitalist class naturally produces its managers, econometricians, market researchers, business consultants and so forth. They are related immediately to the economic structure of society, and indirectly to general culture. By contrast, 'traditional' intellectuals are those scholars, artists and scientists who feel that they form an independent, unified community, with its own standards of judgement and its own historical ancestry. Gramsci says of the latter that they are characterized by a sentiment of 'historical continuity, uninterrupted by even the most radical and complex changes of social and political systems' (*Gli Intellettuali*, p. 5): the apostolic tradition of the Catholic Church was an extreme example. Traditional intellectuals are normally recruited from the ruling groups in society, but their outlook is not necessarily identical with that of the economically dominant class. In certain circumstances, important sections of them may even defect from it altogether (as they did in nineteenth-century Russia or early twentieth-century China). They are immediately involved in general culture, but have a mediate relationship to the economic structure of society. It is evident that the technicians of production, consumption and consent discussed above are 'organic', or functional, intellectuals of today's capitalist class, while university lecturers or professors – at least in the older disciplines – are in England usually 'traditional', or classical, intellectuals. But the line of demarcation is not absolute, and does not coincide with institutional boundaries. Many of the ideologues and apologists of the newer social sciences whom Robin Blackburn examines in his essay are undoubtedly 'organic' intellectuals, while the figures discussed by Perry Anderson in his complementary study are mostly 'traditional' intellectuals. In Britain, the cultural discrepancies are considerable, but there are no major political differences between the two.
   This is not the case, however, in contemporary France or Italy, where the Left has conquered important positions within the 'traditional' intelligentsia. It should be noted that Gramsci always emphasized that a revolutionary movement needed both 'assimilated' traditional intellectuals and the organic intellectuals of the proletariat itself – militants and organizers who embody political leadership within workers' councils, trade unions and the party of the working class.

7. André Gorz, 'Capitalist Relations of Production and the Socially Necessary Labour Force', *International Socialist Journal*, 10 August 1965.

8. In this context, it is important to remember that the theory of Marx and Lenin encompasses both the unique *economic* position of the proletariat in capitalist society – the class whose labour provides the industral core of the system – and the complex *political* alliances which it forges in the course of successful revolutionary struggle. Students and intellectual workers are excluded from the former, but included in the latter. The specific role of revolutionary intellectuals within a socialist movement – the theme of Lenin in *What is to be Done?* – is an important but separate problem. Revolutionary intellectuals will, of course, often come from the ranks of past and present students. The potential contribution of students to a revolutionary culture in England is discussed elsewhere in this volume.

9. Goran Therborn, 'From Petrograd to Saigon', *New Left Review* 48.

10. Herbert Marcuse, 'Repressive Tolerance', in *Critique of Pure Tolerance*, USA 1967.

11. Alaistair Hennessy, *The Politics of Conformity in Latin America*, ed. Claudio Veliz, UK 1967, p. 130.

The Condition of Higher Education

Roots of the British Crisis/David Adelstein

To understand the significance and potential of student action it is essential to examine the nature of higher education through its historical development and in its immediate structure. Higher education only reflects, as do other branches of education, the society within which it functions. Hence conflicts in higher education at the same time mirror wider social conflicts. The prime function of higher education used to be the recruiting and cultural buttressing of the social elite. Nowadays it has an added dimension – the fundamental role it plays in the economy. For skilled manpower is the scarcest resource of a modern capitalist society. It is this fact that collective student action can exploit.

Because of its history, Britain is the last industrial country to begin to technocratize its higher education. This makes the conflict between the older, traditional style of higher education and the new technocratic model more extreme than has been experienced elsewhere. It also engenders particular intellectual characteristics in the various disciplines, making the resolution of the conflict all the more difficult.

Such an abrupt confrontation, with students as its main victims, is bound to provoke student awareness of their situation. In this possibility lies the potential for students to assault all that is rotten in both the old and the new forms of education. For the arousal of student consciousness confronts us with the opportunity of obtaining a more authentic education.

Higher education is divided into three sectors, neatly piled in a prestige pyramid. At the top are the universities and below them the colleges of education and further education (the technical, commercial and art colleges). How did this structure develop, and what are the main features of each sector?

Development of Higher Education

1. The outstanding historical characteristic of higher education is the continual cultural dominance of Oxford and Cambridge from the Middle Ages to the present time.

When change has come to Oxbridge it has taken place slowly, usually well after the stimulus for change. Oxbridge has shown itself always ready to absorb the cream of what is new on the academic scene – so long as it has been new for quite some time and provided it is only the cream. But while open to change, the central ethos has remained the same: to educate the whole man in nothing specific, so that he can do anything specific, better than anybody else. In the seventeenth century, for instance, the scientific revolution was led by Puritanism and Oxbridge experienced a serious cultural challenge in the form of the nonconformist academies. These were set up by dissenters when the Act of Uniformity (1662) excluded them from the universities. They achieved such high standards that non-dissenters often sent their sons to them. These academies offered a more scientific and commercial education than the universities. According to Joseph Priestly, 'the object of education [was] not to form a shining and popular character, but a useful one, this being also the only foundation of real happiness', a remark which shows the already existing tension between the utilitarian, vocational type of education and the non-specialized, general sort. By the end of the eighteenth century, however, the universities were able to do the academies out of business by reforming themselves in order to take in dissenters. By doing so they preserved themselves and prevented any successful assault on their superiority.

Newman, the most influential university thinker of the nineteenth century when the Oxbridge hegemony was firmly socially welded, specified the values of whole-man education. 'Such a community,' he said of the residential university,

will constitute a whole, it will embody a specific idea, it will represent a doctrine, it will administer a code of conduct and it will furnish a principle of thought and action. It will give birth to a living teaching, which in the course of time will take the form of a self-perpetuating tradition as a genius loci, as it is sometimes called, which haunts the house where it has been born, and which imbues and forms more or less one by one, every individual who has been brought under its shadow.[1]

But Newman's thought represented more than an image of the educated man. It stressed the need for authority to mediate between the antagonisms of different disciplines. His liberalism had in fact a profoundly anti-liberal thrust for it sought to deaden any specific intellectual challenge in a welter of spiritual mystique. Furthermore, his view of an all embracing culture, of education as a means of moulding individuals in a particular direction, has proved extensively useful as a model of social control in all levels of education. Such ideas, of course, riddle our education.

2. Although the beginnings of a particularly utilitarian technical education existed by the turn of this century, Britain's technological education was well behind that of other industrialized countries.

At this time full-time higher education comprised the Scottish Universities, London University, the University of Wales and the older civic universities, all, to a greater or lesser extent, under the influence of Oxbridge. Britain as the first country in the world to begin industrializing experienced the most spontaneous, least planned of all industrial revolutions.

Hence industrial skills were taught within the relevant industries. So while continental countries and the USA were developing special colleges to teach new technological subjects, British universities remained singularly aloof from such developments.

Formerly in Europe and the USA the universities were primarily for the training of the top elite in all round education, as they were in the English system. But these countries, in order to compete economically, set up at various stages new, more vocational types of institutions within their systems of higher education. In Germany these were the Technische Hochschulen, in France the Polytechnics, and in the United States such institutions as the Massachusetts Institute of Technology or the California Institute of Technology. These institutions were able to rise to the status of the old universities, providing in contrast a coordinated managerial–vocational and scientific–technological education.

In England, however, the system had, by the end of the nineteenth century, hardly begun to respond to technological change. The mechanics' institutes, which in the 1840s represented the beginnings of a mass, working-class educational movement, had been taken over by the middle class and were moribund by this time.[2] Evening institutes had been established to provide technical education for those with little schooling, but it was only after the turn of the century that courses were extended into the daytime and the institutes developed into technical colleges as we now know them.

The London Polytechnic Movement never constituted a challenge to the structure. Regent Street Polytechnic, founded in 1821 for the purpose of providing a 'rescue operation' for working-class boys, initially taught only a variety of technical subjects. But university subjects soon penetrated the polytechnics after which they assumed a lower-middle-class status within the educational structure.

3. The colleges of education have retained a conservative inferiority complex owing to their religious origins and their geographical and organizational segregation from other institutions of higher education.

Hence the colleges of education are perhaps the most blatantly authoritarian and culturally subordinate of all educational institutions. These colleges were started in the nineteenth century by voluntary, mainly religious bodies, before school education was a public right. Local Education Authorities began taking them over in 1902, but the colleges have never shaken off their church origins. Their rules are often stricter than school rules and they are intellectually the most isolated and muzzled of institutions. New developments in various disciplines often take years to penetrate to the colleges.

This is the basic pattern in which higher education developed up to 1963, the year of the Robbins Report. New layers of universities were added at various times. The younger civic universities of Reading, Nottingham, Southampton, Hull, Exeter and Leicester were founded before and after the First World War.

After 1958 seven new universities were founded: Sussex, East Anglia, York, Kent, Essex, Warwick, and Lancaster. Although often more liberal, scientific and occasionally professional in outlook, they always focused on the central Oxbridge model. Whilst there is an old scientific tradition which transcends present-day limitations, most scientific and technological subjects are taught with a utilitarian and vocational bias, remaining devoid of meaningful intellectual content.

Symptoms of the Crisis

By looking at higher education historically one can begin to see the foundations of the crisis. Highly qualified manpower is now an increasingly essential asset of neo-capitalist society, best attained through the democratization of education plus the operation of a selection process. While the selection process operates very strongly in Britain, democratization resisted at every point by the class structure, is a long way off. A consistent pattern emerges from numerous investigations: A Ministry of Education Report in 1954, the Crowther Report 1959–60, Kelsall on University Application 1957, The Robbins Report 1963, and the Plowden Report 1967 all confirm the deep-seated inequality of opportunity in British education. Epitomizing this situation is the public schools–Oxbridge nexus which retains as its essence an unspecialized, gentlemanly elitism.

There are two very commonly discussed symptoms of this crisis. The most prominent of course is the severe shortage of scientific and technologically trained people. This is not entirely due to inadequate training facilities. It is partly caused by insufficient applicants for these subjects, and partly by the 'brain drain'. Recent estimates suggest that the numbers of qualified engineers required by industry, government and education must increase by 24 per cent every three years. Yet the Dainton Committee, investigating this problem, predicts that in 1971 there will only be 30,000 to 35,000 applicants for such places, compared to 40,000 in 1964. Not only will the rapid increase not be forthcoming – there will actually be a drop. That there are many more places than applicants for degrees in applied science subjects, is a function of the uncritical and anti-intellectual presentation of science and its associate disciplines in most schools and university departments, an approach deeply embedded in the country's tradition. It is a sad paradox that theology is nowadays taught in an enlightened spirit of critical inquiry, while scientific knowledge is leadenly imparted as though it were theological dogma. Students interested in more stimulating study know from their school experience not to apply for science. On the other hand the 'brain drain' affects those in the science side partly through lack of internationally competitive salaries, but mainly because of inadequate research facilities. Because the gap between science and humanities, the 'two cultures' phenomenon, manifest in early schooldays, has its origins in the intellectual and social history of the country, the educational structure at the higher level cannot hope to be altered without a profound shake-up of the entire system.

In addition there is an increasingly critical shortage of teachers. An optimistic figure from the Economist Intelligence Unit estimated that Britain will be short of 36,000 teachers in 1972. Wastage rates amongst teachers are high and the National Union of Teachers has up till now miserably failed to better the salaries and status of teachers. A trained teacher at twenty-one takes home less than £15 a week. When one compounds this with the conditions in colleges of education it is not hard to understand why the country finds it difficult to provide enough teachers. Many students go to training college because they have failed to get into university. Here they are usually isolated from social and cultural centres, and are subject to the most archaic disciplinary rules. No wonder it takes new ideas and teaching methods so long to penetrate the schools. Once again the problem requires not only a complete reallocation of governmental expenditure priorities, in itself an immense political task, but also a revolution in the intellectual climate of teaching education.

This, briefly, is the general situation which has existed in higher education for some time. What 'solutions' have been offered, what are the likely trends and how might students play a part in these affairs? Firstly it is necessary to consider the implications of the Robbins Report, the most significant landmark in the growth of higher education.

The Robbins Report: A Liberal Technocracy?

The Robbins Report with its numerous appendices appeared in October 1963, more than two years after it was commissioned. It is the only major and coherent work on higher education, yet its recommendations have been, in effect, entirely negated. Almost every basic argument contained in the Report has been subsequently discarded by the Government; all that remains is a mass of statistics. Why has this central work been so thoroughly jettisoned?

The Report fully documented the state of full-time higher education, showing how very backward we might soon be in terms of numbers of trained students. It showed the expansion that had taken place in higher education. At the turn of the century 1 per cent of the nineteen-year-old age group attended university (universities were then the only full-time colleges), whereas in 1962 7 per cent of the age group were in full-time education. In sixty years the student numbers had gone up by more than eight times and doubled since the war. On the basis of the numbers likely to be qualified for full-time courses, the committee recommended that the availability of places be drastically increased to avail 558,000 students (17 per cent of the age group) of the opportunity of higher education in 1980–81. These estimates, the committee recognized, were biased on the conservative side and in fact the number of qualified school-leavers has greatly exceeded the Robbins estimates.[3]

The Report did not attempt to reach its recommendations on the basis of the needs of the economy (perhaps because it didn't know how), but based them purely on estimates of the number of qualifying sixth formers – the so-called 'pool of ability'. This is not to say that an economic case was not made for expansion. It was, but only in the general sense that higher education helps the economy and that in order to maintain our place in relation to other countries it was necessary to expand student numbers. In this sense the Robbins Report was 'student oriented' – it catered for apparent student demand. In so far as it based its case on the inherent value of expansion rather than upon economic demands, the Report represents possibly the last 'liberal' document that a government commission will produce for some time. Indeed,

Robbins as an educationalist is very much a liberal heir to Newman. Both favour universities as cosy, intimate communities. Although Newman viewed knowledge as man's most fundamental relationship with God and Robbins views it as man's relationship with man, both conclude that there must exist some overriding 'spirit of universality'.[4, 5] Robbins says that universities 'must emphasise the common element in civilisations rather than the minor variations', that the most important value is the 'transcendence of values'. Thus, despite his 'modernity', the essence of Robbins's concept of a university community is very similar to the aristocratic tradition which Newman extolled: it is the fostering of a common identity that is all important in higher education, i.e., the socializing process. This explains one of the main problems with the Robbins recommendations: their university orientation. One of the deliberate intentions of the committee was to abolish rigid structural differences between the sectors of higher education. It thus recommended that all institutions be given the potential to become universities and that as many as possible form links with existing universities. Expansion of the university sector was to be greater than the other sectors. It posed the university style of education as the ultimate, envisaging technical colleges and training colleges beneath this umbrella. Unfortunately there was a problem here. The further education sector is inextricably tied to large numbers of part-time courses, so, unless part-timers are to be included in the system, a line has to be drawn somewhere. Furthermore, the Robbins committee naïvely assumed the Government would be prepared to pay for its proposals, which would have involved an increase in real costs from £206 million in 1962–3 to £506 million in 1980–1. With a matching naïvety the committee thought that more scientists and technologists could be provided by merely increasing the number of places. The significant decisions are made in school at about the age of fourteen but the school system went unchallenged in this respect, as indeed it was in most others. The Report revealed that 45 per cent of the children of fathers in the higher professional groups enter higher education compared with 4 per cent of the children of skilled manual workers and 2 per cent of the semi- and unskilled workers. Yet, how was this problem to be solved? – the committee had no idea. Finally it might have been argued that a corollary of basing student numbers on student demand should have been a recommendation that the content of courses be determined by student demand. There is, however, no such recommendation in the Report, nor in any of its appendices. In fact the Report ignores the content of education in favour of organizational proposals designed to preserve the buoyancy of the universities.

To summarize: the Robbins Report attempted to direct old liberal notions into a new technocratic programme. It recommended substantial changes in the structure of higher education and indeed in society at large: 'The expansion we recommend will bring with it a very extensive transformation of the social and economic picture.'[6] Such a transformation could hardly occur without at least a vast change in the school system, let alone in the political climate of the country.

The Binary System: Divide and Rule

How has the Labour Government responded to the problems in higher education? The Government's policy was enunciated in a speech by Anthony Crosland, then Secretary of State for Education and Science, at Woolwich polytechnic on the 27 April 1965. In it he outlined what quickly became known as the Binary System, the implications of which involved an absolute reversal of the Robbins philosophy. Where the supreme principle of the Robbins Report was that there should be no rigid distinctions between types of institution in higher education, the Binary System, as its name suggests, involved the segregation of institutions into two completely discrete compartments: the autonomous sector and the public sector. The autonomous sector comprises the universities, including colleges of advanced technology which had become universities by that date, all receiving their finance from the Universities Grants Committee and accountable only to themselves in their spending. The public sector is all the rest: polytechnics, technical colleges, other colleges in further education such as art colleges and colleges of commerce, as well as the colleges of education. These receive their money from the local education authorities and are directly responsible to them in their spending. According to Crosland there would be no more new universities or ascensions to university status for at least ten years. Here is how he justified the policy:

On the one hand we have what has come to be called the autonomous sector, represented by the universities, in whose ranks, of course, I now include the colleges of advanced technology. On the other hand, we have the public sector, represented by the leading technical colleges and colleges of education. The Government accepts this dual system as being fundamentally the right one, with each sector making its own distinctive contribution to the whole ... we prefer the dual system for four basic reasons.

First there is an ever increasing need and demand for vocational, professional and industrially-based courses in higher education. ... This demand cannot be fully met by the universities ... it therefore requires a separate sector with a separate tradition and outlook. ... Secondly, ... if the universities have a 'class' monopoly as degree giving bodies and if every college which achieves high standards moves automatically into the University Club, then the residual public sector becomes a permanent poor relation. ... This must be bad for morale, bad for standards, and productive only of an unhealthy rat-race mentality. Thirdly, it is desirable in itself that a substantial part of the higher education system should be under social control, directly responsible to social needs ... Fourthly ... why should we not aim at ... a vocationally oriented non-university sector which is degree giving and with an appropriate amount of post-graduate work and opportunities for learning comparable with those of the universities, and giving a first-class professional training? Between [these sectors] we want ... mutual understanding and healthy rivalry where their work overlaps.[7]

It is more than unfortunate that such schizophrenic pragmatism is so often duplicated in other Government policies. Nevertheless it is necessary to pull out the single strand of valid argument, an implicit criticism of Robbins, contained in the second point. Under the Robbins proposals the residual public sector undoubtedly assumes the position of 'poor relation'. In fact the Report's structure was not a fully comprehensive one, for whilst it was to be without rigid barriers, the universities would be always more equal than the rest. Hence, after the Report was published, there ensued a scramble for university status amongst the large non-universities, which thereby left all the other colleges out in the cold. Why is it though that the Government opted for the Binary System? For, by so doing, it has used a seemingly progressive criticism of Robbins to introduce in disguise an incredibly backward-looking policy. The Government's real problem is how to encourage a technocratic ethos of sufficient status to rival the university tradition, how to break the old liberal stranglehold of the universities and replace it with a new managerial–technological culture. Yet the Secretary of State consciously devised a policy which has not the slightest hope of doing this. It might have had the glimmering of a chance if the colleges of advanced technology, the only potential spearhead of the new technocracy, had not immediately prior to the announcement of the policy been absorbed (in keeping with tradition) into the universities.

Again, as with Robbins, the sort of social change demanded by the Binary System is not something that occurs merely by the Government's recommending it. Nor is this point understood by the Association of Teachers in Technical Institutions which originally urged a form of Binary system from a slightly more radical position. To the ATTI the universities were the enemy and a Binary system was conceived as a means of isolating them in the hope that they might eventually wither away through social obsolescence. The Association had this to say about its feelings towards universities:

The tradition of following knowledge wherever it beckons, the emphasis upon institutional independence and the unwillingness to allow outside interests to influence the curriculum, all of which are characteristic of the university tradition, are not easily reconciled with professionally oriented courses in which theory and practice are closely interlocked, especially if the courses are to be designed for student members and course contact based upon the employment prospects in the profession concerned.

And it envisaged the public sector as follows:

We see the possibility of a single institution with a rich and varied intellectual life, closely connected with the life of the community and in which the study of the arts and the sciences are closely interwoven. Young people preparing for a profession will have their studies made more real by the presence of experienced practitioners of the profession returning for refresher courses and the experienced practitioners will be stimulated by the idealism of youth. Men and women from different professions will rub shoulders with mutual advantage within a single college and the everyday life of the community will be richer because of the existence in its midst of a college, which, through a varied provision of full- and part-time courses has, in one way or another, made direct contact with citizens in every way of life.[8]

Despite its professional pieties this conception does contain some worth-while ideas: the relationship of the college to the community; the anti-two-cultures position in the combination of arts and sciences; the mixture rather than segregation of part-time, full-time and adult education; the unity of theoretical and practical disciplines. These are all elements of what, I think, ought to be contained in a student viewpoint. (It is interesting to note here that of all the 'staff-side' views the ATTI is the only one to contain any real recognition of potential student contribution. The body has shown itself regularly more pro-student than any other.) But the Binary System as the institutional means to the ATTI's education millennium is doomed from the start, in the same way as is the Government's less concise picture of the future. A structural device cannot, by virtue of being officially decreed, change the present relations. Any contemplated change must take account of the interest groups behind, and the differentials dividing, the two sectors. It is worth looking into these.

There were 184,000 students in forty-three universities in 1967; 202,000 full-time and sandwich course students in over 300 technical and other colleges and 87,000 students in 200 colleges of education. In fact there are about three million students of different sorts in further education. In what sense is there 'healthy rivalry' or 'parity of esteem' between the universities and the rest? An average of £581 is spent per year on a university student's academic facilities compared with £249 for a trainee teacher. The average union fee for universities is £8 per head; in the public sector it is £3.[9] Living accommodation hardly exists for technical college students. The size and location of colleges in the public sector make them both more physically and more intellectually isolated. Staff–student ratios are more equal in universities whilst university staff enjoy greater sums of money for research. In fact a tidy picture of financial privilege emerges.

Oxford and Cambridge, of course, are the most endowed. In St Catherine's College, Oxford, each student has in his room a new chair costing eighty guineas to cushion him against life and student radicalism. The Robbins Report found that 29 per cent of university undergraduates came from manual working families as opposed to 44 per cent of the full-timers in technical colleges of education. The prestige of the universities, the low educational image of technology and the lower status of teaching, ensure that there are many more applicants for university places; those attending a non-university college have often failed to gain admission to a university. To complete the pattern, university graduates have in general higher social destinies than those from non-university colleges.

Underlying the Binary System is the fundamental gulf between theoretical and applied subjects, between the abstract and the practical, such that the one side veers towards dilettantism and the other towards mechanical specialism. This is the profound cultural schism that the Binary System creates and reinforces.

This aspect indicates how the Government is using the Binary System: to provide as cheaply as possible middle- and lower-grade technicians for the economy and teachers for schools. The infusion of thirty polytechnics as academic focal points into the public sector does not change this a bit. The system is such that even Robbins could say

I can sincerely say that nothing has astonished me more than that a Government with an egalitarian background and actively engaged at the school level in an attempt to reduce unnecessary and invidious distinctions, should be energetically supporting, in the field of higher education, a separation which must have exactly the opposite effect.[10]

Robbins is right. The logic of the Government's case is of course the same as the 1944 Education Act which it so strenuously attacked in opposition. Parity of prestige, each section pulling its weight, is as much bunk in the higher education system in 1967 as it was in the lower in 1944. But the Government takes as much notice of Robbins in the Lords as it does of a monkey ranting in a cage. No longer is there any toying with the old policy of assimilation. Instead, educational apartheid is unwaveringly pursued, stratifying, fragmenting, and dividing the student body on all levels: social, economic and intellectual.

Contradictions Within the System

It is now possible to describe more precisely the conflict that exists within higher education. It is basically a conflict, embodied in the Binary System, between social forces, in which neo-capitalist economic demands are pitted against the power structure and culture of existing society. The old education trained the unspecialized person to apply himself, with managerial qualities, to non-standard situations. The new requires the specialist to do the same. But the old education belongs to a previous century whilst the 'new' produces universities and colleges which one critic has called 'battery factories for broiler technicians'.

By isolating the inherent shortcomings in the whole structure and seeing how these problems inflict themselves on student existence, it is possible to define a third and alternative model to the two competing currently. There are three interrelated contradictions affecting students: [11]

1. The contradiction between the economically necessary expenditure to ensure output of trained personnel and the Government's persistent failure to meet its responsibility for this investment.

The economic system requires the Government to limit severely spending on the social services and education. Education, the third largest sector of public spending, cost about £1,936 million in 1967. The Government's meagre projections expect educational expenditure to rise in real terms at about 5 per cent per year. Yet even this rate of growth will be impossible to obtain. For although education is an urgent social and economic investment it is argued that the rate of increase of spending on the social services cannot exceed the rate of growth of the economy (and we all know the latter is not bounding along), a view which implicitly accepts that the alignment of priorities of Government spending is static and unchangeable. Here the Binary System displays its latent utility : to economize – the move to obtain more student places without more money. Expansion of student places is to be concentrated in the public sector which is financed through the local authorities from rates, a source hardly sufficient for an expanding sector of expenditure. And so we find the comparatively extravagant university finance being contrasted against that of the public sector and 'healthy rivalry' resulting in the literal impoverishment of our education.

Education on the cheap hits students in many ways. Facilities, teaching and living accommodation are bad, whilst the size of the institutions increases. All sorts of measures are now presented or discussed to reduce student income. These range from the introduction of loans, or increasing the parental contribution in the means test to the freezing of student grants by withholding the customary compensation for inflation. To foster such policies numerous myths about the irresponsibility of students, living idly off the State and the taxpayer, are publically encouraged. Making the student's financial life harder ties him more to the *status quo*. Hence, in opposing measures to worsen his financial lot the student adopts a position of challenge to the *status quo*. He is forced to argue in terms of socially necessary investment and to think in terms of his social, rather than individual, existence. Hence there develops a student consciousness as a particular type of skilled worker and this must produce a total challenge to the Government's spending priorities and economic policies.

2. The contradiction between the stratifying functions of the educational system and the need to make opportunity really equal.

Educational progress has always been hindered by this conflict. In the nineteenth century the great fear of the reactionaries was that compulsory elementary education would encourage the working class to mistake its social place. This apprehension proved unfounded and it is now gradually being learnt how to practise supposedly egalitarian policies yet maintain fairly rigid social stratification. Comprehensive secondary schooling is meaningless whilst streaming persists and class differentials begin in early primary school.[12]

It is in school that the individualizing competitiveness of the whole education system is instilled in the most obviously authoritarian manner. From school the fittest go on to university or college where the authoritarianism manifests itself less physically and more academically. The prime instrument of this process is the examination system. Its function is to atomize and stratify, to produce with a label so that prospective employers know the value of the product. Yet because the examination system embodies the most invidious element of the system, rejection of it opens up to students a very powerful tactic: the threat of refusing to sit examinations which would jeopardize substantial sections of the economy.

In higher education the specific thrust comes from the inchoate technocratic education challenging the old liberal form for supremacy. The classical tradition, ensconced as it is in the entire social structure, will not easily be budged. But although at present the universities control the intellectual heights, the expansion of higher education makes the foundations more irrational, and thereby gives the further education sector an interest in making its students aware of their own inferior situation. Hence the student demand for a truly comprehensive structure of higher education develops, coupled with an attack on all stratifying procedures.

3. The contradiction between the collective and autonomous nature of productive work and the individualist and authoritarian structure of contemporary education.

This contradiction pervades most work situations. The conflict is particularly active, though, in higher education as it is in this sphere that the technocratic capitalist society demands its greatest changes. Consumer society has one characteristic dimension: that only the products of work should be regarded as gratifying. Work itself must remain only a means to an end. Intellectual work must be motivated by individual careerism. Never can the process of productive work become meaningful in itself for as soon as this happens its structures may be challenged on a different basis. In the France of 1968 it was the students and the young, especially skilled, workers who were in the forefront of the rebellion, their demands being not for better material rewards but for control over their work situations. Furthermore, consumer society requires trained people for the unproductive tasks of promoting consumption which in turn heightens the contradictions.

There are two contradictory pressures increasingly exerted upon students. The examination system requires students to show themselves solely as individuals, but at the same time students and young graduates are more and more frequently being required to work together as teams, although quality of this sort is untrained and untested; collective work involves an appreciation of other disciplines yet interfering in another's subject is strictly frowned upon. Students are expected to examine critically the first principles of their own disciplines whilst remaining entirely impervious to important intellectual questions outside their own spheres. Their minds are required to be pungent and penetrating in one direction and totally blunted in all others. No wonder more students are wishing to study sociology which at least touches on the implications of all other disciplines and attempts a synthesis, than the natural sciences which are so often intellectually one-dimensional.

This inner contradiction permeates our education. The Binary System calls on some students to study abstract, theoretical disciplines and others applied and practical subjects, but the economy demands productivity, which in turn demands the combination of these two extremes. The System categorically segregates them yet simultaneously requires a fusion.

It is in this context that the demand for student power arises. For students cannot question critically and at the same time blindly accept what their educators say. The teachers have a vested interest in preserving the compartments in their disciplines; the students are interested in removing this atomization. The staff are bent on moulding the students to their own image; the students are concerned with deciding for themselves what the crucial questions are and how they should combine to study them. In this conflict, then, is the embryo of the demand for students to participate in, or even control the decisions affecting their academic lives.

The ATTI depicted the universities as 'following knowledge wherever it beckons'. This is misleading. The motivation towards knowledge is not an autonomous process – rather the direction of inquiry is produced by specific conditions of study. The 'ivory-tower' view of universities, especially of Oxbridge, is therefore a misleading one. These so-called ivory tower institutions do in fact produce highly functional and highly ideological knowledge. It is therefore essential that the student position be grounded not in the traditional myth of confined academia, but in social reality. It must not, however, descend into the narrow utilitarianism of the public sector. This would be to stultify the intellectual meaning of education. A critical awareness of the social forces behind the 'knowledge industry' is needed. The response to problems must not be to retreat into self-deceiving isolationism but to challenge the actual social forces creating the problems.

The problem with the present system is not that it mixes the ingredients in the wrong ratios: the theoretical with the applied: the sciences with the humanities: the vocational with the intellectual. The fault is that the intermediate and connecting areas, what C. Wright Mills called 'sensibilities' are lacking. Wright Mills wrote:

Skills and values cannot be so easily separated as the academic search for supposedly neutral skills causes us to assume. And especially not when we speak seriously of liberal education. ... To train someone to operate a lathe or to read and write is pretty much the education of a skill; to evoke from people an understanding of what they really want from their lives or to debate with them Stoic, Christian and humanist ways of living is pretty much a clear-cut education of values. But to assist in the birth among a group of people of those cultural and political and technical sensibilities which would make them members of a genuinely liberal public, this is at once a training in skills and an education in values. It includes a sort of therapy in the ancient sense of clarifying one's knowledge of one's self; it includes the imparting of all those skills of controversy with one's self, which we call thinking; and with others, which we call debate. And the end product of such liberal education of sensibilities is simply the self-educating, self-cultivating man and woman.[13]

Thus what is required is a new education for the whole man;

one which rejects the compartments of the technocratic model and transcends its functional requirements, but at the same time exposes the false sense of independence of the classical tradition and redirects its theoretical heritage, one which does not inflict its values from above but consciously adopts them through independent and critical study, intimately entwined with practical activity.

Such a position is most likely to be properly assumed only by students. The government, we have seen, has its own economic masters. The staff have, to a greater or lesser degree, invested their careers in the *status quo*. Students on the other hand are less career bound and generally less tied to established institutions. Moreover, because the contradictions of the system tend to concentrate on students and because students are undergoing such a formative period in their lives it is highly probable that the most combative force will be the students.

Before passing on to a more detailed consideration of the concept of student power it is necessary to review the response of student institutions on a national level to the problems in higher education outlined above.

Student Power

At its base 'student power' must mean the ability of the students' bloc to inflict, if necessary, sanctions of sufficient economic, social, or political magnitude to force its opinions to be heeded. At a more operative level it implies the participation of students in, or the joint control by students and staff of, the internal authority structure. 'Student power' is a difficult concept to use, linked, as it currently is, to all the other power slogans on the scene. 'Student control' might have been more appropriate but it excludes the defensive aspect of the power concept.

It is necessary to consider initially the way in which national developments affect students in their local environments. Here there are two main factors: the expansion of higher education itself, and the actual direction of the change, i.e., from a traditional–liberal model to a technocratic–managerial one.

The rapid expansion of a higher education automatically brings about a change in the students' view of the process.

Whereas higher education was previously seen as a privilege, it is now taken as a right.

Because the ideology of expansion is based on social need and equality, even though this is not the objective case, students respond as though it were. The ideological 'structure' of expansion inevitably constitutes a determinant of behaviour in its own right. Nor are students' career prospects as secure as before.

This transformation of student attitudes takes place even though students are still, despite the vast expansion in numbers, a relative elite. Previously, as only a tiny element of the national elite, graduates were assured of automatic status and self-enhancement through the possession of a degree, no matter what its quality.

No longer is this the case. A good or a higher degree is now the deciding factor for social status and the possibility of irrational rejection by the system is thus greater. The student who regards his study as a privilege or a means of social mobility is likely to be very passive towards the system, to assiduously learn what he is told, never questioning its validity. In contrast, the student who takes higher education as a right will respond much more assertively. He will demand his 'rights', adopting a generally critical approach to all he is taught or expected to know. Methods of teaching, the content of courses, the entire system of examinations will all be called into question.

The second factor is the direction of the expansion towards a technocratic–managerial society. The old system educated the whole man; the new processes only that part of him which is economically functional. The rest must remain dormant because whole-man education is now too expensive. With this, the cushy surroundings of student life necessarily dwindle and it becomes harder to chloroform students with their former luxury. It is, moreover, no longer possible to control the student's social life as before. In return for the privilege of the old whole-man education the student had to endure strict hierarchical social relationships between himself and the staff. But with social and informal relationships now much more egalitarian, the actual disparities in formal relationships are highlighted, resulting in the student's demand for equality on a formal level as well. By illuminating the actual power differentials between staff and student, and even between staff, the debate focuses upon those who make decisions in the college. Here the students might often encounter the staff as the enemy. For, although there are often contradictions within in the staff's own ranks, especially between the junior and the senior staff, power invariably lies in the hands of the senior staff. Academics are essentially conservative in relation to affairs within in their own institution even though they might be well-known progressive figures externally. Staff interests, in research and teaching require security and stability. Hence student demands sometimes assume menacing proportions in the eyes of the teachers.

Before any demands can be seriously launched, there are a number of prerequisites in the form of student rights. The first is the right of the students' union to be completely self-governing. Very few unions are fully autonomous at the moment but it is obvious that if students do not at least have full control over their own organization the strength of any other control they might have is likely to be gravely weakened. Similarly the rights of free speech, discussion and expression are essential. For if the student voice is to carry any significant weight, it must have absolute freedom to raise whatever matters it wishes. (At LSE not only were students forbidden to discuss a particular matter but they were even forbidden to discuss whether or not they should discuss this matter.) Finally there are disciplinary rights. The old education, aimed at moulding the whole personality, inflicted a complete social range of disciplinary strictures on the student. But students will be prepared to submit to the semi-legality of *in loco parentis* only so long as they feel higher education to be a privilege. The fact is that students ought to come neither above nor below the ordinary law of the land — there is no ounce of justification for academic authorities to have non-academic disciplinary powers.

Undoubtedly basic social changes are needed to make higher education ideal. Yet this must not inhibit students taking action for an improved system. The French National Students' Union declared in its manifesto on the democratization of higher education:

We are not reduced to the absurd dilemma in which we wish to do nothing towards improvement if we can't achieve everything, and in which we must wait, in order to act, for a radical change in society without preparing it in any particular field and without preparing for the future society, the instruments which will permit it to solve the problems it faces. Moreover there is not any chronological order which concerns education : it would appear wrong to affirm that the solution to these problems of higher education should necessarily precede the solution to problems of other sorts. The opposite proposal also ... seems to us illusory. One can therefore express a point of view on the reform of higher education alone without for that reason being accused of putting the cart before the horse.[14]

The demand for democratic control must not be reserved for institutions of higher education. It should embrace all socially necessary work. There is a danger that student power might become a conservative force if confined to the campus. The movement must widen its horizons in order to link up with other struggles for democratic self-control. At the same time it must never become divorced from its own environment. The specific demand for student power must rest upon the work conditions of students – educational and intellectual. It must be guided by the knowledge that the most rewarding study is inspired by authentic interest rather than social aspiration, that the most stimulating learning is that in which the student himself decides what he wants to learn, that the most productive education involves critical, collective work unfettered by disciplinary boundaries, but extending to, and linking, all subjects.

It is the solution to the fundamental contradiction that productive intellectual work, which ought to be the most exciting and rewarding of activities, is in fact dehumanized by the individual careerism that the system forces upon it.

REFERENCES

1. *The Idea of a Liberal Education*, J. H. Newman.
2. *Studies in the History of Education, 1780–1870*, B. Simon.
3. *The Times*, September 1967.
4. *The University in the Modern World*, L. Robbins.
5. *The Idea of a Liberal Education*, J. H. Newman.
6. The Robbins Report, 1963.
7. Speech at Woolwich Polytechnic.
8. 'The Future of Higher Education within the Further Education System', ATTI Policy Statement, 1965.

9. 'Binary System *v.* the Comprehensive University', an NUS leaflet.
10. L. Robbins, House of Lords speech, December 1965 .
11. 'Capitalist relations of production and the socially necessary labour force.' A. Gorz, *International Socialist Journal*, 1965.
12. The Plowden Report, 'Children and their Primary Schools', 1966. Also : *Streaming: an education system in miniature*, B. Jackson.
13. *The Power Elite*, C. Wright Mills.
14. 'Manifesto for the Democratic Reform of Higher Education', UNEF, 1965.

Learning One's Lesson/Linda Tinkham

Life and Prospects in a College of Education

To argue from the particular to the general is usually dangerously misleading. A statistical account of the national situation in the colleges of education would doubtless be more objective, but for most people less forceful or interesting than a personal one. My own experience cannot be defined as typical, in that – as much as anyone else, I suppose – I do not care to regard myself as a typical student. All the same, my account is tempered by the knowledge of other colleges of education which I have acquired by working within the University of London Institute of Education Students' Association and the National Union of Students.

The changes in training colleges, reflected in their new title 'colleges of education', have resulted ostensibly from the recommendations of the report of the Robbins Committee: but social pressures too have brought about rapid and lasting changes in the pattern of teacher education, and changed some of the colleges from the remote and inaccessible places with their 'monastic rules and fierce matronly assemblies'[1] that they once were.

A Woman's Place ...

It is normal to discuss equality of opportunity in education in relation to social class or financial status. But available statistics demonstrate that greater consideration should be given to educational opportunities for women. Are there innate or environmental causes to support the allocation of the majority of college of education places to women, while allowing them only 25 per cent of university places? [2] Are there valid reasons for giving women a minority of places in the medical or legal professions or for giving them only a small number of apprenticeships? Why in 1961 were 593 women admitted to Oxford and Cambridge when places were available for 4,002 men?[3]

The attitude that education is wasted on a girl still prevails, particularly if such an education does not train her to do something 'useful'. Hence the large numbers of girls who get their higher education on the side while really training to be a teacher. Almost half the entrants to colleges of education possess university entrance requirements but have obviously been persuaded that university is not for them, so they fail to apply.

The first training colleges were established in the nineteenth century by voluntary, mainly religious bodies to train teachers for the schools they had set up. Local education authorities entered this field in 1902 and are now responsible for ninety-eight of the present total of 146 colleges. The Robbins Report[4] remarked that 'because the system grew up piecemeal, the colleges have tended to be scattered, variously housed and small'.

This does not go far enough. Colleges have occasionally been purpose-built, but many still occupy premises that were formerly schools or country residences; one college is still 'temporarily' housed in an ex-army camp and another occupies the first floor of a Northern Co-operative store. Recent building programmes have helped but are still inadequate: expansion for some colleges has meant the use of annexes – at distances of between twelve and thirty miles in the case of colleges in Yorkshire and Northumberland.

Until recently, almost one hundred colleges had fewer than 250 students, a mere handful in relation to the size of the universities. In these tiny, remote institutions, the students were 'very intensively taught'.[5] Even in 1963, 70 per cent of all students in the colleges were residential, the college believing itself responsible not only for the students' education and professional training, but also for their cultural and social life, their physical and moral welfare. Most colleges took this responsibility extremely seriously, and imposed restrictive regulations. The Local Education Authority colleges in this respect were no more enlightened than those governed by religious bodies. In such a sheltered, cloistered atmosphere any rebellion was crushed at the start. From the outset, the Principal's notes in the prospectus indicated that no nonsense would be tolerated. This quotation is from a prospectus published for the academic year 1962–3:

> Students may neither prepare for nor take any other examination during their training ... students are expected to continue their studies during the vacations, and may be required to join expeditions on Saturdays. ... Candidates must satisfy the Principal as to character, probable suitability for the teaching profession, health and physical capacity for teaching.

It takes a strong will to oppose such resolution. Most colleges seem to have been, and many still are, hybrid institutions descended from boarding schools, ladies' colleges and convents. The situation for men has always been slightly better, particularly in the LEA colleges, where regulations are not so strict or so rigidly enforced.

It must be a great shock to some retired principals to see the present student generation, trouser-suited and articulate, taking part in the general protest against the concept of 'in loco parentis'. It is against this traditionally limiting background that the larger, co-educational colleges are now developing.

The college at which I trained was controlled by a Local Education Authority. There are now about one hundred Local Education Authority colleges and half as many independent voluntary colleges. The voluntary colleges tend to be more generous in the amount of money they allow to their student unions, to have greater control of the Union, more restrictive regulations and oddly, more purpose-built accommodation. In most cases the life of the students is much the same as in LEA colleges, the more marked differences being apparent in the Catholic colleges.

When I entered college in 1963, there were just over 300 students; currently there are 450, typical of the expansion being carried out nationally. Those 300 students were all women, taught and administered by women. The one obsession of 90 per cent of the students was to get away into mixed company at weekends and in the evening. The notion of single-sex education for eighteen to twenty-one-year-olds is a little archaic, and yet the situation is changing only very slowly.

I was resident in a small hostel (an annexe), ten minutes' walk from the main college. This hostel had been a luxurious residence and more recently a small private hotel. Thirty of us, fresh from school, shared rooms there, usually in twos and threes, but one room accommodated four. This made studying, entertaining and even sleeping difficult, but the situation was remedied by the regulations. Visitors in rooms were limited to Saturday and Sunday afternoons and Wednesday evenings. This prevented inconvenience to your room-mates. There was no noise after 10.30 p.m. during the week (any undue noise was investigated), by which time everyone was safely locked in. On Sundays we were in at 11 p.m. and on Saturdays at midnight. This allowed us all to get sufficient sleep. Apart from our half-term we were allowed leave of absence on two additional weekends. This helped us to settle in.

Nothing was ever so bad as that first term. Eleven p.m. was our normal time of return (Saturdays excepted) and our weekend leave was unrestricted. Our weekend extended from Friday evening until Sunday evening: in many colleges it did not begin until Saturday morning. Throughout the first year, late extensions were unknown, except on one famous occasion of a rag ball.

Our restricted existence and our temperamental warden engendered a strange community spirit (perhaps its purpose). This spirit moved us to enter a team in a race to Brighton on toy scooters, to be followed by the Rag Ball at Tunbridge Wells. The twelve who were involved were granted an extension until 1 a.m. After the Ball, the delay in collecting coats, waiting at traffic lights and losing our way made us twenty minutes late. By this time we were exhausted and wanted only to go to bed, but the Warden was waiting for us. We were refused permission to park our scooter in the Hall and asked to lock it in the garage. After some discussion, the scooter stayed – until before breakfast on Sunday. Then the leader of the group was cross-examined. Had she studied the route on an Ordnance Survey map? Had she assessed the time of the journey (allowing for lights, diversions and Acts of God?). The Warden considered it extremely irresponsible not to have done so. As we were travelling in a hired dormobile we had not attempted to plan the route – evidently we should have done so. The repercussions continued in interviews for several days.

Every student I have ever met has one such experience to relate. Most demonstrate the lack of understanding existing between students and wardens, and the intolerant bureaucracy of the rule makers. Why should a student newly arrived in London be allowed to visit a cinema or theatre only on Saturday (the only day permitted by time regulations)? Should eighteen-year-olds training to be responsible for the moral education of children be cosseted like pet lambs?

In my own experience there was no disciplinary action taken against students who were late – the ensuing lecture on the doorstep was punishment enough for most. The sin of unpunctuality was considered as great for a two minute lapse as it was for twenty, and as a result the student attitude was 'you might as well be hung for a sheep as a lamb'. Our warden was so conscientious that she frequently checked her watch by telephoning TIM at 11 p.m.

In other colleges the most frequent punishment for this particular offence was 'gating' a student for a week or weekend. The college atmosphere tends to dull the student's righteous indignation; it was not until I had been at college for some weeks and had joined a local political group, that I realized how ridiculous my abrupt departure at 10.20 p.m. seemed to other young people. Many colleges continue to treat their students as if they were children. How is a young teacher to know how to conduct herself when she has lacked the opportunity of being responsible for her own actions for three vital years?

The most striking contrast apparent in my first weeks at college was that between college life and sixth-form life. My sixth-form education was reasonably good – it encouraged us to think for ourselves, to question values, to be outward-looking and independent. In our preparation for 'A' levels we had learnt to work alone, to be critical and to go as deeply into any subject as we were able.

The reverse was true of the first year of college study. We were required to listen and accept: there was little opportunity to question. The course seemed less concerned with thought and independent judgement than with amassing facts, receiving opinion and studying mechanically. The day was long and crammed with compulsory lectures at which our presence was checked. We were involved in gaining a mass of knowledge of every subject under the sun which we were likely to teach, both practical and theoretical. We supposed the method lectures would follow, but in many cases they did not. There was little time for private study: we rarely saw the library except to collect an occasional novel. In addition we had to spend one evening a week at a nearby technical college, learning to operate a film projector. We had normal lectures from 9 a.m. to 5 p.m., travelled to the college for lectures there for a further three hours, and finally travelled back.

My main complaint about the first year was the lack of choice in any subject. Yet, we were being told simultaneously in our Education course that to encourage responsibility in children and allow them to be free it was necessary to offer them a choice. What the Education Department preached no one practised.

One particular incident illustrates the unwillingness of many college of education students to seem different from the mass, or to make a protest. During our second week we were required to go to the first in a series of lectures on the teaching of Religious Instruction. We had already discussed this among ourselves, and many were doubtful about their own beliefs, apart from being worried about the place of religious education in schools. But when the crunch came only two out of ninety insisted upon their right to opt out – myself and a girl who left a little later to go to university. The others comforted themselves with the excuse that they were 'going along to see what it's like'. They did so for two years and constantly complained about the unhelpful and evasive nature of the course.

To be fair, the situation slowly improved throughout the course: the second and third years allowed us more time for private study and encouraged depth study of our main subject and of education.

Colleges of education compare unfavourably with universities and the colleges of advanced technology (currently becoming the 'new' universities) in both the quality and quantity of their teaching staff. These figures are taken from the Robbins Report:[6]

	Percentage of Staff with Degrees	Staff/Student Ratio
University	almost 100	1:8
CAT	80	1:8
College of Education	60	1:10

Although degrees do not imply an ability to teach, they do usually ensure that the staff have sufficient knowledge to help the student to learn. In my college I gained little sense of new developments in the disciplines of psychology or comparative education from several of the lecturers; and it seemed to me that their own knowledge of philosophy or philosophical thinking was virtually non-existent. By the time we reached our final year many of us were do-it-yourself experts, often seeking help from friends in the men's colleges where the situation seemed to be better. I was at first appalled at the general academic standard of the Teachers' Certificate and spent much of my first term investigating the possibility of transfer to a university. Later I accepted the standard and turned my energies to things outside the course. Only one of my contemporaries went to university, although another left to become a nursery nurse. The rest of us had a state-aided social and cultural education between the periods we actually spent in teaching.

The saddest part of all this is that these three years could have been very profitable had we been even sufficiently stimulated to study for ourselves and to forget the monotonous lectures – often regurgitations of books we could have read for ourselves, but were rarely required to. Nothing much was in fact required of us so eventually we did nothing much. I know that in my own college the situation is now much improved, partly as a result of our own efforts: the pattern of the first-year course has changed completely, there are younger, better-qualified lecturers, a new library, and staff/student relations are better than before. I wish I could say that this was generally so.

Two helpful signs exist: one is the advent of the Bachelor of Education degree, which at present suffers from an over-academic bias, but which brings with it a re-examination of the three-year course and better-qualified staff. The other is the longer period students now spend in schools on teaching practice, though this is also a convenient means of cramming more students into the already overcrowded colleges.

Both corporate life and extra-curricular activities present opportunities for personal development, for doing things together in a creative, communal way, for active leadership, and participation in societies and clubs, or in a responsible and free Students' Union.[7]

This is the view of the Department of Education and Science (DES) of what should be the case in colleges of education, but then, it is doubtful if anyone in the top echelons at the DES was ever in a college of education. Faced with a controlled and restricted personal life, a full time-table of monotonous and compulsory lectures which stunted the critical faculties, how could any student muster sufficient enthusiasm to run a club or accept Union office?

In some institutions the conditions I have already described would have produced a militant rebellion, a determination to remove restrictions and to participate in college government. The opposite is true of almost every college of education. The student population is so small and so politically immature that it is easily stifled by the pervasive authoritarian atmosphere. The Union struggles along, its Executive often the only people successfully crawling out of the swamp of apathy and resignation. The Union usually receives very little encouragement. The General Meeting first has to overcome the problem of bringing together students of the same sex who live and work together for so much of their time that they are sick of the sight of each other. The clubs and societies suffer this even more acutely and are generally moribund. Both Union and societies suffer financial difficulties and are sometimes subjected to restrictions by the principal or academic staff. Many Student Union treasurers have bowed to the wishes of the Staff Senior Treasurer.

Some principals actually retain the prerogative of 'requesting' that certain students do not stand for Union office. In one college the Union Executive is not elected solely by that Union.[8] The strength of the Union is often minimal. If a simple request fails, then a Union resolution may recommend the same minor change in college procedure (in one instance, a change of meal-time): if the principal is not in agreement with the Union's wish, then the matter rests there. When this situation has existed for a number of years, a belief grows with it that the Union is useless and the student support it once commanded will turn to apathy. This is another manifestation of the general desire not to 'cause a fuss' which in this case means that when the Union says 'Yes' and the principal says 'No', it is the Union which immediately backs down.

The degree of political naïvety in most women's colleges is remarkable, considering the general level of education and liberal enlightenment. This is not only the partial cause of the failure of the Unions, but it also engenders a lack of support for any kind of political society. Most women's colleges do not have these, so the societies which exist are therefore mixed or in men's colleges. In some cases political societies are banned; though how widespread this practice is is difficult to judge since in many cases such a ban has never been tested. In this matter the voluntary colleges are worse than the LEA controlled ones: a religious community obviously cannot endure a Communist Society, or in some cases, a Socialist one.

The effect of political naïvety is that no one realizes the full potential of the student unions, or in some cases their real function. So often female student leaders are good at organizing open days or bringing together the students to be addressed by the principal. They are capable of giving votes of thanks and after-dinner speeches, and are nice, respectable girls who make favourable impressions as typical students on visiting dignitaries. I have never met a student who saw the Union as one side in a 'us and them' battle, or even as an instrument for radically changing conditions of work. Most executives do not realize what they could or should be doing; most students do not know what they should ask of their Union. The Union is a debating society or an administrative convenience; the student is the recipient of whatever is benevolently dropped from above: this is the view most widely accepted. The change can, and will, come when students have responsibility for their own welfare and a choice in their academic commitments.

The Examination System

Our self-regulated life in hostel was particularly important to us during the autumn term of our third year as this was our final period of teaching practice (TP), when normal TP pressure was increased by the knowledge that this was a part of our assessment for the Teachers' Certificate examination. The strain of teaching practice normally made us more temperamental, not to say neurotic, so we were grateful for the opportunity to mix only with fellow sufferers, or to shut ourselves away, rather than to be burdened with normal relationships in lodgings.

There were many reasons for our highly charged emotional state. Firstly, the teaching situation is false: students are never accepted by a class as 'real teachers' and consequently have extra difficulty with discipline. Secondly, there is inevitably a certain friction between the student and class teacher, who patiently bears your mistakes and witnesses a slow disruption of her good work. Thirdly, we were now teaching an almost full time-table and did more preparation, used more visual aids and launched more topics than is usual in a full year of teaching. Fourthly, in addition, we wrote detailed and abundant notes about what we did, how and why we did it, and how successful it had been. Fifthly, many of us had long or complicated journeys, mine took just an hour on two buses this time, and I was fortunate. (My second TP journey was across Central London, took two hours and needed four changes between all the available kinds of public transport.) Journeys of great length or complexity were inevitable as we used schools in north and east London, and in Essex, Kent and Surrey.

For us, each day began before 7 a.m. and ended well after 10 p.m. There was little possibility of a mid-week break, and weekends were spent in collecting information for lessons, arranging visits, planning lessons or making visual aids. Some students even struggled to maintain a certain amount of normal academic work. During this period (and this is true of all teaching practices) we did more work than in all the other months of the year. The constant pressure was exhausting, and not altogether necessary – certainly the note-writing could have been cut down. The amount of work and notes would have met less fierce resentment if its purpose had been more obvious. In many cases notes compensated for inadequate visits by supervisors, but the current staff/student ratio prevents any real increase in these visits.

College of education students obviously cannot maintain an organizational position in the Union during this TP period. Most colleges operate an elaborate deputation system – ours was built into the constitution. Colleges have not yet succeeded in overcoming the great problem of losing up to a third of their population regularly throughout the year, although the problem is increasing in proportion to the length of teaching practices.

Complaints about teaching practice are numerous, and in my college the mature students were especially articulate (though not usually through any official channel). Teaching practice for the married women, who comprised 25 per cent of our year, is almost impossible. The long hours of work and travelling involved made cooking, shopping and taking young children to and from school Promethean feats. Such complaints and the others listed, are regular features of college life and every year another college prepares another report or survey of the problems. It is difficult to see a solution to the problems as student numbers grow and teaching practice lengthens.

The one advantage that college of education students have over their fellows in the university is the more enlightened examination system which, apart from the torture of TP, is fairly diverse and allows candidates to show their ability in other ways than in written, timed papers. The amount of freedom depends on one's main subject to a certain extent. Apart from mathematics students everyone prepares a long essay on a subject of his own choice within his main field of study. In the case of history students, this involves the use of original documents to propound new theories and geography students usually prepare an environmental study of their home area. Such an essay is also required in the education course in addition to the practical teaching and three written papers.

Main subjects required in addition one or two papers, essays on work done during the three-year course, some practical work (e.g. a dramatic production or exhibition of paintings) and an oral examination. The permutations of choice were mainly left to the students although this may not be so in other colleges. In some ways this structure lessened the pressure normally produced by a series of papers but it also tended to extend such pressure throughout the entire third year of the course.

This type of examination suits the diverse nature of the course and allows most students to do well in some aspect of it. The standard is not very high: the failure rate varies nationally, I believe, from 2 per cent to 10 per cent. I am not convinced, as some are, that the Teachers' Certificate is of pass degree standard, nor do I believe that the three years of study are always merely equivalent to Part I of a degree. The Certificate falls somewhere between these extremes. Many universities will not even accept the Certificate as matriculation requirements. In a ULIESA survey of some nineteen universities, only six accept it, six others will accept it if distinctions are gained, but the rest will not consider it.

The status of the three-year Teachers' Certificate and indeed of the new BEd. degree is a continuing thorn in the side of college of education students which will continue to produce a good deal of resentment.

College of Education Students in Student Politics

The apathy and isolation of some student unions in London has been reduced by their cooperation in the University of London Institute of Education Students' Association. Although this Association was founded by a former Director of the Institute, it has performed a valuable service in providing information and a forum for discussion to Union leaders, and has helped the individual Unions to become an effective joint pressure group with direct contact with the Institute's Committee of Principals and with the Department of Education and Science. A similar body exists in Leeds, but it does not receive the same degree of cooperation or financial support. Other college Unions are active members of area and regional committees within the National Union of Students, but many are forced to rely on the annual Colleges of Education Conference or on the twice yearly NUS Councils to come into contact with other student leaders.

Until 1966, the Colleges of Education Conference was a non-political discussion group. It was an annual social gathering to discuss such pressing student issues as 'The Place of Religious Education in School' or the 'Structure of the BEd. Degree'. Last year the Conference spent one of its sessions discussing motions to be put forward at the full NUS Council. This was a minor (great) leap forward for the colleges although they are still concerned only with the issues directly affecting them and not wider, more general student issues.

Preparation for the Profession?

It has always seemed to me very possible that perhaps the three-year college course was purpose designed to produce a semi-profession of docile, institution-respecting teachers. On the whole, teachers face their situation with continuing resentment or with resigned acceptance. Many spend their years feeling that they are getting a raw deal, others do not even recognize that they are getting a raw deal in being organized and controlled by laymen in so many aspects of their job. The heat recently generated by the salaries issue also rises from long-felt grievances about status.

It is fashionable to compare the teaching profession with the medical profession. The advent of the National Health Service gave doctors a large degree of self-government as a reward for their cooperation in the system. Conversely, teachers are appointed by laymen on school governing bodies or management committees. Their conditions of service result from negotiations with employing authorities of laymen. Their professional life is controlled by inspectors appointed both locally and centrally. More simply they are told what to do, and where and how they are to do it by a body of people with little or no teaching experience. Their lack of self-government is the reason for their lowly professional status.

If teachers fought for greater involvement in running their own profession, their status would rise and a pay rise would be more or less automatic. The teacher's traditional path of pay now, power later, is a typical working-class trade union one. In spite of this the teachers' organizations have always regarded themselves not as trade unions, but as professional associations.

They are now being forced along a more militant path by young teachers who form 50 per cent of the profession as a result of the great expansion of the training programme in recent years. Perhaps, to look at the whole pattern, a student struggle for greater participation in college government will have its repercussions on the teaching profession.

The Changing Pattern

The national need for more teachers has been the greatest single factor affecting the development of colleges of education during the last ten years. The methods employed during this expansion have also been the subject of much discussion but have as yet produced no strong reaction. This final section specifies some of the more obvious effects of the very rapid growth of the colleges.

The Student Population

There are more students, more men students, more mature students and their qualifications are better than before. Firstly, the over-all increase in student numbers is phenomenal: in 1955 just 12,200 students entered the colleges in England and Wales, the estimated number for 1966 was 33,400.[9] This was about the Robbins target for 1971: as there has been only inadequate capital expenditure on college building, this increase has produced sardine-like overcrowding in many colleges.

Almost 30 per cent of the college population are men, but the former women's colleges have not become co-educational just to accommodate them: they have done so to attract more women into the profession. As my own college now has its first intake of men, I can report that they have re-awakened interest in the Union and encouraged criticism of lectures. There has been a greater degree of discussion in groups in which they participate, and the girls are becoming more articulate in these seminars.

Mature students are not flocking into teaching (the disincentives are too great) but the numbers are increasing. The *Guardian* of 25 July 1967 reported a letter from Crosland to educational authorities in which he states that the numbers of students over the age of twenty-five have risen from 1,930 to

6,100 over the last five years – a proportional increase from 11 per cent to 18 per cent of college entrants. This is good for the colleges: mature students are usually less willing to accept opinions, resent the more monotonous and time-wasting lectures and bring into college a wide experience of life and occasionally of trade unions, valuable to the student community. Their close links with society have 'opened up' some colleges. Their age and status have, in some cases, made the academic staff more willing to accept the validity of student opinion.

Resident Students

The student housing situation is now critical. The colleges of education, unable to conjure up more halls of residence, are competing with the universities and technical colleges to find lodgings for their students. A recent report made up of information from sixty-four colleges of education showed a significant change in the pattern of residence since 1963 (the year of the Robbins Report). Whereas in 1963 15 per cent of students were at home, in 1967 the figure was 23·4 per cent. Students in lodgings had increased from 15 per cent to 29 per cent, while the number of students in residence had fallen from 70 per cent to 47·6 per cent.[10] Such a change has some beneficial side-effects. Certainly the matriarchal ties will be severed; other benefits may include a greater awareness of the world outside the college, and subsequently a more demanding attitude to the organization of the college.

Teaching Practice

The accommodation problem is finding a more subtle and harmful solution in the introduction of Box and Cox schemes. Both methods of increasing 'the productivity of Colleges of Education', suggested by the DES in Circular 7/65 involve an extension of teaching practice. The methods have either a whole year, or half-year group out of college on teaching practice for two half terms in each year, for a whole term in each year, or possibly for three consecutive terms during the three-year course. This presents enormous problems which have not yet been fully investigated although many colleges have already started on some such plan. The one advantage the lengthy period of teaching practice may have is that increased contact with the schools may show the students a more realistic teaching situation.

Academic Advances

The re-examination of the three-year course and new blood on the academic staff came in the wake of the BEd. degree. Principals are being forced by sheer weight of student numbers to organize their lecturing staff more efficiently and to reappraise their time-tables. There is less repetition of lectures, less regurgitation of book-learnt fact and more joint staff/student committees engaged in minor time and motion studies. The advent of bibliographies and more detailed schemes of lectures enables some students to prepare for lectures beforehand and makes them generally more critical of the lecturer's approach. This shakeup is what colleges have needed for years : it is also the first step in the direction of mass-produced graduates on the American system.

Student Representation

Larger colleges can no longer be run on the basis of pleasant, or unpleasant, confrontations between principal and president. Neither one can be fully conversant with all the various aspects of college life, try as he may.

The indignation produced by the Weaver Report on the Government of Colleges of Education could provide the necessary impetus to student demands, and the Report also brought to light the unhappy position of the lecturers. At the moment they are in a similar predicament to the students. They too lack elementary rights of representation and appeal in disciplinary matters. The change needed in representation is a drastic one, but the way has been paved.

Organizational Changes

At the same time as the Box and Cox increased productivity schemes were announced, the introduction of a four-term or 'modified' three-term year was suggested. All these schemes are having, and will continue to have, severely disruptive effects on the residential, academic and corporate life of students. Unions will almost be organized out of existence, and students may not be accommodated in the same place for more than five weeks at a time. These schemes are being introduced at a time when the student situation is changing very rapidly, when there are effective and controlled demonstrations elsewhere – but the colleges of education remain relatively calm and silent. The sufferers still work very slowly, with reports and negotiations, following a policy of wait and see. They have already seen enough to make them voice their criticisms and prepare for action.

Now that it is clear that the DES have no intention of retracting their intensive farming schemes for training teachers, will the students react? Perhaps the constant comparison between college of education conditions and university conditions will drive the colleges of education into the arms of the long-suffering technical colleges and together they will fight for a better deal.

There are now numerous factors which could provoke the colleges of education to react – but they will need a great deal of encouragement from other students and student organizers before they finally take action to assert their rights and better their condition.

REFERENCES

1. *Education and the Working Class*, Brian Jackson and Dennis Marden, Penguin Books, 1966.
2. *Robbins Report*, London, 1963.
3. ibid.
4. ibid., Chapter IV.
5. John Vaizey, *Education for Tomorrow*, Penguin Books, 1966.
6. *Robbins Report*, Chapter XII.
7. *Conditions in Colleges*, University of London Institute of Education Students Association.
8. Vaizey, op. cit.
9. *Statistics of Education 1965*, Part II, HMSO.
10. *The Residence Pattern in Colleges of Education*, NUS, January 1967.

Education or Examination?/Tom Fawthrop

'To be a success in our society one has to learn to dream of failure'
R. D. Laing
'Examination = Servility, Social Climbing, Hierarchical Society'
(Paris wall, May 1968)

Last year 18 per cent of men and 12 per cent of women studying at British universities failed to complete their courses. At other further-education establishments the failure rate was 30 per cent for men and 25 per cent for women in the same year. These are the facts of failure in higher education today. Why is there this enormous wastage rate?

One common argument is that such students did not meet the required standards, and thus were justly failed. But when some universities have 30 per cent failure rates and others 3 per cent rates, the failure from one institution would clearly have been a success at another. The huge fluctuations between various failure rates indicate one thing clearly: that the existing system of examinations is a *random process of selection*.

Now most discussion of examinations has concentrated on the issue of what type of test to set the student. But the more pertinent question is: a test of *what*? So often educational aims are assessed in terms of examinations instead of examinations being assessed in terms of aims; the assessment system at present dominates the academic community. Examinations not only define for the student what his course is about, but further, what education itself is concerned with. It would be more rational if first the aims of a university education were defined, and an assessment system subsequently designed to coincide with these objectives.

Examinations can be specifically attacked from two vantage points: firstly, the *reliability* of examinations. This approach accepts the assumption of the present system, but challenges the accuracy of the results; and secondly: the *relevance* of examinations, in that they do not test intellectual ability and what they do test conflicts with the liberal aims of the education.

To take briefly the criterion of reliability: marking – the examiner's judgement – is a notoriously hazardous business. Among the factors undermining the authority of the practice of marking are discrepancies in the range of marks awarded, differences in marking criteria, differences in the standards expected by various markers, and of course other marginal but relevant factors such as the temperament of the examiner, his mood and health at the time of marking any one paper, and again, the order in which the papers are marked. The subjectivity of examinations was summed up by Peron – one of the few educationists who have studied examinations thoroughly:

All the experimental data has shown that for a particular performance assessed in terms of an examination script, assessment by different examiners produces marks with considerable variability – such that in the determination of these marks, the part played by the examiner *is greater than that of the performance of the examinee.* (1963)

One way of judging the factitious nature of the three-hour stint in the examination chamber is simply to reflect on the extensive folklore that has sprung up around it: ways of deceiving the examiner, of deploying a careful hoard of quotations, of pandering to his known prejudices, and so on and so forth; and of course within the folklore the occasional wretched tale of those who could not even last through the masquerade, but who collapsed either before or during these conclusive and ridiculous marathons.

At most colleges the normal process of education, the collective pursuit of learning, is undermined and disrupted by examinations. Interest and involvement in the course for its own sake is drained away by the demands of the educational machine, in which education is no longer an end in itself but becomes relegated to the means of acquisition of a certain commodity of great value in the educational market – namely a degree. The priority of the teachers is generally to 'get them through', of the taught 'to get through': the crammers cram as the final hour approaches.

Nervous breakdowns occur, insomnia, suicide: all students, whether winners or losers, are subjected to the same strains. And after it all, there is the final irony: that the individual student is held responsible if he fails, and not the system with its methods, teachers and advocates. But lives are determined on this basis; by peoples' assent to the rules of this particular game and this grotesque memory orgy. The system itself is a mirror image of capitalist society as a whole, with its criteria of educational productivity and the growth rate of degrees.

The issue of examinations is also the issue of who shall control education and beyond this the liberation of man.

To suggest some alternatives:

Clearly a rational system of assessment must be flexible, and there should be a variety of means by which assessment is arrived at: from termly work standards to dissertations. Examinations may operate as a minimum incentive to construct tunnels of knowledge leading to the examination room, but this can never be a substitute for a genuine interest in education or at least in one's own subject. The only incentives to work hard – aside from the odious pressures of the degree mill – are interest in one's work and a sense of public obligation that this work must take priority over private pleasures.

Three basic principles underlie the new system advocated:

1. The student decides which stimuli to learning are appropriate to his own educational needs.

2. Evaluation of work is neither arbitrary nor status-oriented but is open to discussion and challenge by all concerned and the ensuing discourse between staff and students will be conducted between equals in terms of power, assuming the reality of student power.

3. The results of evaluation procedures will have little permanent significance except as aids to learning. Assessment must always be subordinated to the demands of the process of learning and the degree itself would become an automatic award for three years spent at college.

But to change the system requires more than the desire to change it: it requires the *power* to change it. Since the number of sympathetic lecturers is not yet sufficient, change will primarily depend on student initiative. Yet students lack the power, for power lies in the hands of the examiners. However lightly authority is imposed in the lecture room or tutorial, in the examination hall it is all-powerful. The exam is taken, and the student's academic trial is over, prosecution, defence and judgement all now in the hands of the examiner. When the results are placed on the notice board there is no doubt where the real power lies. Examinations are, in this sense, the 'control centre' for the manipulation of the lives of the students. They present one aspect of an academic conditioning process which induces the acceptance of arbitrary authority geared to a society which needs to perpetuate academic hierarchy because it is itself based on privilege and inequality.

The aim must be to overthrow the university 'management' and replace it by a democratic power. Student power is the only solution for us as it is primarily the students' lives that are at stake.

At present the more alert defenders of the *status quo* are promising to look into the whole question of examinations and to introduce any reforms which seem necessary to them. We must remember that in the last analysis the bureaucrats always support every reform except the next one – real change will not come from above. It rests on the students to transform the present degree factories with their academic division of labour power and authority into liberated centres of education.

Education without exams must be open to all. The degree factories are based on the dominant assumption that every society must have its rulers and ruled, its masses and its elites, those who give the orders and those who carry them out. The abolition of exams and of all other forms of grading and stratifying has profoundly subversive implications for our society.

Chaos in the Art Colleges/Tom Nairn and Jim Singh-Sandhu

Art students occupy a specially chaotic corner in the chaotic scene of higher education. The specific contradiction of this corner could perhaps be put like this: by the very nature of what they do, art students ought to be able to contribute towards the democratization of education; and yet, the fatal combination of their own inherited attitudes and the educational chaos in which they have to work prevents them from doing so. One of the main themes of this book is the need for a general transformation of higher education from the authoritarian model (teachers as rulers, students as subjects; teachers as priests, students as acolytes) to the democratic one (teachers and students as partners in the same task). Now art, as a type of creative activity, always lent itself very poorly to the authoritarian model. Much of the time – as all art students know – it makes nonsense of it. The essential situation of art training ought in fact to lend itself particularly well to the development of democratic forms: the concept of a shared creativity, where the learner is more 'inspired' than 'taught' by the older and more experienced practitioner. Unfortunately, the potential of this situation is obscured by a great deal of what goes on in today's art colleges.

In order to chart this contradiction in more detail, and see how student politics should act towards it, we must first of all look at the background to British art education. Then, secondly, at the obstacles to the positive evolution of art education, represented by the inherited attitudes of students and teachers (the 'ideological' barriers). Then at the formidable confusion of Government and other official policies in this field, which seem designed to sabotage everything of value in it (and demonstrate the absolute necessity of initiatives from below). Lastly, at the challenge to student educational politics which the situation provides.

The Background

The problems of art education in this country centre around the enigmatic initials 'Dip.AD'. This stands for the degree now conferred by authority after four years' attendance at our leading colleges of art: the Diploma in Art and Design. This degree was created recently, and its introduction was supposed to herald a revolution in the whole business of art and design training.

Traditionally, art colleges were the gypsies of educational society: a dubious fringe, with a certain romantic appeal for the more misguided sons and daughters of the bourgeoisie. They produced easel-painters by some ill-understood hit-and-miss method inaccessible to reason; and also design technicians, by a simpler and more medieval process of apprenticeship. Rebels and the not-so-bright congregated there. In the 1920s and 30s the Bauhaus had tried to unify the two approaches in a coherent and contemporary philosophy of design. But the majority of British establishments drifted on, unaffected by such over-clever foreign adventures.

The Dip.AD was intended to change all that. Not before time. The enormous technological revolutions of this century, the obvious increase in the importance of design of all kinds (especially for the British economy, with its particular need to export and its traditional insularity and poverty of design), and the move of the 'fine arts' away from the old message-in-a-frame towards abstract total environments – all made the need for changes in educational practice more and more pressing. Whether one rates these changes as amounting to the creation of *la société du spectacle* (in Situationist terms), or just as a growth in the significance of appearances for our society, the old order was obviously defunct. The gypsies had to be brought in and given useful jobs, somehow.

All the current dilemmas follow from the attempt to do this. As a result of it, art education has been plunged out of its long sleep into a process of very rapid and chaotic change – which is certainly only in its earliest stages, as yet. This, of course, provides a situation which is extremely unsettling. One often hears laments for the good old days of comfortable unimportance, when nothing much was achieved, but everyone was happy and

They left us alone, and the Life class was held in the local pub. However, everyone also knows that the change is irreversible. In fact, the very chaos of the new scene provides objective possibilities for intervention from below that are greater than in any other sector of higher education.

The central problem – so far quite unresolved – of the new order is itself quite an old one. As was recognized at the Bauhaus, it is necessary to work out an integrated programme of 'art education' which is not education in 'art' in the familiar sense: rather, it must be a flexible and generalized training in forms of expression and self-expression, both intellectual and emotional, where a high degree of mental culture and manual skills are reconciled. Such a programme will not produce the 'geniuses' of bourgeois myth, nor the silent idiot craftsman-who-sticks-to-his-job so popular with employers; this is the whole point. It must produce the more sophisticated designer of the social environment, aware of the wider meaning of his work and able to match the great creative challenges presented by changing materials and techniques. Unfortunately, the development of such an educational programme accords ill with the British make-do-and-mend temperament. It involves much theory, an effort to reconcile theory with practice, and (therefore) much experiment in order to work things out. These are not elements in plentiful supply in any sphere of higher education. Perhaps it is not surprising that they are still largely absent from the art colleges; which are consequently in the position of trying to conduct a revolution with little idea of where they are going, and less of how to get there – a large-scale, despairful Happening, in fact, poised in the realm of the absurd, and held together by dogged British hope that it will all turn out all right in the end.

Art Ideologies

Objectively, the situation may be revolutionary. Subjectively, it is a mess, and the Aesthetic revolutionaries (who we must hope will soon appear on the scene) will have a hard time sorting it out. Art students are at present torn between two contrasting attitudes, and neither have a great contribution to make to the revolution.

On one hand, the debilitating traditional set of beliefs about 'the Artist' is still powerful. According to this philosophy, derived from nineteenth-century practice, creative people are an elite set apart from society by their mysterious inner fire. While it is decent of society to provide somewhere for them to go – the art college – all they want to do there is burn away in peace, undisturbed by education. Education is liable to be phrased in words, which are irrelevant. Indeed, it is practically an insult to the indwelling visual spirit. Needless to say, this 'superman' philosophy is associated with the defence of other traditionalist notions of elite and minority culture. Its most damaging aspect is the pseudo-revolutionary complacency which goes with it. That is, it usually contains the assumption that just by having become a would-be 'Artist' in this sense, grown hair, donned the appropriate garb, and so on, an effective revolt against the *status quo* has been carried out. So there can be nothing else left to do. Discussion of the theory of art education, ideas about changing curricula, all forms of student protest and politics, encounter chilling contempt: 'Why don't we just get on with our work, man?'

On the other hand, quite different from this idiot quietism, but almost as destructive, there is what one could call the New Ideology. This represents, in fact, a response on the part of students to precisely those new pressures of the environment which gave rise to the Dip.AD and all the problems. But it is a crude, unmediated response which underlines the need for a new and better programme. Society's sharp new interest in many forms of design has created a violent new careerism in these design-arts. Youthful fortunes can be made overnight, through the right ideas, the right scene, aggressiveness in the right place. The high-pressure professionalism of fashion has replaced the old doddering philosophy of the artisan. This has had immediate repercussions among art students, producing in some quarters a kind of counter-revolution against the old image of the inspired misfit. Here, the hard-boiled competitiveness of the neo-capitalist environment outside, its concern with 'image' and 'public relations', its frank commodity-fetishism and cult of flash success – all tend to be reproduced in startling miniature in today's art college.

So while some students dream of being Rembrandt, more assume they are going to be Mary Quants, David Baileys, or David Hockneys. The ethos of art colleges is part a fossilized old world, part the bitchy new one of the ad-man, the teen-age glossy, and the newest gimmick. This battle between bohemians and swingers goes on so ruthlessly just because art colleges are such limp, neutral institutions. They have no traditions, no implanted conventional culture of their own, capable of forming an insulating barrier against the outside environment. Admittedly, in the universities such traditions are often irrelevant and stifling, and the barrier may be too high. But from the vantage-point of art education, the need for a certain amount of detachment is very clear.

Egoism is one powerful factor common to both the philosophies described. This of course means that art students tend to be unclubbable. They are rebellious, but in a small, individual way quite refractory to any sort of organization. The lack of solidity in their institutions and the lack of coherence in their programmes of study means that no model of cooperation is presented to them – they very often feel that all they can do is further their own ambitions, and damn the rest. Shutting their eyes to a chaos they feel is beyond them, they concentrate on being a Great Artist, or a Success (or, with any luck, both). Bright-eyed and open-minded in the first year, they are doubtful by the second, cynical by the third, totally hard-boiled, aggressive, and indifferent by the fourth (and so, ready for the world, but not prepared to change it creatively, as they should be).

Schools of art were thought of as remote hot-houses of the aesthetic spirit, once upon a time. The fact is, they are still partly like this; while on the other hand, they have become more crudely and directly linked to the demands of a certain sort of industry than any other part of the educational system. They are being torn apart in this way, because so far they have been unable to build up their own educational world, their own kind of unity between theory and practice, their own ethos and traditions. Of course, Britain is Britain, and here situations of this kind are never as bad as they might be, simply because of the fragmentation and incoherence that are prevalent. The chaos implies some freedom, and some colleges use such freedom much better than others. Over and over again, one finds that the creative initiative of individual teachers, of particular principals or departments, have overcome the sterility of official policy and the absence of an intelligent curriculum.

The Art Establishment

Just how much such initiatives have to overcome is best shown by a brief résumé of Establishment politics in art education, a dizzying tale of confusions.

The story begins in the late fifties, when a body known as *The National Advisory Committee on Art Examinations* advised that a new and more prestigious degree ought to be awarded in the art field, to raise standards (presumably in response to the pressures of change mentioned above). The advice, accepted by the Government, issued forth in the august shape of *The National Advisory Council on Art Education*, chaired by Sir William Coldstream. This, in the fullness of time, brought forth the *National Council for Diplomas in Art and Design*, presided over by Sir John Summerson. In 1961, this genteel saga led to the launching of the new courses, which were supposed to take students from 1963 onwards.

One would scarcely expect too radical a change from such a genesis. In fact, the general pattern of the new Dip.AD courses prescribed by these bodies were an immaculate compromise between academic traditions and the new needs the Art Schools were supposed to be meeting. As such compromises are apt to do, this one reconciled everything and everyone quite satisfactorily, amid much mutual congratulation – and missed the entire point of what was at stake.

For the liberal bureaucrats and Distinguished Persons on these committees, improving art education meant – laughable as this must appear to many readers of this book – making the art colleges more like the universities. The new degree was supposed to be 'degree-equivalent', on a par with the ultimate in status symbols, the BA. How was this to be done? Obviously, by injecting a bit of university into the training of the mute mechanics: 'Liberal Studies', or 'General Studies', as it is usually and unconvincingly called. In other words, a few hours a week of some orthodox academic discipline (Philosophy, English, or Sociology), taught by university-trained people in the appropriate fields. Of these fields, by far the most important was the History of Art, which in fact became the academic mainstay of the Dip.AD. The art history exam is the principal constituent of the academic part of the Dip.AD. Final Assessment (naturally equipped with the proper grades, first, second, pass and fail). History of art was chosen because of its apparent closeness to the needs and interests of art students; but of course, in its usual forms it is among the most academic of subjects.

Apart from laudably providing jobs for graduates (especially art historians), this was a perfect recipe for educational suicide. It consisted in tacking on an academic sector ('Theory') to a wide assortment of traditional forms of training in art and design (the 'Practice'), and piously hoping that it would all fit together. How could it? The actual shape of the Dip.AD curriculum varies widely – and again, in some places the fit is not too bad, as a result of good luck, good personnel who develop some awareness of the real problems of art education and work piecemeal to cope with them, and so on. But more often, and on the whole, the result of this poorly thought out and timidly conventional policy is chaos.

The most exasperating feature of the mess is that there *is* indeed one vital respect in which the Dip.AD colleges should be made like universities. Naturally, no attention whatever has been paid to this, while they have been academicized in the way described. It is really indispensable that art colleges should have something of the independence and the self-respect as institutions which the universities take for granted. Most of them in fact are dependent upon Local Education Authorities, and (while Authorities naturally vary, and the one for Inner London is quite exceptional) for many this is a severe handicap. There are two reasons why such a change is necessary. Firstly, some security and a reasonable freedom from interference are required in the difficult process of building up art education. Secondly, an integral part of this process – indispensable to more sophisticated forms of art training – is *research*. This, however, is something of which Local Education Authorities tend to be suspicious. In general, one might claim that facilities for research, and its fertilizing influence on teaching, were part of the definition of any education which is really 'higher'. In the case of ·the Dip.AD schools, the need is urgent: for the business of developing art education itself requires so much research into the nature of design, and so much experiment, simply to get under way beyond the bland and useless formulae of officialdom.

Thus, the contemporary 'revolution' in art education has been provoked from above, according to largely irrelevant criteria (which are exquisitely summed up in the Royal College of Art's new-found right to award the Grail itself – the BA – to its students, complete with newly designed academic robes, parchments, and ceremonies), and in a way that betrays its true sense. But perhaps the most revealing thing about these abortive changes, in the general perspective of British higher education, is the larger meaning which is gradually becoming clear. This does not seem to have been planned. Indeed, it contradicts many of the intentions formally expressed by Ministers – and yet, unmistakably, everything contributes towards this ultimate pattern of art education.

Polytechnics and Elites

Art colleges are being developed within a general programme for the evolution of higher education, whose purpose is avowedly democratic: more and better educational opportunities for everybody. Yet, unmistakably, this formal commitment is nullified by the fundamental tendency of the social system towards the formation of hierarchies and elites on the old Oxbridge–Redbrick model. Art education in fact is particularly menaced by this trend.

The form in which this problem presents itself to the art colleges is through the Department of Education and Science's new scheme for 'Polytechnics'. This is a plan to group together various scattered institutions of higher education (technical colleges, colleges of commerce, and so on) into larger, concentrated units with one administration and – eventually – the same facilities and buildings around one campus. The theory is that this 'rationalization' will offer better facilities than small colleges could on their own, and will promote a more rapid expansion of student numbers in this sector. In fact, the slogan advertising the scheme (now under way in most parts of the country) is the familiar one of 'separate but equal development' for the non-university sector.

The precise weight to be attached to the term 'equal' in this context was suavely defined by Minister Crosland in a speech at Woolwich Polytechnic two years ago:

The Polytechnics ... will provide full-time and sandwich courses for students of University quality who are attracted by the more vocational tradition of the Colleges, and who are more interested in applying knowledge to the solution of problems than in pursuing learning for its own sake.

The message was rubbed in more recently by a Mr French of Her Majesty's Inspectorate, addressing Technical College teachers from the Greater London area:

the emphasis would be on teaching of a high standard rather than on research. ... In this emphasis on excellent teaching as the primary objective, with research as a secondary consideration there was a marked difference to the Universities ... the removal of time for research would mean there was more time for teaching, and timetables would not be the same as in the Universities, nor in these circumstances was it to be expected that the salaries structure would be identical with that of the Universities.

In other words, the new polytechnics will be the lowest known form of the 'higher' education, devoted to solid nine to six cramming, under the direction of less well-paid instructors uninterested in research. Above them will be the CATs, doing research into technology and high-level technical teaching. Above them again, Redbrick. And above that, Oxbridge and a few other centres in London devoted earnestly to 'pursuing learning for its own sake'.

For art education the problem was, where exactly did it fit, in this imposing hierarchy? The answer generally provided by officialdom is, on the lowest rung. They are supposed predominantly to integrate with the technical and other colleges, into the new polytechnics. The admirable tidiness of this solution from the bureaucratic point of view is plain. But so is the utter contradiction between the whole concept of the Dip.AD, with its 'degree status', and the qualitative revolution which was supposed to proceed from it, and this assigning of art colleges to the outermost fringe of educational civilization. In other words, in the last ten years governments have with one hand launched an ostensible 'revolution' in art education; and then, with the other hand, apparently aborted the 'revolution' by removing the conditions necessary for it.

However, there is a logic even behind contradictions of this order. At a meeting in a college threatened with 'polytechnicization' last year, someone asked the DES representative who had materialized to defend official policy why it is that a certain number of well-known London art colleges are being so unfairly deprived of the glowing advantages of amalgamation with polytechnics. Mr X, after all, had been painting a dazzling picture of these great poly-universities-to-be: their new Californian-style campuses, their rich cross-fertilization of disciplines, their escape from arid academicism. Why weren't St Martin's, Camberwell, Central, and Royal College complaining bitterly at their exclusion from paradise? The truth is, naturally, that these are the elite colleges of art education, and they will be rendered still more of an elite by the polytechnic scheme. They will be the Oxbridge of art education. Thus, the real effect of the programme of 'progressive' reforms is the very opposite of what was declared and (perhaps) intended.

The most effective apologist for the polytechnics has been Eric Robinson. His vision of them, in *The New Polytechnics* (Penguin), sees new, American-style popular universities which will finally destroy the congenital elitism of British education. But he himself makes perfectly clear that the realization of this mission goes against the whole natural trend of the system. How can it be realized, therefore, without a far more profound educational and social revolution than Robinson apparently envisages?

Art Politics

It is the revolutionaries of the art sector who have in fact launched the movement which could – amongst other things – make the polytechnic development into something significant and worthwhile.

Not long before the revolution, Jim O'Connor (NUS secretary at the Royal College of Art) declared: 'It is becoming evident to everyone that the present state of affairs cannot continue. We must not let any gospel of defeatism get us. Trends in art students' indifference and their abdication of personal responsibility must not be allowed to develop undirected.' But events since then have shown just how deceptive this old quietism was.

The agitation at Hornsey and Guildford was one long dramatic illustration of the truth about 'apathy'. Far from being what it was generally taken for – a kind of hopeless natural state – it was clearly revealed as a response to the peculiar alienations of art-student existence. When the right situation was created it peeled off with remarkable swiftness and completeness.

The right situation was one where a sense of collective existence and power was generated, and where some common conception of a possible alternative had time to emerge in collective discussion. At Hornsey – a college which suffered from all the diseases of art education in their most extreme form – such a sense of communal being was created originally by the officially-sponsored student demonstrations against inclusion in the proposed North London Polytechnic. Although smiled on by authority, this agitation had the effect of generating the one thing the system normally conspires to keep hidden: a feeling that it was *possible* to change things by intelligent, direct common action. A few months later, the fruit was harvested in the shape of the famous sit-in from May 28 until July 12.*

This sit-in, and the one at Guildford, which very quickly followed, produced a great response throughout the art-school world. At least for a time, the notorious apathy disappeared overnight, and there were sit-ins, active discussions and demands for radical reform in a large number of colleges. The Hornsey and Guildford students founded a national movement, the Movement for Rethinking Art and Design Education (MORADE), which held a conference in the Roundhouse in London in July,

* A very full, collective account of the Hornsey affair has been written by those who took part in it. This is shortly to be published by Penguin Educational Books, edited by David Page, Tom Nairn and Victoria Hamilton. This book tries to draw the lessons from the episode and its many repercussions, and contains a selection of the Hornsey documents and a vivid description of what happened and why.

1968. And although both pioneering colleges are at the time of writing in the grip of a counter-revolution which has undone a lot of what was fought for and led to considerable victimization (especially at Guildford, where the staff has suffered heavily for its participation in the revolt), there is no reason to think that this is more than a passing phase.

The underlying causes of revolt in this hot-bed of discontent remain, and are only likely to be aggravated by further efforts at 'reform'. The art colleges will continue to be in the avante-garde, and future developments in this sector now have a rich inheritance of thought and action to build on. The material miseries formerly accepted passively – as things to be turned away from into 'apathy' – are now seen more and more in a true light, as intolerable insults to the creative values of art and design.

Art students account for about a quarter of the whole student population in higher education (about 120,000 students, in 159 colleges of different kinds). It is clear from what we have just said that the challenge to organization among them is colossal. The tasks of such organization are very far-reaching – indeed, they are more evidently global (involving every aspect of education, curriculum, ideology, the higher political strategy of educational affairs than in any other sector. In the past, in spite of this challenge, organization was very poor in most art colleges. Back in 1960, the NUS Council was moved to comment on the lack of student facilities at very many art colleges, and the lack of recognition of Union organization and opinion in most of them. Things have improved little since then. Some colleges lack even a common room. Most colleges have no Union offices, and often facilities are restricted to a notice-board, and the occasional use of a classroom for meetings. There is not one journal or magazine in the country worthy of note which reflects student activity in art colleges (*Ark*, the Royal College magazine and by far the best-known, is consecrated to slick self-adulation and displays of technique). The Local Education Authorities agreed to contribute Union fees for each student, some years ago, and these are now normally between £1 and £3 per head in art colleges – a figure to be compared with the £8 10s. of the Royal College of Art, or with (to take an arbitrary example) the £17 of Liverpool University.

The Future

In 1968, the avant-garde role of the art student movement was often acknowledged with some reluctance elsewhere in the student world, because of its novelty and its failure to conform to certain political schemata of the left. But presumably as the whole movement develops, and theory is revivified by practice (not drowned by it in the old British 'empirical' way), these problems will disappear.

In the wider perspective of the revolutionary movement, it should not be forgotten that there are two vital reasons for hoping that the art students will remain in the vanguard.

Firstly, by its very nature, art and design education militates against the authoritarianism of the old teacher-student relationship. In it, the concept of education as a shared creative task where in certain respects 'teachers' and 'students' stand on a really equal footing – a concept essential to any programme of student power – is quite natural and fairly easily attainable. Hence art training constitutes a viable model for the education revolution, a point of reference which should be employed far more by revolutionaries in the other sectors. Far more than any other, art (and art education) represents the type of creative, collective, action to which all revolution aspires.

Secondly, within the larger revolution towards which student revolt tends, the effective presence of this kind of cultural upheaval is an invaluable guarantee against philistinism. It is – and we must hope it continues to be – the necessary counter to the rigidities of thought and action into which any movement will fall, unless the cultural revolution is continuous and cumulative.

The Failure of Student Institutions

NUS – The Student's Muffler/David Widgery

The National Union of Students has 336,000 members and is the sixth biggest union in the country. The NUS offers, in the stirring words of its President, 'service provisions in the fields of personal and life insurance, entertainments, concessions, vacation work, cultural activities such as drama and debating and a number of other such issues'.[1] The NUS has bored a generation of students to political death.

The backwardness of British students, their political isolation and docility, and the conceit and self-indulgence which passes so often for 'university politics' is directly reflected in the world picture of the leadership of the NUS. For these leaders, the submission of evidence and the preparation of reports has been a substitute for mass activity and commitment on the campus. Policy is equated with the text of those motions passed at Council, and is left to moulder in the Minute Book as proof of the Union's liberality. Militancy is 'the last refuge of the politically impotent'.[2] *Tio Pepe* diplomacy becomes the only conceivable form of student action. The NUS has all the passion of an ashtray. Today, a verbal war between the radicals and the Union escalates as its President complains of the 'liberal use of sweeping and seemingly fashionable cliché' and 'one sided trouble-shooting'.[3] Beneath the rhetoric of this bitter and complicated struggle, lies a deep political crisis in the nature of British class society as it is worked out in higher education.

Where are the real differences and what are the alternatives the NUS faces?

1. Geoff Martin, 'Focus', Home Service, 25 May 1967.
2. Tom McNally, Liverpool Council, Easter 1967.
3. See T. W. Savage, 'NUS, the First Forty Years'.

In the Beginning

The NUS was formed in 1922 as an outgrowth of various inter-university organizations. It was mainly created for international cooperation and this preoccupation with international affairs has remained with its leadership. In the early period it proselytized in the Dominions urging them to form National Unions and affiliate to the Imperial Conference of Students and then the CIE. From the late twenties, it concentrated on a massive travel department with visits and vacation holidays. Out of these service concerns grew interest in welfare in the university; the familiar pattern of consultation with staff unions, drives for student health schemes, text book concessions; motions on the iniquities of the tutorial system had begun. Concern for exclusively student welfare and conditions remained at the core of NUS throughout the fifties – even as late as 1961, the Council was still debating the opening hours of the British Museum.

After the war, the definition that discussion could only relate to the 'student as such' was enlarged to allow the Union to discuss the whole of educational policy. The remaining provision, that the Union should under no circumstances 'become a general political Forum' was rigidly enforced. The NUS Council asked for 'representation of consumer interest on all committees reporting into matters of study' and the submissions to Robbins, Plowden, Newsom, Hale (university teaching methods) and Anderson (student support) were the source of great pride. The union's leaders were increasingly welcome at the tables of under-secretaries; the NUS leaders' delight at their own respectability must have been equalled by the gratification of the Department of Education and Science at finding students so eager to participate in their own subordination. 'NUS is of course an educational pressure group and this can be measured in terms of the support that we gain from other educational organizations and from the trade unions. In addition to which our representations to the Department of Education and Science are noteworthy for their frequency and their positive results,'[4] said President Geoff Martin last year.

Much of NUS ideological underpinning is in fact contained in

4. Geoff Martin, op. cit.

these reports to the Royal Commission which are prepared by single executive members and the Research Staff. The draft document 'Student Rights and Responsibilities' which amounts to NUS philosophy, contains twenty-eight references to Union Policy, only seven of which refer to motions discussed in Council. Up to 1964, the union's main policy concerns were the abolition of the means test on student grants, payment of student national insurance dues, lodgings and sports facilities and the pay and conditions for teachers. Some mass involvement was generated around the campaigns against apartheid (educational) in South Africa and racial discrimination in Britain. In 1965 a large meeting and march was held in protest against the level of teachers' salaries. The liberalization proceeded dizzily; Council called for the retraction of the Immigration White Paper (because of its effects on education). At the present rate we can expect a condemnation of the deleterious effect of napalm on text books and mortar boards in North Vietnam by the early seventies.

Recently, the tripartite secondary education pattern of grammar, secondary and public streams and the Binary System's division into public and autonomous sections of higher education have been attacked as 'socially divisive' and the vision of a 'comprehensive university' was offered. The various campaigns against the means test, for teachers' salaries, for student housing were never linked to make intelligible the structure of educational spending. While meeting after meeting deplored the cutbacks in building, overcrowding and crash expansion of the colleges of education, the inadequacy of teachers' pay, the condition of school buildings and the low grant levels, the total picture of a Labour Government quite unwilling to meet even the modest programme of the 1964 election manifesto was never drawn together. The state of the economy flitted through delegates' contributions but the assumptions of Wilson's deflation and freeze were never challenged. The economy and education's input into it were taken as given. In short, the main body of NUS thought would not have frightened the Townswomen's Guild.

NUS and Democracy

The structure of the Union makes it especially vulnerable to ruling minorities. The rapid turnover of delegates and their lack of political experience leaves procedure and the direction of the Council in the hands of the old men and ex-students on the Executive and the Steering Committee. (The last two presidents have both been twenty-seven, a clear generation older than the students entering the universities they presided over.) The infrequency of Council Sessions, (it meets only twice a year and there is no middle tier of representation) and its unwieldy size in plenary means that the Executive alone takes the fundamental decisions about policy implementation and initiation. While confused delegates wallow in documentation from the Executive, attempts by constituent unions to bring forward their own information seemed to be slowed down from the platform (Newcastle Memorandum on Voting, UCL on Means Test, GLCS on the London Differential, LSE on the crisis negotiations).[5]

Members of the Executive themselves have attacked its level of political morality, especially in relation to the elections. Michael Stern found 'the most distasteful aspect is the use of the Union machinery they control, by the incumbents, to elect their successors'. Roger Lyons, Union Vice President and later Treasurer, attacked what he called 'corruption' from the platform at Margate in 1966. When challenged by the remainder of the Executive to substantiate his allegations, he listed eighteen examples of Executive malpractice which were confidentially circulated to NUS secretaries. Even then three of the examples were not reproduced, 'on the advice of the Union's Solicitor'. *The Times* reports Lyons, who was elected against the ticket, as accusing the Executive of 'using its prior rights to have information in order to contain members and stop them taking part in discussions'.[6] The most obvious example of abuse is NUS's unique voting system which has survived the repeated wishes of over half the Council to introduce a more representative election system. The particular dangers of the present Multiple Transferable Vote system is that an organized group of 51 per cent can control all

5. Voting Commission Report, October 1966, paragraph 56.
6. *The Times*, 26 January 1967.

ten Executive seats if they operate a 'ticket'. While weak candidates can, with the support of the ticket organizers, be dragged on to the Executive, independent candidates have to break the ticket list entirely. The system leads to a polarization of radical and conservative opinion in the Union and effectively forces groups within the Council, say the 'political' universities, to adopt takeover tactics to get any representation on the Executive at all.[7] Since the Executive plays such a crucial role in the whole policy creation, direction and campaign, it is inevitable that radical opinion in the Union will want at least a voice on that Executive.

The Executive acromegaly and all-or-nothing election system has produced in our view a particularly low level of campaigning based on various modifications of a basic smear, the calling of anyone left of the Rotary Club 'Communists'. Discontent came to a head at Exeter in 1966 where one of the listed ticket supporters of the executive was changed within minutes of the election. Geoff Martin, who was reported as 'dedicated to reducing Communist influence',[8] has admitted, though it was scarcely necessary, to using a ticket on this occasion. An emergency motion at this Council led to a Commission which introduced new methods to make tickets and blatant abuses more difficult without actually changing the voting system. The new system will cramp smear canvassing: militants will find it easier to run for election without being libelled as mentally sick, sexually deviant or politically motivated.

One of the most nauseous aspects of the election smears has been the intervention of Fleet Street. The *Sunday Times* in particular has devoted five articles over the last two years to the danger of 'extremist takeovers' of the NUS. The paper has exposed 'a determined left wing bid for power', 'closely organised extremist plan' and 'far left's attempt to seize power'. When militants were Labour Party Members, the *Sunday Times* simply said 'that they deny being Communist Party Members'. A recent article boldly named three, 'self-declared Communists', none of whom had any connexion whatsoever with the Communist Party.

7. For general discussion of the Executive's role in policy and implementation, see op. cit., paragraphs 77–89.
8. *Guardian*, 12 April 1966.

The *Observer* tagged along rather less energetically, in an article headed 'Union Fights Communist Bid For Power'. Alan Hunt was quoted, for example, as saying that he did not mind who got elected to the executive, as long as they are 'aggressive', when what he actually said was, 'progressive'. The rest of the press has been more straightforward; any remotely progressive move is immediately labelled a plot from the Kremlin. Thus after attempts to introduce a 'Student Charter' summarizing NUS student policy had failed, at Easter 1965, the *Evening Standard* trumpeted 'Communists defeated in First Round'. In the week that RSA held its founding convention, Bruce Kemble, the *Daily Express*'s Education Reporter, posed the question 'that worries every responsible don and student in Britain'; 'who will capture the students' ears in the next few months – the lively young Liberals or the Moscow-organized militants? ...'[9] Peregrine Worsthorne was less alliterative. 'The result is a growing body of bloody minded students who poison the university climate by setting teachers and taught at each other's throats and generally embroiling the universities in an endless caterwaul of puerile protest.'[10] When an NUS conference decision was taken to pursue a neutralist international policy in November 1966, the reaction of the press was such that, as *Tribune* commented, 'anyone who thought that the idea that non-alignment meant pro-communism had gone out with Senator McCarthy would have been proved wrong by the press this week.'

NUS and its Activists

The Executive's paranoia about student Communist Party members is a very revealing aspect of their political outlook. For those who see politics as essentially manipulative, opposition becomes subversion. Any attempt to alter the present situation is sedition, the result of a minority plot and a mass gullibility. The evidence of Battersea CAT to the NUS Voting Commission aptly commented : 'It is unfortunate that the people who fight to keep poli-

9. Bruce Kemble, 'Crisis among the angry Students', *Daily Express*, 1 February 1967.
10. Peregrine Worsthorne, 'Too easy to go to university', *Sunday Telegraph*, 5 February 1967.

tics out of the National Union are the same people who go round to you at election time and say, "Don't vote for him he belongs to the ..." ' For the Executive, CP members have provided suitable scapegoats. In practice, Communist students have been simply too few to operate blocks and 'control' delegations and have had to rely on their ability. Precisely because of the smear barrier in most colleges, elected Communists are not only able but down-right pedantic about obeying mandates and observing delegation responsibility. What characterized UCL or Leeds when they had CP secretaries was their painstaking and informed motions and speeches: UCL used to manhandle a three-tier filing cabinet into Council floor; Leeds intervention on teacher training and the National Plan verged on the academic. Clause Three of the Union specifies that 'it is not the role of the Union to become a general political forum.' [11] In this demonology, politics is seen as something that threatens to bring the conflicts of the real world into the educational enclave which is the student's only arena. Those from political backgrounds, it is implied, wish to super-impose the ideology of their parent party on the virgin neutrality of NUS thought and reproduce the pantomime of parliamentary debate in NUS Council. In practice, of course, the 'apoliticism' appears to conceal a principled adherence to the assumptions and aims of Fabian Labourism. NUS Executive members pass fluently and regularly into Transport House and the Union bureaucracy. The 1964/6 Secretary went direct to the editorship of the Amalgamated Engineering Union Journal whose (unsuc-cessful) role in the 1967 AEU elections is notorious: the heads of Transport House Research and of its Overseas Department were both until recently members of the NUS oligarchy. The last two personal assistants of Sir Ronald Gould of the NUT have also been NUS Executive members. The present Executive and right-wing floor organizers are active supporters of the London Fabian Society. They are our social engineers, nudging and anticipating capitalism. There is no secret about this. Only they themselves bother with the polite fiction of their 'apoliticism'.

11. *Sunday Times*, 5 February 1967.

The Radicals Emerge

The assumptions of a centralized bureaucratized Union with local militants attacked and the central machinery increasingly inducted into central planning mechanisms are explicit and highly political. NUS's 'sane and sensible policy to get at the levers of power' [12] has involved respectability at all costs and converted it into a listless company union.

It was inevitable that students would eventually come to revolt against the menopausal leadership of NUS and its flaccid policies. For the last eight years the larger universities have tended to be an awkward squad with the NUS, continually advocating more radical policies. Universities with a strong and democratic union came to Council with an elected delegation fully briefed and mandated on all issues by general meetings. Universities like Leeds, Manchester, UCL and, more recently, Birmingham, Hull, LSE, Keele, York and Sussex, have sent sophisticated delegates who have generally voted and organized against the Chair. The main areas of Executive support comes, by contrast, from the backward areas which have tended to rely on national leadership rather than local initiative; the traditionally conservative universities and colleges of education which command a quarter of the votes. The Technical Colleges have become increasingly disenchanted with the Chair and provide rather an unpredictable and truculent bloc.

The pattern of growing opposition to the NUS style and leadership, however, depended on the growth of parallel organizations which were concerned with the type of politics which NUS insisted on ignoring. In October 1965, a new London based student newsletter called *Snap* was started by NUS activists, for distribution among student unionists. It had been originally conceived as a group called Students Now For Action and Progress, but this thirties-sounding alliance never lasted as far as its launching. The first issue declared, in the sort of prose that seemed necessary at that time, 'We believe in the value of intercollegiate communication. Students in this country have never had psychological unity – not because common student concerns and action do not exist but because most students are simply

12. Ian Cunningham (NUS Executive) Surrey University, 5 June 1967.

unaware of them.' [13] The news service scooped the first Department of Education and Science mutterings on student loans on 6 October, 1965 – although NUS took no action until 22 October when they sent a confidential letter to union presidents, a tactic which managed to let sleeping dogs lie. *Snap* readers' groups discussed their own problems rather than those that NUS had in mind for them. The Establishment reacted by barring its reporters from NUS Margate Council 1965, and attacking it. Alan Evans announced from the platform that it was edited by lying Communists, despite the well-known fact that both editors were Labour Party members. Tom McNally called it a 'despicable rag'. Both went on to enter the Executive ticket. Frank Fuchs, the editor of *Sennet*, the London University newspaper, who had supported *Snap* editorially, was asked to resign, refused and was physically barred from the office. Two libel writs were sent to the paper, one in the name of the NUS solicitors, and it was repeatedly attacked in *Student News*.

The pattern of journalistic agitation continued both in the increasingly disenchanted student press and in specifically insurrectionary papers like *The Agitator* at LSE. The party-political groups begun to issue joint statements. The first was a mild rebuke to the Americans in Vietnam signed by officials from the Liberal, Labour and Communist student groups and drafted at NUS Margate 1965 Council. It was at this meeting that the first left-wing NUS breakthrough came, when the Council decided overwhelmingly to reject the proposal of the Majority Report on International Affairs which advocated full membership of the ISC (see Alan Hunt's and David Triesman's article), the CIA financed, anti-Communist organization with which NUS had been traditionally identified. The Report's advice was not accepted. Usually the Executive was prepared to accept the occasional defeat as a tolerable dissonance in their overall fugal pattern. But this reverse undermined their central stance in Cold War student politics and they fought it with ferocity.

Immediately after the decision, delegates were told that they would lose their travel concessions and that anyway the defeat was engineered by left-wing journalists. Over the following six

13. *Snap*, 8 October 1965.

months, a great deal of interest was stimulated in colleges all over the country as the international question was debated. The Establishment found the lobbying of the student hierarchy more to their taste. Selected students were taken on an expenses paid weekend at a Maidenhead hotel by an organization called 'The Fund for International Student Cooperation' where they were gently told the facts of life about world politics by lecturers flown in for the weekend.[14] The pressure on the Union Balls and Banquets was unrelenting; at a reception at Endsleigh Street held immediately before the UCL Foundation Ball, two past presidents of NUS were there to support the Executive's canvassing. Eventually, the 'swingometer' which the UCL NUS Committee had installed in their Gower Street office moved slowly in favour of the ISC and the Executive. The Council decision was reversed at Exeter.

But during these six months radical counter-networks developed; left-wing centres had kept in daily telephone contact and this enabled the cooperation behind attempts at national student opposition to the Rhodesian UDI centred on LSE and York. Throughout this period there was increasing concern with the growing pace of student activity in Europe and the USA where the universities were spearheading the opposition to the Vietnam War. The syndicalism of the French students and the Direct Action of the Provo movement increasingly became part of British students political syntax. Just as the Americans had studied the tactics and literature of the CND movement, so FSM and SDS literature was shipped back to English activists. There was a sudden growth of motions moving no confidence in the philosophy of the National Union of Students, an approach which would have been unthinkable two years ago. The first of these debates was in Hull on 25 January 1967, where David Adelstein's attack on the inadequacies of NUS's vision was supported by 208 of the 250 student unions. *The Times* described the vote as 'essentially a victory for the union's politically active element which has successfully exploited a widespread dissatisfaction among students who feel that they are not being given enough say in how their union is run'.[15] Geoff Martin's reaction

14. See *Private Eye* and *Essex Left*, May 1967.
15. *The Times*, 26 January 1967.

was 'philosophical', he continued to attribute these reversals to minor and temporary discontents. The *Guardian*'s summary was more realistic, 'in constituent unions there has been criticism of misuses of executive powers, lack of militant leadership, a decision to double membership fees, internal voting procedures and divisions of opinion among the executive.'[16] Over the following months motions of no confidence proliferated in Swansea, Keele, Birmingham, Essex and both the London technical colleges and colleges of education. The Executive remained complacent; Martin told *New Society*, 'that he expects to see unions "trot in and out" for a time'.[17] The first signs of a nationally organized alternative to the NUS's unrepentantly non-militant politics came when twelve student leaders, six of them primarily active in ULS, NALSO and the CP, and the rest local union celebrities, signed a manifesto which they offered the waiting student movement as 'a basis for discussion and action'. The Radical Student Alliance was thus launched. The actual content of the manifesto was moderate and basic, stressing student rights to control their own union and union funds and have a say in disciplinary matters. It demanded an end to the means test and declared that education must be 'classless, integrated (not tripartite or binary) and comprehensive at all levels'. It asked for more pay for teachers and solidarity with foreign students, especially those who were the victims of oppression. It even went as far as to mention collective student action on 'matters of social concern ... for example in opposition to racialism wherever it occurs.' For those without knowledge of the turbulent conflict within NUS, it would appear innocuous; for those convinced of the need for a revolutionary challenge, it was scarcely fiery. For most of the winter term things were quiet. Meanwhile however, the attack on Walter Adams's desirability as Director of LSE had begun; LSE students boycotted lectures on the day of Adelstein's trial (for writing to *The Times*). At the NUS Margate Conference in November, Bill Savage, the outgoing President, skilfully endorsed the LSE action in terms of an attack on 'educational Colonel Blimps', a typically golf club image, and managed to use LSE as a codpiece for the NUS's lack of militancy over less spec-

16. *Guardian*, 24 January 1967.
17. *New Society*, 16 February 1967.

tacular discipline problems. Every time Adelstein spoke he was received with rapturous applause, but an LSE motion advocating the use of direct action in cases where negotiations broke down, failed to reach the floor. Mike Thomas, Vice President, said angrily, 'Some of those concerned were not protesting solely about the suspensions.'[18] The NUS response was further proof of their ability to miss the point as they stumbled through the wood of injustice trying to find the legal tree. The most heated debate was over the much vaunted change in the voting system. In a bitter debate the platform was clearly split in its attitude to the whole relationship of Executive with membership. The Treasurer attacked 'corruption' from the platform. The 58 per cent vote for a change in the election system against the strong advice of the platform reflected a growing independence and radicalism.

The next period is worth some examination to plot out the Executive's responses to a fluid situation. The RSA pressed ahead to its first conference which was held at LSE over the weekend of 28/29 January. The press release promised that the meeting would be 'the first public testing of a common front student alliance which has so far been influential but ambiguous ... it can be expected that the convention will dramatize the growing split in the leadership and local membership of the national union.' About 500 students arrived from all over Britain with strong Union contingents from Birmingham, Manchester, Leeds and Hull. Not a single official from NUS was apparently visible. The discussion was energetic and volatile. Procedure was dispensed with and formal motions scarcely occurred. The meeting had a very strong antipathy to organization; the phrase 'grass roots' could be guaranteed to enter every speech. RSA speakers pledged themselves, as the *Guardian* put it 'to a brand of political involvement which NUS has studiously sought to avoid'.[19] The central discussion was on the government's announcement of a discriminatory fee increase for overseas students which was decreed on the first day of the Christmas vacation without any consultation whatsoever. After electing twenty members of a council to act as a coordinating body to service student radicals, the

18. At St Mary's College of Education, Strawberry Hill.
19. *Guardian*; David Gowlay, 'The Shape of Student Politics'.

meeting called for a day of mass student activity in the form of strikes, boycotts, meetings, and town rallies on 22 July 1967 and massive participation in the NUS parliamentary protest rally organized for 1 July.

The NUS's absence from the meeting did not prevent their attempting to nullify it with the sort of press release which they so much prefer to dialogue. On Sunday, Geoff Martin put onto the Agency tapes the most hackneyed ploy ever used by the NUS. It took the form of a letter to the Russian Student Council, complaining about an alleged meeting between two Russian students visiting this country as guests of NUS and Communist students in Britain. This offence took place in November and although it took two months for the President to decide that a rebuke was deserved, it was also deemed necessary to release its contents to the British Press before it had been received in Moscow. The press rose beautifully; stories headed 'Students Protest Against Russian Interference' all mentioned RSA as the subject of discussion between the Russians and the British Communists. The notion that militancy can be imported from Moscow and student radicals stagemanaged from the Kremlin could only occur to an antiquated Cold War bureaucrat.

Despite the assault in the press, students arrived in massive numbers for the July lobby of Parliament, and despite the deliberate attempts of the NUS leadership to confine it to two union officials from each college, like a coach trip to *The Sound of Music*. Martin walked out of the lobby after twenty minutes but the rest of the 3,000 students waited patiently and in spite of the painful movement of the queue and the rain, the lobbiers remained determined. The National Press gave it the widest coverage that a student lobby has ever had. The *Evening Standard* editorial described the protest as 'symptomatic of a fairly modern phenomenon. The development of an obsessive and direct interest in political action among students.'[20]

Subsequent NUS activity was centred on manoeuvring with the Conservative Party to have a motion sufficiently mild to encourage Labour rebels, placed on the House's business. The plan was to stage a one-day protest on the day before the debate in the House but the letters to their local NUS secretaries were en-

20. *Evening Standard*, 1 February 1967.

tirely concerned with the dangers of militancy. Rather than any rash talk of strikes, they suggested what the *Guardian* called 'a moderate policy of lobbying and letter-writing' and were obsessed that any action that was taken should have the full approval of the college authorities and local newspaper editors. Aware that on the campus the radicals were forcing the pace, the Executive chose this period to dissociate itself from the RSA and its activities.

On Sunday 5 February, the *Sunday Times* reported that 'a group of hard-line moderates will demand the proscription of the RSA, a popular front ginger group within the NUS' and went on, 'a hard-line member of the Executive ... said yesterday "This would be a crushing blow for the Union, but we believe it necessary to prevent Communist control."' The article then attempted to list 'self-declared Communists' naming three well-known non-Communists, members of the Labour and Liberal parties, to whom the *Sunday Times* apologized the following week. Although there is no constitutional means for proscribing anyone, the Executive, meeting the same day, busied themselves in the composition of a letter officially, 'disassociating themselves' from the RSA. In Manchester, the right wing forced a filibuster through three Union meetings and the Union ran a referendum before the strike action was agreed on. The NUS had still not committed themselves to a date for their action, indeed could not, till the date of their parliamentary debate was decided on by the Whips. They continued with their anti-militant pleas; on no account was any action to be called a 'strike' since, 'preliminary response from the national press to this sort of action has been highly unfavourable'. On 18 February, the Executive chose, lo and behold, 22 February for their activity too, although the parliamentary debate was on the same day. In their letter which announced this, they sternly warned against any lobbying of Parliament in case it would distract and anger previously sympathetic MPs and insisted that 'under no circumstances should the word strike be used' ... all these admonitions despite the apparent knowledge that any mass activity would have been planned for three weeks now. On the eve of 22 February, the NUS began the final stage of its desk-bound protest and started to claim that it was the radicals who had procrastinated and had 'attached them-

selves to our shirt tails because it's the only way they can get publicity. They have called for strikes and pickets which we think
frankly ridiculous'.[21] Having heaved themselves on to the band-
waggon some three weeks late, they proceeded to denounce the
drivers and announce that it was all a mistake. These anti-militant
tactics had some success. The claim that strike action might alien-
ate press and parliamentary opinion confused some unions and
Lancaster, Hull, Glasgow and Strathclyde called off boycotts. But
The Times still calculated that ten universities took effective
strike action and quoted a RSA leader as estimating that as many
as twenty were officially involved. The only meeting that NUS
could claim to have taken a direct hand in organizing was the
'orderly and attentive meeting' at the Friends House, Euston
Road, where Lord Arran called the decision 'a highly morally
distasteful action'. That evening, Geoff Martin was once again
on television where he devoted his time to another attack on the
RSA's motives. At the NUS Easter Council in Liverpool, the Executive's 'timing' of their protest action was censured and the
RSA, the Northern Presidents' Meeting and the Coordinating
Committee of Overseas Student Organization were congratulated.

The point of this examination of dates and decision is to show
that in a real context the NUS leadership lack both the desire
and the political structure to mobilize protest on this sort of
scale. For in practice, the people who care enough to organize
strikes and lead protests are precisely those militants the NUS
Executive has constantly attacked.

Now the Grants

The same pattern was repeated with an identical script when the
Government announced its intention to halve whatever increase
might be recommended by the Triennial Grants Review due to
report in 1968. This vicious cut in the value of grants came at a
time when the Margate Conference of the NUS (November
1967) had discussed and rejected the notion of a student wage.
Discussion of the idea of the 'student worker' was widespread
among radical students at the RSA's Second Conference,
NALSO's Student Power meeting and the National Workers'

21. *The Times*, 23 February 1967.

Control Conference. The concept did challenge student loyalty to the ruling class ethic of the old universities and the power structures of the new. But it is evident that students do not occupy the same position within capitalist relations of production as do workers – whose daily life drums into their consciousness the fundamental conflict over the division of the product. The remoteness of much of this discussion became obvious when – after the freeze, devaluation, the highest bank rate for forty years and a new £3,000 million international loan – the January 1968 measures turned to the business of dismantling the social services. The ruthlessness of the cuts of school building, school milk and teacher expansion made complete nonsense of the NUS proposals for educational growth. The international needs of British capitalism made it essential to depress domestic living standards to the point where even British business might increase its share of world trade. Some of the cuts were economically gratuitous: school milk and prescription charges were attacked entirely for the benefit of foreign bankers. The severity of the assault on student grants showed up the optimism of those militants who felt that the main problem confronting the NUS was whether to dub inevitable increases a grant or a wage. The impossibility of considering student conditions apart from the larger social crisis had never been clearer.

The NUS reactions which ensued follow too closely those of the Overseas Fees Campaign to need repetition here. Martin argued that students were prepared, like anyone else, to make sacrifices for Britain in crisis, although *his membership was constitutionally prevented even from discussing the nature of this crisis*. In his public appearances, he competed with the Government in proposing possible attacks on educational spending, denouncing student militants and urging better discipline. Various meetings were held with Gordon Walker.

Aware of the opposition by even the Right to his earlier enthusiasm for the grant sacrifices, Martin now tended to decorate his statements with appeals to protect the 'children of less well off families'. The usual rallies and marches produced some mobilization, but the NUS leadership relied on inertia to cover the traces of a defeat they had no intention of fighting. Indeed the circumstances of the cut in grants placed them in a very difficult position. For either they accepted the cut and the 'Back Britain' logic that went with it, or they had to accept that the attack on education and student conditions was merely the climax of a sequence of attacks on working-class wages, living standards and industrial organizations – and could only be fought alongside the other groups attacked.

An attempt to move No Confidence in the Executive's handling of the grants issue failed at the NUS's Leicester Conference despite a wide backing from local unions. This setback and the defeat of radical candidates in the 1968 elections depended largely on skilled handling of delegates. The elected President for 1968–70 is Trevor Fisk, previously Union Secretary, who publicly announced that he was running to stop the radical candidate. The Elections Commission ruled that he was ineligible for candidature because he only signed on to his law course at the Inns of Court six days before the election papers were due. This decision was then startlingly reversed in a second overnight session. It is an index of the general level of political and intellectual credulity within the NUS that even these gymnastics were not seriously challenged. In 1962, Fisk was listed by David George, then President of Debates at London University, 'as one of the signatories to George's own proposed constitution of a University of London Chapter of the John Birch Society'. While there is little doubt that his views have been suitably modified since those days, Fisk remains the product of the right-wing, elitist Union dynasty that is one of the worst bureaucratic cliques in the country.

The international chain of student insurgency in the spring and summer of 1968 began to transform the perspectives of the British student movement. Occupations and sit-ins occurred in a wide range of colleges on a wide range of issues (the examinations system, the nature of courses, disciplinary powers of university authorities etc.). Events such as these prompted some student radicals to abandon their tussle within the NUS and to strengthen revolutionary student power agitation at the base. At the same time those socialists who had formerly condemned student movements as irredeemably petit-bourgeois began to acknowledge that they might have a genuinely revolutionary potential after all. The inauguration of a Revolutionary Socialist Student Fed-

eration in June 1968 was in part the product of these re-orienta-
tions. This promises to be a crucial initiative in the development
of a revolutionary student movement in Britain. The reaction of
the NUS leadership to the stirring events of this period was to
tell anyone who cared to listen that student insurrection could
be avoided in Britain if only the Government and the Vice Chan-
cellors would concede the petty ameliorations proposed by the
NUS. Nothing could be more loathsome to Fisk and his kind
than a revolution which promised to strangle the last capitalist
with the entrails of the last bureaucrat. Their reflex appeared
merely to use the student insurrections to apply a little pressure
to the authorities and present the NUS as the champion of the
reasonable majority of students.

The Future

The NUS oligarchy will certainly never reform itself. Despite
opportunities for even a diplomatic shift to the Left, it has remained wedded to a deeply conservative vision of society and
human action within it. It has refused to reassess its 'apoliticism' and, if anything, has intensified its fetishistic concern with
the niceties of non-involvement. The politics of NUS still remain manipulative, managing the press and manufacturing debate; the only hope for mass democracy is bigger parties and
more sherry. The Executive's stained-glass minds concentrate on
methods of reforming the Union without allowing any of their
top-down power into the hands of the active membership. Externally there is no attempt to unite the fragmented policies of the
Union into a single intelligible critique, far less to link this to a
strategy for change in British education and society. A phoney
consensus with genuine differences glossed over, is still preferred
to the admission of fundamental divisions. The feebleness of
NUS consensualism in student crises, like LSE and the Overseas
Student Fees decision, emphasizes the gap between it and a
genuine student union.

What is needed is a programme which would enable the students to experience new rank and file alliances and a much higher
level of demands and activities. This is precisely what happened
in the USA, where the direct contact of the activists with the

machinery of segregation in the South, and the Northern Ghettos, expanded their outlook into a wider picture of the American power structure. A real student movement will grow out of real struggle, not *vice versa*. The sort of transitional projects that activists could increasingly launch should have as their central aim enlarging the arena of student activity to include the Trades Council and the Stewards Committees as well as the Union and University. A national Housing Campaign could, for instance, link up with local housing struggles and Tenants Associations in a way which would enhance all three activities. For they are all reflections of the same failure to divert adequate funds into public housing.

The particular situation of the student in lodgings and flats which are quite useless for serious study and cost him two-thirds of his grant, is merely one consequence of the same crisis which forces council rents up and allows the domination of the Rachmans of Islington, Moss Side and Liverpool 9. The 'sustained programme to provide more houses at prices that ordinary people can afford' of which the Labour Party Manifesto spoke has utterly failed to change the basic situation. Three and a half million houses lacking basic amenities; four million houses over eighty years old; land prices up 40 per cent over the last five years; the student has lived all this problem. Any demand that university students should jump the queue of stagnation may make educational sense in terms of 'output and efficiency' but it would be the effort of a fragmented interest group to evade the general crisis by a partial solution. Wilson's satellitism to Washington forces an attack on Government spending. It does not distinguish between student building or local authority building. The new Rent Act, welcomed by NUS as another lever to decent student accommodation at reasonable prices, has turned out to be controlled by precisely those landlords, lawyers and estate agents it was designed to attack. Of the 1,100 cases going to appeal in the GLC area, many of them by students, only 357 had a decrease in rent upheld and 480 had their rent levels increased. What is needed is student evidence which can link the students' housing conditions to the general social situation and then use this factual background not just on the shelves of the DES, student union files and newspaper editors' waste paper baskets, but in a campaign at tenant meetings and council house protests. A housing campaign for students which does not take the plight of the rest of the community into consideration will get the contempt it deserves from the working people. Students should not be asking for special treatment and university cubicles but fair housing and a council house for students as well as any other young worker. By uniting their experience of the need for decent living conditions with the fights and organizations of other groups who are demanding dramatic improvements in their housing conditions, students give meaning to their demands to be treated like ordinary people and ordinary people will respect them for it.

Equally, the radicals' demand for militancy and involvement can be made concrete action over the teachers' pay claim. Teachers' real wages have been steadily falling, in relation not only to manual workers but also to white collar and other professional groups. A comparison with ten other European Countries puts Britain at the bottom (except for Eire) in some categories. The combination of a non-militant Union, desperate overcrowding and absurd salaries has long caused an exodus from the profession. In one year alone, 2,000 newly qualified students never even took up a position. If the Government were serious about increasing the leaving age, reducing classes to statutory size and implementing the staffing recommendations of the Plowden Report, it would need to increase the number of teachers by about 200,000, some 70 per cent of the current teaching force. Yet the blame for the present situation lies very largely with the teaching unions, which have used any and every excuse to evade any militant action. They have followed the ATTI and the AUT's concept of a white collar union with its 'professional ethic' (which never cramps the BMA's style), isolated from their own rank and file and other unions. The correct models of course, are the white collar unions like DATA, ASSET and AScW, which use selected strike action, intensive negotiations and a high level of strike pay to great effect. Employers are powerless against militant wage bargaining in one sector with the whole area resources behind it. Afterwards the neighbouring sectors can fight to drift their wages up to the new differential levels. The selective sanctions that teachers have agreed to apply make possible this form of sectional attack especially if the areas of militancy were already

Plowden designated 'positive wage discrimination' areas. The NUS has always had a formal policy for increasing teachers' pay, but militant action is now needed on the picket line and the school hall.

In many respects the alternatives which are said to confront student militants – the industrial struggle or the university – are simply a function of the comparatively small number of student militants. A developed, autonomous student movement with a clear theoretical perspective would be able to obtain wide inroads of control within the university while at the same time participating in anti-imperialist and workers' struggles. This is already true of Japan and increasingly so of Germany. Without experience of mass political struggle, above all in the Labour movement, the best criticism of colour-supplement culture, the most complete blue-print for students' control or the grooviest anti-university might all be sponsored by the Arts Council. The Left within the university has got to find a bond with those parts of the system which are able to halt and change it fundamentally, such as tenants and unofficial strikers. The campus cannot become a citadel of advanced political consciousness if the same old lies of national unity, social peace and racial difference are steam-rollered over the rest of society. The Revolutionary Socialist Students Federation could play a vital role here, in clarifying and generalizing the political content of student struggle.

For either radical or revolutionary, work in the NUS is depressing and seldom rewarding. The sheer dead weight of an organization defined by the absence of militants is difficult to exaggerate. Debate appears so infantile, organization appears so manipulative and elections appear so deeply conditioned by hucksterism that the value of enlarging the radical enclave within NUS is very questionable. At present, given the wide range of interest-groups within the union and their uneven level of political development, it is unlikely that a radical Executive would be able to give the advanced political militants in the universities what they want and at the same time service the entirely different attitude of the apolitical small colleges. The NUS does represent some kind of expression for the activists in the small colleges without any socialist formation, and the NUS Council is their main chance to make contact with other militants, especially those in local universities and bigger colleges who can make available their experience. This has happened in Leeds, Manchester and Essex on a very political basis. RSA was welcomed by precisely these people as a way to overcome the isolation of radicals marooned in backward colleges; it allowed them to gain invitations and thus foot-holds in colleges that would ban the Conservative Party. But it is also true that the leadership of the NUS could change hands without anything like a majority of British students being aware of it; unless a radical Executive had some mass backing at the roots, a well-organized Right deprived of power would be in a strong position to counter-attack.

Perhaps the most important of the current developments is that the increasingly frustrated militant universities are talking of disaffiliation. The NUS at present remains almost unique in Europe as a single national union. What is more frequent is one militant union and a sorry service organization. But where an autonomous revolutionary student movement emerges outside the national union, such as the SDS in Germany or the SDS in the USA, the latter often trails belatedly after it. If a genuine lead is given, it will oblige the national organization to follow – as the VDS and NSA had to some extent to do in West Germany and the USA.

Beyond all these questions of organization, it is clear that out of the ideological wreckage of social-democracy and Stalinism, a new student revolutionary perspective is emerging – international, extra-parliamentary and returning militant politics to the street. These students have seen through the fancy dress of modern capitalism and found the irrational violence and the hopelessness which is its core. They have seen their community of interest with the working class – a community which should concern us as much as it should frighten those who rule us. There is a spectre haunting Europe and its banners read, in Berlin and Warsaw and Paris and London: 'Today the Students, Tomorrow the Workers'.

The CIA and Student Politics/David Triesman

1.

Three years ago, it could not be said that the most consuming item of interest to British students was the problem of the international student organizations. Its spiral to notoriety as an 'issue' was, in the best James Bond tradition, owing to the discovery that behind the entire Western set-up of cheap holidays, glossy student magazines and half-price admissions to the Louvre which characterized the International Student Conference for most of us, lay another world of melodramatic intrigue, the whole being financed by the Central Intelligence Agency of the United States. As with most chronic patients, once the disease in the ISC had been diagnosed, only the enthusiasts wait for the latest bulletin on the hopeless case. And yet the question is still important, not only for the lessons it teaches about international student cooperation, but also because it looks very much as though this country is to play nursemaid to the ISC.

The ISC, its Secretariat having rested its filing cabinets for the last decade in Leiden, Holland, has now been asked to leave by the Dutch students' union. Having lost the base of its operations it finds itself in the embarrassing position of being disowned by former staunch friends in Switzerland, El Salvador and Costa Rica, treated with extreme reserve by the Scandinavians, and almost inevitably forced to turn for a home towards London. The situation is a stark reminder of the state of international relations in the student world, and illustrates why we should decline to receive the guest. The answer to the question, 'Why this isolation?', says something about the ISC, and it also says something about the National Union of Students in Britain, the last major union to back the ISC.

The answer to the question lies in the answer to two other questions. The first is, what is the truth about the CIA infiltration? The second is, how has the international student complex operated over the past twenty years, how has the Cold War come to mark a generation of student unionism? Intermingled with these questions lie the threads of suspicion which surround the Western International Student Conference and the peculiar, equivocal position of our National Union, itself now the subject of considerable distrust. Undoubtedly, the most crucial factor in the twenty-year history has been the CIA infiltration, now proved and accepted by everyone. We cannot, however, dispense with a brief resumé of this history.

The storm which finally made the international student organizations an inescapable problem broke in February 1967. The American West Coast magazine *Ramparts* announced in a full page advert in the *New York Times* that in its March edition it would reveal how 'the CIA had infiltrated and subverted the world student leaders'. Before the issue appeared the State Department admitted a link between the CIA and the American student organization USNSA,[1] dating back to 1952.[2]

We may summarize the *Ramparts* report on the CIA machinery which it unveiled. The first hint of a liaison had come in 1964 when Texas Congressman Wright Patman was investigating tax dodges employed by foundations. He suggested that the J. M. Kaplan Fund was a CIA financial channel. Despite his retraction of the information, some facts emerged. Like the Kaplan Fund, which served the CIA from 1961 to 1963, five other 'foundations' which supplied money to Kaplan were not listed by the Inland Revenue as tax exempt foundations. They were the Borden Trust, the Price Fund, the Edsel Fund, the Beacon Fund and the Kentfield Fund. They also gave money to two other foundations, the F. Frederick Brown Foundation and the Independence Foundation, which in turn supported the past programmes of NSA. The Independence Foundation was a significant contributor, paying the down-payment on NSA's headquarters, receiving $247,000 in 1962, of which it collected a mere $18,500 from individuals, and over $100,000 from the Funds named. Like the Kaplan Foundation, another which had initially depended on the largesse of its founder, the Rabb Foundation was suddenly fortunate enough to receive two large gifts from the Price Fund which it passed intact to NSA.

As soon as the scandal broke, NSA's Supervisory Board issued a statement: 'Officers from the NSA negotiated for these funds directly with the Agency (the CIA). The funds were passed from the Agency to USNSA through the Catherwood Foundation, Fund for Youth and Student Affairs (FYSA) and the San Jacinto Fund.' The NSA officers who made the statement had been attempting for some time to break out of the strangle-hold, but were continually forced to deliver the goods. One NSA President, Phil Sherburne, did rebel, staging a fight for NSA's autonomy. Although initially friendly to the Agency, he demanded complete control of the international programme which exerted considerable influence on the affairs of the ISC. Until then, the policy was planned by NSA staff members and the CIA, whether in the fields of scholarships, conferences, publications or exchanges.

Sherburne's non-cooperation led to the first ever delays in grant schedules by FYSA or San Jacinto, which were now emerging as the major contributors. The money eventually started flowing again, but Sherburne admitted that the CIA's Covert Action Division No Five had become so alarmed by his behaviour that they considered cutting all ties with NSA. Besides, Sherburne was already in their bad books. He had written to the Soviet National Union of Students suggesting that he meet their leaders and discuss opening bilateral agreements, and exchange schemes. The CIA, on finding out about the approach, explained that Soviet Intelligence assumed NSA took its orders from the US government, and Sherburne's letter would be taken as an official change in CIA policy on bilateralism. In future, before diplomatic overtures, he must get permission from the Agency. One could scarcely find a more poignant illustration of how closely NSA was tied to the CIA and how remote it was from student life.

Although it is important to see what happened to NSA, British students were obviously more concerned about ISC, of which they are still members. Not only did ISC get much of its money from NSA,[3] but it was also provided for by the same foundations which looked after the prosperity of the latter. The two funds which provided 90 per cent of the ISC budget were FYSA and San Jacinto, FYSA giving by far the most – $1,826,000 between 1962 and 1964, without which ISC would have been impotent as an international body. That is not to imply that San Jacinto was mean; they delivered nearly half a million dollars for ISC's glossy magazine *The Student*, which has never been thought of as a firebrand of progress, and a further third of a million for other purposes including several international conferences. San Jacinto, named after a battle in which the Texans massacred the Mexicans, has somehow contrived to avoid any registration for taxation purposes, either in the local offices at Austin, Texas, or in the Federal Tax Office in Washington. Its address leads to a small accountant's office in downtown Houston. No one at NSA or ISC knew the names of any of its directors or its source of finance. FYSA, on the other hand, has a board of directors and an imposing office. The *New York Times* summarizes the career of its Executive Secretary, Harry Lunn, from the time of his Presidency of NSA (1954–5) and subsequent work for ISC in South East Asia: 'After his student work, Mr Lunn was reported to have worked as a research assistant in the Defense Department. He was then assigned to the political section of the American Embassy in Paris, and later worked for the Alliance for Progress, before joining the foundation.' He also worked in the militantly anti-Communist Independent Research Service, while employed in the Department of Defense. When asked by the *New York Times*, Lunn 'declined to say whether he had been an intermediary between the Agency and student groups'. His boss, the President of FYSA, and Steuben Glass Inc., Arthur A. Houghton Jnr., 'conceded in a statement that he had cooperated with the government but refused to discuss the extent'. Houghton was more elaborate in a reply to the French union, UNEF, when he cabled 142 words of eloquent corroboration mingled with intense chauvinistic pride in the work of FYSA, which was 'started by me some years ago to assist in philanthropic activities in which I am interested'. Towards the end he writes: 'At the moment, some of the activities of FYSA are being questioned. I do not intend to give answers to these allegations. I have never sought public recognition in my philanthropic activities, nor disclosed my contributions to any organization. I do not intend to do so now. If at any time I have cooperated with my government on matters affecting the national interest, that is my own affair.'

Many other papers have taken an unequivocal view of the infiltration. The *Economist*, not commonly associated with the international Communist conspiracy, remarked: 'It turned out last week that the Central Intelligence Agency had for about fifteen years been a principal source of finance for both NSA and the ISC' (25 February 1968, p. 725). *The Times* commented: '*The Washington Star* reported that the ISC in Leiden have received millions over the last decade. The money was said to have been channelled through public foundations, among them FYSA of New York.' It went on to say that the CIA 'has used students to spy, it has used students to pressure international student organizations into taking cold war positions ...' (15 February). *Time Magazine* also named the ISC as a major recipient of CIA money.

As the evidence left no loopholes, there was little the American students could do except make a full statement. Already the French and Irish unions were threatening to leave (they subsequently did) and it was commented in London that the one thing you could say about the International Student Conference was that it had little to do with students, was no longer a conference, and at the present rate of disaffiliation, wouldn't be international much longer. So USNSA, with no doubts about the identity of ISC's wealthy benefactor said: 'unless the ... ISC completely dissociate themselves from the CIA and make a public disclosure of the nature of their previous relationship, the National Supervisory Board will recommend to the next NSA conference that NSA withdraw its membership.'

This as might be expected stimulated feverish activity in Leiden. NSA President Gene Groves flew to the headquarters of ISC, where an emergency summit meeting took place with other leaders. He told them that NSA had to make a confession, but urged his Leiden colleagues to say as little as possible. Where Foundation personnel were available, they either made no comment, or made no attempts to deny the allegations; many of them incriminated themselves.

The initial statement from ISC headquarters said, 'the ISC knows no evidence to suggest that any of its funds have come from clandestine bodies in any country.' The Indian Secretary General, Ram Lakhina amplified this, telling the *New York*

Times: 'We receive our money from sources in many countries, but not from the CIA or any other Government Agency, including the State Department. To the best of my knowledge, our financial sources are tied to business interests. ... There are several in the USA but I cannot discuss them.' Geoff Martin, however, had told the Conference of the NUS [4] in England that the money came from individuals, not business interests.[5]

2.

The explosive impact of these revelations in the USA was tremendous. The American students decided to leave the ISC at their 1967 Conference. The move was recommended by President Gene Groves and the International Affairs Vice-President of NSA who stated that NSA 'should detach itself from the area of the cold war'. A comprehensive coverage of the disaffiliation appeared in the *New York Herald Tribune*[6]; the article also revealed some remarkable data on the link-up, and the emotions it produced both before, and at, the conference at the University of Maryland:

Officers of the International Student Association, which has received financial support from the CIA called today for the organization's 'unilateral withdrawal' from 'the Cold War of International student politics'.

In reports to the Association's annual Congress here, the officers recommended that the student group end its ties with the International Student Conference in the Netherlands.

The International group, like the NSA has received much of its funds from the CIA.

It was also learned that the International Conference and the British Union of Students received funds from a British counterpart of the dummy foundations that channelled the money from the CIA to American student groups.

The NSA said that from 1952 to February 1967, it had received more than $3·3 million as 'an intelligence and operations wing of the CIA'. Eugene Groves, the NSA President said his organization frequently did not even know where its overseas staff members were while they served as 'CIA agents and informers'.

Mr Groves told some 1,500 delegates to the Association's Congress that during the breakaway period, Richard G. Stearns, NSA Vice-President 'was awakened at 4 a.m. to be read out of future service in the US government by a CIA agent over the phone'.

Another NSA leader, Jim Johnson 'was frightened he would be knocked off on the street corner that week in Washington'. ... Mr Groves said that he had been told that Philip Sherburne, former NSA President, 'was threatened with the fabrication of psychiatric records — records which would appropriately turn up at a future date and ruin his career or open him to blackmail'.

'NSA was exploited because it was weak. To the individuals involved, a generation of the most promising student leaders, the CIA taught that spying on fellow students overseas, and being dishonest to close friends and the constituency at home, was serving the country.'

3.

What can be said of Britain where a number of British students have been senior office holders in the ISC? Geoff Martin, who headed the NUS International Affairs section for some time, was deeply involved in ISC and travelled up and down the country for two years allaying the fears among constituent Unions [7] about ISC financing. He told them he had the facts. If he had them, then he knew about the ISC link with the CIA and if he knew nothing of the CIA connexion, then he clearly did not have even an approximation of the facts, and he wittingly or unwittingly misinformed two NUS Conferences [8] and innumerable constituent Unions.

The NUS reaction to the revelation will probably strike the next student generation as amazing. The Executive issued an undistinguished and complacent Report.[9] It launched an intellectually miserable attack on the American students, and made a commitment to 'back' the Third World, whatever that means. Its authors, Trevor Fisk, Mike Thomas and Albert Preston devoted nearly a third of it to attacking the students in this country who had questioned the whole international role of the Union and certain of its finances for years. The Executive fiercely resisted a debate on the question at the Margate 1967 Conference of NUS, and when the debate eventually took place, there was scarcely time for four three-minute speeches. The Conference marginally rejected disaffiliation. Since then, despite the disaffiliation of a number of other national Unions, and the publication of a series of damning reports, the NUS Executive has said and done virtually nothing. Effectively, then, the NUS is the only major Union solidly supporting the ISC. Together with the International Secretariat it is now moving to exclude from all further discussion on ISC, any Union not prepared to pledge full support for the policies and leadership. The stated reason is that there is no longer enough money to invite hostile Unions to conferences. Thus the ISC lurches towards its inevitable demise.

4.

To see what it is that the CIA wanted, and to reach any conclusions about the future, it is necessary to look briefly at the background in which the Cold War stances were taken up.

Following the Second World War, there was a general impetus to establish a democratic, progressive, international union of students. Pre-war organizations were plainly useless, and with the slogans of peace and anti-Fascism, a conference in Prague established the International Union of Students (IUS) in August 1946. It soon emerged that behind the formal slogans lay deep ideological differences, the first of them caused by the British intervention in the Greek Civil War.

The mounting pressures of the Cold War were beginning to make a serious impact on the IUS by the late 1940s. In 1947 the Americans urged the IUS to condemn the Communist takeover in Czechoslovakia after the elections that year, and when the Union refused, the Americans left. In the following years, the Western Unions became increasingly isolated, playing an opposition role, under the leadership of our National Union. IUS finally split over the attitude adopted by the majority in the Union when they expelled the Jugoslav students in 1949 on grounds parallel to the Russian government's position in the Stalin–Tito dispute. This finally drove the Western Unions out into the cold. However, they were not long to be without an organization. In 1950, in Stockholm, the NUS and Scandinavian unions formed the International Student Conference, which coalesced around the fundamental and reificatory tenet that it would only discuss problems of the 'student as such'; it could discuss education but not 'politics', the root cause of the dissent in the IUS. It would be, as the name implies, simply a Conference, without formal structure or organization, students coming together at conferences to discuss mutual problems; there were to be no members, merely participants. In 1952, a Coordinating Secretariat (COSEC) was formed to implement Conference decisions, but it had no executive powers.

During the late fifties, ISC grew rapidly, reaching its zenith with eighty members in 1962. The Western European unions and Americans preserved a controlling interest at conferences and in the COSEC, providing, with the Commonwealth delegations, over half the membership. Australia was even appointed the Asian representative on COSEC. The growth, however, produced the same problems for the ISC leadership that the growth of the United Nations seems to have produced for the USA. Ex-colonial students, like all other emergent peoples, see their political and economic problems, both domestic and international, as of paramount interest, making the tradition of discussing 'education' in the abstract, divorced from a social context, irrelevant. Whilst the idea of conducting this type of abstract discussion, in advanced Western countries, rests on specious logic, in the Third World nations where the creation of an education system was a concomitant of political and economic independence, such an abstraction is absurd. Thus, if the unions from the advanced countries were not to be isolated, leaving the others to the IUS, ISC had to admit 'politics'. It was in this way that the phenomenon of seeing a Western organization passing anti-imperialist motions emerged. Clearly, many of the advanced unions were voting for these motions, and a sprinkling of anti-Communist motions, for the process never resulted in any implementation, and kept the emergent countries happy at very little cost. The political issue only came to a head at Quebec (10th ISC) in 1962, when the question of whether the ISC would give support to students actively engaged in struggles against imperialism was raised. The dispute centred around the proposed recognition of the Puerto Rican Student Union, FUPI, whose major activity was the struggle for independence.

In a way which has never ceased to amaze onlookers, the Secretariat apparently seemed to find, overnight, a rival, non-political union, which claimed to represent the Puerto Rican students, discrediting FUPI. A thirteen-hour debate raged over the recognition issue, in which the Latin American Unions stated that the aims of FUPI were more important than the

bickering about who it claimed to represent. However, it was the
tactical point and constitutionality of the Western Unions which
won the day, and in the face of this conservatism, the Latin
Americans (all but two Unions), the French-speaking Africans,
some southern Europeans and the Indonesians, a total of twenty-
six national unions, walked out. Nor could they be prevailed on
to return.

In fact, the debacle led ISC to turn through a complete circle;
having begun as a non-political debating forum, it now became
a completely political organization. By the 11th Conference of
the ISC at Christchurch, New Zealand in 1964, by which time
other dissident Unions were exluded,[10] a Charter was adopted
which recreated ISC, making it an explicit political counter-
force to IUS. It had a full-time organization with a Secretariat
which it enabled to initiate policy between conferences; it had
formal and binding membership. The Charter also contained a
manifesto condemning Imperialism, Totalitarianism, Colonialism and Racism, this being considered minimal bait to dangle
before the Third World. The NUS played a vital role in this
conference. The mover of the new Charter was Rhys Hughes,
NUS President, a man noted for his hostility to bringing politics
into education,[11] the precise aim of the Charter. The Conference Chairman was a past NUS President, Bill Savage; ex-
President Gwyn Morgan[12] filled ISC's top civil service post,
as Secretary General. This left the job of leading the British
delegation open, and it was filled by Geoff Martin, who thereafter became NUS President.

It soon became apparent that the policies of the 'new look' ISC
had not changed appreciably from the old policies. Its Secretariat made its first independent political act the issue of a leaflet
condemning the Chinese for testing nuclear weapons. It was
not, however, until 1966 that the Conference felt able to express
any opinion on the most crucial world issue, Vietnam, a subject
on which the NSA officers were remarkably radical at home.
Eventually, a catch-all motion, condemning the North Vietnamese 'invaders', the National Liberation Front, and lastly, the
US for intervening, was passed at the 12th ISC in Nairobi.[13]

Because of the non-political policy adopted since the beginning of ISC, and lasting until the Christchurch Conference,

every critical political issue of the decade remained undiscussed by the students in the organization. At the time when the Latin Americans were just entering the international student arena, the types of issue which they found crucial were proscribed. Thus, no mention was made of the CIA's Guatemalan coup in the rarified atmosphere of the ISC. Nor did the Hungarian rising figure as an issue in the organization, at a time when support for the Hungarian students was essential. In one way and another, the policy excluded students from discussing the range of problems which, in the Cold War era, should have stimulated them most. To understand the point of such a policy, one must see it in the context of any student involvement in politics in a Western country. Whilst students are encouraged to join, and even take more than a passive part in the traditional political organizations, they are dissuaded from any engagement in unofficial political channels. Whilst, in this country, the political societies, the Labour Clubs, Conservative Associations and Liberal Unions are delighted to see the influx of new members, and the University and College Authorities are by no means averse to encouraging, even patronizing, this level of involvement, they cannot tolerate, as we have seen in the last two years, involvement on the level of serious commitment to change. The truth is that one can say almost anything in a debating society, but the act of filling out hollow words by doing any more than attending party meetings is abhorrent. The ISC leadership, and the NUS leadership, for that matter, have always asserted strongly that as individuals they have political views. As students they feel it is undesirable to mention them in their organizations. To do so, of course, would be to mobilize students as a body in their places of work and discussion, and this would inevitably produce a radical perspective which these leaders could not control. Similarly, the students who become completely apathetic become impossible to control, because they become less susceptible to established political ideas, traditional demands, and accepted forms of action. The watch-word has become, therefore, involvement, but involvement in the right sort of activity.

On the other hand, the 'non-political' ISC has always been manifestly energetic about getting foreign, sympathetic student leaders flown to the United States for their purely 'educational' Seminars. These costly trips included extended tours of the USA, showing the visitors an encouraging picture of the American way of life. Not only were these students destined to be the ascendant bourgeoisies in their own countries, but they were to become an Americanized bourgeoisie as well. This policy was, as John Gerassi [14] has shown, well developed by American commercial agencies, and the CIA in Latin America. Needless to say, the coloured foreign student leaders were not included in tours of the Southern States. It was by means of these costly holidays that the ISC managed to keep the visiting leaders reasonably happy; we should remember that the organization is a meeting point for leaders as opposed to rank-and-file members, and consequently, the cost of the support of an entire student Union was never higher than the cost of the allegiance of its leaders. We can also see why the 'student-as-a-student' attitude, acting as though 'education' was a social function entirely estranged from the remainder of the society, its economy, and any foreign power's control over its economy, was necessary if sensitive problems were to be continually evaded. The ISC allowed its members to indulge in political activity, privately, as long as it remained meaningless and ineffectual. At the same time, membership was, for the national leaders, like membership of an opulent and exclusive club.

During the latter part of this history, the NUS at home was taking a greater interest in ISC. Now that the Charter had been adopted, every national Union seeking membership had to present it to their own members for ratification. This consisted not only of acceptance of the new structure but also of the principles outlined (anti-imperialism, etc.). The leaders of the NUS, as prime movers behind the Charter, were anxious to achieve speedy ratification from Council.[15] But this same leadership had opposed any change in the NUS Constitution which allowed discussion of matters other than those 'directly affecting education'. The Council was now faced with ratifying political principles while they were at the same time unable to discuss the content of these principles, since the delegates were limited to discussing educational matters. The NUS Executive took the Charter to the November Council, 1964, though without presenting the full text; they were, however, forced to retreat and allow a Commission to 'review the developments'. This Commission comprised four members of the Executive and four elected from the floor. They deliberated for a year and presented a Majority Report signed by seven members and printed in a glossy cover, pretentiously entitled *Britain's Students In Tomorrow's World* and a minority report which the Executive turned out on some duplicating paper. The Margate Council, 1965, forcefully questioned the then International Affairs Vice-President, Geoff Martin, about the discrepancy, refused to accept the explanations offered, and concentrated more attention on the Minority Report.

The Majority Report embarked on an extraordinary historical polemic, based more on the 'Communist conspiracy', Moscow gold and Russians with snow on their boots, tramping through Bradford in the dead of night, than on any semblance of fact. The major issue in Alan Hunt's Minority Report was the financing of ISC. It pointed out that 90 per cent of the funds came from two sources, the Foundation for Youth and Student Affairs and the San Jacinto Fund. It was suspected that these Foundations had close links with American and South African industrial complexes. The evidence was based on the links between the boards of the FYSA and the Corning and Steuben Glass Companies, international cartels with interests in South Africa. At the time it was impossible to get information on San Jacinto, for reasons which are now obvious. What was particularly significant about these foundations was the way in which they passed money to the ISC. At no time were block grants made; ISC had to make a submission to them for each project on their programme, leaving the foundations free to pick the particular activity they wished to support. It was not that the foundations frequently refused funds,[16] but rather that the ISC imposed on its membership a self-limitation in that they did not seek finance for projects that they knew would be refused. The result was a concentration of financial power among the right-wing European and North American Unions.

The Minority Report recommended, in opposition to the Majority, that the NUS join neither ISC nor IUS, but should rather seek limited agreement with both to enable cooperation in giving aid to newly formed national unions or to those suffer-

ing from oppression. The policies of the future were to be formed
by the Council, rather than by the self-styled international
experts on the Executive. This line was endorsed by a two to one
majority leaving the Executive making an inevitable 'fight, fight
and fight again' promise to ignore the Council. They laid aside
most commitments to education for the next six months and
toured the country bearing the story of the red plot which, like
an old time music hall act, brought waves of nostalgia from
older NUS members so often had they heard it. The statements
they made about the purity of ISC's financial sources now looks
a little foolish. However, at the following Council, Exeter 1966,
NUS rejoined the ISC. Thus it is that ISC is still a problem for
British students.

5.

To describe the CIA revelations as embarrassing to the NUS
Executive would be to understate. Together with the Secretariat
they immediately began to spell out explanations, mingling them
with appropriate expressions of horror at the behaviour of the
American USNSA officers. The explanations were essentially of
three types, all seemingly mutually exclusive and contradictory.
They began to indicate the nature of the malaise in our international participation, and they provide concrete reasons for us
to reject any visit by ISC to this country. They also indicate the
new direction.

Firstly, the excuse that 'we didn't know' was widely used. It
can only reflect on the lack of inquisitiveness of a generation of
Western student leaders, none of whom ever questioned the
financial sources despite the strange means of financing. Further,
they attacked the students in this country who did ask the
appropriate questions. Secondly, another line of defence was
emerging from the Secretariat. 'The ISC has never and will never
accept any funds subject to any conditions or pressures.' The
suggestion is that if the money came from the CIA, as it un-
deniably did, the CIA never affected the policy and programme
of the ISC. That is to say, in direct contradiction to the first
explanation, that they did know, but were never constrained by
the CIA. Even when they were aware of the appalling international record of the CIA, and aware of the Agency's systematic

corruption of a generation of American student leaders, some of the less fastidious supporters of the ISC have used this justification: money should be accepted from the John Birch Society itself if it can be freely spent on useful and freedom-loving projects. This almost suggests that the students duped the CIA out of their money.

The truth of the situation is brutally clear; the CIA are not pouring money into Leiden for the sake of their atrophied consciences, or because of a deep-rooted belief in liberal education. The CIA's sole purpose as an organization is to further the interests of the USA, particularly in foreign policy.[17] Needless to say, no spy organization in the world, least of all the CIA, is motivated by philanthropy; the CIA have paid for the ISC for the same reason as they sponsored the Cuban 'Bay of Pigs' invasion, the overthrow of Bosch in the Dominican Republic, the organized coup in Guatemala, and manufactured the general strike which overthrew the left-wing government in Guyana.[18] They do it because the rewards yielded in power and prestige are commensurate with the expenditure. Their methods are the methods of any Government Secret Service. The CIA's Covert Action Division No. Five, which handled the whole arrangement, was unscupulous and ruthless. An NSA officer welded into the information network would be threatened with a twenty-year prison sentence should he reveal the covert arrangement. Where it suited their purpose, the CIA manufactured dissent, bought opposition and even financed the 'moderate' American critics. The occasional liberally worded statement against Franco, Salazar and Vorster scarcely met with objections from the Patron, and in exchange they had a reliable, well-equipped anti-Communist voice in the International student forum.

The whole system worked smoothly. Within the massive International Department of USNSA, the approved American student underwent initial training. The cream of these moved into the intensive course at the International Student Research Seminar (ISRIS), by courtesy of FYSA. Bearing the ISRIS seal of approval, the student 'cold warrior' was released into the world to provide solid, pro-Western leadership under the auspices of ISC. Consider two typical examples. Following the period when ex-NUS President Gwyn Morgan was Secretary General of ISC, before he departed to the greener pastures of the Labour Party International Department, a surprise candidate suddenly emerged for the top job in ISC. Ed Garvey, who won the election, after several popular candidates had been prevailed upon to withdraw, had been an NSA President in the mid-fifties. He knew about the CIA cash. ('Former NSA President Edward Garvey said they were briefed about the CIA's involvement when they were elected to their posts' – *Guardian*, 17 February.) Charles 'Chuck' Goldmark, whose unspectacular career in NSA included a vehement defence of the American Vietnam position at the Madison Conference, became Associate Secretary of ISC. To suggest that the money came without strings and reliable guardians appears blatantly absurd.

The final defence comes nearer the truth. The argument runs that as we are pro-American and anti-Communist, we should be pleased to get the money. This argument is in fact the crucial one since it both tells us why the ISC has had such a scarred history, and how it was that the CIA could infiltrate it. The leadership has been a willing participant in Cold War strategy and will back the policy to the last. Not only does the past attitude confirm this belief, but it tells us all we need to know about the future of international student cooperation, indeed, all international student cooperation within the academic world; it is to be remembered that the great spokesman of the latest vogue in the Senior Common Rooms, *Encounter*, was also found to have CIA as its paymaster. The ISC has been described as 'the child of the Cold War'.[19] Its policies over a fifteen-year period show it fighting 'Communism' which it defines in the vaguest possible terms, terms which usually seem to equate 'Communism' with struggles for national independence. That it passed the odd anti-American motion which it never implemented can only be seen as window-dressing for the Third World. Can we imagine an organization which defended every American foreign policy decision receiving the support of more than a handful of nations, particularly among students? These motions were the sugar coating on the pill.

What we learn is this: we need the possibility of informal exchanges with other students, not at the Executive level, policed by globe-trotting student officers, but at the grass-roots level, involving large bilateral agreements and an open opportunity for exchange visits between students in different cultures. An organization which assisted this would have meaning for the mass of students, cut off, as it must be, from the discredited leadership of the ISC. Only through this type of exchange can we come to understand the problems of other students, in social, political and economic fields. We must not, in these exchanges, allow balkanization of the various social components which have a bearing on education, allow the political to be split from the social, the social from the economic, all elements becoming mutually exclusive and antagonistic, a complete separation of those parts which make a meaningful social whole.

As British students become increasingly radical, increasingly take control of their own environmental and working situations, they are bound to become more outward-looking, both because they will need to compare their performance with others, and because they will perceive the ramifications of what they do, spreading further through society and the world, and the effect of outside situations on them. They will become increasingly internationalist in attitude. Their internationalism will reflect their changing national culture and their social commitments. The generation developing in this country will not want to pay mere lip service to the international struggle against imperialism, colonialism and racism; it will be in conflict with capitalism as the parent of these enemies. It will want to implement the decisions it makes in these spheres, identifying in practical terms with the students of the African National Congress, with the revolutionary Unions in Latin America. It will become an enemy within the fortress of capitalism, identifying the fight of the Vietnamese as a fight of its own. It will recognize, intimately, the comradeship it has with the students of Europe now under intolerable pressure, becoming a home for the emigré Student Unions of Spain, Portugal and Greece, offering concrete support to the proscribed organizations in France who led the preliminary skirmish with an advanced capitalist state in May. Such a development in our international engagement will be, indeed, a severe test of our advancement as a revolutionary social force, capable of, and desiring, an international perspective and role.

To be able to engage in these opening perspectives, we need

to do several things, if we are to keep pace with what we expect to achieve nationally. Initially, we must reject unequivocally any continued buttressing of the ISC. It must not find its last resting place in London. Whilst making this rejection, we must begin to build a genuine international policy based on informal bilateralism, as suggested. Finally, we must continually review and analyse the issues which affect the student organizations of the world, what makes their parent countries so concerned about the problems which became mere catch-phrases in the ISC Charter. A new spirit of student internationalism will have to destroy the lingering influence of ISC, its insidious political infiltration, accomplished in the name of a bogus 'non-political' stance, which was itself the cause of ISC's sterility. A valid move forward, a commitment to student internationalism has become crucial, and we know that it is only attainable by learning the lessons of the last twenty years.

REFERENCES

1. United States National Student Association: sometimes known simply as NSA.
2. This date is significant because it is the same year as the creation of the Foundation for Youth and Student Affairs and the establishment of the permanent secretariat of ISC, known as COSEC.
3. The NSA has not been ungenerous to the ISC. It contributed 50 per cent of the subscription income of ISC and furthermore, not only provided a high proportion of the elected officials of the organization, but most of its full-time paid staff.
4. 'NUS' stands for the National Union of Students of England, Wales and Northern Ireland, which is known internationally as the unpronounceable NUSEWNI; Scotland has its own union, SUS.
5. Minutes of the NUS Conference at Exeter 1966, page 102. Geoff Martin got this information from the FYSA colour brochure.
6. *New York Herald Tribune*, 15 August 1967.
7. The constituent Unions are the Unions of each individual college and university in the country.
8. Until 1967, NUS conferences were called 'councils' and take place twice a year, at Easter and in November.
9. This was presented to the November Council, 1967, at Margate.
10. The dissident group were unable to attend the 11th ISC in Christchurch because they had, with the exception of a penitent few, been refused travel grants (which are normally paid for by the wealthy national unions). The pretext used was that the offenders had not paid their

financial obligations. The accounts show that grants had been made to other non-payers who had remained loyal to the leading group.

11. At the conference, Rhys Hughes pledged a campaign by students to coincide with the General Election in Britain, for majority rule in Rhodesia – a pledge not allowed by the NUS constitution – which was, of course, never implemented.

12. Gwyn Morgan is now head of the International Department of the Labour Party.

13. Discontent at Nairobi reached enormous proportions. A minority group emerged which developed into a consistent opposition to the leading group and its policies. The minority – 'The Sixteen' – issued a statement characterizing ISC as 'a mere Commonwealth student organization, under the conservative leadership of the Anglo-Scandinavian bloc. The ISC is no longer in any way representative of the majority of the students in the world.' This was signed by sixteen national Unions: France, Belgium, Italy, Greece, Ireland, the Philippines, Iran, Palestine, Kuwait, Madagascar, Tunisia, the Ivory Coast, Chile, Bolivia, Nicaragua and Quebec – representatives of five continents.

14. *The Great Fear in Latin America*, John Gerassi.

15. The November Council, 1964.

16. A decision of the 10th ISC to hold a seminar on National Independence in Latin America was never implemented because the funds refused to finance it. On a number of occasions, the ISC has not been able to find travel grants for 'difficult' Unions, while the foundations appear to have provided the money for a variety of pro-American groups from South Vietnam, previously unknown, to attend ISC Conferences and also a string of anti-Communist emigré groups from Eastern Europe (Latvia and Hungary). An emigré group of Cubans from Miami has been similarly financed.

17. See Ross and Wise, *The Invisible Government*, for an account of the CIA's run-of-the-mill activities since 1946.

18. The CIA operation was recently exposed in the *Sunday Times* which described the Agency's involvement in the ousting of the Jagan government in Guyana; since no denials have ever been forthcoming from Harold Wilson or the American Government most commentators conclude that the 'Insight' team got very close to the truth.

19. Alan Hunt's Minority Report to Margate Council, November 1965.

The Repressive Culture

A Brief Guide to Bourgeois Ideology/Robin Blackburn

The first concern of a revolutionary student movement will be direct confrontation with authority, whether in the colleges or on the barricades. But the preparation and development of such a movement has always entailed a searching critique of the dominant ideas about politics and society – in this way practice and theory reinforce one another. These dominant ideas are invariably produced, or reproduced, within the university itself. For many students, to contest these ideas is to question what they are taught. It is therefore not surprising that social science faculties are usually so heavily involved in student revolt. Some of the most articulate champions of academic reaction are professors of sociology, industrial relations or some allied subject. At the same time the social science faculties always provide a prominent contingent in student revolts. In Britain, as elsewhere, the student who takes up sociology, economics or political science finds he or she has to reject the conformist ideas and technocratic skills which his teachers seek to instil.

My intention here is to try to identify the prevailing ideology in the field of the social sciences as taught in British universities and colleges. This ideology, I hope to show, consistently defends the existing social arrangements of the capitalist world. It endeavours to suppress the idea that any preferable alternative does, or could exist. Critical concepts are either excluded (e.g. 'exploitation', 'contradiction') or emasculated (e.g. 'alienation', 'class'). It is systematically pessimistic about the possibilities of attacking repression and inequality: on this basis it constructs theories of the family, of bureaucracy, of social revolution, of 'pluralist' democracy all of which imply that existing social institutions cannot be transcended. Concepts are fashioned which encapsulate this determinism (e.g. 'industrial society') and which imply that all attempts to challenge the *status quo* are fundamentally irrational (e.g. 'charisma'). In short, bourgeois social science tries to mystify social consciousness by imbuing it with fatalism and by blunting any critical impulse. Those aspects of this social science which are not directly aimed at consecrating the social order are concerned with the techniques of running it. They are providing vocational training for future market researchers, personnel managers, investment planners, etc. And all this in the name of 'value neutral' social science. The critique of these notions that follows is not intended to suggest that they are self-consistent or unified by any logic other than their common function within the society which produces them. As Joan Robinson has written: 'The leading characteristic of the ideology which dominates our society today is its extreme confusion. To understand it means only to reveal its contradictions.'[1] The source of the confusion must be sought in its apologetic function. The real achievements of bourgeois social theory for the most part lie behind it in that heroic epoch when the bourgeoisie was destroying an obsolete form of society and inventing a new one. Today it is incapable of understanding the major problems that confront mankind. The plight of the 'underdeveloped' capitalist countries cannot be understood without questioning the viability of capitalism in those lands, and without a preparedness to expose the exploitation of the poor by the rich capitalist countries. The nature of the revolution in Asia, Africa or Latin America cannot be grasped in terms of the philosophy of counter-revolution. Moreover the systematic complacency of bourgeois social science about its own society and its instinctive pessimism about the possibility of creating a civilization which avoids its own misery and servitude blinds it to any understanding of the revolutionary stirrings within the advanced capitalist world itself.

The Assumptions of Capitalist Economics

Let us begin where the capitalist system itself begins, with the exploitation of man by man. We shall see that capitalist economics refuses to consider even the possibility that exploitation lies at the root of inequality or poverty – one can acquire

1. Joan Robinson, *Economic Philosophy*, UK, 1962, p. 28.

a first class degree in economics in Britain without ever having studied the causes of these phenomena. It is now a well established (though not so well known) fact that economic inequality within most capitalist countries has remained roughly constant for many decades. In Britain, for example, the share of national income going to wages and the share going as profits has remained more or less the same since the statistics were first collected towards the end of the nineteenth century: the richest 2 per cent of British adults own 75 per cent of all private wealth, while the income of the top one per cent of incomes is in sum about the same as that shared out among the poorest third of the population. Marx and the classical economists tried to explore the causes of such phenomena in sharp distinction to their neglect by most modern bourgeois economics. The shift in emphasis is stated as follows by a recent historian of the subject:

Marx inherited both the strengths and the weaknesses of his classical forerunners. In both theoretical systems, the central analytical categories were moulded to illuminate the causes and consequences of long term economic change and the relationship between economic growth and income distribution. The tools useful for these purposes were not, however, well adapted (nor were they intended to be) to a systematic inspection of other matters: e.g. the process through which market prices are formed and the implications of short term economic fluctuations.[2]

It is these latter questions which have for so long preoccupied the main bourgeois economists and all too often the conceptual tools developed in these inquiries are then used to tackle the larger issues with predictable lack of success. Thus in the age of attempted 'incomes policies' economic theory is quite incapable of accounting for the share of national income represented by profits. In the most recent edition of a now standard text book we read:

We conclude by raising the interesting question of the share of profits in the national income. We have no satisfactory theory of the share of national income going as profits and we can do little to

2. W. J. Barber, *A History of Economic Thought*, Penguin, UK, 1967, p. 161.

explain past behaviour of this share, nor do we have a body of pre-dictions about the effect on this share of occurrences like the rise of unions, wage freezes, profits taxes, price controls etc.[3]

In his conclusion on theories of income distribution as a whole Professor Lipsey confesses: 'We must, at the moment, admit defeat; we must admit that we cannot at all deal with this im-portant class of problems.' His solution to the impasse is a little lame, faced with all this: 'There is a great deal of basic research that needs to be done by students of this subject.'

A re-examination of the tradition of Marx and the classical economists would have given these researchers the analytical categories they so evidently need. In fact the most promising work in this field is being done on precisely this basis but without acknowledgement from the mainstream of bourgeois economics.[4] For Marx, the tendency of capitalism to generate wealth at one pole and poverty at the other, whether on the national or inter-national scale was a consequence of the exploitive social relations on which it was based. For bourgeois social science, the very con-cept of 'exploitation' is anathema since it questions the assumed underlying harmony of interests within a capitalist society. But of course the rejection of this concept is carried out in the name of the advance of science not the defence of the *status quo*. For example, the whole question is disposed of in the following fashion by Samuelson in the other main economics text book: 'Marx particularly stressed the labor theory of value that labor produces all value and if not exploited would get it all. ... Care-ful critics of all political complexions generally think this is a sterile analysis ...'[5] The tone of this remark is characteristic with its reference to the academic consensus which the student is in-vited to join. A more recent work on this subject makes greater concessions to the 'sterile analysis' but preserves the essential taboo on the key concept: the author writes that we must 'retain the germ of truth in Marx's observation of the wage bargain as one of class bargaining or conflict without the loaded formula-

3. R. G. Lipsey, *An Introduction to Positive Economics*, UK, 1967, p. 481.
4. The work of Piero Sraffa and his school.
5. P. A. Samuelson, *Economics*, Fifth Edition, USA, 1961, pp. 855-6. Samuelson's account of Marx's theory contains numerous factual errors: he attacks Marx's Iron Law of Wages, a concept of Lassalle's

tion of the concept "exploitation".'[6] By excluding *a priori* such ways of analysing economic relationships, modern bourgeois economics ensures that discussion will never be able to question the capitalist property system. Thus Lipsey writes:

> Various reasons for nationalizing industries have been put forward and we can only give very brief mention to these. 1. *to confiscate for the general public's welfare instead of the capitalist's*. In so far as nationalized industries are profitable ones and in so far as they are not any less efficient under nationalization than in private hands this is a rational object. Quantitively however it is insignificant besides such redistributive devices as the progressive income tax.[7]

Lipsey is to be congratulated for sparing a few lines to such thoughts in his eight hundred page tome – most bourgeois economists simply ignore the idea altogether. However, his argument is patently ideological. Firstly, his confidence in the redistributive effects of taxation is in striking contrast to his statements made a few pages earlier, and quoted above, that he cannot with current theory say anything useful about income distribution or the effects on it of taxation. More important is the implicit assumption that capitalists' profits are being confiscated but they are being compensated for the take-over of their property. Nationalization without compensation would have an immediate, massive and undeniable effect on distribution. Even when the bourgeois economist steels himself to consider the prospect of socialism being installed in an advanced capitalist country, he usually finds it impossible to imagine the complete elimination of property rights. In Professor J. E. Meade's *Equality, Efficiency and the Ownership of Property*, he constructs a model where we find that the fledgling 'Socialist State' is burdened from the outset with a huge national debt. It seems that the mind of the bourgeois social scientist is quite impervious to any idea that 'property is theft' or that the expropriators

---

which Marx emphatically rejected; we are told that according to Marx the worker should receive in wages the full fruits of his labour, again a view which Marx explicitly rejected. cf. Karl Marx, *A Critique of the Gotha Program*.

6. Murray Wolfson, *A Reappraisal of Marxian Economics*, USA, 1966, p. 117.

7. R. G. Lipsey, *An Introduction to Positive Economics*, p. 532.

should be expropriated. Instead the only 'rational' objectives for him are ones defined by the rationality of the system itself. A good example of this is provided by Samuelson's discussion of the problems raised by redundancy in a capitalist economy.

Every individual naturally tends to look only at the immediate economic effects upon himself of an economic event. A worker thrown out of employment in the buggy industry cannot be expected to reflect that new jobs may have been created in the automobile industry! but we must be prepared to do so.[8]

The 'we' here is all aspirant or practising economists. Nobody, it seems will be encouraged to reflect that workers should not individually bear the social costs of technological advance, that their standard of living should be maintained until alternative employment is made available to them where they live etc. For the bourgeois economist the necessities of the social system are unquestionable technological requirements. The passage quoted is dedicated to informing the student that: 'the economist is interested in the workings of the economy *as a whole* rather than in the viewpoint of any one group.'[9]

To make his point clear he adds:

... an elementary course in economics does not pretend to teach one how to run a business or a bank, how to spend more wisely, or how to get rich quick from the stock market. But it is to be hoped that general economics will provide a useful background for many such activities.[10]

The one activity to which this brand of economics certainly does not provide a useful background is that of critical reflection on the economy 'as a whole' and the social contradictions on which it is based.

Classical economics could analyse class relationships because it was a constitutive part of 'political economy', the study of social relations in all their aspects. In contemporary social science the economic, political and sociological dimensions of

---

8. P. A. Samuelson, op. cit., p. 10. The complex nature of capitalist rationality is admirably discussed in Maurice Godelier's *Rationalité et Irrationalité en Economie*, Paris, 1967.

9. P. A. Samuelson, ibid., p. 10.

10. P. A. Samuelson, ibid., p. 10.

society are split up and parcelled out among the different academic departments devoted to them. This process itself helps to discourage consideration of the nature of the economic system on other than its own terms. The whole design is lost in the absorption with details. It also allows inconsistencies to flourish within the ideology without causing too much intellectual embarrassment. For example, most economists studying the theory of the firm assume that the goal of businessmen is to maximize profits. Sociologists, on the other hand, assume that since the 'managerial revolution', business decisions are not designed to maximize even long-term profits but are rather prompted by more positive-sounding considerations – public welfare, economic growth, etc. This apparent clash of assumptions reflects only the division of labour between the two disciplines. Economics, the more 'practical' of the two, has to remain closer to the way things actually work in a capitalist economy while sociology provides a justificatory theory which does not interrupt 'business as usual' in the real world. In its turn the economic assumption of profit maximization is validated by the theory that business decisions only reflect the needs ('utility curve' or 'indifference curve') of the sovereign consumer. The naïveté of the utility theory is offensive to sociologists but then it is not necessary to them since they have opted for the (equally naïve) managerial revolution thesis. However, on certain key concepts the same taboos operate in sociology that we have seen in economics. For example,

In the now nearly forgotten language of political economy, 'exploitation' refers to a relationship in which unearned income results from certain types of unequal exchange. ... Doubtless 'exploitation' is by now so heavily charged with misleading ideological resonance that the term itself can scarcely be salvaged for purely scientific purposes and will, quite properly, be resisted by most American sociologists. Perhaps a less emotionally freighted – if infelicitous – term such as 'reciprocity imbalance' will suffice to direct attention once again to the crucial question of unequal exchanges.[11]

11. Alvin Gouldner, 'The Norm of Reciprocity', in *Social Psychology*, Edward E. Sampson (ed) USA, 1964, pp. 83–4. Unfortunately, but not surprisingly those who have followed Gouldner's advice have only succeeded in emasculating the idea in question. cf. Peter Blau, *Exchange*

Gouldner goes on to point out that though this concept has been taboo in macro-social analysis of relations between social groups, this is not the case for micro-social analysis. In studying sexual relations or the doctor–patient relationship the term 'exploitation' does occur in the writings of even the most respectable sociologists. An English social philosopher who finds Marx's usage objectionable proposes that we should consider the ways in which the *weak* exploit the *strong*: 'In some circumstances, as the cases of the beggar and of Dr Moussadek (of Persia) show, weakness can be a favourable position from which exploitation may be exercised.' [12] Sociology's separation from economics, and its rejection of most political economy, produces some curious results. Thus, for example, poverty, an important feature of all advanced capitalist countries, becomes a phenomenon which is dissociated from the way the economic system operates. Instead it is a socially defined 'problem' which can be solved by getting the poor to change their values:

The thesis of this chapter is that disreputable poverty, and not poverty in general, presents a serious social problem to society and a profound challenge to its capacities and ingenuity. ... The disreputable poor may be considered – indeed they may be defined – as that limited section of the poor whose moral and social condition is relatively impervious to economic growth and progress. [13]

and Power in Social Life, USA, 1964. The vacuum created by an absent political economy has allowed a new genre to flourish which seems to be a journalistic amalgam of pop sociology and half-baked economics: see, for example, Andrew Schonfield, *Modern Capitalism*, UK, 1965, or J. K. Galbraith, *The New Industrial State*, UK, 1968.

12. H. B. Acton, *The Illusion of the Epoch*, UK, 1957, p. 243.

13. David Matza, 'Poverty and Disrepute', *Contemporary Social Problems*, Robert K. Merton and Robert A. Nisbet, USA, 1965, p. 619. Of course capitalism creates not only poverty but also a characteristic 'culture of poverty'. Writers like Matza do not see any link between the cultural dimensions of poverty (for example, the poor's resignation and fatalism) and the nature of the social system. Oscar Lewis has provided a most powerful evocation and analysis of the culture of poverty in *Children of Sanchez, La Vida* and other writings. In the introduction to *La Vida* he contrasts Puerto Rico with revolutionary Cuba, suggesting that the latter country, though still poor, has overcome the fatalism associated with the culture of poverty in capitalist societies.

Imperialism and Social Science

The ideological character of a sociology which assumes on
principle a harmonious economic system is particularly evident
when the relations between advanced and backward countries are
being examined. It is now widely acknowledged that the gap
between them is growing and it should be equally evident that
the relations between them involve the domination and exploitation of poor capitalist nations by rich ones. Between 1950 and
1965 the total flow of capital on investment account to the
underdeveloped countries was $9 billion while $25.6 billion
profit capital flowed out of them, giving a net inflow from the
poor to the rich in this instance of $16.6 billion.[14] Yet we are
informed by Professor Aron that 'In the age of the industrial
society there is no contradiction between the interests of the
underdeveloped countries and those of advanced countries.'[15]
Talcott Parsons is also determined to ignore what he calls
'irrational accusations of imperialism'. He writes,

My first policy recommendation, therefore, is that every effort be
made to promulgate carefully considered statements of value commitments which may provide a basis for consensus among both have
and have-not nations. This would require that such statements be
dissassociated from the specific ideological position of either of the
polarized camps.[16]

Parsons's notorious obsession with values is patently ideological in such a context – especially since he goes on to assert that
in creating this consensus atmosphere 'the proper application of
social science should prove useful'. Nowhere in this essay on the
'world social order' does Parsons discuss the role of the capitalist world market or the US Marine Corps as forces acting to
maintain the *status quo*. Further, note the sheer fatuousness of

14. Harry Magdoff, 'Economic Aspects of U.S. Imperialism', *Monthly
Review*, November 1966, p. 39. Of course, there are other aspects of
imperialism than this. See, for example, *May Day Manifesto 1968*, edited
by Raymond Williams, Penguin Books, pp. 66–85, and André Gunder
Frank, *Capitalism and Underdevelopment*, USA, 1966.
15. Raymond Aron, *The Industrial Society*, UK, 1917, p. 24.
16. Talcott Parsons, *Sociological Theory and Modern Society*, UK, 1968,
p. 475.

Parsons's belief that anything would be changed by the promulgation of carefully considered statements, etc. Even Parsons's undoubted intellectual distinction is no protection against the feebleness imposed on its devotees by bourgeois ideology.

The radically distorted perspective encouraged by the Parsonian emphasis on the autonomous efficacy of values shows up very clearly in such studies as *Elites in Latin America* edited by Seymour Lipset and Aldo Solari. In a book supposedly devoted to elites there is no contribution on landowners who have traditionally been such an important element in the Latin American oligarchy. On the other hand there are seven contributions on aspects of the educational system including such topics as 'Education and Development', 'Opinions of Secondary School Teachers' and 'Relations between Public and Private Universities'. The general argument emerging from such works is that development of the underdeveloped regions will ensue if schoolteachers can be persuaded to instil healthy capitalist values in their pupils. The whole programme is offered as an alternative to social revolution:

Although revolution may be the most dramatic and certainly the most drastic method to change values and institutions which appear to be inhibiting modernization, the available evidence would suggest that reforms in the educational system which can be initiated with a minimum of political resistance may have some positive consequences.[17]

Another striking instance of the excessive value emphasis encouraged by Parsonian theory is *The Politics of Developing Areas* by G. Almond and J. S. Coleman. This book, published in 1960, so persistently ignored Mao's dictum that 'power grows out of the barrel of a gun' that the index contains no reference for 'army', 'armed forces', etc, and its discussions have been completely bypassed by the subsequent wave of military coups throughout the underdeveloped zone. The assumption usually made in such writings is that the 'West' provides the model for the development of the underdeveloped world. The fact that the Western capitalist powers were plundering the rest of the world

17. S. M. Lipset, 'Values, Education and Entrepreneurship', in *Elites in Latin America*, ed. S. Lipset and A. Solari, USA, 1967, p. 41.

at the time of their industrialization, whereas the underdeveloped world is in the reverse position, is rarely considered. The profits of the slave trade, the sales of opium to China, the plantations of the Americas etc. (not to speak of the expropriation of the common lands of the European peasantry and the grazing grounds of the American Indian) all contributed to the early capital accumulation of the Western Imperialist powers quite as much as their devotion to a 'universalistic' value system. Curiously enough, bourgeois economists do not recommend underdeveloped countries to follow the Western model in this respect. In all the mountains of literature devoted to the strategy of economic development, writers who urge the poor countries to nationalize the investments of the rich are very rare. Martin Bronfenbrenner's excellent article on 'The Appeal of Confiscation in Economic Development', first published in 1955, has evoked almost no response and most textbooks on development strategy ignore the question altogether.

Not surprisingly the best allies of foreign capital in the underdeveloped regions are the remaining traditional elites and the feeble local capitalist class. At one time it was hoped by Western strategists that the 'middle sectors' could carry through the process of economic development in their respective countries. This ignored the fact that the context provided by the imperialist world market invariably poses an insuperable obstacle to the underdeveloped bourgeoisie of the poor capitalist countries. As a consequence they have usually sought enrichment through battening on a corrupt government or sponsoring a military coup rather than producing the hoped-for economic advance.[18] All this creates most unpleasant dilemmas for the bourgeois social scientist and accounts for the growing acceptance of development strategies based on an analysis such as the following:

I am trying to show how a society can begin to move forward as it is, in spite of what it is. Such an enterprise will involve a systematic search along two closely related lines: first, how acknowledged, well entrenched obstacles to change can be neutralized, outflanked and left to be dealt with decisively at some later stage; secondly

18. The writings of Frantz Fanon, Régis Debray, André Gunder Frank and José Nun, explore different aspects of this process.

and perhaps more fundamentally, how many among the conditions and attitudes that are widely considered as inimical to change have a hidden positive dimension and can therefore unexpectedly come to serve and nurture progress.[19]

This fantasy enables the bourgeois social scientist to ignore the fact that the main obstacles to development are either directly provided by imperialist domination or buttressed by it.

The attraction of the Hirschman approach is increased as earlier illusions about 'underdevelopment' are eroded. The economists, in particular, have often acted as if economic development can be induced as soon as a few well-meaning tax reforms are enforced. The fiasco of Nicolas Kaldor's policies in India, Ceylon, Ghana, Guyana, Mexico and Turkey illustrate this well:

Since I invariably urged the adoption of reforms which put more of the burden of taxation on the privileged minority of the well-to-do, and not only on the broad masses of the population, it earned me (and the governments I advised) a lot of unpopularity, without, I fear, always succeeding in making the property-owning classes contribute substantial amounts to the public purse. The main reason for this ... undoubtedly lay in the fact that the power, behind the scenes, of the wealthy property-owning classes and business interests proved to be very much greater than ... suspected.[20]

On the whole, bourgeois economists only achieve such revelations in connexion with remote places whose local 'privileged minority' appear to impede imperialist penetration. Even then they usually persist in believing that their technical nostrums can be made to work:

In most underdeveloped countries, where extreme poverty co-exists with great inequality in wealth and consumption, progressive taxation is, in the end, the only alternative to complete expropriation through violent revolution. ... The progressive leaders of under-developed countries may seem ineffective if judged by immediate results; but they are the only alternatives to Lenin and Mao Tse Tung.[21]

19. Albert O. Hirschman, *Journeys Towards Progress*, USA, 1963, pp. 6–7.
20. Nicolas Kaldor, *Essays on Economic Policy*, UK, 1964, Vol. 1, pp. xvii–xx.
21. ibid.

The political exclusion of expropriation could scarcely be more unabashed.

The rejection of 'entrepreneural' values by the more militant representatives of the Third World is a problem for Western sociologists like Parsons. He attempts to explain it in terms of 'the inferior status of the rising elements':

Here, precisely because the core elements of the free world have already at least partially achieved the goals to which the developing nations aspire, there is a strong motivation to derogate these achievements. In ideological terms the aim of these nations is not to achieve parity but to supplant certain well-established elements of the 'superior' society, for example, to substitute socialism for capitalism. ... The direction of desirable change seems clear; ideological stresses must be minimized; those aspects of the situation which demonstrate an interest in order which transcends polarity must be underscored. One of the main themes here concerns those features which all industrial societies share in common. ... An exposition of such features would necessarily focus on the standard of living of the masses – for obvious reasons a very sensitive area for the communists. ... This discussion has been based on ... the assumption that one side has achieved a position of relative superiority in relation to the important values.[22]

Parsons goes on to say that the reconciliation of the inferior elements and the core elements of the free world on the basis of the latter's superior values can be achieved partly by drawing on a 'very important resource, namely the contribution of social science'. This explicitly ideological orientation towards underdevelopment has already introduced us to a major theme of bourgeois ideology in the context of advanced countries – namely the category 'industrial society'. The time has come to consider its implications.

'Industrial' Society and Technological Determinism

The category 'industrial society' has now become the accepted definitional concept for modern capitalism. Raymond Aron, who has done much to promote it, makes clear its intention: it is, he writes, 'a way of avoiding at the outset the opposition between

22. Talcott Parsons, *Sociological Theory and Modern Society*, pp. 485–6.

socialism and capitalism and of considering them as two species of the same genus: industrial society.'[23] This way of thinking in sociology owes much to Weber. It contains a large dose of technological determinism since it suggests that the industrial nature of technology dominates social organization as a whole. For pre-industrial societies values may act as an independent variable capable of re-shaping society itself in important ways. But once a society has industrialized the range of significant institutional alternatives available to it is very narrow. Thus the unavoidable concomitant of modern industry will be bureau-cratic organization, the 'nuclear' form of the family (i.e. the family system of the modern American middle class), etc. By deducing social organization from industrial technology bour-geois sociology can portray capitalist society as void of con-tradictions. In the 'industrial society' there is no possibility of a clash between the forces of production and the institutions of the property system since they form a harmonious, non-antagonistic unity. Capitalist social relations cannot be re-jected without abandoning modern technology. Nor with such a view can capitalist relations of production (private property, the sale of labour power as a commodity, etc.) act as a fetter on the development of the forces of production (technology, natural resources etc.).

According to Talcott Parsons, Weber regarded 'capitalism', including bureaucratic organization, both private and govern-mental, as essentially the 'fate' of Western society

23. Raymond Aron, *Eighteen Lectures on Industrial Society*, UK, 1967, p. 42. The term 'industrial society' can be used descriptively, without the intention here acknowledged by Aron, in which case its function need not be ideological. Recently some writers have been trying to popularize the term 'post-industrial society' to describe the most advanced capitalist economy (the USA). Though the inner meaning of both concepts is technological determinism, the sponsors of the notion 'post-industrial society' are right to fear that technological advance may make capitalist social institutions more fragile. As the material pre-conditions for liberation become undeniable in the advanced capitalist countries the defence of repressive institutions becomes more difficult. This is Daniel Bell's nightmare: '... to show that order has virtue becomes more dif-ficult when the appeals to instinct and irrationality, bound up in the coil of pleasure, begin to weave their lure.' Daniel Bell, *The Reforming of General Education*, USA, 1967, pp. 311–12.

clearly to him capitalism in some sense had to be accepted; but equally on a variety of grounds scientific and ethical, the prevailing interpretations were on the one hand inadequate to the phenomena itself, on the other out of accord with his feelings of rightness and appropriateness ... with respect to my own country I have long felt that the designation of its social system as 'capitalistic', even in Weber's highly sophisticated sense, was grossly inadequate.[24]

Parsons eschews the term capitalist, no doubt because its critical overtones are out of accord with his 'feelings of rightness and appropriateness' as well as Weber's. But at the same time he manages to smuggle back the distinctive features of capitalist society in his theory of 'evolutionary universals', that is the universal aspects of all societies as they evolve into modern industrial states. These evolutionary universals, according to Parsons, include 'money and markets' and 'bureaucracy'. The sociological theory of bureaucracy deriving from Weber has marked fatalistic overtones, as Gouldner has noted.[25] It will be convenient to examine this theory in some detail as it is most often cited as one of the forms of social organization made inescapable by modern industrial society. Indeed the more alert defenders of bureaucratic domination, wherever it is found, draw on these ideas.

Bureaucracy and Bourgeois Fatalism

For Weber bureaucratic organization represented a superior and necessary form of rationality. He recognized that the historical origin of modern bureaucracy was to be found in the internal organization of the early capitalist enterprise, and he further claimed that this type of organization was the general destiny of any society which developed an industrial economy. Indeed to some extent it was a prerequisite for industrial development. The bureaucratic mode of organization was characterized as follows:

(1) All official actions are bound by rules with the official subject to strict and systematic control from above.

24. Talcott Parsons, op. cit., pp. 99–101.
25. Alvin Gouldner, 'The Metaphysical Pathos of Bureaucracy' in *Complex Organizations*, edited by A. Etzione, USA, 1964.

(2) Each functionary has a limited and defined sphere of competence.

(3) The organization of offices follows a principle of hierarchy with each lower one subordinate to each higher one.

(4) Candidates are selected only from the basis of technical qualification: 'They are *appointed*, not elected.'

(5) Officials are salaried and have no right of ownership over their job: 'The salary scale is graded according to rank in the hierarchy: but in addition to this criterion . . . the requirements of incumbents' social status may be taken into account.'

(6) The office is the sole, or at least primary, occupation of the incumbent and it constitutes a career: 'Promotion is dependent on the judgement of superiors.' [26]

For Weber the style of work originating in the bureaucratic enterprise would inevitably generalize itself through society in all other institutions (army, church, political parties, state machine, etc.). In this ideal type Weber mixes together some organizational rules which may, in determinate historical conditions, encourage efficient administration, together with others which can only foster the negative effects for which bureaucracies are so notorious (impersonality, manipulation of the administered, evasion of responsibility, empire-building, stifling working conditions, etc.). The whole is then presented as a package which it is fruitless to reject since its imperatives are unavoidable.

The organization which Weber envisages is a pure instrument – its officials are robbed of all real initiative by the requirements of rule obedience, top-down control and hierarchy. The divorce of ends from means appears complete. This is the source of its abstract efficiency or formal rationality. The ends which the organization serve lie outside it, just as the purpose of the capitalist enterprise was not to express the creative energies of those who worked within it, nor to serve the needs of society in general, but rather to make profits and accumulate capital. Weber was aware that the type of bureaucratic organization he was analysing was intimately linked to the existence of a market economy. Thus he argued that the absence of a developed market produced a structural weakness in the traditional type of Chinese Bureau-

26. Max Weber, *Economic and Social Organization*, edited by Talcott Parsons, USA, 1947, pp. 333–9.

cracy – the taxation crisis. Simply to finance the on-going operation of the bureaucracy a money economy was necessary:
without adequate funds a bureaucracy will begin to allow
officials to make money on the side by exploiting their official
position. In some ways the bureaucracy outlined by Weber is an
institutionalization of the imperatives of market society with its
consequent alienations. The capitalist market reduces quality to
quantity, makes human labour power a commodity and ensures
that the exchange value of a commodity dominates its individual
use value. In the same way a bureaucracy reduces both its own
workers and the public it administers to a set of abstract
characteristics (age, formal qualifications, sex, race, etc.). Just as
the market organizes human behaviour according to unquestionable economic laws, so the bureaucracy imposes man-made rules
as if they had some impersonal necessity. For Weber all this was
part of the formal, abstract efficiency which bureaucracy provides. Such efficiency can only serve the powers that be; its
formal rationality is dependent on the rationality of the capitalist
system, of which it is a part. There is however a further ideological distortion involved. Weber's ideal type implies that organizations are more efficient the more they restrict and control the
action and initiative of their employees: with this control and
restriction taking the form of orders and rules transmitted from
above. Experience suggests this is quite simply false. Indeed many
workers in capitalist bureaucracies have discovered that working
to rule is almost equivalent to a strike. Blau's studies of the
workings of a public welfare office have shown that administration is only kept going by an informal network of understanding
between employees who assist one another in all sorts of ways
not envisaged by the rules. Every real bureaucracy only operates
successfully because of the continual adaptations and innovations of its employees.

Charisma – A Pseudo-Concept

If Weber expels innovation from his concept of bureaucracy
where does he find room for it in his sociology? In practice it
seems that Weber identified social innovation and creativity
with the irrational: they are subsumed under the category

'charisma'. This category has become very popular in later sociological writing and tends to be used by leader writers, pundits
and social commentators of all types who wish to discredit popular movements of any sort. Historically 'charisma' was the 'gift
of grace' which early Christian saints were supposed to receive
from God. Weber used it to describe the source of the attraction
wielded by great popular leaders. As such it seems to be a survival in modern bourgeois social science of the medieval doctrine
of essences. This doctrine held, for example, that fire as a physical
phenomenon was to be explained by the fact that every com-
bustible object contained a substance, phlogiston, which was
released when it caught fire. In similar fashion the ascendancy of
every popular leader who rebels against things as they are is
'explained' in terms of his possession of charismatic qualities. In
addition to absolving the social scientist from any real examination of the social forces and circumstances which produce
popular movements it also enables him to lump together quite
disparate types of leader. For Weber, Napoleon and St Augustine
were both charismatic figures: for the modern bourgeois sociologist a typical amalgam might be Hitler and Mao Tse Tung.
Here is an example of how the concept is used:

> Cuba did not prove that a Latin American nation could deliber-
> ately choose Communism; it proved, if proof were still needed that
> a charismatic leader can make a nation choose almost anything even
> in the act of denying he is choosing it for them. . . . Castro's charisma
> . . . cut across all classes; he established a mass relationship primarily
> with his person, not with his ideas.[27]

The term charisma is invariably used in this way, namely to
imply that support for a popular leader is not to be explained
by reference to his ideas, programme or actions, but rather,
exclusively, by some quality of personal magnetism. As Marcuse
has said: 'It reveals the preconception that every successful
ostensibly personal leadership is based on some religious inspiration.'[28] The notion that 'charisma' (initiative, innovation)
could be diffused among all the members of an organization is
quite alien to Weber. For him it is necessarily concentrated at
the summit so that revolutionary movements are reduced to the

27. Theodor Draper, *Castroism*, USA, 1965, p. 127.
28. Herbert Marcuse, 'Max Weber', *New Left Review* 30.

personal qualities of their leaders. Moreover, he insisted that charisma could not sustain itself – it necessarily underwent a process of routinization, ending in some more or less effective form of traditional or bureaucratic domination.

Before leaving Weber let us examine his contention that, 'Under normal conditions the power position of a fully developed bureaucracy is always overwhelming.'[29] The potency of bureaucracy meant that it must be the 'fate' or 'destiny' of mankind to live in this way. But as Marcuse has written:

Weber's concept of *destiny* is an illustration of the substantive content of his formal analysis. 'Destiny' lies in the impersonal laws of economy and society independent of individuals, which can only be defined under pain of self-dissolution. But society is not nature – *who decrees this destiny?* Industrialism is a phase in the development of men's capacities and needs – a phase in the struggle against nature and himself. This development can debouch into very different kinds of organization and goal. Not only the forms of domination but also the forms of technology, of needs and their satisfaction, are in no sense a 'fatality'. They *become* so through their institution in society – as a result of material, economic and psychological coercion. Weber's concept of 'destiny' is derived *ex post facto* from this: he generalizes the blindness of a society, whose mechanism of production occurs behind the backs of the individuals in it, a society in which the laws of domination appear as the objective laws of technology.[30]

To the arm of criticism directed against Weber by Marcuse we may now add the criticism of arms. For Weber, the modern bureaucratic army was a prime instance of the superior power and 'rationality' of this form of organization. Indeed, the whole development of his theory reflects the impression made on him by the apparent successes of Prussian military bureaucracy. Yet the history of this century shows that bureaucratized armies can be defeated by guerrilla armies. Today the highly bureaucratized armed forces of the largest imperialist power in the world have shown their impotence when faced with an authentic popular army. Every guerrilla army of this sort violates the commands of Weber's superior rationality. Conventional differences of rank are abolished; hierarchy minimized; and the individual guerrilla and the local guerrilla commander must be prepared to innovate and take the initiative at any time. One could say that they are bound by rules: but the 'rules' on which all the great guerrilla commanders insist are ones which bind the guerrilla to *the people* as much as to the military and political leadership. The long heroic saga of the people of Vietnam, successively fighting Japanese, French and American imperialism, is surely a decisive refutation of any fatalistic belief in the omnipotence of capitalist military organization. The Weberian aroma of contemporary imperialism should not surprise us and has indeed already been noted by bourgeois admirers. Weber notoriously endorsed the expansionary ambitions of Emperor Wilhelm II's Germany, his enthusiasm only abating as defeat confronted it. An American scholar writes that

(Weber) was convinced that a great political power had special obligations – he called it a 'miserable duty'. He became ever more doubtful whether Germany was morally qualified to be a great nation, and he was prepared to let those obligations fall to the United States. . . .[31]

The Sociology of Revolution as Philosophy of Counter-Revolution

We have seen that the drift of much bourgeois social theory is to undermine the idea that men can ever transform society – its function is to induce a morbid paralysis of social will. In the twentieth century revolutionary disturbances have affected most parts of the world and in areas inhabited by one third of humanity the prevailing order has been completely overturned. Such events have only filtered relatively slowly into the consciousness of mainstream bourgeois sociology. The dominant functionalist school of social theory prided itself on possessing a model whereby social stability could be explained: each part of the social system was analysed in terms of its functional contribution to the maintenance of the social system as a whole. For the Parsonian 'structural-functionalist' the whole edifice is reducible to the basic value system. Power relations are invariably deduced from the possible modes of interaction within small groups (cf. Peter Blau as well as Talcott Parsons) in a society dominated by the

31. Guenther Roth, *American Sociological Review*, April 1965, p. 216.

impersonal dictates of the capitalist property system. Critics from within the camp of bourgeois sociology felt that its weakness was its failure to account for conflict and change, and it was certainly the case that these topics were only treated as an after-thought in, for example, Parsons's *Social System*. In this book Parsons argued, quite correctly, that if he had developed an adequate theory of social integration then he would, at the same time, have provided the conceptual framework for explaining conflict, change, etc. In fact, as we shall see, neither he, nor his critics, have succeeded in either enterprise.

The contemporary discussion of social change and conflict involves a number of strategies towards the theoretical problems involved. A popular one stresses that social conflict can actually promote social integration so long as it is structured and in-stitutionalized.[32] Thus, for example, conflict is seen as endemic in any industrial society because *some people (management) will always have to boss others (the workers)*. The latter will resent this though they cannot change it. The resulting conflict can be institutionalized by the growth of trade unions, reformist politi-cal parties and so forth. This thesis focuses on the conflict be-tween social groups and not that between parts of the socio-economic system. All conflict is, in principle, reconcilable because it relates to a *fatality of social order* not to a *structural contradiction*. Because, for example, industrial society will always breed exactly the same type of conflict between men and management, industrial conflicts can never alter anything. In effect the only significant alternatives are whether to institu-tionalize the conflict or not. A situation of structured conflict is preferable and will promote social harmony by allowing some element of dissensus. By over-personalizing the nature of power this whole approach presents the structural aspect of class power (rooted in the de-personalized potency of economic laws and the collective, cumulative weight of private property) as if it was an ineluctable limit of all social existence in an industrial context. Thus bourgeois ideology has a double face but a single silhouette. There are equilibrium theorists, like Parsons, who are obsessed with social integration and there are so-called conflict

32. See for example: Ralph Dahrendorf, *Class and Class Conflict in Industrial Society*, UK, 1958.

theorists who are obsessed with integration as well. The only problem is that conflict sociology of this sort gets bourgeois theory no nearer a sociology of revolution. Writing in 1955 Professors Bottomore and Rubel wrote:

> It is curious, when one reflects upon the tremendous effects which revolutions have had upon human social organization, that no sociologist since Marx has thought it worth while either to analyse revolutionary movements or to attempt a comparative study of revolutions. The sociology of revolution has so far only one major contribution to record, that of Marx himself.[33]

The few attempts since then to rectify the gap certainly do not make one wish to revise this judgement. A key element in Marx's theory was indicated by the notion of contradiction. Thus the class contradiction of labour and capital was overlaid by the structural contradiction between the increasingly social nature of the production process and the still private character of the ownership of the means of production. Because of the existence of the latter contradiction, the struggle of the working class could, if successful, create a wholly new form of society based on the suppression of class society. Similarly for Marx the bourgeois revolutions had not been just a struggle for ascendancy between two social classes (bourgeoisie and aristocracy) but also a struggle between two socio-economic systems (capitalist and feudal).[34] The coincidence of the two types of contradiction is necessarily the product of a specific historical conjuncture, a 'revolutionary situation'. But for bourgeois social theory the two never coalesce. Some admit the existence of structural contradictions but ignore the possibility that they could relate to class contradictions (e.g. David Lockwood [35]). Others partially acknowledge

---

33. Bottomore and Rubel, Introduction to *Karl Marx: Selected Writings*, Penguin, UK, 1962, p. 40.

34. Thus the Marxist notion of contradiction is necessarily over-determined and not a simple, circular contradiction of the Hegelian type, because of this critical double source.

35. cf. his interesting essay, 'Social Integration and System Integration' in Zollsham and Hirsch, *Explorations in Social Change*. The notion of structural contradiction emerges in Sociologese as 'lack of fit' between, for example, the economy and the 'core institutional framework'. For Lockwood on class conflict see: *The Affluent Worker*, UK, 1968.

class conflict but fail to relate it to structural contradiction (e.g. Ralph Dahrendorf). The confusion all this breeds becomes clear when we turn to the two direct attempts by bourgeois sociologists to construct a sociology of revolution: namely Neil Smelser's *Theory of Collective Behaviour* and Chalmers Johnson's *Revolution and the Social System*. Smelser sums up his analysis by the following equation:

Structural strain + value-orientated movement = Revolution.

The notion of 'strain' used in this formula is the inadequate bourgeois substitute for the concept 'contradiction' – its central inadequacy is that it fails to focus on the problem of whether the crisis in the established society carries with it the possibility of a new principle of social organization. For Smelser a 'value-orientated movement' is the summit of a typology of dysfunctional collective behaviour which runs as follows: panic, craze, hostile outburst, norm-orientated movement, value-orientated movement. Here again there is a flagrantly ideological attempt to present revolutionary movements as necessarily irrational. This assumption is carried over from the typology into the theory itself. For Smelser, revolution is the result of a coincidence and juxtaposition of structural strain and the value-orientated movement. Nowhere does he consider the point that the revolutionary movement may be aware of the nature of the structural strain and act upon it so as to transform the structure. In short, Smelser neglects the conscious element in revolution; the fact that modern revolutionaries do not act in a blind manner but rather try to base their activities on careful analysis and rational strategies. In Chalmers Johnson we find an even less illuminating equation:

Multiple dysfunction + Elite intransigeance = Revolution.

This preference for expressing social processes in equations is itself revealing. For Smelser and Johnson revolutions are not *made*, they just happen. The vulgar bourgeois prejudice that revolutionary disturbances are the work of a small band of troublemakers and extremists is simply inverted to make them the ineluctable consequence of 'multiple dysfunction'. Only the counter-revolution is credited with the possibility of conscious and rational intentions – hence Johnson's concern with 'elite intransigence'. For bourgeois sociology revolutionary movements are not attempts by men to make their own history: they are rather a regrettable malady which afflict the body politic. The weakness of the concept 'dysfunction' is typical here. The categories of functionalist equilibrium theory have simply been turned inside out in the hope that they will thus be adequate to the analysis of revolution. Thus the 1929 crash was 'dysfunctional' for capitalism and so was the Chinese People's Liberation Army 'dysfunctional' for the social order of Nationalist China in the nineteen thirties and forties. Not only does the term fail to convey the 'magnitude' of such phenomena, it also fails to distinguish between the two quite different types of challenge represented by a crisis within the system and a revolutionary challenge to it. But then the entire ideological thrust of such theories is to make both crises and revolutionary movements appear as sort of natural calamities, acts of God disrupting the social system. That residue of revolutionary movements which is not a blind irrational mass response to 'structural strain' is dismissed in the following terms:

Without the background dysfunctions, these movements constitute only a police or mental health problem, as most of them empirically have been.[36]

Regis Debray has suggested that the lumpen-bourgeoisie of Latin America substitute police vigilance for an authentic class consciousness. Perhaps this is already infecting the morale of metropolitan ideologies as imperialism comes under increasing pressure both in the outlying areas and in its heartland. At any rate most supposed investigations of why revolutions occur turn out, on inspection, to be rather pretentious manuals of counter-revolution.

The technique adopted by bourgeois social science to deal with the consequences of successful revolution can be reduced to one basic theme. Basically revolutions change very little. This is often a variation of the bureaucracy argument discussed above. In his accustomed professorial manner Raymond Aron has announced:

36. Chalmers Johnson: *Revolution and the Social System*, p. 26.

We have all become intensely aware of power as the major phenomenon in all societies, and as a problem which no reforms in the property system or in the functioning of the economy can solve.[37]

Crane Brinton, in 'Anatomy of Revolutions', talks of the 'universality of Thermidorean reaction' as a law of revolution. For Talcott Parsons the only aspect of revolutions on which he dwells is the necessity after the 'ascendancy of the charismatic revolutionary movement' for a process of 'concession' to the development of 'adaptive structures'. Of course, this approach is not wholly invalid. As Georg Lukacs has observed, all false consciousness has its own truth: but this truth is partial and inserted into a false overall perspective. In this instance, for example, the one-sided approach of bourgeois sociology renders it blind to the process of radicalization which often occurs in revolution (e.g. the Cultural Revolution, Soviet collectivization, etc.).[38] Carrying out a revolution is a momentous experience of effective social action: if anything it is likely, at one point, to encourage voluntarism rather than a policy of concessions. The post-revolutionary history of Russia, China and Cuba certainly do not substantiate any unilateral adaptive concession theory. In short, bourgeois sociology only begins to understand modern revolutions in so far as they fail – and this is undoubtedly because they want them to fail. The bourgeois social scientists' attempt to deny the efficacy of social revolution by no means inhibits them from proclaiming the existence or necessity of all other sorts of 'revolution'. Indeed revolutions are discovered everywhere: the 'industrial revolution', the 'revolution of rising expectations', the 'technological revolution', etc. This oblique homage to potency of the notion is also to be found in the writings of those who seek to avert them. Nicolas Kaldor, writing on 'under-developed' countries, puts the matter thus: 'The problem which has to be solved, and to which no one has yet found a

---

37. Raymond Aron, *German Sociology*, p. 131.
38. A variant of this approach acknowledges this radicalization but considers it only as an irrational 'totalitarian' phenomenon. (The uses of the concept 'totalitarian' will be discussed later.) Many such studies of post-revolutionary societies argue that revolutions do not so much change them as intensify their basic characteristics: see for example, Karl Wittfogel, *Oriental Despotism*.

satisfactory answer, is how to bring about that change in the balance of power which is needed to avert revolutions without *having* a revolution.' [39]

The Myths of Bourgeois Pluralism

Most bourgeois sociologists predict social peace for the advanced capitalist countries, though they will often concede that 'In the industrializing world, disorder, ideology, and irrational movements will continue to play disruptive though geographically confined roles.' [40] Marx was fond of pointing out that if the appearance of things coincided with their essence then there would be no need for science. Bourgeois social theory assumes axiomatically that everything is exactly as it appears. It is wedded to fundamental conceptual empiricism. This becomes especially clear when we examine the analysis offered by bourgeois political science of power in the advanced capitalist part of the world, where social harmony is expected to prevail. The critical weakness is already evident in the managerial revolution thesis. Economic power, according to this theory, is exercised by men in a direct and unmediated fashion. In the nineteenth century these men were the tycoon capitalists, nowadays they are the corporation managers. On the whole, the new economic despots are thought to be benevolent, balancing the interests of consumers and their own employees. With the divorce of ownership and control, a new power is held to reign in the land. Of course Marx always attacked bourgeois political economists for seeing power in a capitalist society as concentrated in the capitalist as an individual.[41] For Marx, the laws of capitalist accumulation imposed themselves 'as an external co-ercive force' on the capitalist. The more *bien pensant* modern bourgeois economists are liable to get very worried when they discover that capitalist

39. Nicolas Kaldor, *Essays on Economic Policy*, Vol. I, p. 265.
40. Herman Kahn and Anthony Weiner, *The World in the Year 2000*, USA, 1967, p. 25.
41. See Louis Althusser: *Lire le Capital*, Vol. II, p. 138. 'Adam Smith's "enormous oversight" was directly related to the exclusive consideration of the capitalist as individual, that is to say, as economic agent outside the whole, as the ultimate subject of the global process.'

constraints still dominate the 'masterful' modern manager. In her book *Economic Philosophy*, Joan Robinson complains that the recent cumulative spate of take-overs is an atavistic recurrence of *laissez-faire* capitalism. In reality the only justification for the capitalist system is that it does insist on making all individual capitalists and managers the slaves of capital accumulation in this way: this is how it has historically produced a prodigious development of the forces of production.

For the bourgeois social scientist the manager is seen as the controlling force in the system chiefly because he has the immediate appearance of doing so. The notion that he might be only the agent of the impersonal demands of the system itself is not considered. This approach would entail not just a superficial examination of managerial behaviour but also a critical study of the structural conditions of that behaviour. The bourgeois theory of 'pluralism' exemplifies this failure in the field of political sociology. The concept of the 'plural society' is another pleasing euphemism for capitalism. It seeks to suggest that power within contemporary capitalism is not concentrated in a single homogeneous 'power elite' but rather distributed between a number of competing elite groups. Exhaustive studies are made of how given political decisions are made, analysing the different lobbies and interest groups which affected the outcome (see, for example, the work of Robert Dahl). What is neglected is what two American scholars have called the power of 'non-decisions', the role of 'institutionalized bias.' [42] In capitalist society the property regime is installed at the heart of the productive apparatus of the society. Only political forces which are prepared to overthrow it can ignore its dictates. For others political decision making will not just be limited by the capitalist context it will be dominated by it. The actions of the British Labour Government since 1964 are a clear example of this. From the beginning it sought to restore the failing fortunes of British capitalism, even though it probably discharged its function with great incompetence. This path was followed because of the structured exigencies of the situation not because of the evil influence of Treasury officials, Zurich bankers, or City speculators. Short of overthrowing capi-

42. M. Bachrach and Baratz, 'The Two Faces of Power', *American Political Science Review*, 1962.

talism the only alternative is to make it work and this means accepting a very narrow range of choices. (It goes without saying that even the most super-revolutionary leadership could not overthrow even the most flagging capitalist society with a run-down electoral machine like the Labour Party, steeped as it is in the traditional subordination of the British Labour movement to ruling class hegemony.)

The Pluralist Travesty of Politics

I have so far dwelt on the unscientific character of bourgeois 'pluralistic' theory without noting the ideological function to which this is related. Pluralism theory produces a quite new theory of democracy which seeks to justify the way contemporary bourgeois democracies actually operate. Naturally this involves a wholesale revision of classic liberal democratic theory to eliminate its dangerously populist tendencies and to accommodate the elitist features of contemporary capitalist society. The aim is a sort of apolitical politics. S. M. Lipset has summarized his position in the following terms:

> Essentially, I have urged the view that *realistically* the distinctive and most valuable element of democracy is, in complex societies, the formation of a political elite in the competitive struggle for the votes of a mainly passive electorate.[43]

The passivity of the electorate is most important: 'It is necessary to look for factors which sustain the separation of the political system from the excesses inherent in the populist assumptions of democracy.'[44]

For Parsons, the perils of 'populist irresponsibility' are to be reduced by ensuring that 'participation in the selection of leaders' is to be 'structured'.[45] What he might mean by this is indicated by Kornhauser:

> The present study has sought to show that directly accessible elites make ready targets for mass movements. Constitutional and

43. S. M. Lipset, *First New Nation*, p. 208. He is here summarizing views he set out in his earlier book, *Political Man*.
44. ibid., pp. 208–9.
45. Talcott Parsons, *Sociological Theory and Modern Society*, pp. 517–8.

other appropriate institutional devices are needed to regulate access to elites and to reduce pressure on them.[46]

Earlier in this book we have learnt that

Mass politics in a democratic society ... is anti-democratic, since it contravenes the established order. Mass politics occurs when large numbers of people engage in political activity outside of the procedures and rules instituted by a society to govern political action.[47]

It is not surprising that many 'pluralist' theorists have been quick to denounce the student movement in the United States as a threat to their special brand of apolitical, elitist democracy. This approach to politics has recently led Ralf Dahrendorf to reflect that democracy in West Germany would be strengthened by strengthening the elite. This is how he puts it:

The German power elite is not an established elite; it is for that reason incapable of that self-confidence which is a necessary condition of lively competition. ... To create on the basis of equal chances of access, a political class homogeneous in the social biographies of its members, and, in that sense, established, is a task whose fulfilment might give democracy in Germany new and effective impulses.[48]

There is an unwritten premise of this argument. 'Equality of access' to elite membership would only benefit one social class: otherwise their social biographies would not be 'homogeneous'. The wholesale revision of classical democratic theory undertaken by the theorists of the bourgeois 'pluralism' naturally entails re-interpretation of the function of political apathy, ignorance and irrationality. These were vices for the founders of democratic theory but for the pluralists they can be virtues so long as they operate within the bourgeois framework:

Just as the content and significance of voter ignorance and irrationality are often exaggerated, so are the content and significance

46. Kornhauser, *Politics in the Mass Society*, p. 236.
47. ibid., p. 227.
48. Ralf Dahrendorf, *Society and Democracy in Germany*, UK, 1968, pp. 270 and 279.

of voter apathy. Apparently apathetic behaviour ... may reflect widespread acceptance of the way disputes are resolved.[49]

The revaluation is based on the following reasoning:

If the balance of power between the major social groups in society is unlikely to change rapidly or violently, if therefore, political dispute is limited to ways and means of improving the existing structure – and this seems a fair description of the situation in most advanced industrial nations – then there is little to get excited about.

This line of argument rapidly leads to the conclusion that mass involvement and participation in politics is a threat to democracy. The established elites are quite capable of producing the piecemeal reforms required and only passive acceptance is required of the masses. Occasional choice between competing sections of the elite provides them with all the political participation they require, or are competent to provide. The conclusion that there is really 'nothing to get excited about' has a further consequence: 'High electoral participation, massive attendance at meetings, enthusiastic processions and heated discussions may, on the other hand, indicate fever not robust good health.'[50]

This brings us back to Kornhauser's concern lest 'mass politics' should destroy or disrupt the placid workings of bourgeois pluralism. Such writers are continually haunted by the fear that mass interest in politics can only portend an orgy of destruction and fanaticism. Better by far, they say, to become reconciled to the listless, apathetic irrationality of the electorate in a harmonious bourgeois democracy than risk the rampant generalized irrationality of mass politics. We must remember, 'The extreme case of mass politics is the totalitarian movement, notably communism and fascism.'[51]

49. Peter Pulzer, *Political Representation and Elections in Britain*, UK, 1968, p. 129.

50. Peter Pulzer, op. cit., p. 129. Other writers of this sort confess to being worried by apathy if it occurs on too large a scale since it means that the masses are beyond the reach of the control mechanism of pluralist politics. As always contemporary bourgeois society and its theorists want the masses to be energetic in performing the particular role allotted to them but passive with regard to society as a whole.

51. Kornhauser, op. cit., p. 236.

In Kornhauser's use of the word 'totalitarian' we see a very hackneyed theme of bourgeois ideology. We have already discussed the way the category 'industrial society' is used to subsume the social institutions of all societies based on industrial production; this emphasizes that there exist no meaningful alternatives to society as it is. The concept 'totalitarian' is used indiscriminately to refer to all modern societies which are not bourgeois democracies. In particular it seeks to imply that Fascism and Communism have a great deal in common. This involves ignoring the quite evidently 'pluralist' (capitalist) features of Fascist societies.[52] It also involves a patently ideological attempt to identify Marxism and Leninism with the irrationality of Fascist ideology. The most notorious attempt to do this is Eysenck's attempt to prove that Communists and Fascists have a similarly 'tough-minded' personality. He only succeeded in this by wholesale misrepresentation of evidence, errors of calculation and gross violations of his own evidence.[53]

'Totalitarianism'

The scientific level of the main sociological writings on the category of 'totalitarianism' can be judged from the fact that they invariably identified Nazi Germany with Stalin's Russia, and distilled from these the essence of their concept. In this manner purges, forced labour camps, cult of the leader and so forth are converted into the necessary features of all Communist regimes past, present or future.[54] The diverse contemporary evolution of China, Cuba, Romania and Yugoslavia have conclusively demonstrated that Stalin's Russia was an extreme, rather than a typical, instance of a Communist attempt to build a socialist society – no doubt the extreme historical conjuncture which produced the Stalin regime chiefly explains this fact. The error of the bourgeois theorists was again empiricism: that is, identifying the essence of a form of society (socialism) with its

52. cf. G. Roth, 'The Isms in Totalitarianism', *American Journal of Political Science*, October 1964.
53. cf. the critiques by Roszac, Christie *et al.* in *Psychological Bulletin*, 1955.
54. See for example,'Totalitarianism', edited by C. Friedrich, US, 1956.

immediately given forms (Stalinism). Naturally the dialectical approach to the same problematic adopted by such writers as Isaac Deutscher and Herbert Marcuse enabled them to obtain a more lasting insight into the dynamic of Soviet society.

The drift of most bourgeois analysts of 'totalitarianism' is to suggest that the active transformation of their own society and polity by the mass of citizens must threaten a repetition of the horrors of Nazism. The need to portray in such black hues the consequences of any alternative to bourgeois society probably reflects an awareness that its intrinsic attractions are not sufficient to ensure loyalty. The recurring streak of pessimism in contemporary bourgeois thought is also evident here: 'the idea of establishing a self-conscious mastery of all social processes is seen to be as impractical as it is depressing.' [55]

Above all the concept 'totalitarian' seeks to distract us from the fact that for a generation now it has been the so-called 'pluralist' bourgeois democracies which have become the chief practitioners and supporters of wars of extermination, massacres, the use of torture, the bombing of civilian populations and the rest of the grisly catalogue of oppression employed by modern imperialism.

There is an apparent inconsistency between the concepts 'industrial society' and the analysis of 'totalitarianism'. If industrial society tends to be pluralistic then how can there be societies which are both industrial and 'totalitarian'? The answer usually suggested is that 'totalitarian' movements are the by-product of the growing-pains of an industrializing society. Totalitarian society is an aberrant variation which the industrializing process occasionally throws up.

Most bourgeois theorists are confident that all industrial societies, once they reach maturity will begin to manifest 'pluralist' (capitalist) characteristics. Raymond Aron has written:

I am inclined to believe that advanced industrialization in Europe at least, favours individualist rather than collectivist civilization, and diffuses a desire for family life and intimacy: in the future perhaps Europe in this respect will extend as far as the Urals.[56]

55. H. B. Acton, *The Illusion of the Epoch*, UK, 1958, p. 189.
56. Raymond Aron, *Eighteen Lectures on Industrial Society*, UK, 1967, p. 13.

It is no accident that Aron suddenly comes up with 'family life' at this point. Bourgeois theorists regard this as the consolation they have to relieve an otherwise bleak picture of life in the industrial society. Condemned to a trapped existence in anonymous private or public bureaucracies, recommended to political passivity, 'industrial' man is promised the domestic joys of a 'privatized' existence.

The Family and Domestic Mystification

Chiming in harmoniously with the 'home centred' propaganda of the advertising companies and colour supplements the bourgeois sociologist discovers within the tiny compass of the family the realm of self-realization for the citizen of the modern capitalist democracy. Man's world-creating potentialites can here find fulfilment – here is a private refuge from the meaningless routines of the public realms of his life. Britain's two foremost sociological authorities on the question have declared about the family that 'there is enough clear evidence to warrant its description as one of the twentieth century's great success stories.'[57]

Professor McGregor's familistic ideology has achieved its purest expression in a series he wrote for a popular evening newspaper:

In Britain now most families are little democracies and freedom of choice is the essential habit of their lives. The religious, legal, social and economic sanctions which used to buttress the family and marriage have lost their power to cement intimate relationships. Free men and women cannot be coerced into moral responsibility, and the old bonds of matrimony have dissolved into ties of affection, care for children, habit or some other cluster of personal motives. In essence, the integrity of modern marriage rests upon the loyalties of husbands and wives. In a democratic society these cannot be other than loyalties freely chosen. The conclusion of this survey of marriage and divorce is that moral freedom works. (*Evening Standard*, 29 March 1968)

57. O. R. McGregor and Griselda Rowntree, 'The Family', in *Society*, edited by A. T. Welford and others, London, 1962, p. 425.

The bourgeois political theorist is blind to the multiple opportunities for manipulation and concealed oppression in capitalist variants of democracy so it is quite appropriate that the bourgeois sociologist should apply this term to family life ('families are little democracies'). McGregor is *par excellence* a British empiricist sociologist so that one might imagine that his conclusions are based on some sort of research. On inspection one discovers that his resounding conclusions derive from a pedestrian study of divorce statistics. With great laboriousness he and his co-workers seek to prove that the increase in divorce rates in Britain and other advanced capitalist countries reflects changes in the legal and financial availability of divorce rather than rejection of marriage as an institution. McGregor clinches his case by demonstrating the high rate of remarriage among divorcees. It does not occur to sociologists of this tradition to seek out other evidence by which to assess the functioning of the family as the key primary institution of our society. It is, for example, a fact that the family is the main arena of deliberate physical violence as even a cursory look at the statistics on cruelty to children or on murder show. It is also the case that one family in five has some history of 'schizophrenia' that comes to the attention of the medical authorities. David Cooper, a psychiatrist who has investigated this matter together with R. D. Laing, concludes as follows:

> Recent research into the families of schizophrenic patients has shown ... scapegoating procedures to be at the origin of madness. The needs of the Good Folk to define themselves as sane lead them to project their anxiety, disturbance and conflict into a sub-community which is furtively but progressively labelled as mad and then confirmed as such by all the agents (often well intentioned, 'sincere' people) of an alienated society – police, judges, welfare officers, social workers, psychiatrists, and so on, until they become 'chronic institutionalized mental patients'. In this curious dialectic between 'sane' society and 'crazy' individual the mediation is usually provided by the family. In the family the whole bog of social mystification, re-ification, alienation, bad faith is filtered. ... Those who receive less of this precious mess are placed in a situation in which they must rebel and assert the fact of their difference. When they do this they invite the fatal label. A young man has only to look

a little cross with his manipulative incestuously demanding mother to end up on a detention order as 'dangerous to others'. . . .[58]

Even the well-adjusted, happy family creates, by exclusion, those who might yearn for its cosy consolations – the illegitimate child or the unwanted grandparent. Finally the social regulation of sexuality which the family provides is exposed by the proliferation of 'Playboy Culture', which seeks to rob sex of its erotic character.[59]

'Alienation': Destruction of a Concept

As Cooper indicates, the family transmits alienations which originate in the whole structure of capitalist society and one cannot separate its micro-dynamics from this function. Before going further it will be instructive to consider the fate of this concept 'alienation' at the hands of the bourgeois social theorists. Now for the bourgeois sociologist 'alienation' has become an increasingly fashionable concept for discussing certain psychological states. When Marx and the Left Hegelians first used this term in social analysis they wished to achieve a critical understanding of an *objective* social condition. For Feuerbach religion was an alienation of man's essence because in it he projected human qualities on an imaginary Deity. For the young Marx the worker in a capitalist society was alienated because the forced sale of his labour power only served to maintain and expand the alien power of private property. Marx held that even the capitalist was alienated in that he did not control the economic system of which he was the beneficiary. Clearly an alienated mode of existence may not be experienced as such by the individual. The religious enthusiast who has projected himself into his religion or the capitalist who feels himself as realized in his property would in fact certainly not feel estranged. As with many Marxist ideas, the bourgeois social theorist is strongly tempted to plunder the alienation concept so long as its critical, revolutionary edge can be blunted. One way of doing this is to psychologize it until its reference is purely subjective. In an influential article Melvin

58. R. D. Laing and others, *Sanity and Madness in the Family*, UK, 1964.
59. David Cooper, 'Saint Genet', *New Left Review*, no. 25.

Seeman argues precisely that the 'critical, polemical element in the idea of alienation' [60] must be removed if it is to become a scientific and operational concept. Seeman suggests reducing the concept to five psychological dimensions (feelings of normlessness, meaninglessness, powerlessness, isolation and self-estrangement). Once thoroughly 'operationalized' the lifeless remains of the concept can be measured and tested against interview material. With the benevolent encouragement of capitalist foundations, research projects can be set up and yet another team of bourgeois sociologists can make a living extracting the revolutionary essence from Marxism. Thus one is left with such conclusions as the following, guaranteed free from anything critical or polemical: 'Srole finds substantiation of the possible status positioning of the alienated in a negative correlation of .30 between his eunomia-anomia scale and an index of socio-economic status.' [61]

Another concept which appears in this quotation in a thoroughly 'decontaminated' form is that of class or 'socio-economic status'. The same tendency to psychologization is common practice here: 'a man's class is a part of his ego, a feeling on his part of belongingness to something; an identification with something larger than himself.' [62]

Class and Status

In short there is a constant tendency to equate class with some given consciousness of class at a given moment. By these means class is reduced to a register of occupation, income group or 'status' as in Professor Macrae's definition: 'a quasi-group of equivalent statuses is what we call a class.' [63] The UK Registrar General's criteria of class exactly conform to the specifications of bourgeois sociology: they reflect occupational status and thus exclude idle or 'unemployed' capitalists altogether from the classification. Marx was quite alert to these dangers: 'Vulgar common

60. Melvin Seeman, 'On the meaning of alienation', *American Sociological Review*, 1959, p. 784.
61. Gwynn Netler, 'A measure of alienation', *American Sociological Review*, December 1957.
62. Richard Centers, *Psychology of Social Class*, p. 27.
63. Donald Macrae, 'Ideology and Society', p. 67.

sense turns class differences into differences in the size of one's purse, and class conflict into a quarrel between handicrafts.' [64] Marxist class analysis examines not only the immediate determinations and manifestations of class and class consciousness but also their relation to the class dynamic of the society. Classes are ultimately distinguished by their relation to the mode of production though at a given moment this will be supplemented by cultural and historical influences (an approach which Marx exemplifies in such historical writings as *The 18th Brumaire of Louis Bonaparte*). Thus the best Marxist class analysis charts not only the intricate determinations of class consciousness at a particular time but also the 'possible consciousness' [65] of the class. Once the situation of a class has been objectively examined then hypotheses on the appropriate and adequate consciousness of that class can be formulated. The bourgeois sociologist might ask at this point: how can the Marxist verify these speculative hypotheses about events that lie in the future? Would he not do better simply to stick to looking at things as they are? For the bourgeois sociologist 'things as they are' never point to class conflict unless that class conflict is actually entering its final consummation before his eyes. For him, verification of sociological theories is a perpetual problem since he is uneasily aware that his own scientific procedures leave much to be desired. The Marxist does not seek some lifeless and external correlation between his theories and the results of questionnaires. In the best Marxist class analysis verification is sought in revolutionary struggle itself: an example might be Mao Tse Tung's *Report of an Investigation into the Peasant Movement in Hunan* written in February 1927 and 'verified' in the practice of the Chinese People's Liberation Army (a brilliant account of this will be found in Edgar Snow's classic *Red Star over China*). As André Glucksmann has observed: 'As opposed to the "realism" of vulgar Marxism, Mao Tse Tung's thought, like all theory, claims to be true before it has been realized, and to be realizable because it is true.'

The customary refuge of the bourgeois sociologist when it

64. Karl Marx, 'The Moralising Critique and the Critique of Morals', *Deutsch-Französische Jahrbucher*, February 1844.
65. Lucien Goldmann, *Sciences Humaines et Philosophie*, Paris, 1952.

comes to verifying theory is the questionnaire. The results obtained in this way are thought to have unimpeachable scientific validity. Replies to interviews are invariably assumed to reveal a social consciousness which is homogeneous and consistent. A difficulty rarely considered is that interviewees are known to reply in a different sense to the same questions if these are put in different settings (the home, the factory canteen, the personnel manager's office, etc.). One of the best recent studies of class consciousness to be conducted in England illustrates the pitfalls involved. *The British Journal of Sociology* for September 1966 carried a report of a study of the Luton Vauxhall workers by John Goldthorpe. It concluded that

in spite of the deprivation which their jobs on the line may entail, these men will be disposed to maintain their relationship with their firm, and to define this more as one of reciprocity and interdependence than, say, one of co-ercion and exploitation.[66]

Goldthorpe informs us that 77 per cent of the workers had a 'co-operative view of management' and that conditions in the plant were 'no longer likely to give rise to discontent and resentment of a generalized kind.' About a month after the publication of this report the Luton workers broke into open revolt. Two thousand workers tried to storm the management offices, 'singing the Red Flag and calling "string him up" whenever a director's name was mentioned.'[67]

The possibility that the Luton workers might ever recognize the exploitation to which they were subject never occurred to Goldthorpe. Nor did he consider the probabilities that the workers there had at least two sets of 'attitudes', as do many workers in a capitalist society. On one hand they are quite aware that the owners are profiting from their labour: on the other they know they cannot change the system so they are prepared to go along with it. In a study entitled *The Political Systems of Highland Burma*, E. R. Leach demonstrated that the Highland Burmese held two quite opposed world-views at the same time,

66. John H. Goldthorpe, 'Attitudes and Behaviour of Car Assembly Workers', *British Journal of Sociology*, September 1966.
67. *The Times*, 19 October 1966. I discuss this episode at greater length in *The Incompatibles*, edited by R. Blackburn and A. Cockburn (Penguin Books), pp. 48–51.

bringing forth whichever was most appropriate to the situation. Sociologists rarely entertain the possibility that consciousness in an advanced capitalist country might have a similar ambivalence. Empiricist sociology insists that all attitudes should be neat and tidy. This approach can lead the bourgeois sociologist to refuse to admit as evidence anything which upsets his scheme. For example, a sample survey was conducted of all students at the London School of Economics during the sit-in of March 1967. The purpose of this survey was to discover the attitude of students (including those not taking a direct part) towards the sit-in. Professor Julius Gould has criticized this survey for the following reason: 'It is hardly likely that a serious, scientific study could be carried out in the heated, near-violent atmosphere of the sit-in.' [68]

As this study was precisely designed to investigate attitudes generated during the sit-in this is a most curious objection – to be explained no doubt by the fact that the survey indicated that the majority even of those students not taking a direct part in the sit-in tended to approve of it.

Democracy and the Capitalist Market

The above discussion indicates that bourgeois economics and bourgeois social theory operate in a different but complementary manner. Economics aspires to be a purely technical discipline as if economic categories were not saturated with social significance. Concepts with critical overtones are excluded on principle.[69] Instead of tabooing a concept or problem sociological theory will seek to emasculate it. For example, the academic reading public has an endless appetite for works which debunk Marx and it seems that bourgeois theorists have an unlimited capacity to produce such definitive refutations. Since Böhm-Bawerk published *Karl Marx and the Close of his System*, one year after the publication of the complete *Das Kapital*, a flourishing industry of Marx-refutation has grown up which shows no sign of

68. Julius Gould, 'Politics and the Academy', *Government and Opposition*, March 1968, p. 31.
69. The words 'exploitation', 'contradiction', 'expropriation', etc., do not appear among the numerous entries to A. Gilpen's *Dictionary of Economic Terms*, London, 1965.

slackening. Philosophers and sociologists now produce the bulk of this material, but only rarely achieve Böhm-Bawerk's intellectual level.

The complementary nature of economic and social theory can also be seen in the exchange of analogies between the two. Economic theory often draws on the bourgeois conception of democracy to describe the workings of the capitalist economic system. The theory of consumer sovereignty is often conveyed in such terms. Thus Samuelson explains how 'consumer dollar votes of demand interact in the upper goods market with business-cost supply decisions, thus helping to determine what is produced.'[70]

It is sometimes pointed out that dollars are somewhat less equally distributed than votes but even such a concession still implies that economic growth follows where consumer demand leads. And there is one thing that 'dollar votes' quite certainly are not capable of doing – namely changing the system. Some pseudo-critical bourgeois theorists make a great show of rejecting the conventional wisdom on 'consumer sovereignty' by pointing out that demand is manipulated by the advertising and market research employed by the large companies. Such a commonsense objection implies that capitalist countries where advertising expenditure is low and advertising techniques unsophisticated (e.g. France) really are ruled by consumer sovereignty. When such writers complain that advertising creates 'artificial needs' it quite fails to point out that *repression* of needs is, as Nicolas Krasso observed, a more fundamental characteristic of capitalism. The domination of demand of course takes place at a more fundamental level in the capitalist determination of economic accumulation and of the means available for the satisfaction of demands. As Marx explains:

Private interest is itself already a socially determined interest, which can be attained only within certain socially ordained conditions and with socially given means, and which is therefore dependent on the reproduction of these conditions and means. It is the interest of the private person; but its content and the form and means of its

70. P. A. Samuelson, *Economics*, p. 41, sixth ed. Raymond Aron has a parallel formulation: 'Individual enterprises, are, in a way, the equivalent of political parties in the political order.'

realization are set by social conditions independently of the individual.[71]

What is sometimes called 'methodological individualism' (the bourgeois doctrine that all statements about society can be reduced to statements about individuals) is a device for evading such facts as these. The theory of demand provides a good illustration of the ideological distortion involved.

While economics borrows from social theory to justify the economic system, social theory borrows from economics in the hope of acquiring its supposed technical rigour.

Writers such as Anthony Downs construct a theory of democracy where political leaders are seen as entrepreneurs of the system; they produce policies and sell them to the consumers (the electorate.[72] Given the fact that in a capitalist society, economic modes tend to penetrate everywhere, all this is not without a certain plausibility. Of course it is usually reciprocally linked to some sort of consumer sovereignty idea but even so the logical conclusion of such analogies creates real problems. C. B. MacPherson has given a good summary of the sort of predicament exponents of this approach find themselves in:

Politicians in such a model can normally expect to increase their chances of gaining office by discouraging voters from choosing rationally, for example, by offering ambiguous programmes. The only limit is a degree of voter irrationality that would destroy the democratic system, which party politicians have a stake in. But in each party's calculations, that limit will not appear to be approached by any action the party takes in the direction of greater ambiguity, that is, of greater irrationality imposed on voters. Hence the tendency of the system is to discourage rational behaviour indefinitely.

Another proposition that can be reached from the model is that, although the rules of a democratic system are designed to distribute political power, equally, such equality cannot result if all men act rationally. (The rational voter, to make his demand effective, must

71. Karl Marx, *Grundrisse der Kritik der politischen Ekonomie*, quoted by Martin Nicolaus, 'The Unknown Marx', *New Left Review*, March–April 1968.
72. See Anthony Downs, *An Economic Theory of Democracy*, USA, 1958. The pioneer of this approach was Schumpeter in *Capitalism, Socialism and Democracy*. It now pervades political theory especially of the pluralist variety.

acquire a lot of information. The cost, in time, energy, and money, of acquiring it must, by a rational voter, be weighed against the expected benefit to him, which benefit must be discounted in view of the very small amount of influence one vote has. The amount, and the cost, of the information needed for a rational decision necessarily varies between individuals, because the division of labour in modern society gives direct access to such information to only a few in each policy area. To those farthest removed from the sources of information, the rational decision will be not to pay the cost of informing themselves, but to let some interested agency pay the cost, and accept biased information from it. Hence if all men act rationally their influence on policy must be very unequal).[73]

Of course these consequences of their own mode of thinking are not confronted by the bourgeois political scientists who, on the whole, approve of one-dimensional politics and the benevolent domination of pressure groups. Of course even such conclusions exaggerate the power of interest groups and ignore the structural determination of policy which has already been discussed in the section on pluralist theories.

The production of economic goods and the reproduction of power relationships are a twin mystery for bourgeois social science. As Krasso has observed, bourgeois economics ever since the labour theory of value was abandoned has treated the production of goods just as the Melanesian cargo cults treat cargo.[74] As for the origins of power relationships these are sought everywhere but in the ownership of capital (dead, stored-up labour) which structures the bourgeois social system. Instead of registering capitalist property relations as the structural limit of the political order, the bourgeois theorist seeks to render political phenomena directly intelligible in terms of the 'demand' oriented economic analogy.

73. C. B. MacPherson, 'Market Concept in Political Theory', *Canadian Journal of Economics and Political Science*, 1961, p. 493.

74. The Melanesian islanders observed that the Europeans received ships laden with good things by building jetties, scribbling on bits of paper and so forth. The Melanesians also constructed jetties and waited for the cargo ships to arrive. cf. Peter Worsley, *The Trumpet Shall Sound*, UK, 1958.

Science and Bourgeois Ideology

All the bourgeois social sciences declare their ambition to become 'value-neutral' sciences. Once theories are thoroughly cleansed of all 'value judgements' it is believed that they will be governed only by the wholesome discipline of objective facts. The predictable consequence of this attempted purge of values is to orient theory and research towards certain crude, over-abstracted value notions masquerading as scientific concepts: e.g. 'utility', 'efficiency', 'productivity', 'equilibrium', 'rationality', etc. This reflects an inescapable predicament for positivist social science. It is the hallmark of positivism that it presents a misunderstood account of method in the natural sciences as the model for the social sciences. At its most sterile this theory advocates the patient accumulation of 'facts' leading to the later construction of theories. More sophisticated versions of the theory concede that facts are only meaningful within the context of the theory which constitutes them as facts (theories of identification, verification, etc.). But they go on to insist that theories should be 'falsifiable' and that one contrary instance should lead to the rejection of a theory. Fortunately natural scientists have never followed this advice. A contrary instance leads more often to a questioning or reinterpretation of the evidence than to the rejection of a theory.[75] Theories are in any case so much concerned with discussion about what counts as a fact, and with the interpretation of facts, that the very distinction between the two is only valid if it is sometimes abandoned. In his choice of method the social scientist will necessarily be committing himself to a certain conception of what are the proper values of scientific work. Social scientists often proclaim a commitment to 'scientific values' but rarely consider the nature of such values to be a problematic question. The area chosen by him for research will imply

75. Anyone surprised by this statement should consult the following references which, from somewhat different vantage points, give an admirable introduction to the subject of scientific method. T. S. Kuhn, *The Structure of the Scientific Revolutions*, USA, 1961. T. S. Kuhn's contribution to the forthcoming volume in honour of Sir Karl Popper, edited by Imre Lakatos; Paul K. Feyerabend, 'Problems of Empiricism', in *Beyond the Edge of Certainty*, edited by R. Colodry, USA, 1965; Gaston Bachelard, *La Formation de l'Esprit Scientifique*, Paris, 1966.

further judgements about what is worthy of study. Assumptions must also be made about aspects of the object of study which are not being investigated; thus economic theory must assume a certain psychology, and sociology and so forth. Indeed all activity expresses a certain value commitment. However minimally, all action goes beyond and transcends the given situation. Unless the bourgeois social scientist can theorize or engage in research *without actually doing anything* he must be realizing some value. Perhaps it is a surrender to philosophical confusion even to put the matter in this way. A value is only the congealed residue of dead action: the concept suffers from the same false abstraction as the isolated 'fact'. Of course the 'ought' and the 'is' may be separated in the social world but our vocabulary should not establish this separation as an impassable barrier. The positivist social science can only be its 'purely technical' servant.

Re-ification

The positivist delusion invariably involves 'de-humanization' or 're-ification'. Lenin explains the nature of re-ification very clearly when he writes, 'Where the bourgeois economists saw a relation between things (the exchange of one commodity for another) Marx revealed *a relation between people*.' [76]

The rise of market society rendered immensely plausible the view that 'social facts are things'.[77] An alienated society natur-

76. V. I. Lenin, *Collected Works*, Vol. 19, p. 26. For a useful debate on the nature of this concept see, 'Reification and the Sociological Critique of Consciousness', by Peter Berger and Stanley Pullberg, *New Left Review* 35, January–February 1966. Ben Brewster's criticism, published in the same issue, noted that *avant garde* bourgeois sociologists like Berger and Pullberg acknowledge the existence of alienation and re-ification but insist that such is the inescapable condition of everyday existence that it is only to be overcome in quite exceptional historical circumstances.

77. This slogan from Emile Durkheim's *Rules of Sociological Method* has become the root assumption of much contemporary sociology. In the *Critique de la Raison Dialectique* (Paris, 1961; the first part *Search for a Method* has been published in English), Jean-Paul Sartre inverted Durkheim's dictum to read, 'Social facts are things to the extent that things are social facts', i.e. re-ification is inescapable in a context of material scarcity.

ally encourages a re-ifying vocabulary – that is a vocabulary which accepts at face value the thing-like character which social relations appear to possess. The market is capable of representing any object or anybody's labour in terms of a single scale of exchange (money). The market reduces differences in quality to differences in quantity so that every relation appears measurable. The individual use-values of a commodity are only expressed in so far as they have exchange value on the market. As human labour is also a commodity on the market the same rule applies: this opens the way for the exploitation of labour. The employer buys the worker's labour power at the price of its immediate exchange value: by doing so he acquires its 'use-value', including its power to create exchange values. Given the fact that capitalists own the means of production, and thus dominate employment opportunities, they can, indeed must, always pay the worker less than the value of what he produces.[78] Everything conspires to make these objective social relations of exploitation appear inevitable, natural facts. Since a capitalist economy is not controlled by men, or even a social group, its workings have the force of natural laws.

The trade cycle can be tamed somewhat in the way the effects of natural calamities can be insured against. Moreover the emergence of large public and private bureaucracies only reinforces the de-humanizing consequences of the market. In such a society it can seem very scientific to study social relations as if they were things or processes. Man himself is thought of as a rather complex machine or servo-mechanism – an attitude particularly prevalent among psychologists. For example:

The definition of man we intend to use must be of sufficient generality. We take the following: man is a complex error-controlled regulator, restoring its continually disturbed equilibrium through compensatory actions executed by many superimposed feedback cycles, obeying criteria of efficiency, which are not pre-determined forever.[79] We must be on our guard here

---

78. I have attempted an interpretation of the Marxist theory of exploitation in *The Incompatibles*, op. cit., pp. 36–51.
79. Leo Apostel, 'Can Metaphysics be a Science?', *Studia Philosophica Gandensia*, 1963. On a more serious level, the damaging effects of the sociological approach can be seen in even the best sociological studies

against a complementary aspect of bourgeois ideology – namely an easy humanist vocabulary concealing the reality of an alienated social system. Marx was aware of this danger when he wrote: Doubtless, Ricardo's language is as cynical as can be. To put the cost of manufacture of hats and the cost of maintenance of men on the same plane is to turn men into hats. But do not make an outcry at the cynicism of it. The cynicism is in the facts not in the words that express the facts. French writers ... take an innocent satisfaction in proving their superiority over the English economists by seeking to observe the etiquette of a 'humanitarian' phraseology; if they reproach Ricardo and his school for their cynical language it is because it annoys them to see economic relations exposed in all their crudity, to see the mysteries of the bourgeoisie unmasked.[80]

Bourgeois social science is in error not so much because it perceives the thing-like character of social relations under capitalism but rather because it postulates that they will always have this character. The contradiction inherent in the capitalist mode of production is a consequence not only of its 'inhumanity' but also of its obsolescence. The 'inhuman' social relations of capitalism are historically responsible for an immeasurable enlargement of productive forces. But capitalism is not capable of accommodating the expansion which it has itself produced. In Marx's words:

---

wherever an alternative study of the same subject is available which avoids re-ification. Compare, for example, Neil Smelser's *Social Change in the Industrial Revolution*, UK, 1959, with Edward Thompson's magnificent *The Making of the English Working Class*, UK, 1963; or Robert Blauner's *Alienation and Freedom*, USA, 1964, with *Work*, edited by Ronald Fraser, UK, 1968.

80. Karl Marx, *The Poverty of Philosophy*. Contemporary exponents of a 'humanist' social science include such writers as Peter Winch (for a critique see Ernest Gellner, 'Enter the Philosophers', *The Times Literary Supplement*, April 1968). See also Ben Brewster's critique of Berger and Pullberg in *New Left Review* 35.

Another contemporary example of Marx's point: bourgeois economists once talked about the economically 'backward' countries; then 'underdeveloped' was felt to be a kinder adjective. They now prefer to refer to poor capitalist countries as 'developing nations' abandoning all pretence to scientific terminology.

Capital is its own contradiction-in-process, for its urge is to reduce labour time to a minimum, while at the same time it maintains that labour time is the only measure and source of wealth. So on the one side it animates all the powers of science and nature, of social co-ordination and intercourse, in order to make the production of wealth (relatively) independent of the labour time expended on it. On the other side it wants to use labour time as a measure for the gigantic social powers created in this way, and to restrain them within the the limits necessary to maintain already created values as values.[81]

The specific ways in which private ownership of the means of production enters into contradiction with the socially productive forces of the capitalist economy naturally impinges on the different social classes in a quite distinct manner. In order to maintain and expand the value of capital the working class must continue to be exploited. At the same time the lopsided and inadequate process of capitalist accumulation condemns to poverty entire ethnic groups, whole populations who live in 'depressed' or 'underdeveloped' regions, and a great proportion of the aged even in the most advanced capitalist economy.

These people are surplus to the requirements of capital since their labour power is uneconomic to exploit and since they have too little money to constitute a significant market. The obverse of the exploitation of the working class and neglect of excess populations is the existence of economic surplus. This is absorbed, and the profits from it realized, by government expenditure (especially on armaments), the growing costs of marketing and selling, the fostering of artificial product differentiation, 'built-in obsolescence' and so forth. The Marxist economist is equipped with the critical concept of 'use value' when he analyses the capitalist system and does not rest content with a mere examination of 'exchange values'. With the aid of this concept he can discover in what ways the capitalist property relations warp and retard the economic process. He can focus on the difference between production for profit and production for use. By contrast the bourgeois economist only concerns himself with the immediate, given form of economic phenomena in a capitalist society and does not seek to discover their structural determina-

81. Karl Marx, *Grundrisse*, p. 594, quoted by Martin Nicolaus, op. cit.

tion. By making such concepts as 'wage', 'price', 'interest' and 'rent' the basic categories of analysis, bourgeois economics does no more than

> interpret, systematize and defend in doctrinaire fashion the conceptions of the agents of bourgeois production who are entrapped in bourgeois production relations. It should not astonish, then, that vulgar economy feels particularly at home in the estranged outward appearances of economic relations in which these prima facie and absurd contradictions appear and that these relations seem the more self-evident the more their internal relationships are concealed from it. . . . But all science would be superfluous if the outward appearance and the essence of things directly co-incided.[82]

Marx thus examines the hidden structure of capitalist economic relations from the vantage point of their contradictions. This concept of contradiction is yet another that is generally shunned by all bourgeois social theory.[83] Not only is the materialist dialectic of Marx rejected but so too is Hegel's idealist dialectic. Once again contemporary bourgeois social theory is seen *rejecting the achievements of its own heroic epoch* – the class analysis of political economy, the democratic theory of

---

82. Karl Marx, *Capital*, Vol. III, p. 797. See Maurice Godelier, 'System, Structure and Contradiction in Capital', *Socialist Register* 1967, Ralph Miliband and John Saville (eds.). This essay provides a brilliant if controversial account of Marx's method of analysis: see also Ernest Mandel, *Marxist Economic Theory*, 1968, and R. L. Meek, *Economics and Ideology*, UK, 1967.

83. Here is a bourgeois social philosopher who finds the notion of social contradictions an interesting one:

'There is a good deal that might be inquired about contradictions in human affairs. ... Some have argued that the logic of imperatives is similar to the logic of propositions, while others have said there must be great differences between them – that, for example, while from the conjunctive proposition, "He put on a life belt and jumped into the water", we may validly infer either of the conjuncts, e.g., "He jumped into the water", we cannot, from the imperative, "Put on the life jacket and jump into the water", infer the single command, "Jump into the water". These considerations show that there are some interesting problems to be investigated here, and it is to be regretted that Marxists, whose theory of social contradictions raises some of them have, as far as I am aware, left them unexplored.' H. B. Acton, *The Illusion of the Epoch*, UK, 1958, p. 154.

liberalism and the dialectical method of German idealism succumb to the amnesia of modern bourgeois epigones.

The Dialectic

Of course Hegel himself is coming somewhat back into fashion again in the English-speaking world after years of inaccurate abuse by Popper and others. Needless to say, Hegel's ideas have had to be watered down to suit the weak stomach of the modern bourgeois social theorist.

Some writers domesticate Hegel by portraying him as a Teutonic John Stuart Mill, a good old-fashioned liberal at heart; others think of Hegel as a nineteenth-century Karl Jaspers, a remarkably precocious modern existentialist. Both attempt to ignore or repudiate the revolutionary kernel of Hegel's philosophy – the dialectic. Thus Walter Kaufman claims that 'Hegel's dialectic is at most a method of exposition; it is not a method of discovery.' [84]

Let us compare this strange assertion with Herbert Marcuse's admirable account of the role of dialectic in Hegel's system.

Reality appears as a dynamic in which all fixed forms reveal themselves to be mere abstractions. ... Hegel's philosophy is originally motivated by the conviction that the given facts that appear to common sense as the positive index of truth can only be established by their destruction. The driving force of the dialectical method lies in this critical conviction. Dialectic in its entirety is linked to the conception that all forms of being are permeated by an essential negativity, and that this negativity determines their content and movement. The dialectic represents the counterthrust to any form of positivism. From Hume to the present day logical positivists, the principle of this philosophy has been the ultimate authority of fact, and observing the immediate given has been the ultimate method of verification. ... The protagonists of this (nineteenth century) positivism took great pains to stress the conservative and affirmative attitude of their philosophy: it induces thought to be satisfied with the facts, to renounce any transgression beyond them, and to bow to the given state of affairs.

84. Walter Kaufman, *Hegel*, p. 175. Kaufman is the author of an excellent exposé of Karl Popper's attack on Hegel. See his *The Owl and the Nightingale*, USA, 1963.

To Hegel the facts in themselves possess no authority. . . . Everything that is given has to be justified before reason, which is but the
totality of nature's and men's capacities.[85]

Through this essay I have stressed that contemporary bourgeois social science purges itself of any concepts which might
suggest that capitalist society should be critically analysed in this
way. For the contemporary bourgeois social philosopher capitalism is a fact and no amount of sympathy for Hegel's philosophy
will make him see it as a contradictory or transient form of
society. Thus Kaufman, who believes the dialectic to be a quite
unimportant aspect of Hegel's thought, still feels in a position to
complain of its misuse by Marx:

By depriving it (Hegel's dialectic) of its primary reference to ideas
and applying it instead to modes of production, one cannot make
the dialectic more precise; or materialism, scientific. On the contrary
beliefs are at least *capable* of being literally contradicted and then
subsumed in a higher synthesis, while any dialectic of modes of production or material circumstances is bound to be utterly lacking in
rigor.[86]

The rigour the bourgeois social scientist aspires to is *rigor
mortis*: or what Hegel called 'a moving life of the dead'. To regard capitalist society as fatally undermined by its own contradictions is not rigorous because we have no way of being sure
that it will not last for ever. On the whole, bourgeois social scientists avoid altogether such discussion of the ultimate prospects
for their social system and unanimously shun any dialectical
approach to the object of their investigations. None of this
would have surprised Marx:

In its rational form the dialectic is a scandal and abomination to
bourgeoisdom and its doctrinaire professors, because it includes in
its comprehension an affirmative recognition of the existing state of
things, at the same time also, the recognition of the negation of
that state, of its inevitable breaking up; because it regards every
historically developed social form as in fluid movement, and therefore takes into account its transient nature not less than its momentary

85. Herbert Marcuse, *Reason and Revolution*, USA, 1940, pp. 26–7.
86. Walter Kaufman, op. cit., p. 287.

existence: because it lets nothing impose upon it and is in its essence critical and revolutionary.[87]

The method here described by Marx is the only viable alternative to the confusion and sterility into which post-classical bourgeois social theory has fallen. But this is not to say that Marxism is just some rival school of social science. Rather it is the theory of the practice which is changing the world. Marxism as a science was born in the heat of the 1848 revolutions, though it was to be developed in the British Museum. In the twentieth century the modern classics of Marxism have emerged from the most diverse surroundings all of which emphasize its vocation to change the world: from the Vyborg suburb of Petrograd on the eve of the October Revolution (Lenin's *State and Revolution*), from the embattled Budapest Commune of 1919 (Lukacs's *Change in the Function of Historical Materialism*), from the prisons of Mussolini's Italy (Gramsci's prison notebooks), from the caves of Yenan (Mao's *On Contradiction*) and from Havana, capital of the free territory of America (Che Guevara's *Socialism and Man in Cuba*) and from the Paris students' Marxist-Leninist Study Circle in a Sorbonne soon to be the storm centre of the French insurrection of May 1968 (*Lire le Capital*, Althusser, Balibar and others).

87. Karl Marx, 'Afterword to the Second German Edition of Capital', *Selected Works*, pp. 456–7.

Components of the National Culture/Perry Anderson

A coherent and militant student movement has not yet emerged in England. But it may now be only a matter of time before it does. Britain is the only major industrialized country which has not yet produced one. The immediate priorities for any such movement are obvious: the fight against the authoritarianism of universities and colleges, alliance with the working class and struggle against imperialism. These are the issues which are the natural focus of struggle for a mass student revolt. There is, however, another front which will eventually have to be opened. This is a direct attack on the reactionary and mystifying culture inculcated in universities and colleges, and which it is one of the fundamental purposes of British higher education to instil in students.

Louis Althusser has recently written that within the general system of higher education 'the number one strategic point of the action of the dominant class' is 'the very *knowledge* students receive from their teachers'. This is 'the true fortress of class influence in the university'; 'it is by the very nature of the knowledge it imparts to students that the bourgeoisie exerts its greatest control over them.'[1] An assault on this 'fortress' is, in fact, a necessary condition of the successful take-off of a student movement (the example of the German SDS is eloquent here). For one of the main reasons for the lateness of any student unrest in England is precisely the lack of any revolutionary tradition within English culture. Only where revolutionary ideas are freely and widely available – forming part of their daily environment – will large numbers of students begin to revolt. Hitherto, they have been muzzled and quiescent, not primarily because of their class origins (which are somewhat more democratic than in many countries with violent student upheavals), but more importantly because of their cultural formation. It is not their social recruitment which distinguishes British students from German, Italian or French students – but their intellectual heritage. To unlock their traditional and uncritical attitudes towards university and society, a systematic critique of established British culture is needed. This must not become a substitute for practical struggle against institutions of higher education and the society of which they are a part: it should accompany it. Where is such a systematic critique to be found? The natural source for it is the political Left. Unfortunately, any nascent student movement will not find much immediate assistance there.

Britain, the most conservative major society in Europe, has a culture in its own image: mediocre and inert. The ataraxy of this culture is manifest in any international context. But it is a culture of which the Left in Britain has largely been a passive spectator, and at times a deluded accomplice. Twentieth century British culture was by and large made against it. Yet the Left has never truly questioned this 'national' inheritance which is one of the most enduring bonds of its subordination.[2] But this duty remains on the agenda of any serious socialist movement in Britain, that may emerge from the debris of the past. Without revolutionary theory, wrote Lenin, there can be no revolutionary movement. Gramsci, in effect, added: without a revolutionary culture, there will be no revolutionary theory. A political science capable of guiding the working-class movement to final victory will only be born within a general intellectual matrix which challenges bourgeois ideology in every sector of thought and represents a decisive, hegemonic alternative to the cultural *status quo*. It is enough to say this, to be reminded that in Britain, at present, there is virtually no organized combat of any kind, anywhere along the front. Worse than this, we do not have even an elementary cartography of the terrain that must be disputed. The most influential socialist work of the past decade was called *Culture and Society*. Yet the British Left has few analyses of its own society: it has none of its culture.

The aim of the present essay is to begin a preliminary inventory of the problems involved in considering the total 'set' of contemporary British culture, and its meaning for socialists. Given the complete mutism of the past, any such initial attempt will inevitably suffer from errors, lapses, elisions and omissions. But discussion of the subject is eventually a precondition of political advance by students (and intellectual advance by the Left) and a start must be made somewhere. The risks of haste are obvious; but the fact is that we are suffering from the results of years of delay.

Culture

British culture as it exists today is a profound obstacle to revolutionary politics. What is meant by culture here? A preliminary delimitation is essential. We are not concerned with the anthropological conception of culture, as the sum of social customs and symbols in a given society. The generalization of this use of the term characterized the Left in the fifties, and was responsible for some important insights into British society: this was the moment of Richard Hoggart's *Uses of Literacy*. But this usage also blurred the specificity of the superstructural complex which is a society's original thought and art.

For the purpose of this essay, it should merely be stated at the outset that the concept of culture employed here will be distinct from the usage popularized then. This does not mean that the focus will simply be on the superstructural complex mentioned – the original thought and art of a society. Two large exclusions will be made within this ensemble, leaving the core-phenomenon with which the analysis will be concerned. These two exclusions are the natural sciences at one extreme and creative art at the other. The reasons for this restriction follow from the political point of departure of the enterprise. In effect, the culture that is immediately central and internal to any politics, is that which provides our fundamental concepts of man and society. These are, by definition, essential axes of all social action. Thus the disciplines which are obviously relevant and amenable to a political and structural analysis are history, sociology, anthropology, economics, political theory, philosophy, aesthetics, literary criticism, psychology and psychoanalysis. The natural sciences and creative art are, of course, also intimately linked to the institutional order of society, and the class relations which underpin it. But the articulations are qualitatively different. The problem is a vast one in its own right, which cannot be discussed here. It may suffice to say, very approximately, that the dose of 'objectivity' in the natural sciences and 'subjectivity' in art is symmetrically greater than either in the social sciences delimited above, and they therefore have correspondingly more mediated relationships to the social structure. They do not, in other words, directly provide our basic concepts of man and society – the natural sciences because they forge concepts for the understanding of nature, not *society*, and art because it deals with man and society, but does not provide us with their *concepts*. The autonomy of the three spheres, and the 'central' intercalation of the first, is evident in the history of socialism itself in the twentieth century. Russia in the thirties, during the most sombre years of Stalin's rule, witnessed the atomic physics of Kapitza and the lyrical poetry of Pasternak. But it was relatively devoid of advance in the social or human sciences. The triple combination was no accident. The strategic band of culture for twentieth century politics – the central redoubt of the 'class fortress' – is the segment that lies between creative art and physical science. For procedural convenience – the sake of compression – this will be the scope of the culture discussed here.

Structure

Given this delimitation, there is one traditional socialist approach to the subject. This is the specific denunciation of manifest bourgeois distortions in the *content* of each different discipline. This is a crucial day-to-day task, but it does not constitute a genuinely revolutionary critique of these disciplines if it accepts their present distribution and demarcation; it then renounces any purchase on them as a coherent totality. In other words, it does not achieve a *structural* analysis of them. What is meant by structure here? A recent definition by Lévi-Strauss is pertinent. He writes that a structural method in the study of social facts is characterized by its examination, 'not of the terms (in a system), but of *the relationships between the terms*'.[3] The structure of British culture is thus essentially to be located in the inter-relationship between the disciplines which compose it, and not within each discipline. It is not the content of the individual sectors that determines the essential character of each so much as the ground-plan of their distribution. Of course, the former will inevitably relay the latter in its own space. The cartography of the system as a whole should then indicate its inner articulation.

This regulative principle will dictate the forms taken by the analysis which ensues. It is evident that an exhaustive, immanent account of each sector – given the span of disciplines – is impossible for any one critic. The illusion that this would be necessary is doubtless partly responsible for the silence of the Left on the topic. In fact, no such universal competence is required, once the aim is, not to assess the corpus, but to capture the structure of British culture. This itself demands, of course, some consideration of the character of each sector within it – enough, precisely, to establish its specific articulation with the others into a system. No attempt will be made to give a comprehensive account of any one discipline. The analysis will focus on the general lay-out of the system, and then try to indicate the approximate nature of each segment within it. It will thus be deliberately incomplete and open.

The Absent Centre

Confronted with the wide ambit of intellectual phenomena comprised by British culture, where should a structural analysis begin? The starting-point here will be any observed irregularities in the contours of British culture, viewed internationally. That is, any basic phenomena which are not a matter of course, but contradict elementary expectation from comparative experience and hence seem to demand a special explanation. Such irregularities may provide a privileged point of entry into the culture as a whole, and thereby furnish a key to the system.

If we survey the list of disciplines set out above, and consider them in an international perspective, is there any obvious anomaly among them? History, economics, anthropology, philosophy, aesthetics, political theory, psychology, or literary criticism. All these present nothing abnormal in Britain, by comparative standards. All are represented by departments in universities, which teach courses legitimated by decades of tradition. The local pedigree of each is respectable; the leading practitioners enjoy a certain external reputation, if only (frequently) in the English-speaking world. There is, however, one patent exception in this roll-call: sociology. A trivial, if significant index of a radical disjuncture between it and the other 'terms' of the system is the lack of any chair in sociology at Oxford or Cambridge, the traditional apex of prestige within British university life, and the lack of any course at either (both have part-time papers). The case is unique among the world's major universities. This institutional aspect, however, is merely a remote, mediate consequence of an original and fundamental historical fact.

Britain – alone of major Western societies – never produced a classical sociology.

Events that fail to happen are often more important than those which do; but they are always infinitely more difficult to see. Nothing is so familiar as the absence of an English Durkheim, Pareto or Weber: and nothing is so unnoticeable. Yet the non-emergence of any classical sociology in England, and its consequence, the withered half-life of the subject to this day, are momentous historical events. For sociology was the great intellectual achievement of the European bourgeoisie at the end of the nineteenth and the beginning of the twentieth centuries. It was the birth of a new mode of social thought that – significantly – occurred virtually simultaneously in Germany with Weber, France with Durkheim and Italy with Pareto. These three thinkers founded a tradition that was later dynamically recapitulated by Parsons in *The Structure of Social Action*. It is important to insist on this, for Parsons is the heir of the great European lineage; his work shows that sociology was in no fashion destined to be a merely 'continental' phenomenon, after its origins. Yet Britain not merely failed to participate in the great collective discovery of the new social science that occurred in Europe before the First World War.[4] It also failed in any way to assimilate the massive Anglo-Saxon development of that discovery, which emerged in the USA from the thirties onwards. British university culture has, of course, remained virtually impervious to Parsonian theory to this day. Britain thus completely missed both major moments in the development of the new science. From first to last, no sociologist of any original calibre was thrown up on these shores. The lack of any great theorist of the order of Weber, Durkheim or Pareto is significant enough. That it was no accident is confirmed by a glance at the secondary figures who contributed to what the standard volume on it calls 'The Reorientation of European Social Thought 1890–1930': Stuart Hughes's popular almanac, *Consciousness and Society*, lists some twenty lesser thinkers who represent parallel currents of thought: not one is English. This huge gap has never been filled. To this day, despite the recent belated growth of sociology as a formal discipline in England, the record of listless mediocrity and wizened provincialism is unrelieved. The subject is still largely a poor cousin of 'social work' and 'social administration', the dispirited descendants of Victorian charity.

What is the meaning of this spectacular fault in the English intellectual landscape? Is it an isolated fissure, or does it have wider implications? Classical European sociology was a *synthetic* social science. This is its crucial, innovating importance. Weber's sociology of religion, law and the market, Durkheim's study of suicide and social solidarity, and Pareto's theory of elites, surpassed discrete 'economics', 'psychology' and 'history' by unifying them in a theory of society as a totality. The most distingushed English social thinker of this generation was Alfred Marshall, father of marginalist economics. As Parsons points out, Marshall's eventual impasse may be seen precisely as a failure to develop the categories necessary to transcend analytic economics (Marshall's problem of 'activities' beyond rational economic egoism). It was Pareto and Weber who solved his problem by resituating it within a wider theoretical ensemble. Sociology, in this sense, came into existence as a science which aspired to a global reconstruction of social formations.[5] This was its *differentia specifica*. It is no accident that it later developed into the monumental architectonic of Parsonian action theory, embracing every dimension of social existence in a single schedule of classifying concepts. Whatever the concrete outcome of this enterprise, the ambition to provide such a master synthesis was inscribed in its vocation from the start.

Sociology, however, was itself largely (not exclusively) a response to a previous totalizing system. It notoriously emerged as a bourgeois counter-reaction to Marxism on the continent. All of Weber's work on economy and society forms an immense, oblique contestation of the Marxism which had conquered the working-class movement in imperial Germany; his political hostility to that movement was undying. Pareto sought to combat the primitive 'mob-rule' of socialism by writing a violent attack on Marx; Durkheim sought to domesticate it within the reformist perspectives of French positivism. A profound fear of the masses and premonition of social disintegration haunts the work of all three.

Marxism had preceded classical sociology by fifty years. It was an infinitely more powerful synthesis of discrete disciplines, founded on a scale which no bourgeois social science was ever later able to imitate or repeat. Marx's thought was – to use Lenin's traditional formulation – the summation of German philosophy, French politics and English economics. The démarche of classical sociology was thus anticipated and surpassed, on a much vaster terrain. Marx's itinerary was a spiral critique and reintegration of successive cultural systems of his time. He began by an immanent critique of Hegel's philosophy, showing its inability to elucidate the political order of civil society and the State. He then undermined Proudhon's politics by showing its inability to comprehend the economic structure of bourgeois society. He then overthrew Ricardo's economics by showing its inability to grasp the core element historical of capitalism as a historical mode of production. The final fusion of these successive critiques in the mature Marx produced a theory that was totally revolutionary, in both scope and objective. Marx's concept of totality is quite distinct from that of Weber or Durkheim, however. Marx's great innovation was the idea of a complex totality, *loaded* by the predominance in the long-run of one level within it – the economy, such that genuine, dynamic contradictions were generated by the discrepant hierarchy of its levels. This was a complete rupture with the Hegelian idea of totality, to which Weber, inspired by German idealism, later returned. Weber's social whole is a circular one, in which all the elements are equivalent and enjoy causal parity : religious ethics and economic practice indifferently determine each other. This conception was later to produce the explicit theories of functionalism. A second contrast is equally crucial. Marx's thought was not only defined by a specific concept of the *totality*. It was also characterized by the complementary centrality of his concept of *contradiction*. Althusser has recently shown the interdependence of the two.[6] It is no accident that in its crepuscular version of Marxism, classical sociology too was characterized by a pervasive awareness of contradiction. Once again, the notion underwent a critical dilution. Weber's work revolves endlessly about the twin problems of 'charisma' and 'bureaucracy', and the interversions of one into the other. Despite the surreptitious evolutionism which underlies all he wrote (rationalization as the destiny of the West), the inherent instability of either a bureaucratic or a charismatic political order and the tendency of each to capsize into the other, was a constant for him to the end. Pareto's theory of power posited a continual overthrow of elites, from 'lions' to 'foxes' and back again, in an interminable circular movement. Durkheim's account of the development from mechanical to organic solidarity (primitive to industrial societies) produced the concept of anomie – the unceasing reproduction of subjective rulelessness by a society that is defined by its ensemble of objective rules. In every case, a notion of contradiction is at the very core of the work. But it is always a 'degraded' contradiction, that is *cyclical* in its movement and thereby immobile and eternal. This cyclical contradiction is a logical by-product of the idealist totality. It is not an essential one. Its presence in classical sociology betrays the disquiet of its founders, and the impending disaster of the Great War. Parsons was later to develop an absolutely integrated totality, in which contradictions as such have disappeared: there is only 'tension-control' and 'pattern-maintenance'. This is the main difference between action theory and classical sociology; it indicates all the distance between the forebodings of a declining European civilization on the eve of an international civil war, and the optimism of American capitalism in the epoch of its world supremacy. In either case, the Marxist concept of contradiction, as the disjuncture within a complex totality which produces a singular configuration itself striated with new contradictions, is absent.

Marx's thought was so far in advance of its time and its society that it was unassimilable in the nineteenth century. For fifty years, it was never seriously confronted within European bourgeois thought. It was only when the political rise of the working-class movement became a grave and immediate threat to the social order, that bourgeois culture was finally forced to re-act to the challenge. There were various sectoral attacks and refutations of Marx by marginalist economists like Böhm-Bawerk. But the main creative response was the emergence of a new social science – classical sociology. This did not normally engage in any direct confrontation with the ascendant light of Marxism. It was its silent shadow, in the darkening world of the European bourgeoisie on the eve of the First World War.

Marxism in the twentieth century, after the inevitable delay in its theoretical assimilation within the working-class move-ment which had been politically won to it, generated a new wave of major theory. Lenin, Lukacs and Gramsci were the great, dominating figures of this epoch. Flourishing Marxist cultures rose in Germany, Italy and France, not to speak of Russia. In every important continental country, the impact of Marxism was deep and lasting; it left an indelible imprint on the national culture, despite every political vicissitude and theoretical assault. Today, the serious social science of these countries developed either within, or in tension with, the heritage of Marx.

Britain is solitarily exempt from this tension. It produced no important Marxist thinker. Marxism, in fact, was virtually un-known until the thirties of this century. It then suddenly gripped a new generation of intellectuals, overwhelmed by the experience of the depression and the rise of Fascism. It is difficult in retrospect to make any fair judgement of the thirties. No decade has been so obscured by myth and cliché for later genera-tions. Its memory has been formed by its enemies and renegades. A great deal of historical excavation is needed to re-establish the truth of those years. What is clear is that a spontaneous radical-ization of the traditionally dormant English intelligentsia oc-curred, spurred by the political gravity of the time. It was cut short after a few years, by the German–Soviet Pact and the Second World War.[7] The vast majority of those intellectuals who had briefly been on the Left swung to the Right, and the traditional order of English intellectual life was restored. The collective fever had been ephemeral. It was the passing product of a political conjuncture, and developed no serious intellectual dimension to it at the time. Marx's own work, and the development of his theory after his death, remained virtually unstudied. Contrary as it was to all established and traditional modes of thought in English culture, its genuine assimilation would have needed an immense work of theoretical study and reconversion. Nothing, however, was less imagined by many of the radicals of the time. This was partly due to the urgent political preoccupations of the decade. But there was a cultural reason at work: their inherited liberalism often subsisted quite unaltered, beneath their political allegiance. This persistence was facilitated by their predominant occupations. By and large, the radicals of the thirties were not historians, sociologists or philosophers. By contrast, there was a plethora of poets and natural scientists – the two vocations most unsuited to effect any lasting political transformation of British culture. Where there was a bid to 'apply' their formal beliefs, the outcome was frequently bad art and false science: at its worst, the rhymes of Spender and the fantasies of Bernal.[8] For the most part, however, the leftism of these intellectuals was merely a set of external political attitudes. It was inevitable that anything so provincial and insubstantial would be blown away by the first gust of the international gale. A few years later, most of the rebellious litterateurs were banal functionaries of reaction. This general history does not cancel the courage and fidelity of the individual exceptions who never abandoned the beliefs of their youth: William Empson, Claud Cockburn, Roy Fuller and others. They are rather a reminder of how much was lost in these years.[9]

For the tragedy of the decade of the thirties was that it vaccinated British culture against Marxism to this day. After the war, all was changed. The resistances built up have survived virtually intact. The fifties and sixties saw the proliferation of Marxism on the continent; Althusser in France, Adorno in Germany and Della Volpe in Italy all founded important and divergent schools. England remained unaffected. Marxist theory had never become naturalized.

Britain, then, may be defined as the European country which – uniquely – never produced either a classical sociology or a national Marxism. British culture was consequently characterized by an *absent centre*. Both classical sociology and Marxism were global theories of society, articulated in a totalizing conceptual system. They subsumed traditional disciplines within a synthesis designed to capture the 'structure of structures' – the social totality as such. Britain has for more than fifty years lacked any form whatever of such thought. The whole configuration of its culture has been determined – and dislocated – by this void at its centre. Before examining the multiple, interlocking consequences of this phenomenon, however, it must be asked : what were its proximate causes?

The Sociology of No Sociology

Mannheim proposed a sociology of knowledge; what is needed here is a sociology of ignorance. Why did Britain never produce *either* a Weber, a Durkeim, a Pareto *or* a Lenin, a Lukacs, a Gramsci? The peculiar destiny of the nineteenth century industrial bourgeoisie in Britain is the secret of this twin default. The class which accomplished the titanic technological explosion of the Industrial Revolution never achieved a political or social revolution in England. It was checked by a prior capitalist class, the agrarian aristocracy which had matured in the eighteenth century, and controlled a State formed in its image. There was no insuperable contradiction between the modes of production of the two classes. The industrial bourgeoisie, traumatized by the French Revolution and fearful of the nascent working-class movement, never took the risk of a confrontation with the dominant aristocracy. It never evicted the latter from its hegemonic control of the political order, and eventually fused with it in a new, composite ruling bloc in mid-century. It thus remained socially and politically heteronomous, even in the years of its economic apotheosis. The result was that it never generated a revolutionary ideology, like that of the Enlightenment. Its thinkers were confined by the cramped horizons of their class. They developed powerful sectoral disciplines – notably the economics of Ricardo and Malthus. They advanced the natural sciences – above all evolutionist biology with Darwin. But they failed to create any general theory of society, or any philosophical synthesis of compelling dimensions. The one *sui generis* creed of this class produced by its intellectuals, utilitarianism, was a crippled caricature of such an ideology, with no chance whatever of becoming the official justification of the Victorian social system. The hegemonic ideology of this society was a much more aristocratic combination of 'traditionalism' and 'empiricism', intensely hierarchical in its emphasis, which accurately reiterated the history of the dominant agrarian class. The British bourgeoisie by and large assented to this archaic legitimation of the *status quo*, and sedulously mimicked it. After its own amalgamation with the aristocracy in the later nineteenth century, it became second nature to the collective propertied class.[10]

What was the net result of this history? The British bourgeoisie from the outset renounced its intellectual birthright. It refused ever to put society as a whole in question. A deep, instinctive aversion to the very category of the totality marks its entire trajectory.[11] It never had to recast society as a whole, in a concrete historical practice. It consequently never had to rethink society as a whole, in abstract theoretical reflection. Empirical, piecemeal intellectual disciplines corresponded to humble, circumscribed social action. Nature could be approached with audacity and speculation: society was treated as if it were an immutable second nature. The category of the totality was renounced by the British bourgeoisie in its acceptance of a comfortable, but secondary station within the hierarchy of early Victorian capitalism.[12] In this first moment of its history, it did not need it. Because the economic order of agrarian England was already capitalist and the feudal State had been dismantled in the seventeenth century, there was no vital, indefeasible necessity for it to overthrow the previous ruling class. A common mode of production united both, and made their eventual fusion possible. The cultural limitations of bourgeois reason in England were thus politically rational: the *ultima ratio* of the economy founded both.

Superfluous when the bourgeoisie was fighitng for integration into the ruling order, the notion of the totality became perilous when it achieved it. Forgotten one moment, it was repressed the next. For once the new hegemonic class had coalesced, it was naturally and resolutely hostile to any form of thought that took the whole social system as its object, and hence necessarily put it in question. Henceforward, its culture was systematically organized *against* any such potential subversion. There were social critics of Victorian capitalism, of course: the distinguished line of thinkers studied by Williams in *Culture and Society*. But this was a literary tradition incapable of generating a conceptual system. The intellectual universe of Weber, Durkheim or Pareto was foreign to the pattern of British culture which had congealed over the century. One decisive reason for this was, of course, that the political threat which had so largely influenced the birth of sociology on the continent – the rise of socialism – did not materialize in England. The British working class failed to create its own political party throughout the nineteenth century. When it eventually did so, it was twenty years behind its continental opposites, and was still quite untouched by Marxism. The dominant class in Britain was thus never forced to produce a counter-totalizing thought by the danger of revolutionary socialism. Both the global ambitions, and the secret pessimism, of Weber or Pareto were alien to it. Its peculiar, indurated parochialism was proof against any foreign influences or importations. The curious episode of a belated English 'Hegelianism', in the work of Green, Bosanquet and Bradley, provides piquant evidence of this. Hegel's successors in Germany had rapidly used his philosophical categories to dispatch theology. They had then plunged into the development of the explosive political and economic implications of his thought. The end of this road was, of course, Marx himself. Sixty years after Bruno Baeur and Ludwig Feuerbach, however, Green and Bradley innocently adopted an aqueous Hegel, in their quest for philosophical assistance to shore up the traditional Christian piety of the Victorian middle class, now threatened by the growth of the natural sciences.[13] This anachronism was naturally short-lived. It merely indicated the retarded preoccupations of its milieu: a recurring phenomenon. Two decades earlier, George Eliot had solved her spiritual doubts by borrowing Comte's 'religion of humanity' – not his social mathematics. These importations were ephemeral, because the problems they were designed to solve were artificial. They simply acted as a soothing emulsion in the transition towards a secular bourgeois culture.

In a panorama emptied of profound intellectual upheaval or incendiary social conflict, British culture tranquilly cultivated its own private concerns at the end of the long epoch of Victorian imperialism. In 1900, the harmony between the hegemonic class and its intellectuals was virtually complete. Noel Annan has drawn the unforgettable portrait of the British intellectuals of this time. 'Here is an aristocracy, secure, established and, like the rest of the English society, accustomed to responsible and judicious utterance and sceptical of iconoclastic speculation.' [14] There was no separate intelligentsia. [15] An intricate web of kinship linked the traditional lineages which produced scholars and thinkers to each other and to their common social group. The same names occur again and again: Macaulay, Trevelyan, Arnold, Vaughan, Strachey, Darwin, Huxley, Stephens, Wedgwood, Hodgkin and others. Intellectuals were related by family to their class, not by profession to their estate. 'The influence of these families,' Annan comments after tracing out their criss-crossing patterns, 'may partly explain a paradox which has puzzled European and American observers of English life: the paradox of an intelligentsia which appears to conform rather than rebel against the rest of society.' [16] Many of the intellectuals he discusses were based on Cambridge, then dominated by the grey and ponderous figure of Henry Sidgwick (brother-in-law, needless to say, of Prime Minister Balfour). The ideological climate of this world has been vividly recalled by a latter-day admirer. Harrod's biography of Keynes opens with this memorable evocation:

If Cambridge combined a deep-rooted traditionalism with a lively progressiveness, so too did England. She was in the strongly upward trend of her material development; her overseas trade and investment were still expanding; the great pioneers of social reform were already making headway in educating public opinion. On the basis of her hardly won, but now solidly established, prosperity, the position of the British Empire seemed unshakeable. Reforms would be within a framework of stable and unquestioned social values. There was ample elbow-room for experiment without danger that the main fabric of our economic well-being would be destroyed. It is true that only a minority enjoyed the full fruits of this well-being; but the consciences of the leaders of thought were not unmindful of the hardships of the poor. There was great confidence that, in due course, by careful management, their condition would be improved out of recognition. The stream of progress would not cease to flow. While the reformers were most earnestly bent on their purposes, they held that there were certain strict rules and conventions which must not be violated; secure and stable though the position seemed, there was a strong sense that danger beset any changes.[17]

Such was the solid, normal world of the English intelligentsia before 1914.

The White Emigration

Occupation, civil war and revolution were the continuous experience of continental Europe for the next three decades. Hammered down from without or blown from within, not a single major social and political structure survived intact. Only two countries on the whole land-mass were left untouched, the small states of Sweden and Switzerland. Elsewhere, violent change swept every society in Europe, from Oporto to Kazan and Turku to Noto. The disintegration of the Romanov, Hohenzollern and Habsburg Empires, the rise of Fascism, the Second World War, and victory of Communism in Eastern Europe followed each other uninterruptedly. There was revolution in Russia, counter-revolution in Germany, Austria and Italy, occupation in France and civil war in Spain. The smaller countries underwent parallel upheavals.

England, meanwhile, suffered neither invasion nor revolution. No fundamental institutional change supervened from the turn of the century to the era of the Cold War. Geographical isolation and historical petrification appeared to render English society immutable. Despite two wars, its stability and security were never seriously ruffled. This history is so natural to most Englishmen, that they never registered how praeternatural it has seemed abroad. The cultural consequences have never been systematically considered. But this is the context which has vitally determined the evolution of much of English thought since the Great War.

If one surveys the landscape of British culture at mid-century, what is the most prominent change that had taken place since 1900? It is so obvious, in effect, that virtually no one has noticed it. The phalanx of national intellectuals portrayed by Annan has been eclipsed. In this intensely provincial society, foreigners suddenly become omnipresent. The crucial, formative influences in the arc of culture with which we are concerned here are again and again emigrés. Their quality and originality vary greatly, but their collective role is indisputable. The following list of *maîtres d'école* gives some idea of the extent of the phenomenon:

	Discipline	Native Country
Ludwig Wittgenstein	Philosophy	Austria
Bronislaw Malinowski	Anthropology	Poland
Lewis Namier	History	Poland
Karl Popper	Social Theory	Austria
Isaiah Berlin	Political Theory	Russia
Ernst Gombrich	Aesthetics	Austria
Hans-Jurgen Eysenck	Psychology	Germany
Melanie Klein	Psychoanalysis	Austria
(Isaac Deutscher	Marxism	Poland)

The two major disciplines excluded here are economics and literary criticism.

Keynes, of course, completely commanded the former; Leavis the latter. But literary criticism – for evident reasons – has been the only sector unaffected by the phenomenon. For at the succeeding level, the presence of expatriates is marked in economics too: perhaps the most influential theorist in England today is Nicolas Kaldor (Hungary), and undoubtedly the most original Piero Sraffa (Italy). There is no need to recall the number of other expatriates elsewhere – Gellner, Elton, Balogh, Von Hayek, Plamenatz, Lichtheim, Steiner, Wind, Wittkower and others.

The contrast with the 'intellectual aristocracy' of 1900 is overwhelming. But what is its meaning? What is the sociological nature of this emigration? Britain is not traditionally an immigrants' country, like the USA. Nor was it ever host, in the nineteenth century, to European intellectuals rising to occupy eminent positions in its culture. Refugees were firmly suppressed below the threshold of national intellectual life. The fate of Marx is eloquent. The very different reception of these expatriates in the twentieth century was a consequence of the nature of the emigration itself – and of the condition of the national intelligentsia.

The wave of emigrants who came to England in this century were by and large fleeing the permanent instability of their own societies – that is, their proneness to violent, fundamental change.[18] England epitomized the opposite of all this: tradition, continuity and orderly empire. Its culture was consonant with its special history. A process of natural selection occurred, in which those intellectuals with an elective affinity to English modes of thought and political outlook gravitated here. Those refugees who did not, went elsewhere. It is noticeable that there were many Austrians among those who chose Britain. It is perhaps significant that no important Germans did so, with the brief exception of Mannheim who had little impact. The German emigration, coming from a philosophical culture that was quite distinct from the parish-pump positivism of interbellum Vienna, avoided this island. The Frankfurt School of Marxists, Marcuse, Adorno, Benjamin, Horkheimer and Fromm went to France and then to the USA. Neumann and Reich (initially to Norway) followed. Lukacs went to Russia. Brecht went to Scandinavia and then to America, followed by Mann. This was a 'Red' emigration, utterly unlike that which arrived here. It did not opt for England, because of a basic cultural and political incompatibility.[19]

The intellectuals who settled in Britain were thus not just a chance agglomeration. They were essentially a 'White', counter-revolutionary emigration. The individual reasons for the different trajectories to England were inevitably varied. Namier came from the powder-keg of Polish Galicia under the Habsburgs. Malinowski chose England, like his countryman Conrad, partly because of its empire. Berlin was a refugee from the Russian Revolution. Popper and Gombrich were fugitives from the civil war and Fascism of post-Habsburg Austria. Wittgenstein's motive in finally settling for England is unknown. Whatever the biographical variants, the general logic of this emigration is clear. England was not an accidental landing-stage on which these intellectuals unwittingly found themselves stranded. It was often a conscious choice – an ideal antipode of everything that they rejected. Namier, who was most lucid about the world from which he had escaped, expressed his hatred of it most deeply. He saw England as a land built on instinct and custom, free from the ruinous contagion of Europe – general ideas. He proclaimed 'the immense superiority which existing social forms have over human movements and genius, and the poise and rest which there are in a spiritual inheritance, far superior to the thoughts, will or invention of any single generation'.[20] Rest – the word conveys the whole underlying trauma of this emigration. The English, Namier thought, were peculiarly blessed because, as a nation 'they perceive and accept facts without anxiously enquiring into their reasons and meaning.'[21] For 'the less man clogs the free play of his mind with political doctrine and dogma, the better for his thinking.'[22] This theme is repeated by thinker after thinker; it is the hallmark of the White emigration. Namier tried to dismiss general ideas by showing their historical inefficacy; Popper by denouncing their moral iniquity ('Holism'); Eysenck by reducing them to psychological velleities; Wittgenstein by undermining their status as intelligible discourse altogether.

Established English culture naturally welcomed these unexpected allies. Every insular reflex and prejudice was powerfully flattered and enlarged in the magnifying mirror they presented to it. But the extraordinary dominance of the expatriates in these decades is not comprehensible by this alone. It was possible because they *both* reinforced the existing orthodoxy *and* exploited its weakness. For the unmistakable fact is that the traditional, discrete disciplines, having missed either of the great synthetic revolutions in European social thought, were dying of inanition. The English intelligentsia had lost its impetus. Already by the turn of the century, the expatriate supremacy of James and Conrad, Eliot and Pound – three Americans and a Pole – in the two great national literary forms foreshadowed later and more dramatic dispossessions. The last great products of the English intelligentsia matured before the First World War: Russell, Keynes and Lawrence. Their stature is the measure of the subsequent decline. After them, confidence and originality seeped away. There was no more momentum left in the culture; the cumulative absence of any new historical experience in England for so long had deprived it of energy. The conquest of cultural dominance by emigrés, in these conditions, becomes explicable. Their qualities were, in fact, enormously uneven. Wittgenstein, Namier and Klein were brilliant originators; Malinowski and Gombrich honourable, but limited pioneers; Popper and Berlin fluent ideologues; Eysenck a popular publicist. The very heterogeneity of the individuals underlines the sociological point: no matter what the quantum of talent, *any* foreign background was an enormous advantage in the British stasis, and might make an intellectual fortune.

The relationship between the expatriates and the secular traditions they encountered was necessarily dialectical. British empiricism and conservatism was on the whole an instinctive, *ad hoc* affair. It shunned theory even in its rejection of theory. It was a style, not a method. The expatriate impact on this cultural syndrome was paradoxical. In effect, the emigrés for the first time systematized the refusal of system. They codified the slovenly empiricism of the past, and thereby hardened and narrowed it. They also, ultimately, rendered it more vulnerable. The transition from Moore to the early Wittgenstein exemplifies this movement. Wittgenstein's later philosophy reflects an awareness of the antinomy, and an attempt to retreat back to a non-systematized empiricism, a guileless, unaggregated registration of things as they were, in their diversity. On the political plane proper, Popper's shrill advocacy of 'piecemeal social engineering' lent a somewhat mechanistic note to the consecrated processes of British parliamentarism. Apart from this aspect, however, the tremendous injection of life that emigré intelligence and elan gave a fading British culture is evident. The famous *morgue* and truculence of Wittgenstein, Namier or Popper, expressed their inner confidence of superiority. Established British culture rewarded them amply for their services, with the appropriate apotheosis: Sir Lewis Namier, Sir Karl Popper, Sir Isaiah Berlin and (perhaps soon) Sir Ernst Gombrich.

This was not just a passive acknowledgement of merit. It was an active social pact. Nothing is more striking than the opposite fate of the one great emigré intellectual whom Britain harboured for thirty years, who was a revolutionary. The *structural* importance of expatriates in bourgeois thought is confirmed by the symmetrical pre-eminence of a foreigner within its antithesis: Marxism. Both obeyed the *general* determinations of British culture. Isaac Deutscher, the greatest Marxist historian in the world, was the only major contributor to that international system of thought resident in Britain. A much larger figure than his compatriot Namier, Deutscher was reviled and ignored by the academic world throughout his life. He never secured the smallest university post. British culture accepted and promoted what confirmed its fundamental set: it censored and negated anything which departed from it. The White emigration accentuated and crystallized its whole character. But it did not significantly alter it.

Configuration of Sectors

What was the intellectual constellation thus produced? Two fundamental anomalies of British culture have been indicated – the central absence of any classical sociology, and the ubiquitous presence of a White emigration. It is now possible to sketch an answer to the question with which this inquiry began. In a cultural system specified by these coordinates, what are the relations between the different sectors which compose it? In other words, what is its structure? The ensuing comments are merely a pilot-project. They are designed to show the possibilities of an inter-sectoral analysis, not to constitute a model of one. Thus they will consciously omit and select material, aiming only to discuss the essential for the current purpose. It should be emphasized at the outset that no attempt will be made to give a comprehensive account of any given discipline. A recent essay on English history by Gareth Stedman Jones furnishes an exemplary analysis of this type.[23] Here, by contrast, the focus will be on the general cultural nexus of which each discipline is a part. To control the span of material, the method adopted will be to discuss only a single, dominant thinker in each sector, and the themes of his work which relate it to the configuration as a whole. (It should be repeated that not all of these thinkers are of equal intellectual stature.) Such an approach will provide one specific illumination of the subject; it will not encompass or reveal it at all completely. Collective study and critique on a much wider scale would be necessary for this. Meanwhile, any contribution must of its nature be corrigible and limited.

Philosophy

English philosophy since the nineteen-thirties has been dominated by Wittgenstein. In his youth, Wittgenstein was a philosopher who sought a one-to-one fit between a reducible language and a fragmentable reality: basic propositions mirrored atomic facts. This was in essence a monist theory of language, which implicitly excluded 'metaphysical' statements from the realm of the intelligible, because they lacked correspondence with verifiable, molecular entities. After the *Tractatus*, the Vienna Circle proceeded to a much bolder and cruder attack on all forms of discourse which did not conform to the prescriptive model of the physical sciences or mathematics. Any propositions not verifiable by their procedures were written off – not as mistaken, but as meaningless. The distance from Logical Atomism to Logical Positivism was – despite the abandonment of Wittgenstein's notion of granular 'facts' – a short one. The nihilist implications of the latter, however, were too comprehensive to be acceptable to any Western bourgeois society, with its functional need for a consecrated morality and a macro-ideology. This social antinomy reflected an epistemological one. Empiricism pushed to this extreme was subversive of the very experience it should have underwritten: the criterion of verifiability was itself notoriously unverifiable.

Wittgenstein's *Philosophical Investigations* provided an elegant and delphic solution to these problems. In his later philosophy, Wittgenstein constantly asserted that language was a heteroclite collection of games with discrete rules governing them. No 'absolute' standpoint outside them was conceivable. Each game was separate and valid in its own right; the great intellectual error of philosophers was to confuse them, by using a rule for one in the context of another. The meaning of a concept was its conventional use, and the true philosopher was the guardian of conventions. Formally, this doctrine conceded the possibility of 'metaphysics' (i.e. the traditional concerns of philosophy) as one game among others – if an esoteric one.[24] In practice, significantly enough, only religion was ever substantially accorded this status. The main effect of Wittgenstein's later philosophy was simply to consecrate the banalities of everyday language. The anodyne assertion that no *external* purchase on existing language was possible (attack on ideal languages) was coupled with the implicit assumption that existing language was effectively a complete sum of usages, in which any *internal* elimination or addition of one game by another was precluded. The duty of the philosopher, on the contrary, was to ensure the identity and stability of the system, by preventing unorthodox moves within it. This bizarre notion amounted to a massive, undifferentiated affidavit for the conceptual *status quo*. Its logical product was a mystique of common sense, and the ordinary language which reflected it. Wittgenstein, a thinker of great – if narrow – integrity and originality, despised the 'impotence and bankruptcy of *Mind*' and denounced Oxford as a 'philosophical desert'.[25] But Oxford was to be the home of the philosophical school inspired by him.

The linguistic philosophy of the forties and fifties represented a deliberate renunciation of the traditional vocation of philosophy in the West. General ideas about man and society had been the hallmark of all the great philosophers of the past, no matter what orientation. Hume no less than Kant, Locke no less than Spinoza, Descartes no less than Leibnitz, Mill no less than Hegel, wrote social, ethical and political works as well as epistemological and logical treatises, as part of an integral enterprise. English philosophy after the Second World War systematically rejected the very notion of intellectual innovation. Wittgenstein had written: 'Philosophy may in no way interfere with the actual use of language; it can in the end only describe it. For it cannot give it any foundation either. It leaves everything as it is.'[26] The final results of this credo were Austin's exquisite, obsessional classifications of syntax. His famous address to the Aristotelian Society, *A Plea for Excuses*, presents their justification:

Our common stock of words embodies all the distinctions men have found worth drawing, and the connexions they have found worth marking, in the lifetimes of many generations; these surely are likely to be more numerous, more sound, since they have stood up to the long test of the survival of the fittest, and more subtle, at least in all ordinary and reasonably practical matters, than any you or I are likely to think up in our armchairs of an afternoon. . . [27]

The social meaning of such a doctrine is obvious enough. Gramsci once wrote that common sense is the practical wisdom of the ruling class. The cult of common sense accurately indicates the role of linguistic philosophy in England. It functions as chloroforming ideology, blotting out the very memory of an alternative order of thought. 'Philosophy begins and ends in platitude' wrote Wittgenstein's pupil Wisdom. It is difficult to conceive a more explicit and blanket endoresement of the categories of the ongoing society. The intelligentsia who were the principal practitioners of the new 'therapy' have been well situated by Gellner:

> We have here a sub-group consisting of people who belong to, or emulate, the upper class in manner; who differentiate themselves from the heartier rest of the upper class by a kind of heightened sensibility and preciousness, *and*, at the same time, from the non-U kind of intelligentsia by a lack of interest in ideas, argument, fundamentals or reform. *Both* of these *differentiae* are essential to such a group, and both are conspicuously present.[28]

The assiduous praise of ordinary language and aversion for technical concepts paradoxically produced a purely technical philosophy, entirely dissociated from the ordinary concerns of social life.

The technicism of contemporary English philosophy has thus necessarily been a philistinism. Its most striking general characteristic, in this respect, is a complacent illiteracy. Wittgenstein knew virtually nothing of the history of philosophy, was devoid of any sociological or economic culture, and had only a very limited repertoire of literary reference. A vague religiosity and naïve moralism form the barren backdrop to his work, as his memorialists show: yearnings for Tolstoy mingled with echoes of Schopenhauer. This impoverished personal culture determined his thought quite centrally, as will be seen. The intellectual life of the twentieth century by and large passed Wittgenstein by. His outlook is well summed up by his friend Paul Engelmann, who writes of 'his loyalty towards all legitimate authority, whether religious or social. This attitude towards all *genuine* authority was so much second nature to him that revolutionary convictions of whatever kind appeared to him throughout his life simply as "immoral".'[29] This pathetic conformity evokes a stupefied peasant of Central Europe, not a critical philosopher. Wittgenstein's successors were on the whole no better equipped. Nothing reveals the intellectual void in which English philosophy has developed more than its basic premise of timelessness. The whole Wittgensteinian theory of language, in effect, presupposes an unchanging corpus of concepts and an unalterable pattern of the contexts governing them.[30] Only a total historical amnesia could produce such a view. The whole intellectual evolution of the West has been a process of concept-formation and rejection. No extra-terrestrial, absolute standpoint is needed to establish the intertemporal contingency of language. The truth is the opposite. It was Wittgenstein who evacuated time from language, and thereby converted it into an a-historical absolute. He was able to do this because he lacked any notion of contradiction. The idea that linguistic change proceeds by an *internal* dialectic generated by incompatibilities between different rule-systems within it, which give rise to radically *new* concepts at determinate historical moments, was beyond his horizon. It presupposed an idea of language as neither a monist unity (*Tractatus*) nor a heteroclite plurality (*Investigations*), but as a complex totality, necessarily inhabited by different contradictions. It is striking that today, French philosophy is largely concentrated on the problem of the *conditions of appearance of new concepts* – precisely the problem that English philosophy is designed to avert. The work of Canguilhem and Bachelard is a close study of the historical emergence of the scientific concepts of the eighteenth century, which revolutionized biology. Such an inquiry is a diametric opposite of the whole drift of Wittgenstein's philosophy, and indicates its parochialism. To emphasize the social nature of language, as he did, is not enough : language is a structure with a history, and it has a history because its contradictions and discrepancies themselves are determined by other levels of social practice. The magical harmony of language affirmed by English philosophy was itself merely the transcript of a historically becalmed society.

Political Theory

An a-temporal philosophy produces a disembodied political theory. Berlin, a contemporary and intimate of Austin, gravitated towards the study of political ideas early in his career . His conviction of their importance, anomalous in his professional milieu, perhaps derived from his adolescent experience of the Russian Revolution. At all events, his concern was largely prophylactic. Philosophers, he argued, ought to criticize political doctrines. If they do not, these ideas 'sometimes acquire an unchecked momentum and an irresistible power over multitudes of men'.[31] The dangers of such 'fanatically held social and political doctrines' could only be conjured by philosophical vigilance. Berlin thought his colleagues, preoccupied by 'their magnificent achievements' in analytic philosophy, tended to 'neglect the field of political thought, because its unstable subject-matter, with its blurred edges, is not to be caught by fixed concepts, abstract models and fine instruments suitable to logic or to linguistic analysis.'[32] Thus the difference between his method and theirs was merely one of the degree of precision of their respective objects. Ordinary language, in this curious argument, was stable and exact; political concepts were, alas, unstable and blurred. Hence philosophical study of the latter was assimilated to a vaguer variant of the analysis of the former. Nothing else changed. Political theory became a timeless elucidation of concepts, divorced from any historical or sociological context. The *locus classicus* of this procedure is Berlin's essay *Two Concepts of Liberty*, the most influential text of its genre. Here Berlin counterposes two hypostasized constructions: 'negative' freedom – the ability to act without interference, and 'positive' freedom – the achievement of self-determination by the subject. The argument proceeds by a constructed 'logical' development of ideas, projected into some ethereal empyrean, and dispenses with anything so mundane as quotation. The result is two opposed lineages, which function very much as mythical genealogies in the Bible. The idea of negative freedom is attributed to Bentham, Mill, Constant and de Tocqueville; the ideal of positive freedom to the Stoics, Spinoza, Kant, Rousseau, Fichte, Hegel, Marx and Green. Neutrality between the two is momentarily feigned: 'The satisfaction that each of them seeks is an ultimate value which, both historically and morally, has an equal right to be classed among the deepest interests of mankind.'[33] The true intention, however, is not long hidden. A few pages later, Berlin writes: 'The negative liberty seems to me a truer and more humane ideal than the goals of those who seek in the great, disciplined authoritarian structures the ideal of "positive" self-mastery by classes, and peoples, or the whole of mankind.'[34] This blatant self-contradiction is inherent in the intellectual method itself. For the same ideal which inspires 'Kant's severe individualism', we are told, now informs 'totalitarian doctrines' today. Why is this genealogy necessary? The design of the whole exercise, in fact, is to discredit a prefabricated notion of 'positive freedom' – responsible for modern dictatorship and the extinction of liberty, by its separation of the concept of self-determination from the empirical attitudes of the individual. But the very insubstantiality of this entity is precisely what demands the hallucinating amalgam of thinkers alleged to have fathered it: the accumulation of names is all that lends the illusion of substance.

Political theory, thus conceived, extrapolates ideas from history and transforms them into weightless counters that are manipulable at will in the space of ideology. The end-product is typically a mythical genealogy in which ideas generate themselves in a manichean morality tale, whose teleological outcome is the present struggle of the free world against totalitarian communism. It is no accident that Popper, on a much vaster canvas, exemplifies the same procedure in *The Open Society and its Enemies*. The problematic and its answer are the same; only the tone and terminology differ. The dualism of 'negative' and 'positive' freedom is repeated in that of the 'open' and 'closed' society. The latter culminates, predictably, in 'modern totalitarianism', which itself is 'only an episode within the perennial revolt against freedom and reason'[35] – a law of human nature that is mysteriously exempt from Popper's strictures against the formulation of invariable historical laws. The same supra-historical conflation is used: Plato, Aristotle, Hegel and Marx are all enemies of the same Open Society. Popper was obsessed by these mythical constructions. *The Poverty of Historicism* is dedicated to the 'countless men and women of all creeds and nations' who were victims of 'the fascist and communist belief in Inexorable Laws of Historical Destiny'. Who are the philosophical culprits of this historicism? Conflation here produces the same grotesque results as with Berlin. Much of this work dedicated to the victims of Fascism and Communism is devoted to attacking – John Stuart Mill. This *reductio ad absurdum* of the method indicates the complete vacuity of the concept itself. Popper defines historicism as follows: 'I mean by "historicism" an approach to the social sciences which assumes that historical prediction is their principal aim.'[36] Hegel, of course – arch-historicist for Popper – explicitly refused all historical prediction. Historicist prophecies are said by Popper to include belief in absolute laws in history, whereas scientific predictions are based on trends. Marx and Lenin, of course, repeatedly emphasized that they analysed tendencies of social development, not absolute laws, and that therefore the predictions of natural science were impossible in history.[37] Popper's innocence of sociology, which he championed as an antidote to historicism, was equally total. His cherished advocacy of methodological individualism (all statements about society are reducible to statements about individuals) would have been impossible had he been aware of the classic texts of the discipline: Durkheim's discussion of 'social facts' (*Rules of Sociological Method*) and Parsons's discussion of 'emergent properties' (*The Structure of Social Action*).

Hypostasization and conflation were normal in English social philosophy. Popper, however, a competent philosopher of science, was an amateur at even the rudimentary skills of this form of political theory. His discussion of Hegel recalls the idiom of the Third Reich. The German philosopher was a 'paid agent', a 'servile lackey', a 'charlatan', a 'clown', whose works were a 'farce', written in 'gibberish' that was a 'despicable perversion of everything that is decent'.[38] The paranoia here was genuine: it produced its own pathological imagery. 'The Hegelian farce has done enough harm. We must stop it. We must speak – even at the price of soiling ourselves by touching this scandalous thing.'[39] Popper's rantings – inconceivable outside England at the time – are significant, because they provide a limiting case of the possibilities of dehistoricized political 'theory'. His entire diatribe against Hegel, in fact, was based on complete historical ignorance, as has been meticulously shown by a fellow-liberal, Kaufmann.[40] Yet this travesty was never challenged within England for a decade, because it was so natural to the methodological framework of English political theory.

It should be emphasized that the extrapolation characteristic of the discipline is not merely from the political or social history as such. It is also, and crucially, from the other social sciences adjacent to political thought, and which have traditionally been so integrated with it as often to be inseparable. The most striking case is economics. Berlin mentions the word 'property' exactly twice in his whole treatise on liberty. It is totally absent from his conceptual analysis. Yet it is overwhelmingly clear that no serious discussion of the various political theories of liberty can be dissociated from the concomitant theories of property. The classic demonstration came from a Canadian, four years after Berlin's essay, MacPherson's *Political Theory of Possessive Individualism* showed conclusively that the very meaning of freedom in Hobbes and Locke was unintelligible outside their notion of property: freedom, for them, *was* property of one's own person in a market society where he who sold his capacities (his labour) ceased by their definition to be free, and entitled to political suffrage. The inextricability of liberty and property in seventeenth-century England was decisively established by MacPherson. He did not reinstate Hobbes and Locke into their social class and interpret their theories in the light of their origin: he reinserted their theories into their integral intellectual context, and thereby illuminated their relation to their class. He did this simply by remarrying politics and economics. He thereby revolutionized the subject. MacPherson's subsequent work on Mill, Green and marginal economics, has amply vindicated the central importance of 'economic assumptions in political theory'.[41] By doing so, it has potentially redrawn the discipline. But the dominant pattern in English political theory is proof against solitary and alien dissent. It continues to operate a permanent abstraction of political ideas from economic ideas, and from either political or economic history.

History

Ideas divorced from history are matched by a history voided of ideas. Namierism is the obverse of English political philosophy. In this case, however, a powerful and original intelligence produced genuinely new knowledge. The very inability of his disciples to reproduce Namier's achievements is testimony of their novelty. This novelty was never systematized by Namier, who studded his own thought with cultural and political curios.

Namier was an expatriate in England who became a superpatriot. He believed in the paramount attainments of the English and expressed a general contempt for any other peoples and cultures. Thus he could write of 'German political incapacity and deadness',[42] 'French ideas, adaptable in their rootless superficiality'[43] and Austria, where 'Vienna has never produced anything truly great or creative'.[44] A functionary in the Foreign Office during the First World War, he vigorously advocated the liquidation of Austro-Hungary and the elimination of German influence from Eastern Europe. 'The future of the white race,' he wrote 'lies with Empires, that is those nations which hold vast expanses of land outside Europe.'[45] These attitudes were not accidental or tangential to his work. They determined its distinctive binary structure. One half of it was devoted to a meticulous and reverent study of the power structure of landed England in the eighteenth century. The other half was devoted to brilliant and acrid reflections on the history of continental Europe in the nineteenth and twentieth centuries. Namier's studies of the epoch of George III were a milestone in English historiography, because they constituted, for the first time, a truly *structural analysis* of the power system at that date, and of the composition of the ruling class. Demolishing the myth of two antagonistic political parties divided on social-ideological lines, he showed the class unity of eighteenth-century parliaments, and the immediate material interests which governed political fortunes and allegiances within it (corruption and clientelage). For the first time, history was written which virtually ignored chronology: Namier disdained the babble of narrative. His massive, stony edifices were acceptable to British historians, because of the immense infrastructure of factual minutiae on which they were founded. His empirical standards were above reproach. Namier's structural method was perfectly adapted to the tranquil social stability of eighteenth-century England. He saw it as a society which miraculously had achieved a territorial nationality,[46] based on freedom from foreign invasion, and the gradual growing together of different ethnic and linguistic communities made possible by it. Namier thought that only such a territorial nationality could produce liberty. This he identified with parliamentary sovereignty. Parliamentary institutions in turn demanded a hierarchical social structure: England was uniquely blessed in possessing these conditions of freedom. The eighteenth century saw the birth of the political system which was the token of its privilege.

Nineteenth- and twentieth-century Europe provided a diametric contrast to this idyllic picture. Namier analysed the whole evolution of continental Europe from 1789 to 1945 as the deleterious triumph of nationalism and democracy. He regarded both as the enemy of liberty. All the terms of his argument were reversed on the continent. There, territorial nationality on the English model was absent. There was first the dynastic, denationalized State that was the multifarious property of its ruler – the Habsburg Empire, *par excellence*. Then there was its equally pernicious opposite – the linguistic and racial nation preached by Mazzini, Kossuth and the German Parliament of 1848. This idea was the historical content of nationalism, and it was indissolubly linked to democracy. Democracy for Namier was 'a levelling of classes' and not 'constitutional growth'. Social equality he believed to be flatly incompatible with political liberty. 'Oligarchy is of the essence of Parliament, which requires an articulated society for basis. Elections presuppose superiorities ...'[47] The insistence that 'acknowledged superiorities there must be' naturally produced a vision of modern European history as an unrelieved process of decline. Namier's analyses of the France of Louis Napoleon, the Germany of the Hohenzollerns, the Austro-Hungary of the Habsburgs, the Europe of Versailles, are all equally mordant and sombre. An inexorable deterioration sets in after the French Revolution, which works its effects in Europe until after the end of the Second World War, Namier thought the concept itself had disappeared: 'Indeed,' he finally asked, 'what remained of Europe, of its history and its politics?'[48]

Namier executes this fresco with the greatest artistry. But what is striking about it is that it records a decline that it never explains. Namier was not mystified about the existence of classes or the conflict of their interests: indeed his awareness of them was the core of his analysis of the power structure of eighteenth-century England, and of his candid appraisal of the sociological character of British parliamentarism. But he lacked any dynamic theory of historical movement. This was a consequence of the peculiar character of his materialism. The charge that he 'took the mind out of history' was one that he proudly accepted. It meant that he radically devalued the importance of ideas in promoting historical change. Mindless history here complements timeless philosophy: the mediate symmetry of Wittgenstein and Namier is evident. The career of an intellectual like Berlin provides the middle term. What Namier substituted for 'mind', however, is what is important here. 'What matters most is the underlying emotions, the music, to which ideas are a mere libretto, often of very inferior quality; and once the emotions have ebbed, the ideas, established high and dry, become doctrine, or at best innocuous clichés.' [49] Ideas were thus reduced to emotions. The ultimate instance of history is psychology. Namier thought that his work was inspired by his appreciation of Freud, but in fact he showed little knowledge or understanding of Freud's work, and never made any serious application of it to his historiography. His credo was actually a vulgar psychologism – as Gareth Stedman Jones has pointed out, much more akin to Nietzsche's notions of the base motive behind the lofty sentiment. Now such a psychologism inevitably presupposes a fixed human nature. It is therefore totally inoperative as a principle of change. Hence the curious paradox of Namier's passionate belief in psychology. It is both central to his theory, and quite marginal to his practice. For by underlying everything, it explains nothing. It is consequently only introduced as a banal coda, when the work of concrete analysis is done.

I refrain from inquiring into the sense of the envenomed struggles we have witnessed; for such an inquiry would take us into inscrutable depths or into an airy void. Possibly there is more sense in human history than in the changes of the seasons or the movements of the stars; or if sense there be, it escapes our perception.[50]

The role of Namier's psychologism is manifest in this formulation. It precludes any general theory of historical change. The absence of meaning in history has a dual signification. It indicates that purposive human action, controlled by ideas, does not govern the course of events: 'there is no free will in the thinking of the masses, any more than in the revolutions of the planets, in the migrations of birds, and in the plunging of hordes of lemmings into the sea.'[51] But it also indicates that Namier, once he had adopted the premise of an immutable substratum of irrational emotions and passions, had no principle of *explanation* available to him. Thus the gathering avalanche of nationalism and democracy in Europe after 1789 was depicted and denounced by Namier; but it was never rendered causally intelligible. In this sense, the dictum that 'history has no meaning' is a translation of the fact that Namier's history had no *motor*. The distance between this materialism and that of Marx is obvious. Marx emphasized precisely the importance of ideas within any social structure, and dialectically related the two in such a manner as to centre his theory on the historical changes produced by the disjunctures between them.

In Namier's European writings, time exists only as dilapidation. His insights persist: but their context has altered. His superb structural examination of the Austro-Hungarian Empire closes with its disintegration. His secular account of the geopolitical pattern of European diplomacy – an extraordinary *tour de force* generated by his peculiar perception of the State as a historical entity – ends with the submergence of Europe. Namier's legacy to English historiography was thus inevitably equivocal. His structuralism was rapidly suppressed from memory. The two best-known historians today divide his minor bequests. Trevor-Roper inherited Namier's acute sensitivity to the State, as a material complex of power and prebends. He used this to sketch perhaps the most coherent general interpretation of seventeenth-century politics yet produced – the crisis of the Renaissance State.[52] Elsewhere, his writings are erratic and electric. Namier's main self-proclaimed disciple has been his public opponent in controversy. Taylor's works show Namier's philistinism about ideas, and his xenophobia, and caricature them. He converted the microscopic study of structures into its opposite –

a trivial and conventional narrative. The apparent accumulation of minutiae link the two, as if Namier had merely produced a census. Few disciples have ever betrayed their master so completely. Namier's political outlook was frankly regressive, but in England his approach to history was intellectually advanced. Its virtues have generally been forgotten, and its faults exaggerated. A new school of history has in the last decade emerged on the left, quite outside this tradition – but this is another subject. Within the dominant orthodoxy that followed Namier, history without ideas slowly became a drought of ideas about history.

Economics

The insulation of political theory from economic thought duplicates an earlier division: the emergence of 'economics' after the disappearance of 'political economy'. This time, the shift was general, in all Western countries. The advent of marginalism marked the birth of an economic science, ostensibly free from political or sociological variables. What this meant, of course, was that they were pushed outside the conscious focus of the system, and became its silent, unconscious preconditions. Equilibrium theory claimed to be a pure logic of the market: in fact, it underwrote it ideologically by relegating the notion of monopoly to a special case and excluding the very idea of a planned economy: socialism. Neo-classical theory rationalized laissez-faire at the very historical moment that it had been superseded, with the new economy of imperialism. It was incapable of providing any solution to the crises to Western capitalism after the First World War. Keynes's enormous merit was to have seen that the whole categorial system of neo-classical economics needed to be recast. At first prompted by elementary political pragmatism, he merely advocated the practical measures necessary to stabilize British capitalism: then, a decade later, he provided the theory for them. *The General Theory of Employment, Money and Interest* represented a tremendous intellectual advance, precisely because it integrated two conceptual systems that had previously been quite separate, into a new synthesis. Monetary theory and employment theory were regarded by neo-classical economics as completely distinct topics, with no intrinsic connexion between them. Only two years before the publication of *The General*

Theory, Pigou had written his *Theory of Unemployment* without seriously discussing the problem of investment. Keynes's achievement was thus a 'retotalization' of his field. He was well aware of this:

> When I began to write my *Treatise on Money* I was still moving along the traditional lines of regarding the influence of money as something so to speak separate from the general theory of supply and demand. . . . This book, on the other hand, has evolved into what is primarily a study of the forces which determine changes in the scale of output and employment as a whole; and, whilst it is found that money enters into the scheme in an essential and peculiar manner, technical monetary detail falls into the background. A monetary economy, we shall find, is essentially one in which changing views about the future are capable of influencing the quantity of employment and not merely its direction. But our method of analysing the economic behaviour of the present under the influence of changing ideas about the future is one which depends on the interaction of supply and demand, and is in this way linked up with our fundamental theory of value.[53]

This synthesis naturally produced its own concepts. The ideas of liquidity preference and the multiplier were not simply additions to the existing canon. They reformulated the whole system, by knocking away the assumption of a stationary equilibrium. Both concepts, of course, presuppose a dynamic framework. Keynes thus effectively reintroduced time into orthodox economic theory, thereby revolutionizing it. This was the mark of the greatness of his thought. It was also its ambiguous limitation. For the Keynesian temporality is a very restricted one: it is brief and cyclical. 'In the long run, we are all dead.' Keynes accepted capitalism, but without zeal or sanctimony. He was mainly concerned with assuring its immediate stability, not justifying it *sub specie aeternitatis*. This both prevented him from ever becoming an official ideologue of the *status quo* like so many economists, and from developing a deeper and longer dynamic perspective. His contemporary Kalecki, who in contradistinction to Keynes was aware of the work of Marx, achieved some of the same countercyclical insights, albeit in fragmentary form, but saw the ulterior implications of them. By reinserting Keynesian categories into a rudimentary political economy, he was able to predict what he called the 'political trade-cycle', which has since become the principal economic contradiction of advanced capitalism: the conflict between full employment and inflation.

After Keynes, it was no longer possible to develop economic theory within the old equilibrium framework. The temporal dimension he introduced was there to stay. The next step was logical: the emergence of growth theory as such. Here, however, the inherent limits of orthodox economic theory checked its own spontaneous trajectory. The preoccupation with growth which is the distinguishing feature of post-Keynesian economics should logically have returned it to political economy (and its apex, Marx). For the reproduction of capital was central to Marx's concerns. But political economy was forbidden, for obvious reasons: it by definition put the socio-economic system as a whole in question. The result was that growth theory developed on an essentially *ad hoc* basis, with an accretion of hypotheses wherever possible abstracted from the property regime. This is particularly clear in its initial formulation by Harrod. He simply added technical invention – the least *social* variable available – to the Keynesian model, to produce an equation for progress.[54] Subsequent demonstrations that technology does not determine the rate of capital accumulation merely scattered the arena into divergent and piecemeal hypotheses, which have never been unified into any general theory. Time now haunts orthodox economic theory, but it is unable to dominate it. Patent evidence of the failure to effect the transition from Keynes's short-run economics to a true long-run economics is the impotence of British economic orthodoxy to provide any coherent theory of Britain's present economic crisis. The national predicament has obsessed public debate for five years now; all political discussion has revolved on it. In that time, innumerable unrelated or contradictory explanations for the crisis have been advanced by British economists. The most influential has doubtless been Kaldor's, which attributes Britain's post-war economic decline to a shortage of cheap labour from the primary sector, due to the uniquely rationalized English agriculture of the last century.[55] The generalized inadequacy of these accounts is patent. It is as plain as day that Britain's economic crisis has more than one major cause; that these causes are not randomly or equivalently related, but form a complex *hierarchy*; and that they englobe the socio-political structure of contemporary Britain. But orthodox economics has proved completely unable *either* to construct a hierarchical model of the causality of the crisis (not merely a plural one), *or* to integrate the economic end-product into the political and historical totality from which it is so manifestly articulated. The physical cooption of so many economists – Kaldor, Balogh, Neild, Seers and *tutti quanti* – into a foundering government has merely underlined its intellectual bankruptcy. The crisis persists, unabated.

Despite all its technical advances in mathematization, formal economics in England has been unable to grapple with the practical issues which confront it. Retrospectively, Keynes's magnitude has grown. He was perhaps the last great social thinker produced by the English bourgeoisie, with all the largeness and generosity of once confident liberalism. His theoretical system was validated practically; yet he never became a fanatic advocate of the social order to whose temporary salvation he contributed so much. He never hesitated to pronounce outside his subject, on a gamut of topics which recalls that of his contemporaries, Russell and Lawrence; it is characteristic that he could write a brief memoir of them which situates that trio perhaps better than any work of cultural history since.[56] Keynes was an intellectual in the classical tradition.[57]

His international reputation lent British economics a peculiar status among its fellow-disciplines. But, as has been seen, it was unable to enhance it after him. His own definition of the qualities necessary to be a great economist is a standing indictment of his successors:

The master-economist must possess a rare combination of gifts. He must reach a high standard in several different directions and must combine talents not often found together. He must be a mathematician, historian, statesman, philosopher – in some degree. He must understand symbols and speak in words. He must contemplate the particular in terms of the general, and touch abstract and concrete in the same flight of thought. He must study the present in the light of the past for the purposes of the future. No part of man's nature or his institutions must be entirely outside his regard.[58]

This statement of faith has been quietly forgotten. Today, routine and mediocrity have settled over the discipline. Its superior pedigree has not enabled it to produce so much as a Galbraith – an average economist bold enough to formulate some general propositions about the structure and tendency of monopolized capitalism. Sraffa, its one genuine pioneer, has been ignored. Technique has become a substitute for theory. Dissociated from political economy, and checked short of secular history, British economics has visibly stagnated.

Psychology

Namier believed that ideas were merely rationalizations of emotions. Political ideas, in particular, were the camouflaged expressions of unconscious attitudes and passions. This reductionism was independently reproduced, with the utmost fidelity, in the discipline of psychology itself. Eysenck, who presided pervasively over English psychology after the Second World War, tried to classify political beliefs systematically by relating them to psychological attitudes. *The Psychology of Politics* is a monument to crude psychologism. It opens with this classic credo :

Psychology so conceived has one advantage over other disciplines which makes it of particular interest and importance. Political actions are actions of human beings; the study of the direct causes of these actions is the field of the study of psychology. All other social sciences deal with variables which affect political behaviour indirectly.... The psychologist has no need of such intermediaries; he is in direct contact with the central link in the chain of causation between antecedent condition and resultant action.[59]

This characteristic illusion has never been more clearly expressed : the belief in a fundamental psyche which is prior to societal determinations, and which may therefore be considered the immediate pivot of social action.

Eysenck constructed an attitude chart destined to show the emotional convergence of extremisms (left to right) and counterpose them to a solid centre of moderation. Politically, the effect of this was to establish an identification between Fascism and

Communism – contrasted with 'democratic' creeds such as conservatism or liberalism: a typical enterprise of the Cold War. The pseudo-categories of 'tough-mindedness' and 'tender-mindedness' were superimposed on the categories of 'radicalism' and 'conservatism' to achieve this result. Totalitarians of all persuasions proved, of course, to be 'tough-minded'. Eysenck dilated at length on the similarity of test-scores between Communists and Fascists, which showed the temperamental peculiarities of those with these beliefs. Eysenck dedicated his work to the hope of 'a society more interested in psychology than politics'. This inimitable declaration is a self-definition. Eysenck is a special case in the gallery of expatriates. All the others show some intellectual originality; Popper himself, however jejune his political writings, was a respectable philosopher of natural science. Eysenck is not of the same category. A crusading publicist, he has dominated his subject more by prolific output than by any unanimously acknowledged pre-excellence. But this should not lead to an underestimation of his historical importance. After the war, Eysenck developed the use of factor analysis, a basic methodological tool of experimental psychology, in England. He thereby rapidly achieved wide prestige and influence. In these years, Eysenck became the symbol of a new, aggressive scientism. The success generated by the initial lack of any serious challenge to him bore fruit in an ample range of works, pronouncing on the psychology of: politics, crime, intelligence tests, mental illness, smoking and numerous other topics. No other psychologist in England can rival a fraction of this output.

In the course of its production, however, Eysenck undoubtedly over-reached himself. Today, his works have been subjected to criticism by colleagues even in this positivist discipline *par excellence*. The erosion of his relative immunity started, appropriately enough, with the devastating exposé by three Americans – Rokeach, Hanley and Christie – of *The Psychology of Politics*. Subjecting it to scrupulous statistical, methodological and conceptual checks, they concluded that Eysenck had misinterpreted his data, miscomputed his statistics, and misconstrued his results. In particular, they showed that there was no similarity between Communists and Fascists, even on Eysenck's own unscientific evidence:

Eysenck arbitrarily lumps communists and fascists together in an attempt to indicate their similarity.... It is clear that Eysenck's communist samples are neither 'tough-minded' nor 'authoritarian' when the data produced as evidence by Eysenck are carefully examined.[60]

The very concept of tough-mindedness was fictive – a product of Eysenck's arbitrary statistical procedures.

Our analysis leads us to the conclusion that tough-mindedness–tender-mindedness, as conceived and measured by Eysenck, has no basis in fact. It is based on miscalculations and a disregard for a significant portion of his data. It conceals rather than reveals the attitudinal differences among existing groups.[61]

Eysenck's reply did not convince his critics. Christie's restatement of his judgement is memorable. *The Psychology of Politics* contains:

Errors of computation, uniquely biased samples which forbid any generalizations, scales with built-in biases which do not measure what they purport to measure, unexplained inconsistencies within the data, misinterpretations and contradictions of the relevant research of others, and unjustifiable manipulation of the data. Any one of Eysenck's many errors is sufficient to raise serious questions about the validity of his conclusions. In toto, absurdity is compounded upon absurdity, so that where, if anywhere, the truth lies is impossible to determine.[62]

The Psychology of Politics is an expression of the discipline from which it emerged and which permitted it. It is symptomatic that Eysenck's book was eventually denounced, not by English colleagues, but by American psychologists.[63] Discrete criticisms of other aspects of his work followed. But it is significant that his public renown in England – built on innumerable broadcasts, articles and paperbacks – has been virtually unaffected. To a greater extent than any of the other of the emigrés discussed here, he is popularly identified with his subject. There is good reason for this. Despite various reservations about Eysenck's writings, no English psychologist has yet written a critique of his work as a whole. Scattered objections do not constitute a considered intellectual rejection. Eysenck thus continues, from his chair at the Maudsley, to symbolize psychology and preach psychologism in

England. His very defects are his significance: the quality of his work is an index of the receptivity of the culture to its assumptions.

Aesthetics

The model sector for psychology as a discipline has traditionally been perception. The psychological study of perception has yielded the most rapid and reliable scientific results, and has consequently exerted a general influence on the orientation of the discipline. In England, however, a significant reprise has occurred. The dominant aesthetics has been derived from the psychology of perception. Gombrich's *Art and Illusion* – an intelligent and erudite development of theories of perception – is today the consensually acclaimed orthodoxy. Gombrich may be said to dominate the theory of pictorial art as his companion Popper did the theory of the natural sciences.

This influence is not self-explanatory. Art history and aesthetics have been an enclave in British culture much more completely colonized than any other by expatriates. Given the time-honoured philistinism of the intelligentsia delineated by Annan, this is not particularly surprising. The great majority of scholars who have produced serious works on painting, sculpture or architecture in England have been Germans or Austrians: Saxl, Wittkower, Wind, Antal, Pevsner and others. The primacy enjoyed by Gombrich is not explicable merely by reason of his merits. Once again, the filtering mechanism already discussed has been at work. Traditional British culture has an elective affinity with certain types of expatriate and not others. It promotes what is attuned to its own inherited nature, and suppresses what is dissonant with it. Antal, one of the greatest contemporary historians of Florentine art, was a Marxist scholar; he never received official honours and appears never to have been offered a university appointment. Gombrich, intimate and associate of Von Hayek and Popper, has been canonized by established culture. Why? The answer is that Gombrich's theory of art is a variant of the psychologism which is a recurring component of the culture as a system. This is not to deny its sophistication. It undoubtedly represents the most rewarding example of the phenomenon, and one which has achieved a definite advance on its terrain. Gombrich's central problem has been the relation of perception to painting. What accounts for the diversity of styles in the history of art? Basing himself on experimental psychology, Gombrich showed that perception itself is predetermined by stable schemata. There is thus nothing natural in naturalism, as a mode of painting. The literal transcription of reality was a long and arduous achievement, after aeons of endeavour: it was never a spontaneous, unreflective gift. The difference between one age of painting and another is primarily one of *technique*, whereby closer approximation to mirror-like accuracy becomes possible, via innumerable rectifications of the perceptual schemata which govern the painter's vision. In the course of his argument, Gombrich unfolds many acute local demonstrations. But the theory as a whole is evidently vitiated by the closed parameters of its discussion. The problem of any psychologism is to account for historical change, since the initial assumption is a self-contained, universal psyche. Gombrich solves the dilemma for his theory of art, by means of the indispensable notion of technique. Technical progress, in effect, is the minimum dose of history possible for such a problematic. For it is the most easily conceived as an a-social movement. Thus, in the case of painting, it becomes a continual amelioration of the individual's perceptual equipment, abstracted from the social structure of which he was a carrier. Gombrich's use of technique as a central concept radically dehistoricizes art, and renders it ultimately interchangeable and incomprehensible. It is one matter to show that Ancient Egyptian art was not a voluntary refusal of faithful naturalism, but preceded the very capacity for it. It is another to explain the concrete and unique deformation of representational reality which was the visual art of Ancient Egypt. Gombrich, indeed, is at a loss to comprehend it. For the principle of explanation lies, by definition, outside his range of concepts. Why is Ancient Egyptian art totally different from Ancient Chinese art that was coeval with it? Only the structure of the historical society in which it was produced can render this intelligible. Gombrich himself is obliged to have recourse to *ad hoc* sociological explanations to block in the gaps in his scheme. This Ancient Egyptian art was perhaps influenced by the priesthood, and Ancient Greek art by the rise of trade. These random hypotheses are quite external to the categories of his system. They are thrown in to buttress its incoherence – that is, where it evidently fails to account for the specificity of a form of art. It is no accident that Gombrich's chronological study is called *The Story of Art* – not its history. In it, succeeding modes of painting are described, not explained: at most, a vague action–reaction of fashion and generation are evoked, as in the literary criticism of fifty years ago. Thus Gombrich constantly produces such formulae as this:

> We remember the feeling of uneasiness created by the brilliant messiness of impressionist 'snapshots' of fleeting sights, the longing for more order, structure and pattern that had animated the illustrators of the *Art Nouveau* with their emphasis on decorative simplification no less than such masters as Seurat and Cézanne.[64]

The flaccid circularity of such comments is evident, and the futility of their psychologism ('feeling of uneasiness', 'longing for more order' and so on). This is a popular manual, not a scholarly work, but it conveys the narrowness of Gombrich's substantive theory.

Early in his career, Gombrich was uneasily aware of the inadequacy of his psychological problematic. He admitted the validity of Vasari's famous definition of the task of the art historian: to investigate the causes and roots of style – *le causi e radici delle manieri*. He had to confess a general blankness here: 'We have no theory of style which might account for its stability or its changes. ... Psychology alone can never suffice to explain the riddle of history, the riddle of particular changes. ... For me, at least, the enigma of style is wrapped in a thrilling mystery.'[65] But no sooner had he said this, than he suppressed the thought. A moment later he was dismissing Vasari's classical query as by definition unanswerable: 'I do not think we can ever hope to produce a final explanation of this type of problem.'[66] In its place, he proposed the theme which was to become the itinerary of *Art and Illusion*: 'the role of skill, of the learning process involved' in art; 'the individual and particular works of art as the work of skilled hands and great minds in response to concrete demands.'[67] The transition from one position to another eventually produced a complete and unconscious regression to the very belief which he had once formally rejected. A few years later, he was tranquilly writing of 'the shifting urges, the psychological pulls and counter-pulls that result in changes of taste and style within the context of civilization.'[68] This is exactly the formula for the vacant undulations of *The Story of Art*. In the closed space of Gombrich's preoccupations, the psychology which was once exorcized is a revenant which necessarily returns to rule.

Theory and history have a different relationship in a true aesthetics: Vasari's question insistently demands an answer. The iconology of Erwin Panofsky approached the problem much more closely because it focused on the *meaning* of paintings and sculptures, not merely their technique.[69] For the rules of perception and the march of technique – the individual psyche and its immanent evolution – are insufficient to differentiate the art of any society or epoch from another. The very schemata which Gombrich correctly insists govern perception are not alignable on a linear time-track. Their origin must be sought in the diverse societies in which they existed, and which themselves are amenable to no mono-evolutionary classification. Gombrich's psychologism – the construction of a theory of art based on the psychology of perception plus the accumulation of technique – simulates time, the better to abolish it. It is no accident that it lacks any purchase on twentieth century art: the problematic of representation is extinct today. An aesthetic which erases society necessarily precludes a concept of temporality. A historical sociology of art – the examination of its concrete mode of production – is a condition of its differential intelligibility. The 'psychology' of art is ultimately an interdiction of its meaning.

Psychoanalysis

The sectors hitherto discussed have formed an interconnecting and self-confirming cultural circuit. A verification of the analysis sketched here is provided *a contrario* by the fate of the one entirely *new* discipline to emerge within the previous orbit of the traditional 'human sciences'. This discipline was psychoanalysis. In Britain, it did not escape the general law of expatriate dominance. Melanie Klein, an Austrian who came to London after working in Berlin, formed a school or generation of psycho-analysis which after the war became the distinctively British contribution to the international spectrum of the discipline. The power and originality of Klein's work makes it perhaps the most important systematic development of psychoanalytic theory since Freud. Freud had revealed the structural significance of childhood in the formation of human character, by his epochal discovery of the unconscious. Klein extended this revolution beyond the limits of what Freud thought were possible: she pioneered a theory and a therapy capable of capturing the psychic structures of infancy – the aboriginal first months of life which precede and found the original experience theorized by Freud. Klein invented a new therapeutic practice for this radicalization of the scope of psychoanalysis. It is no accident that the two together produced a theoretical development, which provided one of the first coherent attempts at a solution of a fundamental problem left unanswered by Freud. Freud's clinical revolution was to 'produce' the intelligibility of the conduct of neurotics – previously regarded as a meaningless, physiological pathology. In his theory, it became significant human action. Freud, however, never provided a comparable general theory of the psychoses. He insisted on the fundamental conceptual difference between the two disorders, but beyond a brilliant sketch of a case of paranoia (The Schreber Affair), he never formulated an inclusive theory establishing the differential bases of neuroses and psychoses. He left his inheritors the unsolved problem of a unified theory of the two, bequeathing them only some crucial but cryptic signposts. The Kleinian bathysphere into the most submarine recesses of infancy unexpectedly produced a *sui generis* solution. By pro-ducing the concepts of successive 'paranoid' and 'depressive' posi-tions, universally experienced in the course of infancy, Klein was able to reunite psychoses and neuroses along an evolutionary axis. Psychosis became a reversion to the paranoid position, which the patient had never properly passed; neurosis to the depressive position. The criticisms that may be made of this evolutionism are evident. There is no doubt that it represents a 'naïve' synthe-sis. Glover and Anna Freud subjected Klein's work to a violent environmentalist criticism in the forties, much of which was for-mally justified.[70] Klein's capacity for scientific formulation was not equal to her signal intellectual courage and practical intuition. The weaknesses in any linear genetic account of psychological disorders need little demonstration. The objective merit of Klein's work, however, was to retable the question of a unified theory. Today, the work of Laing, Cooper and Esterson represents an advance towards the production of the specific 'intelligibility' of schizophrenia which makes no concession to evolutionism. This is an uneven development: it has been accompanied by a silence on Freud which has precluded any general theory. But the preconditions of this excentric progress derive from the psychoanalytic problematic generated by Klein.

Psychoanalysis in Britain has thus in no fashion been a mediocre or infertile phenomenon. On the contrary, Klein's pupils and associates – Winnicott, Isaacs, Bion, Rosenfeld and Riviere – form one of the most flourishing schools in the world; not to speak of separate cases such as Laing or Cooper. It is now time to ask: what has been the impact of psychoanalysis on British culture in general? The irony is that it has been virtually nil. It has been sealed off as a technical enclave: an esoteric and specialized pursuit unrelated to any of the central concerns of mainstream 'humanistic' culture. There is no Western country where the presence of psychoanalysis in general culture is so vestigial. The USA, Germany, and France – three very different examples – provide a unanimous contrast. The whole cultural matrix of these societies has been affected and transformed by the advent of psychoanalysis, which has penetrated to the centre of the common intellectual inheritance. One has only to think of such diverse figures, in different disciplines, as Parsons, Jakobsen, Adorno, Lévi-Strauss or Althusser, to see the direct impact of Freud on their thought. There is no comparable English thinker who has been remotely touched. A trivial index of the fundamental situation is, in fact, the mere availability of Freud's work. The English *Standard Edition* is the best in the world; its twenty-four volumes are the model for all other scholarly editions. Naturally, its circulation is very limited indeed. The converse of this specialist instrument is the virtually complete absence of central works by Freud in paperback. This astonishing fact contrasts with the millions of copies of his major works published and sold in Germany, the USA and France. It is, of course, the overt sign of a deeper cultural set. To some extent, the isolation of psychoanalysis in England was historically self-imposed. Jones and Glover, the two men most responsible for its institutionalization, were determined to prevent the confusion and vulgarization of Freud's thought that had occurred else-where. The consequence of such a policy was the very limited diffusion of Freud's ideas and writings outside the professional milieu. But this, of course, was only one factor responsible. Much more important, undoubtedly, was the intellectual context which confronted psychoanalysis in England, and to which it eventu-ally adapted by becoming a tolerated but segregated enclave.

Freud often compared his discovery to that of Copernicus. Althusser has recently definied the nature of his revolution :

It was not in vain that Freud sometimes compared the critical impact of his discoveries with the upheaval of the Copernican revolu-tion. Since Copernicus, we know that the earth is not the centre of the universe. Since Marx, we know that the human subject, the economic, political or philosophical ego is not the centre of history – we even know, against the Enlightenment and against Hegel, that history has no centre, but possesses a structure without a centre. . . . Freud has shown us in his turn that the real subject, the individual in his singular essence, does not have the form of an I centred on the 'ego' 'consciousness' or 'existence' – that the human subject is decentred, constituted by a structure which itself has no centre.[71]

The implications of this overthrow for the social sciences were and are vast. There is nothing surprising in the fact that it has affected sociology (Parsons), anthropology (Lévi-Strauss), philo-sophy (Althusser), linguistics (Jakobsen) or aesthetics (Adorno) on the continent and in the United States. English culture, how-ever, has – uniquely – resisted any serious impingement. The significance of this blankness may be assessed by one critical area. The school of linguistic analysis, in England, has been defined by the ambition to align philosophic truth on the rules of ordinary language – ultimate arbiter of the very possibility of social com-munication. The profoundly a-historical conception enshrined in the very notion of a stable 'ordinary language' has already been discussed. Linguistic philosophy may be defined as a flight from the emergence of new concepts. It so happens, however, that psychoanalysis is perhaps the most dramatic example in the century of a conceptual revolution which radically overthrows the rules of everyday discourse. The dethronement of the cogito is the end of the grammatical sovereignty of the first person. The emergence of the unconscious as a central concept produces a 'language' in flagrant contradiction with the ego-centred syntax of everyday speech. 'I' is no longer I in the opaque, metonymic *double-entendre* of Freud's patients, their roles governed by a script that escapes them. No appeal to the conventions of drawing-room conversation can controvert the paraproxes of the couch. The unconscious is not fittable into the language of a colloquial cogito – the quotidian speech to which we have been trained since childhood. Taken seriously, psychoanalysis strikes at the very basis of linguistic philosophy.[72]

What has been the reaction of English philosophers to it? By and large, they have repressed all consciousness of it. None have confronted psychoanalysis as a central issue for the operational assumptions of their philosophy. A few have tried to deal with it as an anomaly or special instance. Austin, in *A plea for Excuses*, it will be remembered, asserted that: 'Our common stock of words embodies all the distinctions men have found worth drawing, and the connexions they found worth marking, in the lifetimes of many generations.'[73] But he later admitted two special 'source-books' – law and psychology – whose concepts might be additional to those of ordinary language. His formulation of the problem is, in fact, particularly clear:

Some varieties of behaviour, some ways of acting or explanations of the doing of actions, are here noticed and classified which have not been observed or named by ordinary men and hallowed by ordinary language, though perhaps they often might have been so if they had been of more practical importance. There is real danger in contempt for the 'jargon' of psychology, at least when it sets out to supplement, and at least sometimes when it sets out to supplant, the language of ordinary life.[74]

Austin illustrates his comment with the technical concepts of 'compulsion' and 'displacement', for which he admits there are no equivalent adverbial expression in colloquial speech. How, then, is the ideology saved? The answer is, by means of the simple device of proclaiming this class of phenomena of no 'practical' importance. Ordinary language 'embodies the inherited experience and acumen of many generations of men. But then, that acumen has been concentrated primarily upon the practical business of life. ... Compulsive behaviour, like displacement behaviour, is not in general going to be of great importance.'[75] The candour of such philistinism is almost admirable. No attempt is made at an intellectual argument: the mere invocation of the 'practical business of life' (the cramped routines of any *bien-pensant* bourgeois) is enough to dispatch the problem. Freud's concepts explicitly capture normal and abnormal behaviour in their contradictory unity (neuroses are the obverse of perversions): they represent a general theory of the unconscious, not a pathology of special cases. Quite apart from this, however, what is evident is the renunciation of any attempt to *relate* the concepts of ordinary language to those of 'psychology' (when does the latter not merely 'supplement' but 'supplant' the other? i.e. – to what extent is the latter a radical critique of the former?); the structural relations between the two are replaced by a mindless summation of different 'sources'.

Wittgenstein's pupil Wisdom has assayed another type of solution. Here the concepts of psychoanalysis are integrated wholesale into the philosophy of ordinary language, despite their incompatibility with it, by the ingenious device of dubbing them 'paradox' and then asserting that paradox is a special but legal language-game.[76] This latitudinarian position – both use and misuse of language are significant – has been devastatingly criticized by Gellner. It represents the classic antinomy of this empiricism, where it becomes an all-purpose permissiveness, thereby cancelling itself. Another approach to the problem has been tried by Hampshire. His Ernest Jones lecture of 1962 is avowedly concerned to build 'the shortest possible bridge' between everyday language and psychoanalysis.[77] For this purpose, Hampshire selects the concept of memory, and argues that psychoanalysis posits a total memory, the greater portion of which becomes unconscious and thereafter generates repressed motives and purposes. No *new* concepts are therefore needed: the existing notion of memory merely needs to be 'extended'. What is striking here is the open and *a priori* assumption that the task of the philosopher is to provide the easiest reconciliation of new concepts with common-sense. It is this extraneous goal which determines the analysis of psychoanalytic theory, not the internal necessity of the object. Banalization becomes the public vocation of philosophy. Hampshire's text is in many respects an astonishing document. He actually says: 'It would be an intellectual disaster if theoretical discussion of psychoanalysis were to be confined to clinical contexts, and if at this stage the philosophy of mind went on its way unheeding.'[78] Fifty years after the advent of Freud, an English philosopher suddenly discovers that it would be an 'intellectual disaster' if his work 'were' to be forgotten by philosophy! What restrospective description is possible, then, for the intervening half century, since the maunderings of Moore in *Principia Ethica*? Hampshire solemnly adds: 'The substitution of a scheme of explanation depending on an extended concept of memory for explanation by causal laws will not be fully understood and evaluated by philosophers for many years.'[79] The ineffable ignorance of English philosophy is thus assured an indefinite respite. These avowals, by the most liberal ornament of the school, are a suitable epitaph for it. They accurately define the fate of psychoanalysis, and the character of philosophy, in Britain.

Anthropology

An interim summary of this rapid survey is now possible. Throughout this desolate panorama, the very notion of the totality is banned. The various traditional disciplines discussed cluster about an absent centre – what should have been the emergence of a classical sociology or a national Marxism. Lacking this centre, they form a vicious circle of self-reproducing fragmentation and limitation. The record of mediocrity has been overwhelming. When neither society nor man are anywhere put in question, culture stops. In England, it has gradually slowed towards zero point. But the notion of totality can never be completely banished from an advanced industrial society. If it is suppressed in its natural loci, it will inevitably be displaced into abnormal or paradoxical sectors. So it has been in Britain.

It has been seen how modern British society was distinguished by its failure to produce any classical sociology. It is now time to consider the bizarre obverse of this phenomenon. For the same society produced a brilliant and flourishing anthropology. It is true that the decisive 'founder' of this anthropology was yet again an expatriate: Bronislaw Malinowski, a Polish aristocrat from the Galician szlachta. ('Rivers is the Rider-Haggard of anthropology: I shall be its Conrad,' he said.) But his contemporaries and pupils were to constitute one of the strongest and most influential schools in any Western country. Radcliffe-Brown, Evans-Pritchard, Fortes, Firth and Leach all won world-wide reputations. Their distinction throws into yet greater relief the collective anonymity of British sociology. This strange contrast is an evident indication of a major problem, which demands an explanation. Yet it has by and large passed unnoticed. The career of Durkheim, who was the most powerful foreign source of inspiration for British anthropology in its formative decades, serves as a reminder of how anomalous the British situation was. Durkheim's work was equally and inseparably 'sociological' (*Suicide*) and 'anthropological' (*Elementary Forms of Religious Life*): the division did not exist for him. Why did it exist, as a virtually absolute datum, in England?

The answer is to be found, not in the aims and methods of the two disciplines, but in their objects. British culture never produced a classical sociology largely because British society was never challenged as a whole from within: the dominant class and its intellectuals consequently had no interest in forging a theory of its total structure; for it would necessarily have been an 'answer' to a question which to their ideological advantage remained unposed. *Omnia determinatio est negatio* – the very demarcation of a social totality places it under the sign of contingency. The British bourgeoisie had learnt to fear the meaning of 'general ideas' during the French Revolution: after Burke, it never forgot the lesson. Hegemony at home demanded a moratorium on them. By the end of the nineteenth century, however, this class was master of a third of the world. English anthropology was born of this disjuncture. British imperial society exported its totalizations, on to its subject peoples. There, and there only, it could afford scientific study of the social whole. 'Primitive' societies became the surrogate object of the theory proscribed at home. British anthropology developed unabashedly in the wake of British imperialism. Colonial administration had an inherent need of cogent, objective information on the peoples over which it ruled. The miniature scale of primitive societies, moreover, made them exceptionally propitious for macro-analysis as Sartre once commented, they form 'natural' significant totalities. British anthropology was thus able both to assist British imperialism, and to develop a genuine theory – something sociology in Britain was never able to do. The class core of this contrast is not an arbitrary construction. The least suspect of sources has innocently admitted it. Macrae, symbol of British sociological orthodoxy ('a rather splendid amateurism'), writes:

British social anthropology has drawn on the same intellectual capital as sociology proper, and its success, *useful to colonial administration and dangerous to no domestic prejudice*, shows at what a high rate of interest that capital can be made to pay.... The subject.... unlike sociology, has prestige. It is associated with colonial administration – traditionally a career for a gentleman, and entrance into the profession and acceptance by it confers high status in Britain.[80]

Useful to colonial administration and dangerous to no domestic prejudice – the formula is brief and exact. These were the twin conditions of existence of British anthropology, as it developed.

The scholars themselves, of course, were nearly always liberal within the paternalist framework of their vocation. But the sensibility produced by it is graphically indicated by Evans-Pritchard, whose classic study of the Nuer contains this calm aside, after a lengthy and often lyrical account of Nuer life:

In 1920 large-scale military operations, including bombing and machine-gunning of camps, were conducted against the Eastern Jikany and caused much loss of life and destruction of property. There were further patrols from time to time, but the Nuer remained unsubdued. ... From 1928 to 1930 prolonged operations were conducted against the whole of the disturbed area and marked the end of serious fighting between the Nuer and the Government. Conquest was a severe blow to the Nuer. . .

Needless to say, the passing reference to this brutal war is completely dissociated from the analysis of Nuer society itself. Later developments modified the role of outright violence. But the context of anthropological work had not changed greatly twenty years later, when a volume of tributes to Radcliffe-Brown, edited by Fortes, could include the following contribution on the uses of anthropology to more 'modern' notions of imperial control:

It is only after months or years of administration, and sometimes not even then, that a Military Government officer or colonial administrator learns the virtues of 'opposition face'. By this is meant that the native leader or appointed official must be allowed some leeway to oppose the occupying administration for the purposes of his public, in order that he may the more successfully carry through the main and essential necessities of government for the maintenance of law and order. This is simply good political horse sense. One good reason for giving native leaders some sense of responsibility (not necessarily for policies but rather for methods and procedures of carrying them out) is to avoid too much paternalism. The latter is stultifying and may lead to complete lack of co-operation on the part of the people. A reasonably alert and satisfied population is amenable in terms of labour procurement and any other problems of administration requiring the co-operation of the people.[82]

This, then, was the practical historical setting of the growth of imperial anthropology. What were its theoretical achievements? The formidable research carried out by two generations of scholars was integrated under the canons of functionalism. Radcliffe-Brown provided the most coherent theoretical explanation of this doctrine, but was himself more influential in the USA than in Britain. It was the original author of the notion, Malinowski, who formed a generation of English anthropologists. The basic idea of functionalism was that the diverse parts of society – economy, polity, kinship or religion – form a consistent whole, unified by the interconnecting functions of each. Functionalism represented the notion of an immediate and simple totality. As such, it was an enormous advance over the atomized empiricism of domestic British thought. It naturally produced a social science of incomparably greater force and insight. To this day, British anthropology towers above its stunted sibling. The limitations of functionalism, however, became increasingly evident with time. Malinowski's founding version of it was a variety of psychologism – the recurring motif discernible throughout this cultural pattern. The function of the different institutions which made up a society was to serve the psychological needs of the population, which Malinowski believed were innate. Parsons has written the critique of this theory; it did not survive Malinowski.[83] But the deeper limit of functionalism persisted. It was a totalization without contradictions. Having posited the compact integration of social segments, it was by definition incapable of dealing with structural antagonisms. Where conflicts were considered at all, they were treated as merely conducive to ultimate order (Gluckmann). Hence the progressive loss of impetus once the pioneering work of Malinowski's pupils was done. No renewal was possible within this framework, which represented the outer limit of a totalizing theory whose vector was a stable British imperialism.

The Second World War provoked the crisis of this imperial system. The emergence of new tendencies within British anthropology coincides with this crisis. The material for the work which represented a new departure was gathered while its author was an officer in the Burmese campaign. Leach's *Political Systems of Highland Burma* was explicitly an attack on the equilibria assumptions of classic British functionalism. The whole of his analysis of Kachin society is focused on the insurmountable contradictions of its political system, which perpetually veered from a hierarchical to an egalitarian pole, without ever achieving a stabilization at either: the hierarchical model necessarily cancelling kin relations and thereby producing revolt, and the egalitarian model necessarily fostering privileged lineages and thereby reproducing hierarchy. It was no accident that Leach invoked Pareto as his inspiration. In effect, the contradiction with which he was concerned was a cyclical one – the exact type which formed the thematic preoccupation of classical sociology. The criticisms that may be made of it are the same; Leach himself, however, supplies a potential corrective, when he comments on a significant asymmetry in the contradiction – the precondition of the hierarchical model is the generation of a reasonable economic surplus. It was consistent with its general advance of theoretical level that Leach's study firmly integrated the imperial administration *into* the anthropological analysis itself, showing how British colonial ideology had insisted that there was only 'one' model of Kachin society – the hierarchical one – because colonial practice repressed the other as subversive, while deliberately intensifying the autocratic aspects of the former, as the mediate instrument of its control (indirect rule). Here political awareness was the condition of scientific progress.

Leach's subsequent development confirmed this radical start. He was the first British anthropologist to understand the importance of the work of Lévi-Strauss, and to use it aggressively to criticize the methodological procedures of the discipline as a whole (*Rethinking Anthropology*). Most recently, he has been the first to produce an exemplary structural analysis of myth. *The Legitimacy of Solomon*, his study of the Old Testament, is perhaps the most exciting intellectual event of the last few years here. Needles to say, it is virtually unknown and was published abroad.[84] In it, Leach once again centres his whole analysis on an insuperable contradiction – the need for the Jews in Palestine to claim endogamy for the purposes of religious unity, while practising exogamy for the purposes of political alliances. In a superb demonstration, he shows that the Old Testament is the mythical drama whereby this contradiction is transformed into a maze of binary oppositions and formally resolved there. With this, Leach re-establishes the concept of ideology as an imaginary resolution of real contradictions. Both in object and method, his analysis is literally an exercise in iconoclasm. The displacement which was at the origin of British anthropology, freeing it from the general rules of the national culture, has thus born fruit to this day. Both traditional functionalism and the structuralism of Leach's later work are anomalies for English empiricism. Anthropology has formed a deviant sector within English culture, because its application was outside it. The exception here is a corollary of the rule.

Literary Criticism

Suppressed and denied in every other sector of thought, the second, displaced home of the totality became literary criticism. Here, no expatriate influence ever became dominant. Leavis commanded his subject, within his own generation. With him, English literary criticism conceived the ambition to become the vaulting centre of 'humane studies and of the university'. English was 'the chief of the humanities'.[85] This claim was unique to England: no other country has ever produced a critical discipline with these pretensions. They should be seen, not as a reflection of megalomania on the part of Leavis, but as a symptom of the objective vacuum at the centre of the culture. Driven out of any obvious habitats, the notion of the totality found refuge in the least expected of studies. The peculiar status of literary criticism, as conceived by Leavis and his pupils, is itself evidence of the global anomaly of the system. A preliminary definition would be to say that when philosophy became 'technical', a displacement occurred and literary criticism became 'ethical'. The two thereafter stood in a relation of structural complementarity. English philosophy, with Wittgenstein, abandoned ethics and metaphysics, for the neutral investigation of language. English criticism, with Leavis, assumed the responsibilities of moral judgement and metaphysical assertion. A comparison may be relevant here: France has traditionally shown the opposite relationship – a highly technical, hermeneutic criticism (Poulet and Richard) and an ontological and moral philosophy (Sartre). This distribution is the classical one in the West.

Leavis's personal critical achievement, of course, was extraordinary. The rigour and intelligence of his discriminations established entirely new standards: *Revaluations* and *The Great Tradition* alone reconstructed the very order of English poetry and the novel. There is no need here to demonstrate this: the works speak for themselves. As a critic, Leavis is a landmark that has yet to be surpassed.

The paradox of this great critic is that his whole œuvre rested on a metaphysic which he could never expound or defend. Empiricism here found its strangest expression. Leavis, whose work transcended the rut of English philistinism so decisively (and was so hated for it), used its most extreme form to evade open debate of his ideas. His was a metaphysic which refused to justify itself. Wellek, in his famous letter to Leavis in 1937, wrote: 'I could wish that you had stated your assumptions more explicitly and defended them more systematically.' Declaring that he shared most of these assumptions, he went on:

But I would have misgivings in pronouncing them without elaborating a specific defense or a theory in their defense.... I would ask you to defend this position more abstractly and to become conscious that large ethical, philosophical and, of course, ultimately also aesthetic *choices* are involved.[86]

Leavis's reply is a deliberate refusal: 'Ideally, I ought perhaps to be able to complete the works with a theoretical statement' – but in practice, he declined to do so.[87] The critic does not judge by an external philosophical norm, he achieves a complete internal possession of a work and then fits it into his assessment of other works. 'We were empirical and opportunist in spirit', he later wrote.[88] Wellek had pointed out the constancy with which certain key formulations and epithets – 'healthy', 'vital', 'plain vulgar living', 'actual' and others – recurred in Leavis's writings, forming the systematic substructure of his works. The most important, and notorious, of these was the idea of 'life' which was central to Leavis's thought. His book on Lawrence, his most important intellectual statement, exemplifies with particular clarity the logical paradox of an insistent metaphysical vocabulary combined with a positivist methodology.

> *The Daughters of the Vicar*, I say, is profoundly representative of Lawrence, and class-distinctions enter as a major element into its theme.... The part they play in the tale is a sinister one, and the theme is their defeat – the triumph over them of life. It is one of the difficulties of criticism that the critic has to use such phrases as that last. It is one of the advantages of having such a creative achievement as *The Daughters of the Vicar* to deal with that the phrase gets its force in the tale, the movement and sum of which define 'life' in the only way in which it *can* be defined for the purposes of the critic: he has the tale – its developing significance and the concrete particulars of its organization – to point to.[89]

The circularity of the argument is complete. Leavis repeats the same procedure again and again: 'We are made to judge that she has chosen life. The sense in which she has done so it takes the tale to define, and in defining it the tale justifies that way of describing her decision.'[90]

How did Leavis justify this logical circle? The answer is that Leavis's criticism did not contain a very specific epistemology, which in its turn implied a particular interpretation of history. When challenged for the rationale of his critical statements, Leavis always replied that they did not properly speaking have an affirmative but *an interrogative form*. The latent form of all literary criticism was: 'This is so, is it not?' Thus Leavis wrote that his method in *Revaluations* was to get his readers 'to agree (with, no doubt, critical qualifications) that the map, the essential order of English poetry seen as a whole did, when they interrogated their experience, look like that to them also.' [91] The formal circularity of the criticism of a text was the elliptical sign of a substantive exchange between its readers.

The central idea of this epistemology – the interrogative statement – demands one crucial precondition: a shared, stable system of beliefs and values. Without this, no loyal exchange and report is possible. If the basic formation and outlook of readers diverges, their experience will be incommensurable. Leavis's whole method presupposes, in fact, a morally and culturally unified audience. In its absence, his epistemology disintegrates. Hence, doubtless, the enormous nostalgia for the 'organic community' of the past which pervades his work. The illusory nature of this notion – its mythic character – has been often criticized: correctly. But its function within his work has not often been understood. It is not a whimsical ideal, but a validating reference for the actual operation of the criticism. For nothing was less obvious or to be taken for granted in Leavis's day than a stable, shared system of beliefs. Indeed, his very epistemology is the explanation of Leavis's own famous inability to understand or sympathize with *either* avant-garde *or* foreign literature (with a very few exceptions, such as Tolstoy). His complete incomprehension was built into his method: it should not merely be attributed to arbitrary traits of his personality. For once time (avant-garde) and place (country) changed, the cultural basis for a shared interrogation collapsed. Blank prejudice and bafflement were the predictable products of his disorientation before them.

Leavis's epistemology was necessarily accompanied by a philosophy of history. The organic community of the past, when there was no division between popular and sophisticated culture, died with the Augustan age: Bunyan was among its last witnesses. Thereafter, history for Leavis traced a gradual decline. The industrial revolution finally swamped the old rural culture. But it did not initially undermine the existence of a cultivated and elite minority, the creators of literary culture. The nineteenth century produced such romantic poets as Keats or Coleridge, and the great tradition of the English novel – Eliot, Conrad and James. With the twentieth century, however, the inexorable tide of industrialism began to invade the very precincts of humane culture itself. Leavis saw the new media of communication – newspapers, magazines, radio, cinema and television – as the menacing apogee of commercialism and industrial civilization. They threatened to obliterate every critical standard, on which the existence of culture depended, in a new barbarism. The duty of the literary critic was to fight uncompromisingly and unceasingly against any dilution or degeneration of these standards. Defying every convention of the British intelligentsia, Leavis lent a violent zeal and fury to his role.

The pages of *Scrutiny* are pervaded by an immense pessimism: a sense of inexorable cultural atrophy, and of a dwindling minority aware of it. This is the memorable and unifying theme of the review. Article after article laments an increasing deturpation of literary standards and a triumph of the meretricious. Leavis became obsessed with the commercialism of the new media and the corruption of the metropolitan world of letters. His commination of them became more strident with every year. *Scrutiny* never paused in its campaign against them. But this was only one of its two central ideological concerns. The other was anti-Marxism. Leavis is the only intellectual in this survey to have been deeply affected by Marxism. This will appear a paradoxical statement to those who only know his latter-day reputation. But the fact is that *Scrutiny* was born in close relation to Marxism – its predecessor, *The Calendar of Letters*, was edited by a Communist – and it developed in a permanent tension with it thereafter. Leavis wrote in its first year: 'I agree with the Marxist to the extent of believing some form of economic communism to be inevitable and desirable.' [92] Antagonism rapidly grew after this, when the metropolitan literary world was suddenly seized with radicalism; Marxism became fashionable among young writers, although many of them were only remotely acquainted with it. This wave has already been discussed. The point here is that it became the intellectual pole against which *Scrutiny* defined itself. Leavis and his colleagues constantly attacked the illiteracy and shallowness of this vulgar leftism. In doing so, they had no difficulty in establishing their superiority over it: the intellectual disparity between a Leavis and an Auden was, after all, self-evident. By the end of the decade, modish literary leftism had virtually disappeared. In *Scrutiny*, Leavis wrote its obituary: 'Marxist the decade certainly was. It was also, in literature, a very barren decade.' [93]

The rout of this opponent did not alleviate Leavis's general cultural diagnosis. If anything, his forebodings deepened after the Second World War. Leavis saw himself as the spokesman of traditional humane values, a critic determined to safeguard the great heritage of English literary culture and the classical English university. Yet he himself was rejected by the very institutions which he exalted. Cambridge, model of his idea of a university, rejected and ignored him. Isolated in this hostile environment, *Scrutiny* finally drifted to a halt in the fifties. The retrospect that Leavis wrote ten years later is an extraordinary document. In it, Leavis defines his relations both to Marxism and to Cambridge.

We were anti-Marxist – necessarily so (we thought); an intelligent, that is a real, interest in literature implied a conception of it very different from any that a Marxist could expound and explain. Literature – what we knew as literature and had studied for the English Tripos – mattered; it mattered crucially to civilization – of that we were sure. It mattered because it represented a human reality, an autonomy of the human spirit, for which economic determinism and reductive interpretation in terms of the class war left no room. Marxist fashion gave us the doctrinal challenge. But Marxism was a characteristic product of our 'capitalist' civilization, and the economic determinism we were committed to refuting practically was that which might seem to have been demonstrated by the movement and process of this. The dialectic against which we had to vindicate literature and humane culture was that of the external or material civilization we lived in. 'External' and 'material' here need not be defined: they convey well enough the insistence that our total civilization is a very complex thing, with a kind of complexity to which Marxist categories are not adequate.

Cambridge, then, figured for us civilization's anti-Marxist recognition of its own nature and needs – recognition of that, the essential, which Marxist wisdom discredited, and the external and material drive of civilization threatened, undoctrinally, to eliminate. It was our strength to be, in our consciousness of our effort, and actually, in the paradoxical and ironical way I have to record, representatives of that Cambridge. We *were*, in fact, that Cambridge; we felt it, and had more and more reason to feel it, and our confidence and courage came from that. . . . Only at Cambridge could the idea of *Scrutiny* have taken shape, become a formidable life and maintained the continuous living force that made it hated and effective. It was (to deepen the emphasis) a product, the triumphant justifying achievement, of the English Tripos. I express, and intend to encourage, no simple parochial enthusiasm or loyalty in dwelling on these truths. I had better, in fact, add at once the further testimony that *Scrutiny* started, established itself and survived in spite of Cambridge.[94]

This astonishing passage contains the core of Leavis's intellectual position: it is a precise, binary exposition of its structure. Marxism is the 'doctrinal challenge'. It is rejected because it partakes of the very society which it claims to condemn: it is materialist and therefore a 'characteristic product of capitalist civilization'. Against it, Leavis proclaims 'literature and humane culture' which are essential to 'civilization', but which are factually negated by its 'external and material drive'. The essence of civilization becomes inner and spiritual. It is represented supremely by Cambridge, and Cambridge is represented supremely – indeed coincided with – *Scrutiny*. 'We were Cambridge.' But the actual Cambridge – inner and spiritual essence of civilization – negated *Scrutiny*, which only survived 'in spite of Cambridge'. Reality becomes completely volatilized in this multiple regression towards the ideal. The logical structure of the argument reveals the intolerable strain that Leavis's concrete experience imposed on his preconception. It becomes a vertiginous spiral of antinomies, in which the flight from one merely produces another which in turn reproduces another. Marxism seems to be a critique of capitalist civilization; in fact it is merely an exemplification of it. This civilization seems to confirm economic determinism; in fact, only its external and material drive does, not its spiritual essence. The inner spirit of civilization seems to be exemplified in Cambridge, and Cambridge in

Scrutiny; in fact Cambridge systematically rejected *Scrutiny*, which was created against it.

What was the meaning of this desperate and impossible syllogism? It was, obviously, not a mere error. It was the manifest sign of genuine impasse in Leavis's thought. Alone of the thinkers in this survey, he was acutely aware that something had gone wrong in British culture. Indeed, this idea obsessed him. *Scrutiny* is the record of a 'barren decade'. But he was unable to explain the decline he denounced. The fate of culture was attributed to the drive of 'mass' civilization and its corrupt accompaniment by modish literati. Against these enemies, Leavis posed older ideals – Cambridge: but Cambridge itself was complicit with them. Hence the fixation on trivial targets which gradually took such disproportionate space in his work – the British Council, *The Times Literary Supplement*, Bloomsbury, the fashionable literary world and so on. They were the aberrant symptoms of his failure to locate the true causes of the decline. Intellectually blocked, his insight became a displaced acrimony and monomania. Leavis was correctly indicting a cultural landscape of rank mediocrity and conformity. But this was not the inevitable product of industrial civilization, nor even of capitalism as a generic form of society. It had its intelligible origins in the specific history of English social structure and the class which dominated it. It was no accident that the very sanctum into which Leavis retreated refused him. For the unity of British culture naturally included it: Bloomsbury and Cambridge were not antipodes but twins (Forster, Strachey and Keynes were the proof of it). But Leavis's critical epistemology demanded the postulation of an authentic cultural community somewhere: hence the delirious idealism of his insistence on a meta-Cambridge.

Lacking any sociological formation, registering a decline but unable to provide a theory of it, Leavis was ultimately trapped in the cultural nexus he hated. His empiricism became banally reactionary in old age. Like many thinkers, he survived himself to his detriment. But the importance of his achievements remains. It is no accident that in the fifties, the one serious work of socialist theory in Britain – Raymond Williams's *The Long Revolution* – should have emerged from literary criticism, of all disciplines.[95] This paradox was not a mere quirk: in a culture which everywhere repressed the notion of totality, and the idea of critical reason, literary criticism represented a refuge. The mystified form they took in Leavis's work, which prevented him ever finding answers to his questions, may be obvious today. But it was from within this tradition that Williams was able to develop a systematic socialist thought, which was a critique of all forms of utilitarianism and Fabianism – the political avatars of empiricism in the labour movement. The detour Williams had to make through English literary criticism is the appropriate tribute to it.

Summary

The results of this survey may now be briefly summed up. The culture of British bourgeois society is organized about an absent centre – a total theory of itself, that should have been either a classical sociology or a national Marxism. The trajectory of English social structure – above all, the non-emergence of a powerful revolutionary movement of the working class – is the explanation of this arrested development. Two anomalous results followed, the visible index of a vacuum. A White emigration rolled across the flat expanse of English intellectual life, capturing sector after sector, until this traditionally insular culture became dominated by expatriates, of heterogeneous calibre. Simultaneously, the absence of a centre produced a series of structural distortions in the character and connexions of the inherited disciplines. Philosophy was restricted to a technical inventory of language. Political theory was thereby cut off from history. History was divorced from the exploration of political ideas. Psychology was counterposed to them. Economics was dissociated from both political theory and history. Aesthetics was reduced to psychology. The congruence of each sector with its neighbour is circular: together they form something like a closed system. The quarantine of psychoanalysis is an example: it was incompatible with this pattern. Suppressed in every obvious sector at home, the idea of the totality was painlessly exported abroad, producing the paradox of an anthropology where there was no sociology. In the general vacuum thus created, literary criticism usurps ethics and insinuates a philosophy of history. It was logical that it should finally be the one sector capable of producing a synthetic socialist theory.

The void at the centre of this culture generated a pseudo-centre – the timeless ego whose metempsychosis in discipline after discipline has been encountered in this survey. The price of missing sociology, let alone Marxism, was the prevalence of psychologism. A culture which lacks the instruments to conceive the social totality inevitably falls back on the nuclear psyche, as First Cause of society and history. This invariant substitute is explicit in Malinowski, Namier, Eysenck and Gombrich. It has a logical consequence. Time exists only as intermittence (Keynes), decline (Leavis) or oblivion (Wittgenstein). Ultimately (Namier, Leavis or Gombrich), the twentieth century itself becomes the impossible object. The era of revolutions is, necessarily, unthinkable.

The consequences of this total constellation for the Left need no emphasis. The chloroforming effects of such cultural configuration, its silent and constant underpinning of the social *status quo*, are deadly. British culture, as it is now constituted, is a deeply damaging and stifling force, operating against the growth of any revolutionary Left. It quite literally deprives the Left of any source of concepts and categories with which to analyse its own society, and thereby attain the fundamental precondition for changing it. History has tied this knot; only history will ultimately undo it. A revolutionary culture is not for tomorrow. But a revolutionary practice within culture is possible and necessary today. The student struggle is its initial form.

REFERENCES

1. 'Problèmes Etudiants', *La Nouvelle Critique* 152, January 1964, pp. 167–77.
2. In recent years a number of radical critiques of different intellectual disciplines have appeared, one after the other: Gellner's *Words and Things*, Carr's *What is History?*, Robinson's *Economic Philosophy* and Leach's *Rethinking Anthropology*. All of these express an awareness of stagnation, and make effective criticisms of existing orthodoxy. But they are all – strikingly – written from the standpoint of a consequent liberalism; they were not produced by the Left. The result is that they have never aggregated into a cumulative attack on contemporary British culture, and hence have never had their proper impact: discreet criticisms may be ignored or absorbed.

3. *Le Nouvel Observateur* 115, 25 January 1967.

4. *The Structure of Social Action*, New York, 1964, pp. 167–77.

5. The essential texts for this history are Parson's *The Structure of Social Action* and his important recent essay 'Unity and Diversity in the Modern Intellectual Disciplines: The Role of the Social Sciences', in *Sociological Theory and Modern Society*, New York, 1967.

6. 'Contradiction and Overdetermination', *New Left Review* 41. Allen Lane, The Penguin Press will shortly be publishing a translation of Althusser's collection of essays, *Pour Marx*.

7. There are only two moments in English cultural history when a collective defection threatened to create a dissident intelligentsia. Both were snapped off before they had time to develop. The precursor of the thirties was the nineties of the last century, when Bohemianism as a social phenomenon finally emerged in England – sixty years after its advent, celebrated by Balzac, in Paris. Art Nouveau and the aesthetic socialism of Wilde were its product. Events were as ruthless with this revolt as with its successor. There was one hammer-blow after another. 1895: Wilde's trial. 1898: Beardsley's death. June 1899: Catastrophe of Mac-Kintosh's Exhibition. October 1899: Boer War. The torrent of conformity and chauvinism after Mafeking finally submerged the memory of the nineties, just as the Molotov–Ribbentrop Pact eclipsed the thirties.

8. For samples, *Communism and British Intellectuals*, Neal Wood, London, 1959 pp. 108–13 and 138–44. The only existent essay which does justice to the politico-intellectual context of the decade is Alexander Cockburn's 'To and from the Frontier', *The Review* 16.

9. The very end of the decade germinated a group of historians, of which the most prominent at the time was Christopher Hill, who thirty years later were to produce what the thirties so completely lacked – a serious, scientific intellectual achievement. Condemnations of the Left in the thirties today tend to forget this. The complexity of the period is much greater than the standard accounts allow. A symbol: when all was lost, by 1940, two undergraduates at Cambridge were collaborating on a pamphlet defending the Russian invasion of Finland: Eric Hobsbawm and Raymond Williams.

10. For a much lengthier discussion of this history, see Tom Nairn 'The British Political Elite', *New Left Revew* 23 and Perry Anderson 'Origins of the Present Crisis', *New Left Review* 23 and 'Socialism and Pseudo-Empiricism', *New Left Review* 35.

11. A century later, H. B. Acton – editor of *Philosophy*, journal of the Royal Philosophical Society – celebrated its instinct with these revealing words: It is not without interest, perhaps, in this connection to mention that in 1857, two years before Marx published his *Critique of Political Economy*, a body was founded known as the National Association for the Promotion of Social Science. . . . The sort of topics discussed in each section may be seen from the following examples, one from each section, taken from the first Volume of the Transactions: Judicial Statistics; An Inquiry on Early Withdrawal from School in Swansea

and its Neighbourhood; Crime and Density of Population; Houses for Working Men – their Arrangement, Drainage and Ventilation; the Early Closing Movement.... The notions employed are seldom so general as 'society', 'capitalism', 'revolution', etc, but are rather of the relative particularity of 'convictions', 'sentences', 'bankruptcies', 'adulteration of food', 'drainage' and 'penny banks'. ... This would seem to be the sort of approach to social science that is most likely to ensure that its exponents know what they are talking about. *The Illusion of an Epoch*, London, 1962, pp. 185–6.

12. For the purposes of definition: a totality is an entity whose diverse structures are bound together in such a way that any one of them considered separately is an abstraction. It is not an aggregated sum of parts.

13. *The Politics of Conscience*, Melvin Richter, London, 1964, p. 36 and passim.

14. 'The Intellectual Aristocracy', in *Studies in Social History, A Tribute to G. M. Trevelyan* edited by J. H. Plumb, London, 1955, p. 285.

15. The historical reasons for this peculiar phenomenon are complex and over-determined. I have discussed them elsewhere, in *Origins of the Present Crisis*. Two early determinants may be mentioned here. Hexter's famous essay 'The Education of the Aristocracy in the Renaissance' (*Reappraisals in History*, London, 1961) shows how the aristocracy captured public schools and universities in the sixteenth century, preventing the development of a separate clerisy within them. Equally important was the absence of Roman Law in England, which blocked the growth of an intelligentsia based on legal faculties of the universities in the medieval period. On the Continent, the law schools of such centres as Bologna and Paris, which taught the abstract principles of jurisprudence, made an important contribution to the emergence of a separate intellectual group; whereas in England legal training was controlled by the guild of practising lawyers and was based on the accumulation of precedent. Weber's discussion of this contrast is excellent. He writes of the concepts of English law: 'They are not "general concepts" which would be formed by abstraction from concreteness or by logical interpretation of meaning or by generalization and subsumption; nor were these concepts apt to be used in syllogistically applicable norms. In the purely empirical conduct of (English) legal practice and legal training one always moves from the particular to the particular but never tries to move from the particular to general propositions in order to be able subsequently to deduce from them the norms for new particular cases. ... No rational legal training or theory can ever arise in such a situation.' (*Law in Economy and Society*, Cambridge, USA, 1954, p. 202.) The ulterior consequences of this system are evident. Ben Brewster has pointed out that the Scottish Enlightenment – so unlike anything south of the border – may by contrast be traced to the tradition of Roman Law north of the border. (*Cambridge Forward* 40.)

16. ibid.

17. Roy Harrod, *The Life of John Maynard Keynes*, London, 1951, pp. 2–3.

18. Some dates: Klein was born 1882 in Vienna. Malinowski 1884 in Kraków. Namier 1888 near Lvov. Wittgenstein 1889 in Vienna. Popper 1902 in Vienna. Deutscher 1907 near Kraków. Berlin 1909 in Riga. Gombrich 1909 in Vienna. Eysenck 1916 in Berlin.

19. Adorno spent two years in Oxford working on Husserl, unnoticed, before he went to America. A number of the greatest names in modern art spent a similar brief and obscure sojourn here before crossing the Atlantic to a more hospitable environment: Mondrian, Gropius, Moholy-Nagy and others.

20. *Vanished Supremacies*, London, 1962, p. 26.

21. *England in the Age of the American Revolution*, London, 1961, p. 13.

22. *Personalities and Powers*, London, 1955, p. 5.

23. 'The Pathology of English History', *New Left Review* 46.

24. Popper had foreseen this possibility already in the early Wittgenstein, and had taken alarm at it: 'Wittgenstein's method leads to a merely verbal solution and must give rise, in spite of its apparent radicalism, not to the destruction or to the exclusion or even to the clear demarcation of metaphysics, but to their intrusion into the field of science, and to their confusion with science.' *The Open Society and Its Enemies* Vol. II, pp. 296–9.

25. Norman Malcolm, *Ludwig Wittgenstein: A Memoir*, London, 1958, pp. 36 and 58.

26. *Philosophical Investigations*, Oxford, 1953, p. 49.

27. *Proceedings of the Aristotelian Society 1956–7*, p. 8.

28. *Words and Things*, London, 1959, pp. 241–2. All critics of English philosophy owe a great debt to Gellner's classic. It is significant that it has never been answered by linguistic orthodoxy, and so panicked its official representatives that discussion of it was forbidden in *Mind*. Linguistic philosophy wrote its own sociology, in this episode. Gellner has advanced the idea in a later essay that linguistic philosophy must be seen partly as a displaced reaction to the successes of the natural sciences, which have threatened the traditional role of the discipline ('The Crisis in the Humanities and the Mainstream of Philosophy' in *Crisis in the Humanities*, ed. J. H. Plumb, London, 1964). This explanation lacks any international perspective, however: linguistic philosophy is a phenomenon of the Anglo-Saxon world, but the successes of the natural sciences are universal. Gellner's most recent contribution is a demolition of the parasitic creepers from linguistic philosophy onto the socal sciences – 'Enter The Philosophers', *Times Literary Supplement*, 4 April 1968.

29. Paul Engelmann, *Letters from Ludwig Wittgenstein with a Memoir*, Oxford, 1967, p. 121.

30. David Pole's lucid book on *The Later Philosophy of Wittgenstein* (London, 1958) makes the same criticism as that developed here: 'It is clearly possible to change existing linguistic practice; and one can sensibly claim that the innovation is better than the accepted form. Wittgenstein's

account seems to allow no appeal beyond existing practice, and we must ask how it is to accommodate this possibility I speak of. Ultimately, I believe, it cannot; it splits, I shall maintain on this rock. . . . (Wittgenstein) has explicitly laid it down that our ordinary expressions are "in order as they are", and has forbidden philosophers to tamper with them But the difficulty goes deeper. His own system makes no provision for the adoption of any new way of speaking in conflict with existing practice.' (p. 57). Pole's own thesis is centred on the notion that it is rational argument and agreement that produces new forms of language. This is an evidently idealistic solution. Who decides what is 'rational'? Pole's formulation virtually admits its own deficiencies : 'The essence of rational discourse is the search for agreement. Wittgenstein's failure to take account of it, I suggest, prejudices his whole picture of language. . . . Clearly to call a statement rational is not to assert that all men ever will, or even might, agree about it; for some are always too stupid or too prejudiced. It is to assert, we may tautologously say, that all men would agree, supposing they were rational.' (p. 59). The naïve psychologism of 'some are always too stupid or too prejudiced' is not an aberration : it is representative of contemporary English philosophy. So much for the epoch-making turmoil of the Renaissance, the Reformation or the Enlightenment! The obvious fact is that important conceptual disputes have nothing to do with psychological differences – they are grounded in the given structure of knowledge at any moment of time and in social conflicts.

31. *Two Concepts of Liberty*, Oxford, 1958, p. 4.
32. ibid.
33. ibid. p. 52.
34. ibid. p. 56.
35. *The Open Society and its Enemies*, London, 1952, Vol. II p. 80.
36. *The Poverty of Historicism*, London, 1957, p. 3.
37. See 'Technology and Social Relations', Georg Lukacs, *New Left Review* 39.
38. *The Open Society and its Enemies* Vol. II pp. 27–80.
39. ibid. p. 79.
40. 'The Hegel Myth and its Method' in *The Owl and the Nightingale*, Walter Kaufmann, London, 1959.
41. 'Post-Liberal Democracy?', C. B. MacPherson, *Canadian Journal of Political Science*, October 1964.
42. *Vanished Supremacies* p. 49.
43. *England in the Age of the American Revolution* p. 39.
44. *Vanished Supremacies* p. 28.
45. *Germany and Eastern Europe*, London, 1915, p. 128.
46. It is odd that there has been so little awareness of the central role of this concept in Namier's historical thought. His whole work is articulated on it.
47. *Vanished Supremacies*, p. 79.
48. ibid., p. 209.

49. *Personalities and Powers*, p. 4.

50. *Vanished Supremacies*, p. 203.

51. *England in the Age of the American Revolution*, p. 41.

52. *Renaissance, Reformation and Social Change*, London, 1967 (the two initial essays).

53. *The General Theory of Employment, Money and Interest*, London, 1964, pp. vi–vii.

54. 'An Essay in Dynamic Theory', *Economic Journal*, March 1939. The role of technique is implicit, not explicit in Harrod's formula. It is assumed to check the diminishing rate of return on investment, and thereby render output per unit of capital constant. The ostensible focus of Harrod's essay is propensity to save, but variations of this are not explained within the model. Hence the determinant role effectively reverts to technique, which is taken as autonomous.

55. *Causes of the Slow Rate of Economic Growth of the United Kingdom*, Cambridge, 1966. Kaldor explicitly discounts such other causal factors as the balance of payments or the rate of investment (pp. 16 and 25). The idea of an overdetermined crisis has evidently not occurred to him. It is perhaps not surprising that the one reasonably comprehensive and cogent account of the crisis has been produced by an economic historian, not an economist – Eric Hobsbawm's *Industry and Empire*.

56. 'My Early Beliefs', in *Two Memoirs*, London, 1949.

57. Keynes was very conscious of his sociological ancestry. He wrote in *Essays in Biography*: 'I have sought ... to bring out the solidarity and historical continuity of the High Intelligentsia of England, who have built up the foundations of our thought in the two and a half centuries since Locke, in his Essay Concerning Human Understanding, wrote the first modern English book.' p. viii.

58. *Essays in Biography*, London, 1933, p. 170.

59. *The Psychology of Politics*, London, 1954, pp. 9–10.

60. 'Eysenck's Treatment of the Personality of Communists', Richard Christie, in *Psychological Bulletin* Vol. 53, November 1956, p. 425.

61. 'Eysenck's Tender-Mindedness Dimension: A Critique', Milton Rokeach and Charles Hanley, in *Psychological Bulletin* Vol. 53, November 1956, p. 175.

62. Christie, 'Some Abuses of Psychology', in *Psychological Bulletin*, Vol. 53, November 1956, p. 450.

63. There is a parallel with Kaufmann's exposure of Popper here. In both cases, these standards of scholarship were never challenged within England, because of the fit between their authors and the culture. Eventually, foreigners of orthodox liberal persuasion were obliged to attack the fact, but no general self-criticism or reappraisal followed in Britain.

64. *The Story of Art*, London, 1950, p. 433.

65. 'Art and Scholarship', in *Meditations on a Hobby-Horse and other essays on the theory of art*, London, 1963, pp. 117–18.

66. ibid., p. 118.

67. ibid., pp. 117 and 119.

68. *Meditations on a Hobby-Horse*, p. 43.

69. Thus Panofsky wrote: 'The art historian will have to check what he thinks is the intrinsic meaning of the work, or group of works, to which he devotes his attention, against what he thinks is the intrinsic meaning of as many other documents of civilization historically related to that work or group of works, as he can master: of documents bearing witness to the political, poetical, religious, philosophical and social tendencies of the personality, period or country under investigation.' *Meaning in the Visual Arts*, New York, 1955, p. 39. It is no accident that his discussion of the Egyptian–Greek contrast mentioned above is incomparably more illuminating than Gombrich's. See 'The History of the Theory of Human Proportions as a Reflection of the History of Styles' in *Meaning in the Visual Arts*. Panofsky's recent death passed virtually unnoticed in Britain.

70. 'Examination of the Klein System of Child Psychology', Edward Glover, in *The Psychoanalytic Study of the Child*, Vol. 1, London, 1945, and the references there to the discussion of 1943–4.

71. 'Freud et Lacan', *La Nouvelle Critique* 161–2, December–January 1964–5, p. 107.

72. Equally it undermines the possibility of certain forms of literature. The novel has declined as a coherent genre, not – as is often alleged – because it was the product of the rising bourgeoisie of the nineteenth century and could not survive it. The true reason is that it has disappeared into the abyss between everyday language and the technical discourses inaugurated by Marx and Freud. The sum of objective knowledge within the specialized codes of the human sciences has decisively contradicted and surpassed the normal assumptions behind exoteric speech. The result is that a novelist, after Marx and Freud, has either to simulate an arcadian innocence or transfer elements of their discourse immediately into his work. Hence the now entrenched bifurcation between pseudo-traditional and experimental novels. Both are doomed as genres (which does not exclude individual successes). The ingenuousness of the former is always bad faith; the past will never be recreated. The opposite solution – the inclusion of frontier concepts from Freud or Marx within the novel – has no viable outcome either. Ideas cannot be transposed into an art without mediation. The missing mediation is – precisely, ordinary language. As long as this is untransformed at base, these concepts remain 'technical' and 'esoteric'. They run against the grain of spontaneous speech. Hence they are strictly *unusable* for the artist. If they are imported into the novel, they crush it: there have been no successful psychoanalytic tales. The novelist can only forge his art from the material of ordinary language. If there is a radical discordance between this and objective knowledge of man and society, the novel ceases. It has no ground between the naïve and the arcane. The gap will only be closed by the reintegration of revolutionary ideas into unreflective linguistic practice, which would make possible a coherent novel once again. Such a change, of course, presupposes a changed society. The point here is that the problem from which linguistic philosophy is in constant

flight is solidly and visibly installed across the destiny of literature: the birth of new concepts.

73. Feyerabend has commented aptly on this notion: 'The firmness, the solidity, the regularity of usages are a function of the firmness of the beliefs held as well as of the needs that these beliefs satisfy: what is regarded linguistically as the "firm ground of language" and is thus opposed to all speculation is usually that part of one's language that is closest to the most basic ideology of the time and expresses it most adequately. *That part will then be regarded as being of great practical importance.*' 'Problems of Empiricism', p. 188, in *Beyond the Edge of Certainty*, ed. Robert Colodny, USA, 1965.

74. *Proceedings of the Aristotelian Society 1956/1957*, p. 15.

75. ibid., pp. 11 and 30.

76. 'Philosophy, Metaphysics and Psychoanalysis', in *Philosophy and Psychoanalysis*, Oxford, 1957.

77. 'Disposition and Memory', *International Journal of Psychoanalysis*, January–February 1962.

78. ibid.

79. ibid.

80. *Ideology and Society: Papers in sociology and politics*, London, 1961, pp. 36 and 9.

81. *The Nuer*, Oxford, 1940, p. 131.

82. *Social Structure: Essays presented to A. R. Radcliffe-Brown*, ed. Meyer Fortes, Oxford, 1949: 'American Military Government', John Embree, p. 220.

83. *Man and Culture*, ed. Raymond Firth, London, 1957: 'Malinowski and the Theory of Social Systems', Talcott Parsons.

84. *Archives Européennes de Sociologie* 1966, No. 7.

85. *Education and the University*, London, 1943, p. 33.

86. 'Literary Criticism and Philosophy', René Wellek, *Scrutiny*, March 1937, p. 376.

87. 'Literary Criticism and Philosophy – A Reply', F. R. Leavis, *Scrutiny*, June 1937, p. 62.

88. *Scrutiny: A Retrospect*, p. 4, Vol. XX, Cambridge, 1963.

89. *D. H. Lawrence: Novelist*, London, 1955, pp. 75–6.

90. ibid, p. 93.

91. 'Literary Criticism and Philosophy – A Reply', p. 62.

92. *Scrutiny*, March 1933, p. 320.

93. 'Retrospect of a Decade', *Scrutiny*, June 1940.

94. *Scrutiny: A Retrospect*, p. 4.

95. The influence of Leavis is discernible in its idealism – corrected in some of Williams's later work. Leavis believed that: 'To say that the life of a country is determined by its educational ideals is a commonplace.' *Scrutiny* No. 1, May 1932.

International Experience

Students of the World Unite/Fred Halliday

International Struggles: International Lessons

In recent years the world has seen a wave of student insurgency in which students have taken radical action in many countries. But this international picture of student revolt is a complex one; any naïve attempt to apply the experiences of one area to that of another can only lead to confusion. Even so, a brief and selective survey of student struggles across the world can illustrate unrealized possibilities and systematize the separate accounts that have been given of these movements.

My method will be to select certain examples which illustrate different features of the student revolution, and which are relevant to the potential development of student action in this country. Each of the sections attempts to do two things: to situate the student struggles in the specific conditions of the area where they take place, and then to see what contribution each example can make to a general theory of student movements.

The Latin American students, who are considered first, claim a special pre-eminence in any account of student action. The Cordoba Manifesto[1] of 1918 was the first declaration of student rights; and since that time Latin American students have played a constantly militant role in the politics of their nations. The Latin American experience suggests that academic demands and more general political activity are complementary rather than competitive.

The Chinese experience shows an attempt at radical democratization of the university and represents a totally different type of student movement, one in a socialist society playing an insurgent role in alliance with other groups. Japan was the first major capitalist country to experience a militant student movement and its record is therefore of great relevance. The Spanish student movement is the only one in Europe to have achieved a substantial degree of organizational cooperation with the militant proletariat. The movements in Germany, France and Italy are of special importance for British students because they are advanced capitalist countries, geographically and socially close to Britain. The crucial lessons of the American student movement are explored elsewhere in this volume.[2]

This selection of examples leaves out much. It is a-historical: there have been militant student movements throughout history. In Muslim societies theology students have often been a disruptive political force; and in post-Napoleonic Europe students were the main exponents of the new liberalism. In Russia students were extremely active as Narodniks and Marxists under the Tsars. But although these experiences were historically important, this survey is about the contemporary wave of student action and its immediate historical roots. The student movement has developed and radicalized itself in the 1950s and 1960s. Discussions of NUSAS in South Africa, of the Salisbury students in Rhodesia, of UNEM in Morocco, the Persian and Indian students, and the Eastern Europeans in 1967 and 1968 have been reluctantly omitted because they require lengthier treatment than can be given here.

Latin America: From the Cordoba Manifesto to Guerrilla War

Both in education and in politics, Latin American students have traditionally been extremely active. The causes of this militancy lie partly in the history of the university reform movement and partly in the political and social structure of these countries. The Latin American movement for university reform grew out of the Cordoba Manifesto of 1918, when the students of Cordoba in Argentina presented a manifesto demanding university autonomy and a student share in university administration – *cogobierno*. The manifesto denounced the old administration in which 'there was no reform of curricula, and no reform of rules, for fear that someone might lose his job because of the changes', and it announced: 'we want to eradicate from university organization the archaic and barbarous concept of authority which in the university is a bulwark of absurd tyranny'. The manifesto also declared its complete confidence in the ability of students to run their own affairs, and its opposition to traditional academic corruption: 'To youth adulation of bribery is not equivalent to merit. It must elect its teachers and directors for itself.'

In addition to the demands of the Cordoba Manifesto a subsequent meeting of the Argentinian students' union made eight further demands which were considered as central to the reform movement: optional attendance, abolition of religious restrictions on what could be taught and who could be appointed to university posts, financial assistance to students, social orientation to the university [3] and a democratic system of university organization.

This programme of reform constituted a total break with the conservative view of university life in which the university had autonomy of an authoritarian sort. For the reform movement 'autonomy' meant not what it means to Oxbridge today – the independence of university authorities from government control – but the ability of students to share university power and for the whole academic community to be independent of the government. Since many Latin American universities were situated on a campus this demand for autonomy also took the form of a demand for physical immunity for the university area.

The demands of the Argentinian students spread throughout Latin America in the next twenty years. In Peru they were made in 1919, in Chile in 1920; in Colombia in 1924; in Paraguay in 1927; in Brazil and Bolivia in 1928; in Mexico in 1929; and in Costa Rica in the 1930s. Varying success – sometimes partial agreement, sometimes later revocation – greeted these moves. One of the most stirring epics has been that of the Venezuelan students: from the overthrow of the hated dictator Perez Jimenez in 1958, to December 1966, the campus enjoyed physical inviolability from police and troops, and the students exercised *cogobierno* in the nomination of their teachers. Finally troops invaded the campus during the conservative government's campaign against the Venezuelan liberation movement. A signal victory for the Peruvian students came when, after forty-one years of struggle, a law was passed giving them the right to dismiss their professors by majority vote. In the University of Lima and Cuzco the students now have equal rights with their professors in appointments and other administrative matters.

A similar situation prevailed in Argentina until the Ongania coup of 28 June 1966. Till then the universities were physically immune, and there was a system of tripartite power on the faculty bodies whereby students, graduates and professors had equal share in decisions. This represented a genuine realization of the ideals of the Cordoba Manifesto spread over the nine national universities of Argentina, the largest of which, the University of Buenos Aires, had 81,000 students. On 29 July 1966 the Ongania regime issued a decree abolishing the old system of university autonomy and gave the Ministry of Education all power in university administration. On the same night students and professors met on the campus of Buenos Aires to protest against this repression. Their meeting was broken up by armed police, aided by Fascist thugs of the Tacuara who invaded the campus. The rector of the university, Hilario Frenadez Long, resigned along with the heads of all ten faculties. Many arrests were made. Two days later all nine national universities were closed and before Buenos Aires reopened in August the student union was dissolved. Ongania packed the university with his own nominees, but riots broke out again when the university finally reopened. Seven and a half thousand students clashed with the police in Cordoba and finally three weeks later 100,000 Argentinian students took part in a 'day of resistance and struggle' in protest against the Ongania dictatorship.

In Mexico students have some power and autonomy. Federal law bans police from the campus and the university has its own radio station. However, there is no *cogobierno*, no economic aid to students and no interdiction against students being expelled without a hearing. In April 1966 students resisted the authoritarian policies of the Dean, Cesar Sepulveda, and a strike by 7,000 law students soon brought out all 70,000 students at the National University. They occupied buildings on the campus and forced the rector to resign.[4]

These examples show how Latin American students have made the demands of the Cordoba movement their own though achievement of them has been patchy. Perhaps the most general success has been in having the campus area banned from the police. Because of the political role students play in Latin America, they have often become the target of conservative attack. Occasionally it has even been alleged that joint control has been detrimental to academic standards. There is no evidence of this. The most distinguished universities on the continent have flourished under *cogobierno* since the beginning. Alastair Hennessy, in a recent Chatham House symposium, points out that: 'The acceptance of the university reform in Argentina after its incorporation in the University Law of 1919 ... led to the golden age of Argentine universities.'[5]

Student invitations have often been instrumental in persuading the continent's most distinguished intellectuals to enter the university. However it is undeniable that political preoccupations have sometimes displaced attention from study. This is very understandable in a continent cursed with military dictatorships, foreign domination, illiteracy, curable disease, hunger, police thuggery and government corruption. The main opposition to the Cordoba movement has therefore been political, with conservative forces opposing student intervention in politics. Here is a selection of recent actions to illustrate the scope of this militancy, heightened by internal social contradictions in the various countries, by the growth of external conflict with the United States, and by the insurgency of workers and peasants in those countries:

Bolivia

In October 1964 students rioted against the government of Paz Estensorso in Cochabamba, the second city of Bolivia. Troops fired on them: 600 armed students then occupied the university of La Paz: they were finally displaced by the intervention of the Papal Nuncio, Monsignor Kennedy. The Bolivian students have also made considerable progress in forming a revolutionary alliance with workers. In the mining town of Oruro the students of the technical university and the local miners signed a joint action pact. Under it the students promised to come out when the miners went on strike and support them with money and clothing: conversely the miners agreed to strike in support of all student demands and to march into the town with their weapons to give them material asistance.

Panama

On 9 January 1964 rioting Panamanian students invaded the American-occupied Canal Zone in reply to provocation by American residents in the Zone. The students' federation demanded the nationalization of the canal and the total dismantling of bases in the Zone.[6] The Panamanian government broke off relations with the US: but a compromise treaty in 1967 still left student demands unsatisfied, since a new system of joint US–Panamanian ownership of the canal was announced.

Peru

US Vice-President Nixon was prevented by thousands of students from visiting the University of San Marcos in Lima in September 1958. Between 1961 and 1966 students at the university of Cuzco, many of them from the surrounding area, organized peasant unions to expropriate land and played an important role in the 1965 peasant struggle in Peru.[7]

Venezuela

After growing public discontent, in December 1957 Caracas students rioted continuously against the Perez Jimenez dictatorship from 14 to 17 January 1958 and clashed with the secret police, the Seguridad Nacional. On 21 January the Venezuelan Students' Front called on all students to strike 'from kindergartens to universities'. Popular riots followed in Caracas and Jimenez fled two days later. On the same day students tore up the barbed wire that had surrounced the university and declared their autonomy. When Nixon visited Caracas on 13 September he was stopped by rioting students on his way in from the airport. When the FALN guerrilla movement began in Venezuela in 1962 Caracas University became a recruiting ground and arms depot for it. Some students would spend the week studying in Caracas and then go out into the countryside to campaign or fight for agrarian reform and the FALN. The students successfully defended the autonomy of the university until December 1966 when a government armoured column[8] occupied the buildings after a bitter struggle.

Cuba

Students have played a major role in Cuban politics throughout this century. In 1933 they were mainly instrumental in bringing down the Machado dictatorship in alliance with a group of rebellious army sergeants; and under Batista's second dictatorship, 1952–8, they played a leading role in both the urban and the rural resistance movements. In March 1957 they organized an unsuccessful assassination attempt on Batista and several of their leaders were killed; subsequently they participated in sabotage in Havana and many went to the mountains of Oriente to fight with the Rebel Army.

After the revolution the student organization, the Directorio Estudiantil Revolucionario, formed a tripartite alliance with the Communist Party and Castro's 26 July Movement, and students have continued to play a major role in Cuban life. Within the university student representatives sit on all academic councils and all matters relating to students and the university are discussed in *open* assemblies. Students are also taking a vanguard position in the economic transformation of Cuba. Courses have been restructured to provide the experts necessary for Cuban development, and all students spend forty-five days a year in *trabajo productivo*, productive work in the countryside. The Isle of Pines has been turned over completely to Cuban students and adolescents, and here they combine study with agricultural work. Cuban youth have been mobilized to play a full role in the transformation of Cuban society and the continuing process of revolution. Alastair Hennessy, in the Chatham House symposium on Latin America, concludes: 'Cuba is still the only country in Latin America to have brought the university system into line with the needs of a developing economy, and the Cuban assertion that university reform is impossible without a total social and political revolution has yet to be proved wrong.'[9]

The students of Latin America are well aware that academic reform is itself an insufficient goal and can only be seen correctly achieved by the transformation of the whole society in which the university functions. Until society has been changed, the liberty and rights of all students are insecure.

Japan: The First Industrialized Country

In Japan the most famous political eruption of students occurred in 1960 against the renewal of the security treaty between Japan and the US. This crescendo can only be understood in terms of the Japanese student situation. One of the main results of the American occupation of Japan was the development of higher education. In 1940 there were forty-seven universities in Japan, but in 1957 there were 230 four-year universities and 269 other colleges. This number has increased since then. In Tokyo in 1957 there were 250,000 students – half the national total, but only 30,000 of these were at national universities: the rest were at private ones. Tokyo University itself, founded in 1877, is the main Japanese university and the most difficult to enter: in 1964 it had 15,720 students. Even so many of the private universities are very prestigious.[10]

Students at national universities pay only 5 per cent of their fees, while those at private universities have to pay the full costs. Poorer parents therefore have to get their children into the national universities, whereas those who are richer can send their children to private universities even if they have failed to get in at the national one. Many students who do go to private universities support themselves, particularly by part-time teaching. In the better Japanese universities examinations are frequent and compulsory, and attendance at lectures is often compulsory too. Until recently there was no student representation or institutional power, but in 1966 a minimal concession was made whereby a student representative was allowed to attend the administrative body that runs Tokyo University.

The great expansion in higher education since 1945 has caused many problems: many students have to spend a year between high school and university at special preparatory schools, cramming for university entrance. Those who fail the university entrance examination, the *rōnin* ('masterless samurai'), may spend up to three years trying again and thus even very intelligent students find it increasingly harder to get into the popular universities at the first attempt. The concentration on qualifications has also minimized intellectual spontaneity: rote learning and slavish pursuit of examination qualifications have been common elements in Japanese higher education. There is also a tendency for businesses to look for recruits particularly from universities in the Tokyo–Yokohama area, and so students gravitate excessively to Tokyo each year at examination time, although there are excellent universities in Hokkaido, Kyoto and Kyushu. Another problem associated with this rapid expansion is that the quality of universities varies enormously. The academic standards of Keio, Waseda and Tokyo National University are very high, but many of the private universities instruct badly and the students find that their qualifications are of little use. In Tokyo itself there are some very traditional private universities, like Takushoku and Toyo, where students study little except traditional Japanese subjects like karate and Shintoism. Because of the great variety of standards the actual number of universities is dependent on what criteria are applied.

Since few students go to private universities it is at the national universities that student politics are most radical, particularly as many of the students at national universities are not aiming to get into industry. For the past twenty years the focus of radical student politics in Japan has been the Zengakuren movement (abbreviation for Zen Nihon Gakusei Jichikai Sōrengō or All-Japan Federation of Student Self-government Association).[11] After the end of the war students in universities all over Japan started to develop self-government organizations, and in September 1948 300,000 students from 145 universities joined together to set up the original Zengakuren Federation. Originally closely connected with the Communist Party, the Federation moved sharply left of the JCP in the period 1955–6. In 1958 two new organizations were set up which were to exercise a great influence over the students – the Kakukyōdō (which was a political organization) and the Shagakudō (which was a purely student body). These competed with the original Federation for control of the various university associations, which students joined automatically on entering (in some cases the membership fee being actually deducted and paid in by the university authorities). The word Zengakuren has been used indiscriminately to describe any one of the various groups of individual university self-government associations, and is thus subject to some confusion. The two main advantages of the movement as a whole have been the strong tradition of local organizing (which has produced fluctuating constellations at national level) and the close ties the various student movements have been able to forge with other political organizations (at varying times, the JCP, the JSP, and the General Council of Trade Unions, Sōhyō – this again being a bonus from the Japanese political tradition. Different sectors of the student movement have been active in all the major political struggles of the post-war period: against the MacArthur Purge in 1950, against the Subversive Activities Prevention Law in 1952, against special police powers in 1958, and above all against the renewal of the Japan–US Security Pact in 1959–60. Between 1958 and 1960 the dominant 'mainstream' faction (the Shagakudō) was labelled as 'Trotskyite', a residual term meaning that the group was Marxist but opposed to the official Japan Communist Party line.[12] The JCP groups or 'anti-mainstream' faction regarded the US as the main target; whereas the mainstream were more concerned with internal Japanese issues and the overthrow of the existing power structure.

The central issue of the 1960 demonstrations was the renewal of the Japan–US Security Treaty and hence Japan's alliance with the USA. There had been constant debate and agitation in Japan over this issue throughout the late 1950s and a policy of neutralism had widespread support in Japan. In addition Kishi, the Prime Minister, has pushed the measure of ratification through the Diet on 19 May by means of a parliamentary trick and this enraged much Japanese opinion, especially the bourgeois press, who did not oppose the treaty itself.[13] Other factors contributed to public opposition: Eisenhower was to visit Japan in June, and the U–2 incident had increased Japanese hostility to the US since it was revealed that U–2 planes had been flying from Japan. There were thus three separate issues of the struggle: the resignation of Kishi for his action of 19 May, the cancellation of Eisenhower's visit, and the prevention of the Security Treaty. Many liberal students from the Christian universities in Tokyo demonstrated for the first demand and called for new elections; whereas the anti-mainstream section of Zengakuren concentrated on preventing the visit of Eisenhower. On 10 June James Hagerty, the Presidential Press Secretary, arrived at Haneda Airport. Huge numbers of students swarmed furiously over his path, blocking and besieging his car in a pitched fight. The tempest of student wrath was such that Hagerty had eventually to be airlifted out by helicopter. The students responsible for this were the group who supported the JCP; whereas the mainstream group regarded the assault on Hagerty as something of a diversion and even on 13 June many Zengakuren leaders were not mainly concerned to prevent Eisenhower's visit. However, the treaty was to be ratified on 19 June and as this date approached mass demonstrations escalated. The Japanese government was obliged to ask Eisenhower to cancel his visit after 10,000 Zengakuren members invaded the Diet grounds on 15 June. Then, on the night of 19 June, 300,000 Sōhyō members and 40,000 militants of Zengakuren converged on the Diet in the famous 'snake-march'. As a gesture of contempt, there was a mass urination on the steps of the building. But although they could have prevented the Treaty from being ratified by invading the Diet grounds they did not do this since much of their support arose from those who wanted to preserve parliamentary formality: an invasion of the Diet would have lost their allegiance.

After 1960, Zengakuren suffered an important defeat, when it offered financial aid to striking miners at Miike; the miners refused this and many students then abandoned hopes of a political alliance with the unions. After the shock of the Miike rejection, Zengakuren seemed to decline in influence: many of its former leaders assumed posts in business and ideological splits fragmented the movement. Rival ideas and groups attracted student sympathy. However, there was meanwhile a rise of local militancy in individual instititutions. An example is Mitada University in Tokyo, a Christian insititution staffed mostly by Americans, which was the scene of fierce student resistance when the authorities tried to increase fees: the students fought this, pointing out that it was exploitation to raise fees when library lights were left on all the time.[14] In 1967 a bid to introduce IQ tests was made, but this positivist attack was repelled when students occupied the main building of the campus for two months.

In 1968, violent new conflicts erupted over foreign and domestic issues. Massive student demonstrations against the Vietnamese War clashed continually with police and were able to sustain their momentum because of unprecedentedly solid technical preparation. The students rallied to the demonstrations well armed with helmets, shields and javelins. Hand to hand combat ensued again and again with the security forces over bridges and roads, in scenes reminiscent of medieval jousts. An epic struggle was fought in solidarity with a peasant resistance movement outside Tokyo to the building of a new airport, when the authorities tried to take over land at Narita. A united resistance campaign was waged by workers, peasants and students against the government on this issue. Then, a dramatic wave of attacks was launched against US airbases, military hospitals and aircraft-carriers at harbour in Sasebo.[15] The pitch of struggle has been constantly rising in recent months. The forging of a worker–peasant–student alliance against the Sato regime and against the American aggression in Vietnam is an important step forward in student political action. The temporary decline of the Zengakuren after 1960 has been reversed by the struggle against Japan's complicity in the Vietnamese War and against the scheduled renewal (in 1970) of the Security Treaty.

The Japanese student movement has played a historic role in any world perspective. It pioneered mass revolutionary action in an industrialized country, years before it was achieved in Europe and America. It was radical in methods and aims, and showed the way for uncompromising and unconventional forms of struggle. Lastly, it has demonstrated that students can forge effective links with the most oppressed classes in society – workers and peasants. Students all over the world owe the Japanese militants a great debt.

China: Academic Equality and the Cultural Revolution

The role of students in China has been of pivotal political importance in recent years. It has, of course, been quite different in character from the examples discussed earlier: China is not a capitalist country. But it is not a new phenomenon. The role of students has traditionally been of enormous significance for the life of the country as a whole. Peking University was founded in 1898 with the guiding slogan 'Chinese learning for fundamentals and Western learning for practical application'. It was Peking students who started modern Chinese revolutionary politics when they launched a gigantic demonstration against Japanese imperialist pressure against China on 4 May 1919. The 4 May Movement formed a generation.[16] It succeeded in inspiring a popular nationalist upsurge among workers in the cities, and was the immediate ancestor of the Chinese Communist Party, which was formed in 1920 by leading participants in the 4 May Movement. The first Party secretary, Chen Tu Hsiu, was a professor at Peking University. Mao Tse Tung himself was initiated into politics through the student movements in Peking and Changsha, and one of his first political experiences was a student strike in sympathy with the 4 May Movement, in June 1919. Up to 1925, the Communist Youth Corps was both more radical and more powerful than the Party itself.[17] Students subsequently played an important role in the fight against the Kuomintang and the Japanese.

This historical background is essential to an understanding of the stormy role of students after the Revolution. When China was liberated from the Kuomintang in 1949, fundamental reforms of higher education were carried out. The number of students was expanded from 117,000 undergraduates in 1949–50 to 441,000 in 1958–9. The percentage of students from working-class and peasant backgrounds was raised from 19·1 per cent in 1949–50 to 48 per cent in 1958–59. The allocation of places ensured that university education would increase the technical experts and scientific specialists needed for industrialization, so that by 1958 41 per cent of all students studied engineering courses whereas only 2 per cent studied law and politics. Students were allowed to state options about where to study, although the space available often determined their allocation. They were expected to accept assignment to jobs after graduation. One major institutionalization of student power was achieved in the examination system. Teachers were not allowed to be 'scholar tyrants'. The 'democratic' marking system of examinations involved the students setting their own examination questions with the approval of the teachers who then wrote certain model answers. The answers of the students were then compared with the model answer and marked accordingly; but this was done by the students themselves and decisions were subject to a vote of the students. The teacher was entitled to intervene in case of dispute. These were the main changes in higher education after the Revolution. Students did not immediately emerge as a powerful or separate force within the new system.

Suddenly, in 1966, Chinese students erupted dramatically into the political life of the country once again. Their role in the Cultural Revolution made them famous all over the world. The Cultural Revolution remains an obscure and complex historical movement — little is known of its pre-history and much of its character is in dispute; information concerning its development on a national scale has never been properly available. However, it is clear that university students became the vanguard of the Cultural Revolution for a short period in the summer of 1966 when the main focus of struggle moved from criticism of literary personalities to an upheaval within the University of Peking, where numerous professors and administrators were the object of violent student attacks. When the Cultural Revolution developed into an assault on prominent Party leaders, particularly Liu Shao-Chi, the spearhead position was taken over by a category of students who are as yet only on the threshold of political activity elsewhere in the world — middle-school pupils. When schools and universities were closed down on 13 June 1966 and the Red Guard movement was officially launched in a rally at Peking on 18 August, university students merged into wider currents of youth on the national political scene. The tremendous importance of this age group in current Chinese politics may be assessed by the fact that half of China's population of 750 million people are now under eighteen. Throughout 1966 and 1967, millions of students – both university and middle-school – were occupied in vast rallies, long marches and turbulent struggles throughout China. The uncontrolled character of much of this upsurge was soon evident in the proliferation of antagonistic groups within the student population. A recent report has given a vivid account of the stormy conflicts between the different 'rebel' and 'revolutionary' student organizations on the campus at Canton University.[18] In Peking, squads of militant students from different tendencies criss-crossed the city on scooters, affixing the large *ta tze pao* posters which were the daily bulletins of the general political turmoil.

Student militancy during the Cultural Revolution was initially organized by student Party members against non-Party and anti-Party tendencies on the campus. When the Red Guard emerged, including non-Party militants and school pupils, and its targets became prominent Party leaders, students became involved in national and local struggles between Maoists, Liuists, brigades of the PLA and the local Party organizations. However, it would clearly be incorrect to regard the various Rebel Committees and Red Guard organizations as mere pawns of contending political forces. The Cultural Revolution has had its own momentum and is evidently not merely the instrument of the Central Committee of the Party, or of any of its members. Indeed, the virulently anti-traditionalist zeal of the Red Guards – which aroused the alarm and disapproval of so many foreigners – seems to have been a largely spontaneous affair, which Mao himself was unwilling to check for political reasons (when the masses revolt, he argued as early as 1927, there is always a certain unavoidable amount of damage and chaos) but which he personally reproved. After the sacking of the Central Institute of Arts, a famous poster of the period reported Mao saying to his niece that he deplored the neglect and contempt for classical Chinese literature, and urging her to perfect her English by translating the Bible.[19]

What have been the results of the enormous shake-up of the Cultural Revolution? Academically, there has been a constant debate since 1949 on the relative emphasis to be given to being 'red' and being 'expert'. These have often been conflicting and not complementary moments. Chinese students suffer a constant tension between the pressure to learn more and thus become a better expert and industrializer, and the pressure to abandon study for manual labour or mass involvement. The Cultural Revolution has undoubtedly altered this equation considerably. One student group marching to Peking to see Mao 'told the people that they had come to see that the education they received was basically of a bourgeois character and was utterly divorced from reality, the masses and the class struggle and that this kind of education only made them into hot-house flowers'. They cried: 'We are determined to be tall pines on high mountains: we will never be flowers grown in a hot-house.' [20] In the shake-up of the university system that followed the Cultural Revolution it was decided to induct 'more revolutionary sons of workers and peasants' and students in Peking University wrote the press declaring the need for students to divide their time between military training, manual labour and academic study. The old system of academic training was denounced – as were many academics. Peking University was eventually reopened in July 1967. The removal of traditionalist teachers, the promotion of militancy as a virtue among students as well as academic excellence and the drafting of students into work in the factory and commune have all helped to erode the old divisions between manual and mental labour. The effect of all this on academic production in the long run, however, remains to be seen. Its potential importance in preventing the rise of a privileged caste – heir to the traditional mandarinate which always wielded such power in Chinese society – is evident. So too is the valuable reminder that the need for vigilant and independent revolutionary students does not cease with the attainment of revolution.

Politically, a new generation has entered the arena *en masse*. Its formative memory will be of struggle against bureaucratic authority and privilege. Chinese students became a crucial group in the Cultural Revolution because they were allied to other forces in society, of which the peasant-based People's Liberation Army was often the most important. They were thus able to achieve experience of mass political conflict such as never again occurred in Russia after 1921. The Cultural Revolution was clearly aimed at preventing a repetition of the Soviet experience, and any loss of political momentum after the disappearance of the generation which made the Revolution of 1949. Here the Red Guards have been the descendants of the 4 May Movement – a rebirth of the singular insurgent role of Chinese students throughout twentieth century history.

Italy: The Occupation of the University

In some ways the most surprising student power movement to develop recently has been that of the Italian students. There is not a political void on the Italian left of the same kind as has made the German SDS the main opposition force to the West German regime – both of the left-wing parties, the PCI and the PSIUP have sizable youth movements. Even two years ago on any Italian campus there was total conformity in dress. The students had created virtually no cultural apparatus of their own – no cafés, discothèques or cinemas. Nor was this merely a superficial question of appearances. In matters of sexual freedom there was no intransigent rejection of the dead weight of Catholic morality and male oppression. In short, in Italy there had not occurred the rupture between generations which has in recent years preoccupied *bien pensants* in France, Germany, Britain, the United States, or Scandinavia. Yet in the academic year 1967–8 student revolt swept the campuses – nineteen of the thirty-three state universities were affected, and in thirteen of them the university buildings were occupied. The Italian students extended their control physically over their universities and intellectually over their courses to a greater extent than in any other country.

The first high points of the year's revolts was the seizure of Turin University, which started with a month's occupation from 27 November to 27 December 1967 and continued with a series of occupations, pitched battles, evictions, lock-outs, demonstrations in the streets, acts of solidarity with FIAT workers, mass victimization and brutality on the part of the police, arrests, releases under pressure, and reoccupations throughout the spring of 1968 until the arts side of the university was closed for the year in March. The Turin events acted like a beacon for the other Italian campuses. Delegations sped from all over Italy to discover what the Turin students were achieving.[21] Government spokesmen thundered against them, and opposition journals anxiously arranged round-table discussions on the problem of the university. During the occupation, counter-courses were organized on everything from guerrilla warfare to repression in the family, and what had started originally as a protest in the Architecture Faculty over the siting of a new building became a campaign for a university with a critical function.

The Italian universities have a most authoritarian pedagogical tradition: professors teach courses from manuals they have themselves written, and both set and mark examinations themselves on these courses; this is clearly not a situation in which a critical approach to what the student is offered is advisable if he wishes to get good marks. The antiquated character of the courses is notorious: the political science syllabus at Rome University stops with Rousseau. Hence the charter of demands worked out by the Turin students was principally directed to the content and organization of the curricula.

We think that the University should, and could, provide its students at one and the same time with an adequate professional formation and with critical tools in regard to their professional role.... It is necessary to go further, and transform not merely the *structure of the curriculum* but the *selection of specific subjects for study* within it and the *methods of study*.[22]

For these aims to be realized, the students would have to impose them. The focus of the demands at Turin set the pattern for the rest of Italy – more than in any other country the aim was reform of the *content* of higher education.[23] However, when this aim was frustrated by the rigidly hierarchical and inflexible university structures, the marching slogan became 'Against Authoritarianism'.

After Turin, it was the turn of Pisa, Milan, Trent, Florence, Rome, Naples, Venice, Catania and Palermo – the contagion spread the length of the peninsula during January and February 1968. Yet throughout these two months there was almost complete silence in the Italian (and international) press concerning what was happening. The ruling class viewed them with fear – a good reason for denying them publicity. The opposition parties were alarmed and uneasy at these wild extremists, with their identification with Che Guevara or Mao Tse Tung, and their suspicions of, if not hostility to, the traditional left-wing parties. The students, however, carried on their struggle unabashed. At the beginning of March, in Rome, two months before the general election, they set their mark on Italian political life in a way that nobody could ignore henceforth. From that time on, for weeks, the Italian press gave more coverage to the struggle on the campuses than to the war in Vietnam.

The University of Rome was already occupied. The professors, anxious to avoid an open rupture, agreed to hold the examinations in the occupied university, under the conditions laid down by the students. These allowed (1) for a student to abandon the examination if he or she wished and take it again later; (2) for the examination board to discuss the papers in the presence of the candidates; (3) for the latter to have the right to request examination on questions not included in the papers set. In fact, these provisions were in accordance with the official statutes – statutes which had never previously been put into effect. The examinations started, and went on normally for two hours, but d'Avack, the Rector, could no longer contain his fury at this affront to the dignity of the university hierarchy, and sallied out into the central courtyard and ordered the students through a megaphone to evacuate the buildings. When this met with no response, he declared the examinations annulled and, after a meeting with the Minister of Education, Gui, called in the police, who cleared the buildings brutally.

The next day, 4,000 students gathered on the Piazza di Spagna and marched to the Architecture Faculty at the Valle Giulia. As they marched, their numbers grew. When they reached their destination, they found the police massed and waiting. The police, clearly under orders, attacked immediately. During the previous two months of silence, repression of the students had taken the form of arrest and intimidation of individual leaders; sometimes of obviously framed charges aimed at discrediting them as thieves or delinquents. Now the tactic was changed, and mass violence was to be the new solution. But instead of turning and running, or sitting down and allowing themselves to be beaten up and dragged away, the students fought back with branches and stones. The police were forced back, and had to barricade themselves inside the Faculty buildings; they were only rescued when water-wagons were called in. By the end of the day hundreds had been arrested, forty-seven students and 147 policemen were taken to hospital, ten police vehicles had been burned and many others damaged. In the days that followed, over sixty policemen were charged with allowing themselves to be disarmed by the 'rebels'.

Throughout Italy 2,000 students were charged with various offences. But the very week after the battle of Valle Giulia, the secondary school children of Milan – 10,000 of them – brought the whole city to a standstill in protest at the suspension of two of their teachers who had participated in the occupation of schools by the children and who had tried to introduce new teaching methods. At least ten universities remained under occupation, and in some the academic year was declared over. Government policy was now clearly that the contagion must be checked at all costs. Demonstrations, even of the most peaceful kind, were broken up savagely by truncheon charges. Lawyers at the Palace of Justice in Rome protested at scenes of indiscriminate police brutality which took place in the Piazza Cavour outside and on the very steps of the building – which once again lived up to the name of Palazzo Nero (Black Palace) which it earned under Fascism. Students who went to the FIAT works in Turin in solidarity with strikers there were beaten up pitilessly. But student power has ceased to be merely a slogan in Italian politics – it has become a political reality with which the authorities and the political parties are having to come to terms. One index of this was a long article published in *Rinascita* the official weekly of the Communist Party, by Luigi Longo, the Party Secretary, in early May 1968.[24] This was a bid to come to terms with the new reality, admitting errors in the Party's policy towards the student movement, and speaking of 'a certain erosion of the internal life of the Party, a lack of information about certain events (for example, the Cultural Revolution in China, the Fidelist revolution, the revolutionary movement in Latin America)'. A similar challenge faces the Christian Democrats, for large numbers of Catholic students participated in the struggles, and their hero is Camillo Torres, the Colombian priest who died fighting with the *guerrilleros* in 1966.

The great achievements of the Italian students have been to assert physical control over their places of study, and to have brought the traditional curricula into question. They have also pioneered confrontations with, or trials of, professors, in which the latter have been forced to justify the content and method of what they taught. Moreover, they quickly realized the importance of having their own publications to focus their struggle, and often published daily student papers which kept the students informed of the course of events and the stage which theoretical discussion and strategic planning had reached. Although Italian students developed their movement later than the Spanish, French or German students, and although they have no national organization such as the German SDS, they have made greater advances towards student power within the universities than in any other country.

Spain: The Struggle for Democracy

The emergence of the Spanish student movement has been related both to the crisis of Franco's regime and to specific university conditions. Students in Spain are a very small group: 75,000 in 1965 out of 31 million people. The percentage of students from working-class and peasant backgrounds is tiny: about 3 per cent. The cost of secondary education is often prohibitive, university fees are high and grants are minimal. The standard of education in the secondary schools varies a great deal, and students from some areas are thus further handicapped. Between 40 and 50 per cent of those who do get to university drop out before their final examinations. After graduation there are still problems of employment: a 1962 survey of arts graduates in the years 1940–58 showed that 52 per cent were unemployed and a further 36 per cent underemployed.

In the Civil War one of the Fascist slogans was 'Death to the Intellect'. This violent hostility, and the continual neglect of all levels of education in Spain, partly accounts for the increase in student discontent in the 1960s. The official student union, the *Sindicato Español Universitario*, was founded in 1936 as a youth group linked to the Falange. It soon became the official student union and the only one; a similar organization was forced on the workers. Up to 1961 all officials of the SEU were nominated by the government, but after student opposition increased, a new decree in that year allowed students to elect some representatives to faculty *consejos* in the universities. This did not satisfy student opinion: they were not consulted on the decree, the university authorities were allowed to disqualify any candidates for election, and these elected candidates could only act as counsellors, real power resting with the local *jefe del distrito universitario del SEU*. The national council of the SEU consisted of twelve elected and forty nominated members.

Students protested against this fake concession and in 1962 at Madrid they formed their own clandestine group, the Federación Universitaria Democratica de España (FUDE). FUDE explicitly declared itself opposed both to SEU and to the whole Franco regime and urged mass student activity against the Government. A similar group was set up later at Barcelona University, but this group, ADEC, tried to avoid clashes with the police. Both groups did however join to form a national Confederación Universitaria Democratica de España (CUDE) in December 1963. In contrast to the socialist orientation of CUDE, liberal Christian opposition at Madrid formed the *Unión de Estudiantes Democratas* in January 1964, and a similar group was set up at Valencia University. At Barcelona a separatist Catalan formation also emerged; and groups of Basque students formed in Bilbao.

The first climax of the new movements came in Madrid, early in 1965, when students protested at Government control of the SEU elections. On 24 February a silent march to the university rectorate was broken up by police and in reprisal the Government closed the Faculties of Philosophy and Medicine and suspended four professors. In April a new attempt to demobilize student opposition was made by the Government: SEU was abolished and a new student union, the APE, was set up. Students were now empowered to elect all delegates to the national convention, but this was a counterfeit concession since no student who had suffered disciplinary action was allowed to stand, and the university authorities were empowered to disqualify any candidates. Elections later in the year were boycotted by most students – in the Architecture Faculty of Madrid University only twenty-five of the 2,850 votes were valid. Many of the candidates had to be nominated by the authorities. In December 1965 a meeting of 250 students in the Political Faculty at Madrid was dispersed by armed police. Students retaliated by systematically disrupting traffic in Madrid. In 1966 the focus of struggle switched to Barcelona where a convention of free students was held at the Capuchin monastery of Sarría in March. The meeting was closed when police stormed the monastery. Sixty-eight university professors were suspended, and numerous students banned and fined. Barcelona University was shut. In January 1968 the regime's repression of students took a new form. It was decided to install a permanent university police, the *Policia Universitaria*, on the campus and to reactivate an old system whereby rightist students were formed into 'University Defence Groups'. The effect of this decision was to increase the number of expulsions, closings of faculties and fights within the university – and to radicalize Spanish intellectuals as a group. Many professors, writers and journalists who had previously been outside the movement now came to support it. This growth in the strength of the opposition encountered increased religious and authoritarian reaction: when students hurled a crucifix at a body of University Police, the Catholic and Falangist Press were outraged and religious atonement ceremonies were held throughout the country.

The student campaign for free unions has now escalated into broader political issues. For workers have simultaneously been struggling in Spain for free trade unions. Their clandestine *commisiones obreras* (workers' commissions), which have mushroomed in recent years, are the counterpart of the free student groups. In February 1967, students in Madrid demonstrated specifically to demand workers' representation on a committee discussing a change in trade-union law. In effect, it has become clear to many students that their situation is not an isolated phenomenon and their oppression is just one facet of the Fascist regime in Spain. The underground political parties of the Left – Communist, Socialist and Anarchist – have thus increasingly won members among the students.

The new student–worker unity was sealed by the three days of national struggle declared for 1–3 May 1968. Mobilization unparalleled in post-war Spain occurred on both sides for this confrontation. Heavy detachments of armed security forces were brought into Madrid for May Day. A strike and boycott of all public transport hit Madrid, as workers trooped into the centre of the city for a major demonstration. The clashes with police which followed were marked by the appearance of a completely new phenomenon — mobile 'shock commandos' of young workers and students, attacking the forces of repression from light vehicles and then rapidly withdrawing and re-attacking at different points of the city. Coordination was assured by central radio transmission from the underground. A flood of arrests was made, and the regime succeeded in preventing the spread of disorders, although there were many clashes in provincial towns — Seville, Bilbao, Tarrasa, Alicante, Badajoz and Las Palmas in the Canaries. Prisoners were taken to the notorious gaol of Carabanchel outside Madrid. A trade-union leader in the underground commented:

The prison of Carabanchel has become a veritable popular university, where the known leaders of the workers' commissions form young working-class cadres in a climate of enthusiasm.... Paradoxically, the faculty of Carabanchel is the only one which is functioning normally this season, since the University of Madrid has been closed time and again.[22]

Spanish students have thus scored two notable successes. They have initiated open popular struggle against Franco's military dictatorship — thereby showing that students can temporarily act as a vanguard in conditions of the direst political repression. (Persian students have equally taught this lesson in their long contest with the Shah.) Secondly, the Spaniards have been the first European student movement to achieve an organized, solidarity alliance with the workers. The shock commandos of Madrid are a symbol of the future goals of the continent.

West Germany: The Anti-Authoritarian Movement

There were 272,000 students in West Germany in early 1967. Only 5 per cent of them were working-class, a sinister example of the resilience of traditional German social structures in the Federal Republic and of the reactionary character of West German society. After the war, most of these students were rightist or apathetic: a survey of them in 1966 showed that 81 per cent were opposed to any student say in university affairs, and elections to student organizations had an average of 40 per cent participation. Only 3·7 per cent of the students were members of political groups, whereas 5 per cent were members of the traditional duelling clubs – *schlagende Verbindungen* – which the Allies had tried unsuccessfully to suppress. Many of the students – one third – would abandon their studies uncompleted and less than 40 per cent had grants from the State. Fifty per cent of all students worked during the vacations. The national student union – the Verband Deutscher Studentenschaften (VDS) – was concerned entirely with administrative matters such as cheap travel. Student representatives in senates and academic disciplinary committees were always in a minority, and hence had no power. Politically, many students were conformist in attitude – 47 per cent in early 1967 were against acknowledgement of the Oder-Neisse line, and 50 per cent thought that the West German parliamentary system was working well.[25]

Such was the somnolent and forbidding situation in the early sixties. Apparently, no more unpromising climate for student militancy existed in Europe. However, there was within the claustrophobic conformity of West German higher education a dedicated and far-sighted minority of revolutionaries. The SDS – Sozialistische Deutsche Studentenbund – was formed in 1960 when the German Social-Democratic Party (SPD) followed its enthusiastic adoption of capitalism as the ideal form of society (Bad Godesburg Programme) by expelling its student organization, which had resisted this abject capitulation to the ruling class. The SDS was thereafter virtually the sole political organization on the Left in a seemingly monolithic reactionary society. It was very small – only some 2,000 strong – but hard-working and dynamic. It demanded a high level of political knowledge and commitment from its members. In order to become one an aspirant had both to pass through a series of reading and discussion seminars on Marxism and to participate in concrete struggles. Undeterred by the wholesale integration of West German working-class organizations – political or industrial – into the *status quo*, the SDS set about building a revolutionary base within the university. Intensive theoretical work and study of historical experience provided an indispensable preparation for later events. By 1966, its strongest bastion was within the so-called Free University of West Berlin, a creation of the Cold War, where imitation of the US example had unwittingly produced a somewhat more vulnerable institutional structure than in the traditionalist universities of the Federal Republic. The SDS used its strength there to demand elementary democratic rights on campus. When two representatives were conceded in the Senate, where all proceedings were secret, a Counter-Senate was organized on the lawns outside, and the two student representatives reported back to it every hour, defying authoritarian domination of the university. Tumultuous struggles with the university bureaucracy and professors naturally ensued, as the students fought step by step towards greater mass control.

Into this explosive environment, two flashes were suddenly thrown in early 1967. Together, they produced a major political crisis and the transformation of the SDS into the centre of politics in West Germany. In April, US Vice-President Hubert Humphrey – a notorious spokesman for the Vietnamese War – arrived on a visit to West Berlin. A group of students were promptly arrested for plotting to throw projectiles (flour) at him. The West German press, led by the Springer empire, reported that the students intended to assassinate Humphrey with a bomb. The actual reason for their arrest was that they formed part of the Berlin Commune, a utopian community that had seceded from the SDS in the previous February and which specialized in scandals and *Bürgerschreck* – shocking the bourgeois. No sooner was Humphrey gone than the Shah of Persia – a detested tyrant who had persecuted Persian students for years – was the next guest of the 'Free City'. There are large numbers of Persian students in exile in West Germany, and they had worked together with the SDS for some time. The beginning of the national West German student revolt was thus provoked by a manifestation of *international* solidarity. For when the Shah arrived, the SDS organized a protest outside the Berlin Opera House. The police indiscriminately attacked the demonstrators, and shot one student – Benno Ohnesorg – to death. The impact of this killing, not only in West Berlin but throughout the Federal Republic, was enormous. Ohnesorg's body was taken to Hamburg, where thousands of students attended his funeral, and his death was followed by hundreds of demonstrations throughout West Germany. The volume of anger and protest was such that both the West Berlin Chief of Police and the Social-Democratic Mayor of West Berlin, Albertz, were forced to resign. But this did not lull the students. They were well aware the the roots of police brutality were to be found, not in the pathology of these individuals, but in the ideological and political structures of West German society. For them the juncture between educational and political issues had been made. The unity and universality of repression was clear to the West German militants: American aggression in Vietnam, imperialist control of Persia, police brutality in West Berlin, the systematic lies of the Springer Press, manipulation in the universities – all these were different aspects of one unified authoritarian phenomenon – capitalism.

Throughout 1967 and 1968 the student movement grew in force. An international congress on Vietnam was organized by the SDS in West Berlin in February 1968: delegates came from the youth of all West European countries. The march that followed the Congress blocked the Kurfürstendamm solidly: in the citadel of anti-Communism, a forest of red flags flew over marchers, buildings and construction sites, and the insignia of the National Liberation Front of South Vietnam was everywhere. The City Fathers and the police had so feared this march that they banned it; a judicial decision, however, ruled that this move was illegal. To retaliate, a huge, counter-demonstration approving the US world role was organized by the Mayor, who declared a public holiday for the purpose. A hysterical wave of reaction now swept the city. During the counter-demonstration, a girl student was attacked, knocked to the ground and then kicked by a crowd of bourgeois shouting: 'Cut off her hair, beat her'; a student who looked like Rudi Dutschke, the most famous of the SDS leaders in West Berlin, was assailed by a group chanting 'Lynch him, hang him'; and a parish priest was mobbed and struck by twenty outraged burgers. Thirty-five people were injured during the counter-demonstration, while nobody had been hurt during the demonstration by the students. The violence of the burgers was complemented by the virulence of the press, which was itself largely responsible for their hostility.

One of the major forces in the indoctrination and manipulation of West German opinion is the Springer newspaper empire, which accounts for 90 per cent of the circulation of the national newspapers on Sundays and 40 per cent on weekdays. Springer's press is a clear example of Herbert Marcuse's thesis that ideological manipulation is one of the central means whereby a pseudo-freedom intensifies the lack of freedom of capitalist society. It constantly attacks the students as rowdies, beatniks, communist agents, traitors, and sex maniacs. Representative headlines in Springer's *Bildzeitung* read 'Stop the Young Reds' Terror Now', 'We Shouldn't Leave all the Dirty Work to the Police and their Water-Cannons', 'Dutschke, No 1 Enemy of the People – Throw the Gang Out'. Frequent echoes of Third Reich propaganda were calculated to produce the same hysteria. Not surprisingly, a correspondent of *The Times* reported as characteristic the comment of a taxi-driver: 'Hitler would have soon stopped all these students.' The Springer empire therefore naturally became a main target for student militancy. The SDS launched a broad national campaign for the expropriation of the Springer empire, and set up a Springer Tribunal to investigate his publications and their content.

The damage had been done, however. Whipped up by hysterical press articles, right-wing violence was now unleashed. On 12 April, a young Fascist attempted to assassinate Rudi Dutschke in West Berlin, critically wounding him: Dutschke had been portrayed in the newspapers as the national leader of the SDS. The student reaction was virtual insurrection throughout West Germany. In West Berlin, the students seized the Technical University and declared it a Soviet. A student siege of the Springer buildings led to the installation of barbed wire trenches to guard it by the police, but notwithstanding this twenty distribution trucks of the empire were captured and burned, and the building set alight. Springer offices in Hamburg, Cologne, Frankfurt and Munich were isolated by students: the day after the assassin shot at Dutschke, the distribution of Springer's newspapers was blocked throughout the Federal Republic, except in Munich where a few sacks were smuggled over the roofs. In West Berlin, the SDS marched into the radio and television centre and demanded that they be given an hour a day to explain to the population their demands. Information groups were sent to argue at street corners and factory gates. This tremendous upsurge freed the SDS from its previous social isolation. In such towns as Essen, where there is no university, an anti-Springer demonstration composed of young workers took place. After the Easter riots, a poll in West Berlin showed that 57 per cent of men aged between sixteen and thirty supported the student protests.[26] Potentially, in fact, the students were not isolated at all. Although the over-thirties were unreconciled, the younger generation as a whole, workers and students, was capable of forming a militant political alliance.

How did the extraordinary transformation of West German politics by the SDS take place? Why, in particular, did it achieve such a rapid and deep radicalization of the student body? In the first place, the Germans were theoretically and ideologically prepared for taking the revolutionary road. The examples of the American student movement, of the Persians and of the Dutch Provos had been studied. The West German students were also much more receptive to political theory than, say, the British. Ever since 1945 the influence of the Frankfurt School of sociologists, Adorno, Benjamin, Marcuse, Habermas and others, had meant that students were conversant with Marxism, and were not the victims of a primitive empiricism or hostility to 'jargon'. Concepts such as exploitation, repression, manipulation and liberation were understood and accepted. Subsequently the influence of Mao, Guevara and Debray became important. This general ideological preparedness was of crucial importance in shaping the student movement once it had started and of giving it a definite revolutionary trajectory.

A second material factor that facilitated the growth of the student movement is the length and conditions of study in West Germany. Students have always been free to move from one university to another, accumulating the necessary amount of study. They are free to choose when to take their examinations, and can start their theses before taking them, provided they have attended a small number of seminars. Thus students can take time off to organize and be politically active in a way that would be impossible with a shorter course and more frequent examinations. There is also more time for students to become politically formed, more time for them to think, read and struggle before they are re-absorbed into capitalist society.

Thirdly, the formation of the Grand Coalition at Bonn, uniting the Christian Democrats and Social Democrats in a governmental alliance, had extinguished all pretence of serious parliamentary opposition to the *status quo*. There was thus no mystification about a two-party system – the identity of the two big political parties was blatant. West Germany was also free from the multiplicity of anachronistic rival factions on the Left which has plagued the opposition in other capitalist countries. The Communist Party, moreover, was banned. Hence the SDS was able to emerge unequivocally as *the* national opposition. Its Marxist formation ensured that it persistently strove to overcome its isolation from the working class and there are now signs that it may be beginning to succeed in this.

The situation in West Germany was thus without many of the specific obstacles to a student movement which are to be found, for example, in Britain: short periods of study, a general ignorance of Marxism and aversion to theory in general, proliferation of antagonistic factions on the campus, and the continuing pretence of a political debate between the parties. The West German context was much clearer. The aim of the student movement was thus to disrupt the existing consensus and raise submerged political issues. The exemplary success of the SDS was due to this propitious combination of subjective and objective factors. But in spite of its specificity, the West German experience provides one of the most instructive models of a student movement anywhere in the world today: its theoretical emphasis, its mass mobilizations, its outflanking of the existing student union and its total confrontation of the system are all features of international significance. The SDS has managed to wage a combined struggle on both the academic and political fronts: this unity is an encouragement to all other students who are still confronted with sterile inanities about the unimportance of student protest. The lesson of the SDS is clear: no matter how formidable the ideological and political consensus appears, no matter how integrated the working class temporarily appears to be into capitalism, determined struggle by a student movement is necessary and possible. Its results may be very wide.

France: Rebirth of the Barricades

Prior to the immense upsurge of student militancy which culminated in barricades in Paris and street fighting throughout the university cities of France in May 1968, the French student movement had seen something of a decline from its high point during the Algerian War. In 1961 the student union UNEF had well over 100,000 members, out of a total two hundred and forty thousand students. It had gained great strength and prestige from the fact that during the Algerian War it was the only major organization actively and openly to oppose the war and the *Algérie Française* policy. The students' only firm allies at that time were a section of the left-wing intelligentsia, and this doubtless played an important role in the political formation of the students themselves.[27]

UNEF organized demonstrations, draft resistance, and a propaganda campaign against the torture, bombing, psychological warfare and prison camps systematically used by the successive governments of the Fourth Republic (and during the first years of the Fifth). Students also provided the cadres for the various resistance networks (such as the Réseau Jeanson) which channelled arms, funds and information to the FLN. Their prestige was such that only they were capable, in October 1960, of bringing all the the Left together in the first nation-wide mass demonstrations against the war. Fidel Castro later paid tribute to the courage of the French students and intellectuals at a time when the organized Left stood silent.

However, when the Algerian War came to an end in 1962, UNEF did not succeed in finding demands and programmes to maintain the level of militant commitment which it had achieved during the war. By the beginning of 1968, although the number of students in France had increased to almost 600,000, UNEF's membership had dropped to between forty-five and fifty thousand, and the organization has been riven by internal struggles. Although it had continued to play a significant role as a national organization, for instance in the campaign against American aggression in Vietnam, it had ceased to provide an adequate reflection of student demands or to provide a leadership for their struggle within their universities. The range of these demands and the enthusiasm for struggle were to be demonstrated in the spring of 1968.

Whereas the high point of UNEF was reached when students played a vital role in French national politics, the recent upsurge of militancy among students has been triggered off by their condition *as students*. French students have waged a constant struggle against the discipline in their halls of residence. In 1968 72 per cent of girls and 58 per cent of men were living in these halls. The disciplinary rules were repressive and archaic: political meetings and propaganda were forbidden and men were not allowed into women's lodgings. Students were not allowed to decorate their rooms or affix things to the walls: in many of the halls residents could only receive their guests in common rooms. In early 1967 a campaign was started by the students at Lyons against 'psychological and sexual oppression' and UNEF joined in this struggle. In February 1968 they started a national campaign to liberalize the rules in halls of residence and in particular to obtain that men should be allowed to visit women in their own rooms. In Paris students also demonstrated for better lodgings, since the facilities provided were inadequate and there was great overcrowding in the *cités universitaires*.

This struggle of the French students for greater freedom in their lodgings was indicative of the importance of sexual liberation as an element in the student struggle. One of the most fundamental ways in which an authoritarian society controls its members and its young is by sexual repression. This repression begins from the first years of a child's life and is effected by instilling false fears, by cultivating taboos, by denying adolescents the facilities (rooms, contraception) for sex, and by parents and educators keeping the young under constant surveillance. The effect of this is not so much to prevent sexual activity as to debase it, and to increase the neurotic, clandestine and unhappy aspects of a student's life. Complete sexual freedom is a number one demand for any student movement. All forms of sexual repression and of puritan 'discipline' should be abolished. Sexual freedom is often dismissed as a non-political question, and is not seen as an important right. This is partly because the young are sexually oppressed from about the age of three onwards, and they have tended to accept it as inevitable. But this need not be so. The French students have made clear that sexual freedom, like student representation, is both a demand in itself and a means of activating the student mass. An alert student leadership can show the concealed systematic relationship between sexual controls, university authoritarianism, economic exploitation, and imperialist aggression. Such a theoretical generalization of the student consciousness is difficult to achieve, most notably because it runs counter to bourgeois beliefs. It is not, however, impossible. (See Marcuse, *Eros and Civilization*.)

Dissatisfaction with student conditions – overcrowding, inadequate grants, lack of cultural and other facilities – far from being confined to the students themselves, was widely echoed in criticisms of French higher education among many social groups. In response to this dissatisfaction a new model campus was opened at Nanterre, an outer suburb of Paris, in 1964. By 1968 the number of students at Nanterre had leapt to 11,000. During the autumn of 1967 and the beginning of 1968 the Nanterre students became more and more impatient with conditions even in this 'model' institution, with its new buildings and 'liberal-minded' academic staff. A group of students and young lecturers developed a thorough critique of the role of Nanterre within a rationalist French capitalism – see the pamphlet 'Why Sociologists?' published elsewhere in this volume. The cultural apparatus of Nanterre was woefully inadequate. There was still no library, nor were there cafés, cinemas, or discothèques. What is more there was no freedom for the students to demonstrate on their own campus. On 26 January 1968, some forty activists marched up and down the hall of the university carrying banners ridiculing the police. There was a clash between them and some of the porters, and the Administration called the police. A thousand students gathered to repel them, and the Nanterre student movement was launched. It was attempts to victimize the leaders of the Nanterre movement which subsequently fired the battle for the Latin Quarter of May 1968.

On Friday 3 May 1968 some 400 students assembled in the

main courtyard of the Sorbonne, protesting against the closing of
the Nanterre Faculty and above all against the summoning of six
Nanterre students before the University Council. All the political groups of the student Left were represented. The police
massed outside the university, and prevented students from
entering. When the Rector called on them to clear the buildings,
a largely spontaneous wave of reaction on the part of students
outside on the streets paved the way for the actions which led
the most sedate observers to recall memories of the Commune of
1871. Barricades were thrown up, constructed of overturned cars
held in place by uprooted paving stones. These, sometimes reaching first storey level, were held by students against police charges
with a determination and heroism which led even *The Times*
reporter to speak of their 'great bravery' and 'fearless heroism'.
The students used pneumatic drills to tear up the paving stones,
boards studded with nails to puncture the tyres of the police
trucks, and home-made petrol bombs against the armoured
vehicles of the security forces. The police had to be equipped
with steel visors to protect them against the hail of paving stones
from the students, and flower-pots and roof-tiles hurled down
on them by the local residents, enraged by the police brutality.
Tear gas canisters and percussion grenades used by the police
were hurled back at them before they could explode. Sixty
thousand students fought in the streets of Paris and demonstrations of solidarity took place throughout France.

What had started as the action of small revolutionary groups
swelled into the most significant mass contestation of the State
since the Commune, arousing large numbers of the French
working class. The workers to begin with joined in huge
demonstrations in solidarity with the students: a general strike
was initiated, then, despite the reluctance of the trade union
leadership, it turned into factory occupations by nearly ten
million workers. These events are well known and I will not
give an account of them here. But it is worth emphasizing
that the militant student groups continued to play a key role
during and after the insurrection they had ignited. Action
groups were set up to help workers produce propaganda
materials: a flood of leaflets and posters began to emanate from
the occupied buildings of the Fine Arts School and the Arts

Faculty at Censier. Links between workers and students were forged which were to form the basis of future common actions, and were to survive the post-insurrection police repression in which a wide range of revolutionary organizations were declared illegal. Although police successfully reoccupied the captured university buildings, it also became clear that this promised no permanent solution to the Government. The avowed objective of the student revolutionaries is to convert universities and colleges into liberated base areas: as Alain Geismar has said 'We want to make the university into a bastion from which we can pursue the struggle against capitalism'.

What are the implications of this international survey? Hasty generalization is obviously dangerous, but there are a certain number of lessons which emerge very clearly from this study. They may be taken as established by the turbulent and diverse experience of the last decade.

1. Student power on campus is an attainable goal. Student joint-control of higher education in Latin America works in conditions of political instability and social underdevelopment. It is all the more capable of success in the more developed societies of the world. Experience shows that students mobilizing within universities and colleges can achieve important corporate successes by isolated action. The Latin American students did not need the support of other groups to make their sanctions felt on campus, and they were able to gain and maintain power by them. It is thus not true that unity with workers or other social groups is a necessary condition of a revolutionary student upsurge within higher education. Students can and have gained significant victories on their own. The Latin American concept of *cogobierno* – joint control – is, however, a reminder that students should not make false analogies with class struggle, but true connexions with it. Some students have been led to see themselves as an oppressed class on the model of the proletariat, and hence to work for a complete student overthrow of the academic staff. This is mistaken. The aim of a social revolution is to eliminate the former ruling class. Students cannot aim to eliminate academics from higher education. The Argentinian system involved a tripartite sharing of university government between students, graduates and teachers. Unless some way is found to abolish altogether the distinction between the teacher and the taught, some such joint-control is inevitable. But given this, there is no doubt of the practical and political feasibility of liberated institutions of higher education, acting as base areas for general revolutionary struggle.

2. There is no predetermined formula for the problem of how to campaign on campus. An existing national student union may often have funds, printing presses, buildings and international communications. If these are acquired, they can be used by a radical student group. On the other hand, the radicals may become entangled in an existing bureaucratic organization and thus find themselves unable to act – or they may be more easily separated from the student mass they should represent and lead. A militant student movement is radical in its demands, and radical in its methods. An existing bureaucratic union may not be adaptable to either of these. Therefore the possibilities of control must be weighed against the dangers of atrophy and debilitation. In France, during the Algerian War, UNEF was a national student union led by an extremely militant leadership into a vanguard political role – well ahead of the parties of the Left. But UNEF was not thereafter able to sustain this momentum, and initiative in the late sixties passed out of its control to other student tendencies. In Spain, radical students have fought for the right to create a free national union. In Japan, Zengakuren was for long the only national student organization of any sort. In West Germany and the USA, a minority organization of militants – the two SDS organizations – eventually pushed a conformist national union into a somewhat more progressive stance by the sheer impact of their political driving-power, not by any conscious design: the national union remained unimportant in both cases. The choice of tactics *vis-à-vis* a national student union is thus not a question of principle – it is a matter of the concrete circumstances concerned. In most cases, militancy has been best generated outside – not inside it: but this is not an invariable rule.

3. The relationship between educational and political issues is a dialectical one. It is not a mechanical one-way process. Thus in many countries there has been an initial build-up of militancy on academic issues, which has then escalated into a struggle on political issues. The Cordoba Movement in Latin America, which later developed into revolutionary solidarity with guerrilla struggles, is an eloquent example. The political triumphs of the West German SDS itself were based on an initial campaign for democratizing the campus. Thus it is absolutely incorrect to counterpose educational to political demands – as if the former had no political content. On the contrary, experience shows that the one often naturally develops into the other. Conversely, there are also examples where an initially political campaign by students repercusses back into the campus and detonates an internal revolt within higher education. In the United States, it was the political experience of the Civil Rights campaigns and demonstrations against the Vietnamese and Dominican Expeditions which produced the explosion at Berkeley. Similarly, the huge national–political mobilizations of the Zengakuren in Japan later detonated local educational revolts such as that at Mitada. Political and educational issues must not be contrasted by abstract dogmas but united in concrete struggles.

4. *Militant student movements can play a vanguard political role on their own in conditions of extreme repression.* They have done so in Spain, Persia, Brazil, Morocco and many other backward capitalist countries. Their relatively privileged social status and the functional advantages discussed earlier often make student protests possible, when all other social groups are shackled by military coercion. This vanguard role, however, is an index of the *restricted* level of political development in any given country. For students are not a social class and cannot transform society. Their resistance to tyranny may often be heroic but there are constant limitations. Student consciousness is highly volatile. It is often hard to sustain a student movement beyond the initial provocation. There is no easy way of resolving this difficulty and one of the main weapons of the established order will always be: 'Leave them alone and let the whole thing peter out.' Student organizers should constantly be aware of this danger.

5. *A militant student movement will only succeed in revolutionary objectives where it allies itself organically with the major exploited classes of society – workers and (in poor capitalist countries) peasants.* This fundamental lesson is borne out again and again. The Cuban experience of 1956–8 is a classical example. The Directorio Estudantil had no chance of overthrowing Batista: it was the Rebel Army based on the peasantry of the Sierra Maestra, with which it eventually allied itself, that did so. Within the socialist countries themselves, the Polish students suffered a temporary defeat in their courageous fight against bureaucratic repression in 1968 because they remained socially isolated; indeed some workers were deluded into attacking them. By contrast, Czechoslovak students prior to the Russian occupation set off profound political changes because they succeeded in uniting their protest with the demands of working people, and no demagogic governmental appeals to proletarian anti-intellectualism were able to dam the popular feeling that resulted. *A fortiori*, in capitalist countries students will only topple governments when they are united with the working class. This does not, however, mean that they cannot change national politics first by autonomous student militancy. The example of the SDS in West Germany is conclusive here. Its very success has provided the possibility of inspiring a revolt of young workers and hence of an alliance between the two. If *victory* is only possible within a social bloc dominated by the working class, militant students may everywhere *start* revolutionary politics when they are in abeyance.

6. *Students are the internationalist social group* par excellence *under present conditions.* They have shown an unrivalled speed in learning from and coordinating with foreign struggles in recent years. It is thus an essential *practical* step for British students to study the lessons of international experience. The enormous gamut of different forms of student struggle has been illustrated again and again: few social movements have been so inventive with them. Some of the following are useful ideas that may form part of general student repertoire in the future: the campus red-base (Latin America), democratization of examinations (China), public cross-questioning of academics and

refusal to negotiate in private (Italy), assaults on the press (West Germany), occupation of the campus (USA), resistance on the streets (France), technical defence against police repression (Japan). These are merely aspects of possible campaigns: what they show is the potential richness of forms of protest.

Britain has not yet seen a mass movement of student militants, conscious of their educational and political ends. This is in marked contrast to most other advanced capitalist societies and indeed to most throughout the world. Yet the dominant structures of British society are no less archaic and repressive than those of other capitalist countries where a strong student movement has already emerged. A network of traditional pseudo-democratic institutions protects the fortresses of wealth and privilege. A dead weight of long accumulated customs and beliefs stifles any revolutionary impulse. Such factors may have delayed the appearance of a revolutionary student movement in Britain. They may also make the ultimate explosion all the greater. This will largely depend on the quality of our own efforts. As we prepare for the future we must draw inspiration and experience from fraternal student movements across the world.

REFERENCES

1. See the opening essay by Gareth Stedman Jones.
2. See the essay by Carl Davidson.
3. That is, universities should reflect conditions in the localities where they are situated.
4. *Time*, 6 May 1966.
5. 'University Students in National Politics', Alistair Hennessy in *The Politics of Conformity in Latin America*. ed. Claudio Veliz, London, 1967, p. 130. See also Juan Mier Febles 'La Reforma Universitaria en Córdoba' *OCLAE* No. 18, June 1968.
6. *International Socialist Journal*, No. 13, January–February 1966.
7. *Economist*, 29 January 1966.
8. *Newsweek*, 26 December 1966.
9. Alistair Hennessy, op. cit., p. 119.
10. 'Entrance Examinations: a Challenge to Equal Opportunity in Education', Yoshihiro Shimizu, in *Journal of Social and Political Ideas in Japan*, December 1963.
11. Cole, Totten and Uyehara, *Socialist Parties in Postwar Japan*, Yale UP, 1966, and Usanu Shō 'Zengakuren', *Japan Quarterly*, April–June 1968.

12. Robert Scalapino and Junnosuke, *Parties and Politics in Contemporary Japan*, California, 1962, pp. 137–8, and Philip Altbach 'Japanese Students and Japanese Politics', *Comparative Education Review*, October 1963.

13. *The Times*, 11–20 June 1960.

14. *The Times*, 4 April 1967.

15. *Mainichi Daily News*, 9 October and 13 November 1967, 18 January and 11 March 1968.

16. Immanuel Hsu, 'The Reorganization of Higher Education in Communist China 1949', *China Quarterly* No. 19, July–September 1964, and René Goldman, 'Peking University Today', *China Quarterly* No. 7, July–September 1961.

17. Klaus Pringsheim, 'Chinese Communist Youth Leagues 1920–49', *China Quarterly* No. 12, October–December 1962.

18. John Collier, 'Cultural Revolution in Canton', *New Left Review* 48, March–April 1968.

19. Jack Gray and Patrick Cavendish, *Chinese Communism in Crisis*, London, 1968, p. 128.

20. *Peking Review* No. 48, 25 November 1966.

21. Some of the Turin texts are in *Documenti della rivolta universitaria*, Bari, 1968 : this is the best collection of documents. The best collection of interpretative texts by Italian students is No. 28–9 of *Problemi del Socialismo*. More generally on Italian education, see *Lettera a una Professoressa*, Florence, 1968 (a collective work), and the Feltrinelli booklet, *La Scuola e gli Studenti*, Milan, 1968.

22. *La Sinistra*, 27 January 1968.

23. For a comprehensive analysis, *Quaderni Piacentini* No. 33, February 1968.

24. *Rinascita*, 3 May 1968.

25. *Der Spiegel*, No. 29, 1967.

26. *Der Spiegel*, No. 17, 1968.

27. Marc Kravetz, 'Naissance d'un Syndicalisme Etudiant', *Les Temps Modernes*, February 1964, and 'De l'Algérie à la Reforme Fouchet: Critique du Syndicalisme Etudiant', *Les Temps Modernes*, April and May 1965.

28. For documents on the conflict at Nanterre, *Esprit*, May 1968.

Campaigning on the Campus/Carl Davidson

The materialist doctrine that men are products of circumstance and upbringing and that, therefore, changed men are products of other circumstances and changed upbringing, forgets that circumstances are changed precisely by men and that the educator must himself be educated. Hence this doctrine necessarily arrives at dividing society into two parts, of which one towers above society (Robert Owen). The coincidence of the changing of circumstances and of human activity can only be conceived and rationally understood as revolutionizing practice (Karl Marx).[1]

1. The Present Malaise of Education

'Happiness is Student Power' was the most catching slogan emblazoned on the many banners and picket signs during the Berkeley Student Strike in December 1966. But, as most college administrators know only too well, Berkeley and its rebellious students are not an isolated phenomenon among the vast variety of American campuses. Far from being an exception, Berkeley has become the paradigm case of the educational malaise in the United States; and, in the last few years, that malaise has been transformed into a movement. Indeed a spectre is haunting our universities – the spectre of a radical and militant nationally coordinated movement for *student power*.

Students began using the slogan 'student power' soon after black people in the Civil Rights movement made the demand for 'black power'. Are students niggers? After studying the history of the Wobblies and labour syndicalism, students started thinking about student syndicalism. Are students workers? Power for what? Just any old kind of power? The university is a clumsy and uncoordinated machine, engulfing and serving thousands of people. Do students want to be administrators?

Obviously the cry for 'power' in and of itself is a vacuous

demand. Student power is not so much something we are fighting *for*, as it is something we must have in order to gain specific objectives. Then what are the objectives? What is our programme? There is much variety in the dispute on these questions. But there is one thing that seems clear. However the specific forms of our immediate demands and programmes may vary, the long-range goal and the daily drive that motivates and directs us is our intense longing for our liberation. In short, what the student power movement is about is *freedom*.

But aren't students free? Isn't America a democracy, even if it is a little manipulative? To answer those kinds of questions and many others that are more serious, it is important to look more closely at and come to an understanding of the malaise motivating our movement.

What do American students think of the educational institutions in which they live an important part of their lives? The most significant fact is that most of them don't think about them. Such young men and women made up that apathetic majority we called the 'silent generation' in the 1950s. While the last few years has shown a marked and dramatic growth of a new radicalism, we should not forget that the apathetic and the cynical among the student population are still in the majority. But this need not be discouraging. In fact, we should view that apparent apathy among the majority of students with a certain qualified optimism.

What makes people apathetic? My feeling is that apathy is the *unconscious* recognition students make of the fact that they are *powerless*. Despite all the machinations and rhetoric used by hot-shot student *politicos* within administration-sponsored student governments, people's experience tells them that nothing changes. Furthermore, if and when change does occur, students fully recognize that they were powerless to effect those changes in one way or another. If this is in fact the case, then why shouldn't students be apathetic? The administration rules, despite the façade of student governments, of dorm councils, and of student judicials. And when *they* give us ex-officio seats on *their* academic committees, the result among most students is that deeper, more hardened kind of apathy – cynicism.

The apathetic students are correct *as far as they go*. They are powerless. The forms given us for our self-government are of the Mickey Mouse, sand-box variety. I would only be pessimistic if a majority of students really accepted the illusion that those institutions had meaning in their lives, or that they could significantly affect those institutions. But the opposite is the case. The apathy reflects the reality of their powerlessness. When that reality confronts the lie of the official rhetoric, the contradiction is driven home – and the apathetic become the cynical. What that contradiction – that daily living with a lie – all adds up to is a *dynamic* tension and alienation. And that, fellow organizers, is the necessary subjective condition for any revolution.

It is important to understand that students are alienated from much more than the social and extracurricular aspect of their education. In fact, their deepest alienation is directed at the educational process itself. The excerpts that follow are from a letter written to the *New York Times* by a young woman student:

I came to this school not thinking I could even keep up with the work. I was wrong. I can keep up. I can even come out on top. My daily schedule's rough. I get up at 6.30. . . . After dinner I work until midnight or 12.30. In the beginning, the first few weeks or so, I'm fine. Then I begin to wonder just what this is all about: am I educating myself? I have that one answered . . . I'm educating myself the way *they* want. So I convince myself the real reason I'm doing all this is to prepare myself; meantime I'm wasting those years of preparation. I'm not learning what I want to learn . . . I don't care about the feudal system. I want to know about life. I want to think and read. When? . . . My life is a whirlpool. I'm caught up in it, but I'm not conscious of it. I'm what *you* call living, but somehow I can't find life. . . . So maybe I got an A . . . but when I get it back I find that A means nothing. It's a letter *you* use to keep me going . . . I wonder what I'm doing here. I feel phony; I don't belong. . . . You wonder about juvenile delinquents. If I ever become one, I'll tell why it will be so. I feel cramped. I feel like I'm in a coffin and can't move or breathe. . . . My life is worth nothing. It's enclosed in a few buildings on one campus; it goes no further. I've got to bust.[2]

Tell the truth. Every American student knows that's the way it is. Even our administrators recognize what is going on. In 1963, a year or so *before* the first Berkeley insurrection, Clark

Kerr prophesied, 'the undergraduate students are restless. Recent changes in the American university have done them little good. ... There is an incipient revolt.'[3] Kerr is not only concerned about the students. He also casts a worried glance at the faculty. 'Knowledge is now in so many bits and pieces and administration so distant that faculty members are increasingly figures in a "lonely crowd", intellectually and institutionally.'[4] The academic division of labour and depersonalization among the faculty is more than apparent to the students. Incoming freshmen scratch their heads, trying to understand any possible relevance of many of the courses in the catalogue, some of which they are required to take. Also, some of the best belly-laughs are had by reading the titles of master's and doctoral theses, like one granted a Ph.Ed. at Michigan State University: 'An Evaluation of Thirteen Brands of Football Helmets on the Basis of Certain Impact Measures.'[5] What's worse, even if a course seems as though it might be relevant to our lives, like Psychology or Political Science, we are soon told by our professor that what we'll learn only has to do with the laboratory behaviour of rats, and that 'political science' has nothing to do with day-to-day politics. A student from Brandeis sums it up nicely,

By the time we graduate, we have been painstakingly trained in separating facts from their meaning. ... We wonder that our classes, with few exceptions, seem irrelevant to our lives. No wonder they're so boring. Boredom is the necessary condition of any education which teaches us to manipulate the facts and suppress their meaning.[6]

Irrelevancy, meaninglessness, boredom, and fragmentation are the kinds of attributes that are becoming more and more applicable to mass education in America. We are becoming a people required to know more and more about less and less. This is true not only for our students, but also for our teachers; not only in our universities, but also in our secondary and primary schools – private as well as public.

What should education be about in America? The official rhetoric seems to offer an answer: education should be the process of developing the free, autonomous, creative and responsible *individual* – the 'citizen', in the best sense of that word. Furthermore, higher education ought to encourage and enable the individual to turn his personal concerns into social issues, open to rational consideration and solution. C. Wright Mills put it clearly: 'The aim of the college, for the individual student, is to eliminate the need in his life for the college; the task is to help him become a self-educating man. For only that will set him free.'[7]

But what is the reality of American education? Contrary to our commitment to individualism, we find that the day-to-day practice of our schools is authoritarian, conformist, and almost entirely status oriented. We find the usual relationship between teacher and student to be a disciplined form of dominance and subordination. We are told of the egalitarianism inherent in our school system, where the classroom becomes the melting-pot for the classless society of America's 'people's capitalism', where everyone has the opportunity to climb to the top. Again, the opposite is the case. Our schools are more racially segregated now (1967) than ever before. There is a clear class bias contained both within and among our public schools – not even considering the clear class nature of our private schools and colleges. Within the secondary schools, students are quickly channelled – usually according to the class background of their parents – into vocational, commercial, or academic preparatory programmes. Concerning the class differences among our public schools, James Conant remarks in *Slums and Suburbs,*

One cannot imagine the possibility of a wealthy suburban district deliberately consolidating with other districts to achieve a truly comprehensive high school in which students of all abilities and socio-economic backgrounds will study together.[8]

Even if they did consolidate, the problem would only be rationalized, rather than solved. Who knows? Maybe the class struggle would break out on the playground.

Finally, what about that traditional American ideal that we were all taught to honour – the legend of the self-educated and self-educating man? It seems to me that rather than enabling an individual to initiate and engage himself in a continual and coherent life-long educational process, our public programmes are of the sort where an individual is merely subjected to a random series of isolated training situations.

From individual freedom to national service, from egalitarianism to class and racial hierarchical ossification, from self-reliance to institutional dependence – we have come to see education as the mechanistic process of homogeneous, uncritical absorption of 'data' and development of job skills. But it is something more than that. The socialization and acculturation that goes on within America attempts to mould and shape American youth. This is mainly the result of the declining influence and, in some cases, the collapse of other traditional socializing institutions such as the church and the family. The schools, at all levels, end up with the job of maintaining, modifying, and transmitting the dominant themes of the national culture.

Quantitatively education has been rapidly increasing in the last few decades; but, as it grows in size, it decreases *qualitatively*. Rickover states in *Education and Freedom*: 'We end up where we began a hundred years ago – with an elementary vocational education for the majority, and a poor college preparatory course for a minority of students.'[9] Conant, who is quite concerned with the plight of the 80 to 85 per cent of urban non-college-bound high school students who are 'social dynamite', places as a primary goal of education, giving these students 'the kind of zeal and dedication ... to withstand the relentless pressures of communism'.[10]

What about our schoolteachers? How is the nation faring on that front? Over 30 per cent of the students in US colleges and universities are going into primary and secondary education. However, despite the quantity, Mortimer Smith remarks in *The Diminished Mind*, 'the teacher-training institutions ... are providing us with teachers who are our most poorly educated citizens'.[11] While the job of teachers should command the highest respect in any society, many of us are well aware of the fact that in relation to other parts of the university, the college or school of education is considered to be the intellectual slum of the campus.

It seems clear that bourgeois education in the US is in its historically most irrational and decadent state. Primary, secondary, and university systems are fusing together, thoroughly rationalizing and dehumanizing their internal order, and placing themselves in the service of the state, industry, and the military. Kerr is quite clear about this when he speaks of the 'multiversity' making a common-law marriage with the federal government. John Hannah, president of Michigan State, was even clearer in a speech given in September 1961, 'Our colleges and universities must be regarded as bastions of our defence, as essential to preservation of our country and our way of life as super-sonic bombers, nuclear powered submarines and intercontinental ballistic missiles.'[12] The fact that none of the three weapons systems Hannah mentioned could have been designed, constructed, or operated without college-educated men proves that this is not just Fourth of July rhetoric. Hannah gives us an even better look at his idea of education in an article entitled 'The School's Responsibility in National Defense', where he comments:

I believe the primary and secondary schools can make education serve the individual and national interest by preparing youngsters for military service and life under conditions of stress as well as preparing them for college, or for a job or profession. . . . I would not even shrink from putting the word 'indoctrination' to the kind of education I have in mind. If we do not hesitate to indoctrinate our children with a love of truth, a love of home, and a love of God, then I see no justification for balking at teaching them love of country and love of what this country means.[13]

Hannah's comment about 'life under conditions of stress' is related to a remark made by Eric A. Walker, president of Pennsylvania State University, a few years ago. There had been a series of student suicides and attempted suicides within a quite short period of time. Many students and faculty members started grumbling about the newly instituted 'term' system – a kind of 'speed-up' – relating the stress and strain of the new system to the student suicides. Dr Walker's response to this unrest was to comment on how the increased pressure on the students was a good thing, since it enabled them to 'have their nervous breakdowns early', before they graduated and had jobs and families when having a nervous breakdown would cause them more difficulties.

Despite the crass attitudes of so many of our educators, or the dehumanization of the form and content of our educational institutions, it would be a mistake to think the problems are only within the educational system. While it is true that education has been stripped of any meaning it once had, and Dr Conant is reduced to defining education as 'what goes on in schools and colleges',[14] our system of schools and colleges is far from a point of collapse. In fact, it is thriving. The 'knowledge industry', as Kerr calls it, accounts for 30 per cent of the Gross National Product; and it is expanding at twice the rate of any sector of the economy. Schoolteachers make up the largest single occupational group of the labour force – some three million workers. Twenty-five years ago, the government and industry were hardly interested in education. But in 1960, the aggregate national outlay, public and private, amounted to $23,100,000,000. As Kerr says, 'the university has become a prime instrument of national purpose. This is new. This is the essence of the transformation now engulfing our universities.'[15] In short, our educational institutions are becoming appendages to, and transformed by, US corporate capitalism.

Education is not being done away with in favour of something called training. Rather, education is being transformed from a quasi aristocratic classicism and petty-bourgeois romanticism into something quite new. These changes are apparent in ways other than the quantitative statistics given above. For example, we can examine the social sciences and the humanities. The social and psychological 'reality' that we are given to study is 'objectified' to the point of sterility. The real world, we are to understand, is 'valuefree' and pragmatically bears little or no relation to the actual life-activity of men, classes and nations. In one sense, we are separated from life. In another, we are being conditioned for life in a lifeless, stagnant, and sterile society.

For another example, there is more than a semantic connexion between the academic division of labour and specialization we are all aware of, and the corresponding division of labour that has gone on in large-scale industry. But it is important to understand what that connexion is. It does *not* follow that because technology becomes diversified and specialized, then academic knowledge and skills must follow suit. André Gorz makes the relevant comment:

It is completely untrue that modern technology demands specialization: quite the reverse. It demands a basic 'polyvalent' education, comprising not a fragmentary, pre-digested and specialized knowledge, but an invitation – or, put more precisely, a faculty of self-initiation – into methods of scientifico-technological research and discovery.[16]

If it is not the new technological production that deems necessary the kind of isolated specialization we know so well, then what is responsible? Gorz spells it out again, 'Capitalism actually needs shattered and atomized men'[17] in order to maintain its system of centralized, bureacratized and militarized hierarchies, so as 'to perpetuate its domination over men, not only as workers, but also as consumers and citizens.'[18]

From this perspective, we can begin to understand that the educational malaise we as students and teachers have felt so personally and intensely is no aberration, but firmly rooted in the American political economy. In fact, the Organized System which Paul Goodman calls 'compulsory mis-education' may miseducate us, but it certainly serves the masters of that system, the US ruling class, quite well. As Edgar Z. Friedenberg wrote: 'Educational evils are attributed to *defective* schools. In fact, they are as likely to be the work of *effective* schools that are being directed toward evil ends by the society that supports and controls them.'[19] Furthermore, he continues later in the same article, 'Schools are a definite indication that a society is divisible into a dominant and a subordinate group, and that the dominant group want to teach the subordinate group something they could noy be trusted to learn if left to themselves.'[20] Clark Kerr would accept this, both for the society in general, which he divides into the 'managers' and the 'managed' and for the university. Kerr states: 'The intellectuals (including university students) are a particularly volatile element. ... They are by nature irresponsible. ... They are, as a result, never fully trusted by anybody, including themselves.'[21] But Kerr doesn't dismiss us. Even if we are by nature irresponsible (perhaps because we can perceive the contradictions?) he considers us essential. 'It is important who best attracts or captures the intellectuals and who uses them most effectively, for they may be a tool as well as a source of danger.'[22]

I think we can conclude that the American educational system is a coherent, well-organized, and – to the extent that the rulers are still ruling – effective mechanism. However, it has turned our humanitarian values into their opposites and, at the same time, given us the potential to understand and critically evaluate both ourselves and the system itself. To that extent the system is fraught with internal contradictions. Furthermore, the events comprising the student revolt in the last few years demonstrate the likelihood that those contradictions will continue to manifest themselves in an open and protracted struggle. As Kerr predicted, we are a source of danger and incipient revolt. And the fact that Kerr was fired and the police used in the face of that revolt only goes to prove that those contradictions are irreconcilable within the structure of corporate capitalism. As Quintin Hoare remarked in the *New Left Review* 32, 'a reform of the educational system involves a reform of the educators as well, and this is a political task, which immediately ricochets back to the question of transforming consciousness and ideology throughout society.' [23] The central problem of radically transforming the educational system is that of the transformation of the teaching and the learning body – the faculty and students. And this transformation, while it *begins* with the demands of the students' and teachers' work situation, cannot take place unless it occurs *within* and is organically connected *to* the practice of a mass radical *political* movement.

2. The Political Economy of the Multiversity

The Knowledge Factory

What sense does it make to refer to the university as a factory? Is it just a good analogy? Or is there more to it than that? According to Kerr, 'The university and segements of industry are becoming more and more alike.' [24] He also informs us that, 'The university is being called upon to ... merge its activities with industry as never before'.[25] Furthermore, in terms of control, the merger that Kerr speaks of seems to have been completed. According to a study by H. P. Beck,

Altogether the evidence of major university-business connections at high levels seems overwhelming. The numerous high positions of power in industry, commerce, and finance held by at least two-thirds of the governing boards of these 30 leading universities would appear to give a decisive majority more than ample grounds for identifying their personal interests with those of business.[26]

Indeed, the boards of regents or trustees of almost every college and university in the country read off like corporation directories.

But it is not ample proof to call a university a factory merely because it is controlled by the same people who control industry. We must look deeper. Let us look at a relatively recent development within the US political economy – the 'innovation industry'. This aspect of corporate capitalism, usually referred to as 'R and D', Research and Development, has become a major industry. Since 1940 it has grown twenty-seven times over; and it now accounts for approximately 5 per cent of the overall federal budget.[27] What is important for us to see is that 20 per cent of the work and production of the innovation industry is done directly within the university. In fact, it is this phenomenon that, since the Second World War, has been transforming the academic landscape into what we now call the 'multiversity'. Entirely new areas of work have been created – research assistants and technicians, industrial consultants, research promoters, contracting officers, and research project managers.

While research and development can be seen only as an adjunct to the real business of the university – teaching – the position it occupies is much more strategic.

The men who teach in America's graduate schools determine for the rest of us not only what is true and what is false, but in a large measure what is 'done' and 'not done'. Since the graduate schools are usually a generation ahead of whatever segment of society they lead, their influence at any particular moment always looks modest. Over the years, however, they are perhaps the single most important source of innovation in society.[28]

And those innovations are important in more ways than we might think. According to Mills, 'Research for bureaucratic ends serves to make authority more effective and more efficient by providing information of use to authoritative planners.'[29] In the end the multiversity becomes the vanguard of the *status quo*, providing the know-how to gently usher in the New Order of 1984. The clearest manifestation of this trend can be seen in the sciences. Mills concludes: 'Science – historically started in the universities; and connected rather informally with private industry – has now become officially established in, for, and by the military order.'[30]

As I remarked earlier, the services rendered by American education to corporate capitalism are evidenced by the academic division of labour. According to James Conant, over 1,600 different academic degrees are possible within our diploma mills, most of which parallel the skill demands of the new technology. But it is important to note that not only is the division of labour increasing *within* the universities, but also is occurring *among* the universities. Just as different factories can produce different *kinds* of commodities, different universities can produce different *kinds* of students. A type of educational 'pluralism' has been developing over the last few decades. The traditional and old League Schools shape the sons and daughters of the ruling class and old middle class into the new ruling and managerial elites. The state colleges and universities develop the sons and daughters of the working class and petty bourgeoisie into the highly skilled sectors of the new working class, the middle sector white collar workers, and the traditional middle-class professionals. Finally, the new community and junior colleges serve the increasing educational needs of, for the most part, the sons and daughters of the working class. This division of function both within and among our schools has a further strategic importance for radical organizing that I will comment on later.

So far, we have only seen the connexion between the universities and the factories of industry in a secondary sense. It is true that there are parallels between the form and content of the educational system and large-scale industry. It is true that the same people determine the decision-making parameters of both systems. It is true that the non-teaching intellectual work – the innovation industry – produces a commodity directly consumed by industry. All of this is still not sufficient evidence to call our schools 'factories', except in an analogous sense. Before we can draw that conclusion, we must look at the *primary* function of our educational system – the work of teaching and learning.

A factory is the focus of the machinery of production, social in character, where men work together to produce a commodity for consumption in the market place. At that point, the commodities are purchased either directly by the public or by other sectors of industry. Furthermore, if one is a radical, there are strategic criteria about factories to be considered as well. Is the work done in the factory productive work? i.e. are the commodities produced both socially necessary and useful rather than inherently designed for waste, repression, and destruction? In other words, would work of the same nature, although transformed, be essential to a rational (i.e. socialist) political economy? These are the sort of questions that must be dealt with before we can arrive at a radical understanding of both our educational system and the new characteristics of advanced industrial society.

Work and Alienation within the University

To begin, I will make a number of qualifications for the purpose of resolving disputes with other radicals before they happen. First of all, much of the work done in American education is irrational. Both the learning and teaching of many (but not all) of the manipulative techniques of bourgeois political economy that goes on in our schools of business administration, education, and social science can in no sense be considered productive work. However, while this is true of the university in part, it does not follow that it is true of the university as an *objective whole*.

Second, I am not trying to say that students are workers in the strict sense. At best, so long as he, his family, or his friends are paying for his education, his learning activity results only in the production of *use value*; i.e., the potentially socially useful increase in the *future* productivity of his labour power. However, to the extent to which the student is *paid* by private or state institutions to engage in *specific* kinds of intellectual work, his activity *might in some cases* be seen as commodity production; i.e., the development of the productivity of his labour power as *an actual exchange-value*, rather than as a potential use value. This small number of students might be called workers. However, the position of most students is that of workers-to-be, i.e., trainee or apprentice. But as a trainee, it is important that we recognize that many students share many of the social relations and conditions of production with many of the skilled workers of large-scale industry.

Finally, it is true that many faculty members are becoming more entrepreneurial and developing many interests that are objectively bound up with the ruling and sub-ruling classes. However, to say this is true of all faculty members fails to take into account a kind of class division that is occurring within the faculty in American universities. Clark Kerr distinguishes three functional types within the faculty of the multiversity.[31] The top level faculty – the heads of departments, intellectual administrators, research promoters, and paid consultants – should be seen as petty bourgeoisie and managerial sector constituents who have their interests tied up with the ruling and sub-ruling classes. The second group, the traditional academics, should be seen as middle-class professionals in the classic sense. However, the third and largest group, the lower-echelon faculty who are primarily engaged in teaching in the mass production line of large classes should be seen as members of the new working class. Their objective interests are with the students and the working class in general, despite the significant problem of their false consciousness. This point is also of strategic and tactical importance and will be considered in Part 3.

So much for the qualifications. What is the nature of the teaching–learning activity within our educational institutions that might permit us to call them 'knowledge factories' in other than an analogous sense? First of all, we need to take into account a few historical factors. The growth of the American political economy in the last thirty years has been facilitated in part by the development of a new technology. The development of the new technology itself, the job displacements it created, and the increase in job skills required for its operation, created tremendous pressure on the state for the training of a highly skilled sector within the labour force. The working class, recognizing the need for the new skills, both for themselves and their children, also made demands of the government for both more and better education. Even at present, skill levels are rising at perhaps the highest rate in history. The government responded and is continuing to respond. According to Kerr, 'Higher education in 1960 received about $1.5 billion from the federal government – hundredfold increase in twenty years.' [32] However, while the demand for expanding education comes from both the needs of a developing technology and from the demands of working-class parents, it is the needs of the industrialists that *structure* the form and content of the educational expansion. According to Gorz, the state responds to capital rather than people, 'since the development of education falls under the general head of growing collective needs produced by monopolistic-expansion'.[33] In the last few decades, the expanding reproduction and accumulation of a continuing increase in the *productivity of labour power* is an *objective necessity* of contemporary corporate capitalism. Kerr remarks: 'Instead of waiting outside the gates, agents (of the industrialists) are working the corridors. They also work the placement offices.' [34]

The colleges and universities have gone beyond their traditional task of socialization and acculturation. They are deeply involved in the production of a crucial and marketable commodity – labour power. Again Gorz comments, 'the work of learning (and teaching), of extending and transforming professional skills, is implicitly recognized as socially necessary and productive work, through which the individual transforms himself according to the needs of society (and industry).' [35] It is this aspect of the university that is most crucial for the political economy. The production of an increase in socially useful and necessary labour power is the new historic function of our educational institutions that enables us to name them, quite accurately, knowledge factories. In this process of historical change, liberal education has been transformed into its opposite and what we are witnessing is the advent of training and indoctrination. The core of the university with its frills removed, has become the crucible for the production, formation, and socialization of the new working class.

What does the interior of the new knowledge factory look like? Where are the workshops? Specifically, these are to be found in the classrooms, the faculty offices, the study rooms in the libraries and homes, the psychological counselling offices and clinics, the conference rooms, the research laboratories, and the administrative staff offices. What kind of machinery can we find in these mental sweatshops? What kind of apparatus have our rulers constructed in the name of our enlightenment? The machinery of knowledge-production pervades the university. And, despite its invisibility, it is no less real or tangible. The productive apparatus consists of grades, exams, assigned books, papers, and reports, all the curriculum and scheduling requirements, non-academic *in loco parentis* regulations, scientific equipment and resources, the mechanics of grants and endowments, disciplinary procedures, campus and civil police, and all the repressive and sublimative psychological techniques of fear and punishment. Most, if not all, of this machinery and the purposes it is used for are beyond the control of the students and faculty who work with it. All government, all control, all the parameters of decision-making have fallen into the hands of the administrative representatives of the ruling class. At best, hand-picked 'representatives' of student and faculty 'opinion' are prearranged. For example, female students are permitted to determine how strict or 'liberal' their dorm hours might be; but the underlying assumption of whether they should have curfews at all is beyond question. Or, while some (but not all) college professors are free to teach *what* they please, they are not 'free to decide *how* to teach – whether in large numbers or small, in departmentalized courses or others, one day a week or five.'[36]

In the past the work of teaching and learning was a two-way process with the Socratic dialectic as its purest form. However, with the advent of the corporate state and its corresponding appropriation of the cultural apparatus, education has become increasingly one-dimensional. Teaching is reduced to an uncritical distribution of pre-established skills, techniques and 'data', while learning is transformed into the passive consumption of the same. In its broadest sense, culture – that which is man-made – is turned into its opposite – anti-culture – the creature of expanding production. Education, meaning 'to educe', to draw out from, has become something that the state *gives* to people. Finally, teacher and students, both dehumanized distributors and consumers of the knowledge commodity become commodities themselves – something to be bought and sold in the university placement office.

But it is not enough for the knowledge factory to produce skilled labour power in the form of a *raw material*. The commodity must be socially useful as well. When describing the multiversity's machinery Clark Kerr tells us that academic processes and requirements are 'part of the process of freezing the structure of the occupational pyramid and assuring that *the well-behaved do advance even if the geniuses do not*' (emphasis mine).[37] Our rough edges must be worn off, our spirit broken, our hopes mundane, and our manners subservient and docile. And if we won't pacify and repress ourselves with all the mechanisms they have constructed for our self-flagellation, the police will be called.

Like any good training programme, the knowledge factory accurately reproduces all the conditions and relations of production in the factories of advanced corporate capitalism – isolation, manipulation, and alienation. First, the teaching and learning workers of the knowledge factory are alienated from each other, isolated and divided among themselves by grades, class ranks, and the status levels of the bureaucratic hierarchy. Secondly, they are alienated from the product of their work, the content and purpose of which have been determined and used by someone other than themselves. Finally, they are alienated in the activity of education itself. What should be the active creation and re-creation of culture is nothing more than forced and coercive consumption and distribution of data and technique. Throughout the educational apparatus, the bureaucratic mentality prevails. History and ideology have come to an end. Science, the humanities, even philosophy have become value-free. Politics are reduced to advertising and sales campaigns. Finally government and self-determination become matters of administration and domination.

The Meaning of the Student Revolt

Our manipulators have overlooked one fundamental factor; there is one facet of human history to which the bureaucratic

Weltanschauung is blind. Men are not made of clay. Despite all the official pronouncements asserting the end of this or that, the wellsprings of human freedom still run deep. All the attempts to teach ignorance in the place of knowledge have come to naught. The student revolt is an historic event. Someone (the Berkeley students?) let the cat out of the bag. The emperor has no clothes.

Our rulers are aware of this. The bureaucrats of corporate capitalism must cut back and control the quality of and content of 'liberal' education. They know only too well that a widespread culture rising out of critical thought might challenge, during a crisis, the existing relations of production and domination. The CIA control of the National Student Association and other 'cultural' organizations prove this only too well.

But the corporate ruling class is not primarily interested in containing and pacifying us *as intellectuals*. Their real concern with us lies in our role as the highly skilled members of the new working class. As Gorz points out, 'skilled workers ... possess *in their own right* ... the labour power they lend.' [38] Their skills are an attribute of *themselves* and not just the material means of production. Gorz continues:

> The problem of big management is to harmonize two contradictory necessities: the necessity of developing human capabilities, imposed by modern processes of production and the political necessity of insuring that this kind of development does not bring in its wake any augmentation of the independence of the individual, provoking him to challenge the present division of social labour and distribution of power.[39]

From this analysis, we can understand the student revolt in its most strategic and crucial sense. What we are witnessing and participating in is an important historical phenomenon: the revolt of the trainees of the new working class against the alienated and oppressive conditions of production and consumption within corporate capitalism. These are the conditions of life and activity that lie beneath the apathy, frustration, and rebellion on America's campuses. André Gorz predicted a few years back: 'It is in education that industrial capitalism will provoke revolts which it attempts to avoid in its factories.' [40]

Nevertheless, the 'student power' movement is still vague and undefined. Its possibilities are hopeful as well as dangerous. On the one hand, student power can develop into an elitist corporate monster, mainly concerned with developing better techniques of 'co-managing' the bureaucratic apparatus of advanced industrial society. On the other hand, a student power movement might successfully develop a revolutionary class consciousness among the future new working class, who would organize on their jobs and among the traditional working class around the issues of participatory democracy and worker control. The character of the future movement will depend to a great extent on the kind of strategy and tactics we use in the present. The struggle will be protracted, that is certain. There is no certain or pre-determined victory. We should not forget that 1984 is possible. And not many years away. But we have several years of experience behind us from which we can learn a great deal.

3. The Praxis of Student Power: Strategy and Tactics

Socialism on One Campus – an Infantile Disorder

Perhaps the single most important factor for the student power movement to keep in mind is the fact that the university is intimately bound up with the society in general. Because of this, we should always remember that we cannot liberate the university without radically changing the rest of society. The lesson to be drawn is that any attempt to build a student movement based on 'on-campus' issues only is inherently conservative and ultimately reactionary. Every attempt should be made to connect campus issues with off-campus questions. For example, the question of ranking and university complicity with the Selective Service System needs to be tied to a general anti-draft and 'No Draft for Vietnam' movement. The question of the presence of the military on the campus in all its forms needs to be tied to the question of what that military is used for – fighting aggressive wars of oppression abroad – and not just to the question of secret research being poor academic policy. Furthermore, the student movement must actively seek to join off-campus struggles in the surrounding community. For example, strikes by local unions should be supported if possible. This kind of communication and understanding with the local working class is essential if we are ever going to have community support for student strikes.

Radicalizing the New Working Class

If there is a single overall purpose for the student power movement, it would be the development of a radical political consciousness among those students who will later hold jobs in strategic sectors of the political economy. This means that we should reach out to engineers and technical students rather than to business administration majors, education majors rather than to art students. From a national perspective, this strategy would also suggest that we should place priorities on organizing in certain kinds of universities – the community colleges, junior colleges, state universities and technical schools, rather than religious colleges or the Ivy League.

One way to mount political action around this notion is to focus on the placement offices – the nexus between the university and industry. For example, when DOW Chemical comes to recruit, our main approach to junior and senior chemical engineering students who are being interviewed should not only be around the issue of the immorality of napalm. Rather, our leaflets should say that one of the main faults of DOW and all other industries as well is that their workers *have no control* over the content or purposes of their work. In other words, DOW Chemical is bad, not only because of napalm, but mainly because it renders its workers *powerless*, makes them *unfree*. In short, DOW and all American industry *oppresses its own workers* as well as the people of the Third World. DOW in particular should be run off the campus and students urged not to work for them because of their complicity in war crimes. But when other industries are recruiting, our leaflets should address themselves to the interviewees' instincts of workmanship, his desires to be free and creative, to do humane work, rather than work for profit. We should encourage him, if he takes the job, to see himself in this light – as a skilled worker – and arouse his interest of organizing in his future job with his fellow workers, skilled and unskilled, for control of production and the end to which his work is directed. The need for control, for the power, on and off the job, to affect the decisions shaping one's life in all arenas; developing this kind of consciousness, on and off the campus, is what we should be fundamentally all about.

Practical, Critical Activity: Notes on Organizing

There are three virtues necessary for successful radical organizing: honesty, patience, and a sense of humour. First of all if the students we are trying to reach can't trust us, who can they trust? Secondly it takes time to build a movement. Sometimes several years of groundwork must be laid before a student power movement has a constituency. It took most of us several years before we had developed a radical perspective. Why should it be any different for the people we are trying to reach? This is not to say that everyone must repeat all the mistakes we have gone through, but there are certain forms of involvement and action that many students will have to repeat. Finally, by a sense of humour, I mean we must be life-affirming; lusty passionate people are the only kind of men who have the enduring strength to motivate enough people to radically transform a life-negating system.

Che Guevara remarked in *Guerrilla Warfare* that as long as people had faith in certain institutions and forms of political activity, then the organizer must work with the people through those institutions, even though we might think those forms of action are dead ends.[41] The point of Che's remark is that people must learn that those forms are stacked against them through their *own experience* in attempting change. The role of the organizer at this point is crucial. He or she should neither passively go along with the student government 'reformer' types nor stand apart from the action denouncing it as a 'sell-out'. Rather, his task is that of *constant criticism* from within the action. When the reformers fail, become bogged down, or are banging their heads against the wall, the organizer should be there as *one who has been with them throughout their struggle* to offer the relevant analysis of *why* their approach has failed and to indicate future strategies and tactics.

However, we also need to be discriminating. There are certain forms of political action, like working within the Democratic Party, that are so obviously bankrupt, that we need not waste our time. In order to discern these limits, an organizer has to develop a sensitivity to understand where people are. Many radical actions have failed on campuses because the activists have failed in laying a base for a particular action. It does no good to sit in against the CIA if a broad educational campaign, petitions, and rallies on the nature of the CIA have not been done for several days before the sit-in. It is not enough that we have a clear understanding of the oppressiveness of institutions like the CIA and HUAC before we act in a radical fashion. We must make our position clear to the students, faculty, and the surrounding community.

The Cultural Apparatus and the Problem of False Consciousness

In addition to its role in the political economy, it is important to deal with the university as the backbone of what Mills called 'the cultural apparatus.'[42] He defined this as all those organizations and milieux in which artistic, scientific and intellectual work goes on, as well as the means by which that work is made available to others. Within this apparatus, the various vehicles of communication – language, the mass arts, public arts, and design arts – stand between a man's consciousness and his material existence. At present, the bulk of the apparatus is centralized and controlled by the corporate rulers of America. As a result, their use of the official communications has the effect of limiting our experience and, furthermore, expropriates much of that potential experience that we might have called our own. What we need to understand is that the cultural apparatus, properly used, has the ability both to transform power into authority and transform authority into mere overt coercion.

At present, the university's role in acculturation and socialization is the promulgation of the utter mystification of 'corporate consciousness'. Society is presented to us as a kind of caste system in which we are to see ourselves as a 'privileged elite' – a bureaucratic man channelled into the proper bureaucratic niche. In addition to strengthening the forms of social control off the campus, the administration uses the apparatus on campus to legitimize its own power over us.

On the campus, the student press, underground newspapers,

campus radio and television, literature tables, posters and leaflets, artist and lecture series, theatres, films, and the local press
make up a good part of the non-academic cultural media. Most
of it is both actively and passively being used against us. Any
student power movement should (1) try to gain control of as
much of the established campus cultural apparatus as possible,
(2) if control is not possible, we should try to influence and/or
resist it when necessary and (3) organize and develop a new
counter-apparatus of our own. In short, we need our people on
the staff of the school newspapers, and radio stations. We need
our own local magazines. We need sympathetic contacts on local
off-campus new media. Finally, we all could use some training
in graphic and communicative arts.

What this all adds up to is strengthening our ability to
wage an effective 'de-sanctification' programme against the
authoritarian institutions controlling us. The purpose of de-
sanctification is to strip institutions of their legitimizing
authority, to have them reveal themselves to the people under
them for what they are – raw coercive power. This is the purpose
of singing the Mickey Mouse Club jingle at student government
meetings, of ridiculing and harassing student disciplinary hearings and tribunals, of burning the Dean of Men and/or Women
in effigy. People will not move *against* institutions of power
until the legitimizing authority has been stripped away. On
many campuses this has already happened; but for those remaining, the task remains. And we should be forewarned : it is a
tricky job and often can backfire, de-legitimizing us.

The Correct Handling of Student Governments

While student governments vary in form in the United States,
the objective reasons for their existence are the containment, or
pacification and manipulation of the student body. Very few of
our student governments are autonomously incorporated or have
any powers or rights apart from those sanctioned by the regents
or trustees of the university. Furthermore, most administrations
hold a veto power over anything done by the student governments. Perhaps the worst aspect of this kind of manipulation
and repression is that the administration uses students to con-

trol other students. Most student government politicos are lackeys of the worst sort. That is, they have internalized and embraced all the repressive mechanisms the administration has designed for use *against* them and their fellow students.

With this in mind, it would seem that we should ignore student governments and/or abolish them. While this is certainly true in the final analysis, it is important to relate to student governments differently during the earlier stages of on-campus political struggles. The question we are left with is how do we render student governments ineffective in terms of what they are designed to do, while at the same time using them effectively in building the movement?

Do we work inside the system? Of course we do. The question is not one of working 'inside' or 'outside' the system. Rather, the question is do we play by the established rules? Here, the answer is an emphatic no. The established habits of student politics – popularity contest elections, disguising oneself as a moderate, working for 'better communications and dialogue' with administrators, watering down demands before they are made, going through channels – all of these gambits are stacked against us. If liberal and moderate student politicians really believe in them, then we should tell *them* to try it with all they have. But if they continue to make this ploy after they have learned from their own experience that these methods are dead-ends, then they should be soundly denounced as opportunists or gutless administration puppets.

We should face the fact that student governments are *powerless* and designed to stay that way. From this perspective, all talk about 'getting into power' is so much nonsense. The only thing that student governments are useful for is their ability to be a *temporary vehicle* in building a grass-roots student power movement. This means that student elections are useful as an arena for raising real issues, combating and exposing administration apologists, and involving new people, rather than getting elected. If our people do happen to get elected *as radicals* (this is becoming increasingly possible) then the seats won should be used as a focal point and sounding board for demonstrating the impotence of student government *from within*. A seat should be seen as a soap-box, where our representative can stand, gaining a kind of visibility and speaking to the student body as a whole, over the heads of the other student politicians.

Can anything positive be gained through student government? Apart from publicity, one thing it can be used for is money. Many student-activities funds are open for the kinds of things we would like to see on campus: certain speakers, films, sponsoring conferences. Money, without strings, is always a help. Also, non-political services, such as non-profit used-book exchanges, are helpful to many students. But in terms of radical changes, student government can do nothing apart from a mass, radical student power movement. Even then, student government tends to be a conservative force within those struggles. In the end, meaningful changes can only come through a radical transformation, of both the consciousness of large numbers of students and the forms of student self-government.

Reform or Revolution: What Kinds of Demands?

Fighting for reforms and making a revolution should not be seen as mutually exclusive positions. The question should be: what kind of reforms move us toward a radical transformation of both the university and the society in general? First of all, we should avoid the kinds of reforms which leave the basic rationale of the system unchallenged. For instance, a bad reform to work for would be getting a better grading system, because the underlying rationale – the need for grades at all – remains unchallenged.

Secondly, we should avoid certain kinds of reform that divide students from each other. For instance, trying to win certain privileges for upper classmen but not for freshmen or sophomores. Or trying to establish non-graded courses for students above a certain grade-point average. In the course of campus political activity, the administration will try a whole range of 'divide and rule' tactics such as fostering the 'Greek-Independent Split', sexual double standards, intellectuals *vs* 'jocks', responsible *vs* irresponsible leaders, red-baiting and 'non-student' *vs* students. We need to avoid falling into these traps ahead of time, as well as fighting them when used against us.

Finally, we should avoid all of the 'co-management' kinds of reforms. These usually come in the form of giving certain 'responsible' student leaders a voice or influence in certain decision-making processes, rather than abolishing or winning effective control over those parts of the governing apparatus. One way to counter administration suggestions for setting up 'tripartite' committees (one-third student, one-third faculty, one-third administration, each with an equal number of votes) is to say, 'OK, but once a month the committee must hold an all-university plenary session – one man, one vote.' The thought of being outvoted 1,000–1 will cause administrators to scrap that cooptive measure in a hurry.

We have learned the hard way that the reformist path is full of pitfalls. What, then, are the kinds of reformist measures that do make sense? First of all, there are the civil libertarian issues. We must always fight, dramatically and quickly, for free speech and the right to organize, advocate, and mount political action – of all sorts. However, even here, we should avoid getting bogged down in 'legalitarianism'. We cannot count on this society's legal apparatus to guarantee our civil liberties: and, we should not organize around civil libertarian issues *as if it could*. Rather, when our legal rights are violated, we should move as quickly as possible, without losing our base, to expand the campus libertarian moral indignation into a multi-issues *political* insurgency, exposing the repressive character of the administration and the corporate state in general.

The second kind of partial reform worth fighting for and possibly winning is the abolition of on-campus repressive mechanisms, i.e. student courts, disciplinary tribunals, deans of men and women, campus police, and the use of civil police on campus. While it is true that 'abolition' is a negative reform, and while we will be criticized for not offering 'constructive' criticisms, we should reply that the only constructive way to deal with an inherently destructive apparatus is to destroy it. We must curtail the ability of administrators to repress our *need to refuse* their way of life – the regimentation and bureaucratization of existence.

When our universities are already major agencies for social change in the direction of 1984, our initial demands must, almost of necessity, be negative demands. In this sense, the first task of a student power movement will be the organization of a holding action – a resistance. Along these lines, one potentially effective tactic for resisting the university's disciplinary apparatus would be the forming of a Student Defence League. The purpose of the group would be to make its services available to any student who must appear before campus authorities for infractions of repressive (or just plain stupid) rules and regulations. The defence group would then attend the student's hearings *en masse*. However, for some cases, it might be wise to include law students or local radical lawyers in the group for the purpose of making legal counter-attacks. A student defence group would have three major goals: (1) saving as many students as possible from punishment, (2) de-sanctifying and rendering dysfunctional the administration's repressive apparatus, and (3) using (1) and (2) as tactics in reaching other students for building a movement to abolish the apparatus as a whole.

When engaging in this kind of activity, it is important to be clear in our rhetoric as to what we are about. We are not trying to *liberalize* the existing order, but trying to win our *liberation* from it. We must refuse the administrations' rhetoric of 'responsibility'. To their one-dimensional way of thinking, the concept of responsibility has been reduced to its opposite, namely, be nice, don't rock the boat, do things according to our criteria of what is permissible. In actuality their whole system is geared towards the inculcation of the values of a planned irresponsibility. We should refuse *their* definitions, *their* terms, and even refuse to engage in *their* semantic hassles. We only need to define – *for ourselves and other students* – our notions of what it means to be free, constructive, and responsible. Too many campus movements have been coopted for weeks or even permanently by falling into the administrations' rhetorical bags.

Besides the abolition of repressive disciplinary mechanisms within the university, there are other negative forms that radicals should work for. Getting the military off the campus, abolishing the grade system, and abolishing universal compulsory courses (i.e. physical education) would fit into this category. However, an important question for the student movement is whether or not positive radical reforms can be won within the university short of making a revolution in the society as a whole.

Furthermore, would the achievement of these kinds of partial reforms have the cumulative effect of weakening certain aspects of corporate capitalism, and, in their small way, make that broader revolution more likely?

At present, my feeling is that these kinds of anti-capitalist positive reforms are almost as hard to conceive of intellectually as they are to win. To be sure, there has been a wealth of positive educational reforms suggested by people like Paul Goodman. But are they anti-capitalist as well? For example, we have been able to organize several good Free Universities. Many of the brightest and most sensitive students on American campuses, disgusted with the present state of education, left the campus and organized these counter-institutions. Some of their experiments were successful in an immediate internal sense. A few of these organizers were initially convinced that the sheer moral force of their work in these free institutions would cause the existing educational structure to tremble and finally collapse like a house of IBM cards. But what happened? What effect did the Free Universities have on the established educational order? At best, they had no effect. But it is more likely that they had the effect of strengthening the existing system. How? First of all, the best of our people left the campus, enabling the existing university to function more smoothly, since the 'troublemakers' were gone. Secondly, they gave liberal administrators the rhetoric, the analysis, and sometimes the man-power to coopt their programmes and establish elitist forms of 'experimental' colleges inside of, although quarantined from, the existing educational system. This is not to say that Free Universities should not be organized, both on and off the campus. They can be valuable and useful. But they should not be seen as a primary aspect of a strategy for change.

What then is open to us in the area of positive anti-capitalist reforms? For the most part, it will be difficult to determine whether or not a reform has the effect of being anti-capitalist until it has been achieved. Since it is both difficult and undesirable to attempt to predict the future, questions of this sort are often best answered in practice. Nevertheless, it would seem that the kinds of reforms we are looking for are most likely to be found within a strategy of what I would call 'encroaching control'. There are aspects of the university's administrative, academic, financial, physical, and social apparatus that are potentially, if not actually, useful and productive. While we should try to abolish the repressive mechanisms of the university, our strategy should be to gain control, piece by piece, of its positive aspects.

What would that control look like? To begin with, all aspects of the non-academic life of the campus should either be completely under the control of the students as individuals or embodied in the institutional forms they establish for their collective government. For example, an independent Union of Students should have the final say on the form and content of all university political, social and cultural events. Naturally, individual students and student organizations would be completely free in organizing events of their own.

Second, only the students and the teaching faculty, individually and through their organizations, should control the academic affairs of the university. One example of a worth-while reform in this area would be enabling all history majors and history professors to meet jointly at the beginning of each semester and shape the form, content, and direction of their departmental curriculum. Another partial reform in this area would be enabling an independent Union of Students to hire additional professors of their choice and establish additional accredited course of their choice independently of the faculty or administration.

Finally, we should remember that control should be sought for some specific purpose. One reason we want this kind of power is to enable us to meet the self-determined needs of students and teachers. But another objective that we should see as radicals is to put as much of the university's resources as possible into the hands of the under-class and the working class. We should use campus facilities for meeting the educational needs of insurgent organizations of the poor, and of rank and file workers. Or we could mobilize the universities' research facilities for serving projects established and controlled by the poor and workers, rather than projects established and controlled by the government, management, and labour bureaucrats. The conservative nature of American trade unions makes activity of this sort very difficult, although not impossible. But we should always be careful to make a distinction between the American working class itself and the labour bureaucrats.

The Faculty Question: Allies or Finks?

One question almost always confronts the student movement on the campus. Do we try to win the support of the teaching faculty before we go into action? Or do we lump them together with the administration? What we have learned in the past seems to indicate that both of these responses are wrong. Earlier in this paper, I remarked on the kinds of divisions that exist among the faculty. What is important to see is that this division is not just between good and bad guys. Rather, the faculty is becoming more and more divided in terms of the objective functions of their jobs. To make the hard case on one hand, the function of the lower level of the faculty is to teach – a potentially creative and useful activity; on the other hand, the function of most administrative and research faculty is manipulation, repression, and – for the defence department hirelings – destruction. In general, we should develop our strategies so that our lot falls with the teaching faculty and theirs with ours. As for the research and administrative faculty, we should set both ourselves and the teaching faculty against them. Also, during any student confrontation with the administration, the faculty can do one of four things as a group. They can (1) support the administration, (2) remain neutral, (3) split among themselves, and (4) support us. In any situation, we should favour the development of one of the last three choices rather than the first. Furthermore, if it seems likely that the faculty will split on an issue, we should try to encourage the division indicated above. While it is important to remain open to the faculty, we should not let their support or non-support become an issue in determining whether or not we begin to mount political action. Finally, we should encourage the potentially radical sectors of the faculty to organize among themselves around their own grievances, hoping that they will eventually be able to form a radical alliance with us.

The Vital Issue of Teaching Assistants' Unions

Probably the most exploited and alienated group of people on any campus are the graduate student teaching assistants. The forces of the multiversity hit them from two directions – both as students and as teachers. As students, they have been around long enough to have lost their awe of academia. As faculty, they are given the worst jobs for the lowest pay. For the most part, they have no illusions about their work. Their working conditions, low pay, and the fact that their futures are subject to the whimsical machinations of their department chairmen, make them a group ripe for radical organization. Furthermore, their strategic position within the university structure makes them potentially powerful as a group, if they should decide to organize and strike. If they go out, a large part of the Multiversity comes grinding to a halt. The kinds of demands they are most likely to be organized around naturally connect them with a radical student power movement and with the potentially radical sector of the faculty. Moreover, these considerations make the organization of a radical trade union of TAs a crucial part of any strategy for change. We should see this kind of labour organizing as one of our first priorities in building the campus movement.

Non-academic Employees: On-Campus Labour Organizing

Almost all colleges and especially the multiversities have a large number of blue-collar maintenance workers on campus. Within the state-supported institutions in particular, these people are often forbidden to organize unions, have terrible working conditions, and are paid very low wages. Their presence on the campus offers a unique opportunity for many students to become involved in blue-collar labour organizing at the same time that they are in school. Secondly, since these workers usually live in the surrounding community, their friends and relatives will come from other sectors of the local working class. Quite naturally, they will carry their ideas, opinions, and feelings toward the radical student movement home with them. In this sense, they can be an important link connecting us with other workers, and our help in enabling them to organize a local independent and radical trade union would help tremendously. Finally, if we should ever strike as students, they could be an important ally. For instance, after SDS at the University of Missouri played a major role in organizing a militant group of non-academic employees, they learned that, were the Union to strike for its own demands in sympathy with student demands, the university as a physical plant would cease to function after four days. It is obviously important to have that kind of power.

The Knowledge Machinery and Sabotage: Striking on the Job

One mistake radical students have been making in relating to the worst aspects of the multiversity's academic apparatus has been their avoidance of it. We tend to avoid large classes, lousy courses, and reactionary professors like the plague. At best, we have organized counter-courses outside the classroom and off the campus. My suggestion is that we should do the opposite. Our brightest people should sign up for the large freshman and sophomore sections with the worst professors in strategic courses in history, political science, education, and even the Reserve Officers' Training Corps counter-insurgency lectures. From this position they should then begin to take out their frustrations with the work of the course while they are on the job, i.e. inside the classroom. Specifically, they should constantly voice criticism of the form and content of the course, the size of classes, the educational system, and corporate capitalism in general. Their primary strategy, rather than winning debating points against the professor, should be to reach other students in the class. Hopefully, our on-the-job organizer will begin to develop a radical caucus in the class. This group could then meet outside the class, continue to collectively develop a further radical critique of the future class-work, to be presented at the succeeding sessions. If all goes well with the professor, and perhaps his department as well, they will have a full-scale academic revolt on their hands by the end of the semester. Finally, if this sort of work were being done in a variety of courses at once, the local radical student movement would have the makings of an underground educational movement that was actively engaged in mounting an effective resistance to the educational *status quo*.

Provo Tactics: Radicalization or Sublimation?

There is little doubt that the hippy movement has made its impact on most American campuses. It is also becoming more clear that the culture of advanced capitalist society is becoming more sterile, dehumanized and one-dimensional. It is directed toward a passive mass, rather than an active public. Its root value is consumption. We obviously need a cultural revolution, along with a revolution in the political economy. But the question remains: where do the hippies fit in? At the moment their role seems ambivalent.

On the one hand, they thoroughly reject the dominant culture and seem to be life-affirming. On the other hand, they seem to be for the most part, passive consumers of culture, rather than active creators of culture. For all their talk of community, the nexus of their relations with each other seems to consist only of drugs and a common jargon. With all their talk of love, one finds little deep-rooted passion. Yet, they are there: and they are a major phenomenon. Their relevance to the campus scene is evidenced by the success of the wave of 'Gentle Thursdays' that swept the country. Through this approach, we have been able to reach and break loose a good number of people. Often, during the frivolity of Gentle Thursday, the life-denying aspects of corporate capitalism are brought home to many people with an impact that could never be obtained by the best of all of our anti-war demonstrations.

However, the hippy movement has served to make many of our people withdraw into a personalistic, passive cult of consumption. These aspects need to be criticized and curtailed. We should be clear about one thing: the individual liberation of man, the most social of animals, is a dead-end – an impossibility. And even if individual liberation were possible, would it be desirable? The sublimation of reality within the individual consciousness neither destroys nor transforms the objective reality of other men.

Nevertheless, the excitement and the imagination of some aspects of hippydom can be useful in building critiques of the existing culture. Here, I am referring to the provos and the diggers. Gentle Thursday, when used as a provo (provocative) tactic on campus, can cause the administration to display some of its most repressive characteristics. Even something as blunt as burning a television set in the middle of campus can make a profound statement about the life-styles of many people. However, people engaging in this kind of tactics should (1) not see the action as a substitute for serious revolutionary activity and (2) read up on the Provos and Situationists rather than the Haight-Ashbury scene.

From Soap-box to Student Strikes: the Forms of Protest

During the development of radical politics on the campus, the student movement will pass through a multitude of organizational forms. I have already mentioned several: Student Defence League, Teaching Assistants' Unions, Non-Academic Employees' Unions, and of course, SDS chapters. Another important development on many campuses has been the formation of Black Student Unions, or Afro-American cultural groups. All of these groups are vital, although some are more important than others at different stages of the struggle. However, for the purpose of keeping a radical and multi-issue focus throughout the growth of the movement, it is important to begin work on a campus by organizing an SDS chapter.

From this starting point, how does SDS see its relation to the rest of the campus? I think we have learned that we should not look upon ourselves as an intellectual and political oasis, hugging each other in a waste land. Rather, our chapters should see themselves as organizing committees for reaching out to the majority of the student population. Furthermore, we are organizing for something – the power to effect change. With this in mind, we should be well aware of the fact that the kind of power and changes we would like to have and achieve are not going to be given to us gracefully. Ultimately, we have access to only one source of power within the knowledge factory. And that power lies in our potential ability to stop the university from functioning, to render the system dysfunctional for limited periods of time. Throughout all our on-campus organizing efforts we should keep this one point in mind: that sooner or later we are going to have to strike – or at least successfully threaten to strike.

Because of this, our constant strategy should be the preparation of a mass base for supporting and participating in this kind of action.

What are the organizational forms, other than those mentioned above, that are necessary for the development of this kind of radical constituency? The first kind of extra-SDS organization needed is a Hyde Park or Free Speech Forum. An area of the campus, centrally located and heavily travelled, should be selected and equipped with a public address system. Then, on a certain afternoon one day a week, the platform would be open to anyone to give speeches on anything they choose. SDS people should attend regularly and speak regularly, although they should encourage variety and debate, and not monopolize the platform. To begin, the forum should be weekly, so that students don't become bored with it. Rather, we should try to give it the aura of a special event. Later on, when political activity intensifies, the forum could be held every day. In the early stages, publicity, the establishment of a mood and climate for radical politics is of utmost importance. We should make our presence felt everywhere – in the campus news media, leafletting and poster displays, and regular attendance at the meetings of all student political, social and religious organizations. We should make all aspects of our politics as visible and open as possible.

Once our presence has become known, we can begin to organize on a variety of issues. One arena that it will be important to relate to at this stage will be student government elections. The best organizational form for this activity would be the formation of a Campus Freedom Party for running radical candidates. It is important that the party be clear and open as to its radical consciousness, keeping in mind that our first task is that of building radical consciousness, rather than winning seats. It is also important that the party take positions on off-campus questions as well, such as the war in Vietnam. Otherwise, if we only relate to on-campus issues, we run the risk of laying the counter-revolutionary groundwork for an elitist, conservative and corporatist student movement. As many people as possible should be involved in the work of the party, with SDS people having the function of keeping it militant and radical in a non-manipulative and honest fashion. The party should permeate the campus with speeches, films, and leaflets, as well as a series of solidly intellectual and radical position papers on a variety of issues. Furthermore, we should remember that an election campaign should be fun. Campus Freedom Parties should organize Gentle Thursdays, jug bands, rock groups, theatre groups for political skits, and homemade 8mm. campaign films. Finally, during non-election periods, the Campus Freedom Party should form a variety of CFP *ad hoc* committees for relating to student government on various issues throughout the year.

The next stage of the movement is the most crucial and delicate: the formation of a Student Strike Coordinating Committee. There are two preconditions necessary for its existence. First, there must be a quasi-radical base of some size that has been developed from past activity. Secondly, either a crisis situation provoked by the administration or a climate of active frustration with the administration and/or the ruling class it represents must exist. The frustration should be centred around a set of specific demands that have been unresolved through the established channels of liberal action. If this kind of situation exists, then a strike is both possible and desirable. A temporary steering committee should be set up, consisting of representatives of radical groups (SDS, Black Student Union, TA's Union). This group would set the initial demands, and put out the call for a strike in a few weeks' time. Within that time, they would try to bring in as many other groups and individuals as possible without seriously watering down the demands. This new coalition would then constitute itself as the Student Strike Coordinating Committee, with the new groups adding members to the original temporary steering committee. Also, a series of working committees and a negotiating committee should be established. Finally, the strike committee should attempt to have as many open mass plenary sessions as possible.

What should come out of a student strike? First, the development of a radical consciousness among large numbers of students. Secondly, we should try to include within our demands some issues on which we can win partial victories. Finally, the organizational form that should grow out of a strike or series of strikes is an independent, radical, and political Free Student Union that would replace the existing student government. I have already dealt with the general political life of radical movements. But some points need to be repeated. First of all, a radical student union must be in alliance with the radical sectors of the under-class and working class. Secondly, the student movement has the additional task of radicalizing the subsector of the labour force that some of us in SDS have come to call the new working class. Thirdly, a radical union of students should have an anti-imperialist critique of US foreign policy. Finally, local student unions, if they are to grow and thrive, must become federated on regional, national, and international levels. However, we should be careful not to form a national union of students lacking in a grass-roots constituency that actively and democratically participates in all aspects of the organization's life. One NSA is enough. On the international level, we should avoid both the CIA and Soviet Union sponsored International Unions. We would be better off to establish informal relations with groups like the Zengakuren in Japan, the German SDS, the French Situationists, the Spanish Democratic Student Syndicate, and the Third World revolutionary student organizations. Hopefully, in the not too distant future, we may be instrumental in forming a new International Union of Revolutionary Youth. And even greater tasks remain to be done before we can begin to build the conditions for human liberation.

REFERENCES

1. Marx: *Theses on Feuerbach.*
2. *New York Times*, 29 November 1964.
3. Kerr, Clark, *Uses of the University*, p. 103.
4. ibid., p. 101.
5. Baran and Sweezy, *Monopoly Capital.*
6. Golin, Steve, *New Left Notes*, 7 October 1966, p. 3.
7. Mills, C. Wright, *Power Politics and People*, p. 368.
8. Conant, James, *Slums and Suburbs*, p. 77.
9. Rickover, Human, *Education and Freedom*, p. 145.
10. Conant, James, *Slums and Suburbs*, p. 34.
11. Smith, Mortimer, *The Diminished Mind*, p. 87.
12. Hannah, John, Speech given at Parents' Convocation at Michigan State University, September 1961.
13. Hannah, John, 'The Schools' Responsibility in National Defense', 5 May 1955, quoted in *The Paper*, 17 November 1966, p. 1.

14. Conant, James, *Bulletin of the Council for Basic Education*, January 1960, p. 3.
15. Kerr, Clark, *Uses of the University*, p. 87.
16. 'Capitalist Relations of Production and the Socially Necessary Labour Force', No. 10, August 1965, p. 423.
17. ibid., p. 428.
18. ibid., p. 428.
19. Friedenberg, Edgar Z., *Nation*, 20 September 1965, p. 72.
20. ibid.
21. Kerr, Clark, 'Industrialism and Industrial Man', quoted in *The Mind of Clark*, in Draper, Hal (ed.), *Berkeley: The New Student Revolt*, p. 211.
22. ibid.
23. Hoare, Quintin, 'Education: Programs and Men', *New Left Review* No. 32, pp. 50–1.
24. Kerr, Clark, *Uses of the University*, p. 90.
25. ibid., p. 86.
26. Beck, H.P., quoted in Aptheker, Bettina, *Big Business and the American University*, p. 7.
27. 'The Innovation Industry', *Monthly Review*, July–August 1959.
28. Jencks, Christopher, 'The Future of American Education', *The Radical Papers*, p. 271.
29. Mills, C. Wright, *The Sociological Imagination*, p. 117.
30. Mills C. Wright, *Power, Politics and People*, p. 417.
31. Kerr, Clark, *Uses of the University*.
32. ibid., p. 53.
33. 'Capitalist Relations of Production and The Socially Necessary Labour Force', No. 10, August 1965, p. 423.
34. Kerr, Clark, *Uses of the University*, pp. 89–90.
35. Gorz, André, 'Capitalism and the Labour Force', *International Socialist Journal*, p. 418.
36. Jencks, Christopher, 'The Future of American Education', *The Radical Papers*.
37. Kerr, Clark, *Uses of the University*, p. 111.
38. Gorz, André, *Strategy for Labour*, p. 108.
39. Gorz, André, 'Capitalism and the Labour Force', *International Socialist Journal*, p. 422.
40. Gorz, André, *Strategy for Labour*, p. 107.
41. Guevara, Ernest 'Che', *Guerrilla Warfare*.
42. Mills, C. Wright, *Power, Politics and People*, p. 386.

Acknowledgement: we thank the Students for a Democratic Society for permission to reprint Carl Davidson's piece, which they originally issued as a pamphlet.

Documents

On Revolution/Herbert Marcuse – Interview

FIRST QUESTION: It is said that Marx's concept of revolution, will not stand up to the new facts of industrial society. It has become an anchronism; it no longer has any constituency. The working class, in Marx's opinion the historical subject of all future social upheavals, has dissolved itself *as a class*; the desire to establish a qualitatively different social order has given way to the need for better working conditions, more leisure time and more material goods. In these circumstances, the old theory of revolution, which articulated the economic misery of one class and taught the oppressed to speak, has become impotent and unrealistic; it has turned its back on reality. Anyone talking of revolution nowadays is surely contributing to a mystification?

MARCUSE: The idea of revolution is in fact never a 'mystification'. As a whole the existing situation has always been bad: a force resisting the real possibilities of overcoming misery and inhumanity. The fact that revolution no longer has any identifiable 'constituency' and no organized movement on which it could depend does not remove its necessity. But does it really have no 'constituency' today? Neither the ideological veil of pluralist democracy nor the material veil of extravagant productivity alters the fact that in the realm of advanced capitalism the fate of man is determined by the aggressive and expansive apparatus of exploitation and the policies interwoven with it. The civic rights that are permitted and administered in this system of domination do not diminish the violence of an oppression which has made the world a hell. At the moment hell is concentrated on the battlefields of Vietnam and the other sacrificial lands of neo-colonialism. Of course humanity is concentrated there too: not immediately, in the guerrilla struggles, which meet the horror of the conqueror with the horror of defence, but, via many mediations, in the opportunity to define the inner limit of the system given to those who in their extreme poverty and weakness have for years now kept the richest and technologically most developed destructive machine of all time in check. I say 'inner' limit because there is no longer any outer limit to the global system of advanced capitalism; because even the development of the socialist countries, despite all the contrast in their relations of production, responds to the pressure of world competition and the needs of coexistence. But any romantic idea of the liberation front is incorrect. Guerrilla struggle as such does not present any mortal threat to the system: in the long run it cannot resist a technological 'Final Solution'. The system reserves for itself the right to decree whether and when it will achieve 'victory' by burning and poisoning everything. The 'Final Solution' in Vietnam would be the final consolidation of the power of capital, which would further extend its interests with the help of dictatorships of the military and of property, and would force the socialist countries into an increasingly debilitating defence (or into powerless neutrality).

This tendency can only be broken if the resistance of the victims of neo-colonialism finds support in the 'affluent society' itself, in the metropolis of advanced capitalism and in the weaker capitalist countries whose independence is threatened by the metropolis. (I will come back to the opposition in the metropolis in my answer to question 4.) In any case, in the capitalist countries of the European continent the pre-condition for the efficacy of a serious opposition remains the political revitalization of the working-class movement on an international scale.

SECOND QUESTION: One of the striking aspects of our time is the gradual mutual convergence of capitalism and socialism. In both systems advanced industrialization has altered the social process and the methods of production. To the extent that technology determines the course of things and the social relationships of men, relations of domination can still be defined only in technological terms. Power lies with the apparatus which administers social labour and organizes its adaptation: domination, translated into manipulation, can hardly be recognized any more as political and economic domination. Each person acts in good faith, from his own desire to act in response to general pressures. The conception of freedom, by which revolutionaries and revolutions were inspired, has, so it seems, been taken out of circulation in modern capitalist *and* socialist states. Has the concept of freedom finally lost its revolutionary force in the 'managed mass society'?

MARCUSE: The 'gradual mutual convergence of capitalism and socialism' has found its expression in the cliché concept of the 'technological society' or the 'developed industrial society'. The usual indignant criticism of this concept is itself ideological. It should no longer be necessary to emphasize that it is not technique, but the social organization of the productive forces that determines the difference between social systems. But it appears necessary to repeat that the abolition of private ownership of the means of production and collective control of them does not finalize this difference, particularly when this control is exercised by a working class whose needs and aspirations are dominated by imitation of and adaptation to needs engendered by the capitalist system. Coexistence with advanced capitalism is driving the socialist societies into a life and death competition – into a competition in which the development of the productive forces and of social needs is to a large extent subordinated to politico-diplomatic and military exigencies. Thus, here as well as there, technique is becoming a means of oppression built into the process of production. As such, technique, which has not yet been turned into a means of liberation, prescribes definite modes of conduct within and in relation to the apparatus of domination – here as well as there. Nevertheless, it remains the case that the opportunity for liberation lies where the means of production have been socialized. The political economy of the socialist countries needs peace, not aggressive expansion.

But technological and political competition in the development of the forces of production produces yet another tendency which appears still more pernicious for the future. The present international constellation is leading to an opposition of interests between the 'old' stabilized, technologically advanced and industrialized socialist countries on the one hand and the 'new' and poorer ones on the other. The former are moving into the category of possessors; the revolutionary Communism of the poor on the other side of the border may well appear to them as a new 'revolution from below' and thus as a danger. Not to them alone, of course. For the 'affluent society' also senses danger here: for a long time the American 'struggle against Communism' has become a struggle against the Communism of the poorest.

If it is the case that the 'conception of freedom, by which revolutionaries and revolutions were inspired', is suppressed in the developed industrial countries with their rising standard of living, then it is all the more acute and open where the suppressed are rebelling against the system. It is here that the revolutionary concept of freedom coincides with the necessity to defend naked existence: in Vietnam as much as in the slums and ghettoes of the rich countries.

THIRD QUESTION: In contemporary industrial society the economy is no longer the basis of political decisions, but is itself a function of politics. Economic processes are more obviously under political control now than 50 years ago. In this a new, and long unfamiliar, form of totalitarianism is emerging. Social theory seems not to have adapted to this state of affairs: it slavishly adheres to its own categories and leaves the facts to themselves. It seems that practice has broken with ideas. Can the contemporary development of society still be interpreted with concepts like 'alienation', 're-ification', 'exploitation', 'minimum subsistence level' and 'pauperization'?

MARCUSE: It is not correct to say that 'in contemporary industrial society the economy is *no longer* the basis of political decisions, but is itself a function of politics'. In the *narrow* 'economic' sense, the economy was never the basis. Today too it is 'political economy': the process of production and distribution is largely determined by politics and is itself a determinant of a politics which is dominated by the great oligopolistic interests (they are by no means always in harmony). And the political opinion and position of producers and consumers is more than ever an economic factor: it is an element in the process of exchange, in the buying and selling of labour power, in the marketing of commodities. One must be 'all right' politically to be able to compete in business, in the office and in the factory. Political propaganda and commercial advertisements coincide. The political economy of advanced capitalism is also a 'psychological economy': it produces and administers the needs demanded by the system – even the instinctive needs. It is this introjection of domination combined with the increasing satisfaction of needs that casts doubt on concepts like alienation, re-ification and exploitation. Is the beneficiary of the 'affluent society' not in fact 'fulfilling' himself in his alienated being? Does he not, in fact, find himself again in his gadgets, his car and television set? But on the other hand, does false subjectivity dispose of the objective state of affairs?

FOURTH QUESTION: In an essay in 1965 you put forward the thesis that capitalism has succeeded in bringing its contradictions into a 'manipulable form'; it has absorbed the 'revolutionary potential'. Does this mean that under the given conditions it is impossible to combine critical theory and political practice? In other words, what does 'revolutionary' mean in the context of a society that has, without violence, suppressed the thought of revolution and the need for it?

MARCUSE: The manipulation of the contradictions of advanced capitalism has its own dynamic, whose explosive force is today active in the escalation of the war in Vietnam and in the expansion of American capital into Europe, South America and Asia. It is senseless to see in this tendency the seeds of an armed conflict between the capitalist powers: common interest *vis-à-vis* the common enemy forces the rivals together. But within the nations particular interests are insisting on resistance to American capital; national independence is again becoming a progressive factor. A retreat by American capital – combined with the unemployment created by increasing automation – could lead to serious shocks; it would undermine the unification of antagonistic forces in the USA. It is possible that neo-fascist tendencies would then triumph and that the majority of the organized workers would follow them or remain neutral; it is, however, also possible that opposition would grow and organize itself.

In this situation the opposition of American youth could have a political effect. This opposition is free from ideology or permeated with a deep distrust of all ideology (including socialist ideology); it is sexual, moral, intellectual and political rebellion all in one. In this sense it is total, directed against the system as a whole: it is disgust at the 'affluent society', it is the vital need to break the rules of a deceitful and bloody game – to stop cooperating any more. If these young people detest the prevailing system of needs and its ever increasing mass of goods, this is because they observe and know how much sacrifice, how much cruelty and stupidity contribute every day to the reproduction of the system. These young people no longer share the repressive need for the blessings and security of domination – in them perhaps a new consciousness is appearing, a new type of person with another instinct for reality, life and happiness; they have a feeling for a freedom that has nothing to do with, and wants nothing to do with, the freedom practised in senile society. In short, here is the 'determinate negation' of the prevailing system, but it is without effective organization and is in itself incapable of exercising decisive political pressure. Only in alliance with the forces who are resisting the system 'from without' can such an opposition become a new avant-garde; if it remains isolated it runs the risk of falling victim to inoculation and thus to the system itself.

Interview by *Günther Busch*

Acknowledgement. Günther Busch's interview with Herbert Marcuse was originally published Kursbuch 9, *Suhrkamp Verlag.*

Why Sociologists?/Daniel Cohn-Bendit, Jean-Pierre Duteuil, Bertrand Gérard, Bernard Granautier

We will consider here only the dominant tendencies in contemporary sociology. This must be followed up by more detailed studies: *all boycotts of courses to help us in this are welcome.*

Sociology must be looked at from a historical angle. The crucial date from this point of view is 1930, the date of Mayo's experiment in the Hawthorne factory.

In showing the importance of affective phenomena in small groups, and in suggesting that human relations should be regulated in order to improve the productivity of workers, Mayo did much more than open a new field of sociology. He closed the epoch of social philosophy and speculative systems concerning the society as a whole, and opened the glorious era of empiricism and of 'scientific' data-collection. At the same time, in selling his services to the management of an enterprise, Mayo initiated the age of the large-scale collaboration of sociologists with all of the powers of the bourgeois world – which was then hard put to rationalize a capitalist system strongly shaken by the crisis of 1929.

The transition from an academic sociology, the vassal of philosophy, to an independent sociology, with scientific pretensions, corresponds to the transition from competitive capitalism to organized capitalism.

Henceforth, the rise of sociology is increasingly tied to the social demand for rationalized practice in the service of bourgeois ends: money, profit, the maintenance of order.

The proofs are abundant: industrial sociology seeks, above all, the adaptation of the worker to his work: the inverse

EDITORIAL NOTE: The group of Nanterre students and junior teachers which prepared this pamphlet later helped to found the 22 March Movement. The critique presented by the pamphlet was part of the theoretical preparation for the momentous actions which were to follow.

perspective is very rare because the sociologist, paid by the management, must respect the goals of the economic system: to produce the most possible in order to make the most money possible. Political sociology plans huge studies – most often mystifying – which presuppose that electoral choice is, today, the locus of politics, never asking whether that locus might be elsewhere. Stouffer studies the optimal conditions of the American soldier's morale, without posing the structural problems of the role of the army in the society in which he lives. One finds sociologists in advertising, in the thousand forms of consumer conditioning, in the experimental study of media – there too without attempting to criticize the social function of these media.

On the other hand, how do US sociologists conceive the central problem of social classes? The concept of class, and that of 'discontinuity' (class struggle) are eliminated and replaced by notions of classes and of strata which have status, power and prestige. In this conception, there is a continuous scale in which to each step corresponds a definite quantity of power and of prestige, in increasing stages as one approaches the summit. And, of course, each individual is presumed to have, from the outset, the same chance to climb the pyramid, since we are (here, as everywhere) in a democracy. Besides the theoretical refutations of Mills and D. Riesman, the practical refutation of the sub-proletariat (the ethnic minorities) in the USA, and those of certain workers' groups against their union apparatus, are enough to dispel the dream of an achieved integration.

Just recently, the riots of Black Americans created such a fear that supplementary credits were voted to sociologists so that they could study the movements of mobs and furnish recipes for repression.

Finally – bitter irony! – when the US Secretary of Defense, Mr MacNamara, launched an anti-subversive project in Latin America (the infamous Project Camelot), he could imagine no better way to disguise it than calling it a 'sociological' study-project. . . .

And in France?

The rationalization of capitalism began, certainly, after the war (with the creation of planning), but only became effective with Gaullism and its authoritarian structures. It is not by chance that the 'degree' in sociology was created in 1958. The unequal development of French capitalism compared to US capitalism is seen too on the level of ideas: all current sociology in France is imported from the US, with a few years' delay. Everyone knows that the most esteemed sociologists are those who follow most attentively the American publications.

Sociological 'Theory'

We have seen sociology's tight connexion with social demand. The practice of organizing capitalism creates a mass of contradictions; and for each particular case, a sociologist is put to work. One studies juvenile delinquency, another racism, a third the slums. Each seeks an explanation of his partial problem and elaborates a 'theory' proposing solutions to the limited conflict that he studies. Thus, while serving as a 'watchdog' our sociologist will make his contribution at the same time to the 'mosaic' of sociological 'theories'.

The confusion of the social sciences, which has its source here, can be seen in the interdisciplinary approach so fashionable today (cf. the critique by Louis Althusser). The uncertainty of each specialist when confronted with the uncertainties of other specialists, can only give rise to immense platitudes.

Behind this confusion lies the absence, never stressed, of a theoretical status for sociology and the social sciences. Their only point in common is finally that they constitute 'for the most part methodological techniques of social adaptation and readaptation', not to mention the re-integration of all forms of contestation: the majority of all our sociologists are 'Marxists'. We can mention, in support of our argument the conservative character of concepts currently in use: hierarchy, ritual, integration, social function, social control, equilibrium, and so on. The 'theoreticians' must explain localized conflicts without reference to the social totality which provoked them.

This supposedly objective procedure implies *partial* perspectives (in both senses of the word) in which phenomena are not connected (but, racism, unemployment, delinquency and the slums constitute a unity), and where the rationality of the economic system is taken as given. The word profit having become shocking, one now speaks of growth, of adaptation to a 'changed reality'. But, where does this change lead? Whence does it come? Who organizes it? Who profits from it? Are such questions too speculative to be of interest to science?

These considerations lead us to conclude, simply, that the unrest of sociology students cannot be understood unless one questions the social function of sociology. It appears that, in the present conflicts, the sociologists have chosen their camp – that of business managements and of the State which assists them. In these conditions, what does the 'defence of sociology' recommended by some really mean?

The Case of Nanterre

The preceding general analysis illuminates the particular case of Nanterre. There too: crisis in sociology, uneasiness about careers, confusion in the teaching, and importations of 'theories' made in USA. Those who remain outside the positivist-empiricist current are led to retreat into a verbal critique which has the merit of avoiding a total 'one-dimensionalization', but which confirms isolation and impotence.

Among the 'hopefuls' of French sociology, Parsonian jargon and the cult of statistics (at last! a scientific field) are the key to all problems. The study of society has managed the *tour de force* of depoliticizing all teaching – that is to say, in legitimizing the existing politics. And all of this is joined to a fruitful collaboration with the ministers and technocrats seeking to form their cadres. Our professors, it is true, are considered 'leftists', compared with those flourishing in other departments who yearn nostalgically for the old days. The reason is that these latter give up with regret the mandarinate of the university established by liberal capitalism, whereas the sociologists know where the 'change' is leading: *organization, rationalization, production of human commodities made to order for the economic needs of organized capitalism.*

It is here necessary to refute the conceptions defended by Professor M. Crozier (*Esprit*, January 1968) and Professor A. Touraine (*Le Monde*, 7 and 8 March 1968) about the debates which now concern us. For Crozier, American unrest does not

reside – as some naïve persons would think – in the violence of
the Negroes, pushed to the limit by the conditions of their life,
or in the horror of the imperialist war in Vietnam (that 'accident', that 'folly', as Crozier puts it – one had thought him
more attached to scientific explanation than to magic words).
Neither is it found in the dissolution of all values, as they cede
their place to exchange value, to money. No, this exists, but it is
only an appearance. Violence has always existed in the USA.
What is new, Crozier tells us, is the invasion of rationalism. It is
the change of mentality necessary to familiarize oneself with the
'world of abstract reasoning'. Present history is not a real
struggle between social groups fighting for material interests and
different socio-economic priorities. It is the field in which two
fantasmagoric entities confront one another: rationalism in the
service of growth versus the irresponsible anarchy of those who
are frightened by change. This 'sociological' version is not
worth the trouble of refutation, save for the probable ideological
importance it contains. For Crozier counsels the Blacks not to
demand power, but to undergo 'an intellectual mutation' (sic!),
all of which leads to the Grand Celebration of the American
Way of Life, which, today, produces new, creative and dynamic
individuals.

In his recent articles, Touraine has presented the following
conception: there exists a university system whose function is
to produce knowledge in the service of growth (again!). Changing this system depends on the fruitful contradiction which it
contains between students and professors. The university, in its
conflicts and its essential social function, is analogous to nineteenth-century business enterprise.

But it is false to oppose the nineteenth and twentieth centuries. It is not true 'that knowledge and technical progress are
the motors of the new society'. Knowledge and technical progress
are subordinated to the struggles between firms for profit (or,
which is the same, for monopolistic hegemony), and to the
military and economic confrontation between East and West.
Scientists are not the innocent entrepreneurs that they are made
out to be, nor is science that glorious autonomous activity which
seeks only its proper development.

The unit of reference, the university, is not viable. The contraditions occur on the level of society as a whole, and the university is implicated in them. The majority of professors and students are committed to the preservation of order, and only a minority have taken part in the struggle which is developing in the imperialist countries and in the exploited countries. The recent motion of student groups here at Nanterre (not at all upset by their own servility) in support of the administration and the majority of the teaching corps, is the latest evidence.

Possibilities and Limits of Student Struggle

Within the university, the perspectives are limited: the essential thing to do is to enlighten the rest of the students on the social function of the university. Especially in sociology, it is necessary to unmask the false arguments, throw light on the generally repressive meaning of a career in sociology, and to dispel illusions on this subject.

The hypocrisy of objectivity, of apoliticism, of the innocence of study, is much more flagrant in the social sciences than elsewhere, and must be exposed.

An intellectual minority remains totally inefficacious if it submits to, or even becomes complacent in, the ghetto prepared for it.

While waiting for other actions, we will carry this debate to the conference of 'defence' of sociologists, which should take place before Easter.

Daniel COHN-BENDIT
Jean-Pierre DUTEUIL
Bertrand GÉRARD
Bernard GRANAUTIER

More about Penguins

Penguin Book News, which appears every month, contains details of all the new books issued by Penguins as they are published. From time to time it is supplemented by *Penguins in Print* – a complete list of all our available titles. (There are well over three thousand of these.)

A specimen copy of *Penguin Book News* will be sent to you free on request, and you can become a subscriber for the price of the postage – 4s. for a year's issues (including the complete lists). Just write to Dept E P, Penguin Books Ltd, Harmondsworth, Middlesex, enclosing a cheque or postal order, and your name will be added to the mailing list.

Some other books published by Penguins are described on the following pages.

Note: *Penguin Books News* and *Penguins in Print* are not available in the U.S.A. or Canada

Revolution in the Revolution?

Régis Debray

'Régis Debray has been arrested by the Bolivian authorities, not for having participated in guerrilla activities, but for having written a book – *Revolution in the Revolution?*'
– Jean-Paul Sartre

'The most interesting and relevant piece of Marxist theoretical writing that has appeared for some time'
– *Guardian*

'Debray's intellectual importance stems from his being one of the few major theorists . . . to analyse what seems to be becoming the Third World's dominant pattern of social revolution' – *Ramparts*

'His book is of tremendous importance' – *New York Review of Books*

'Deserves to be read even by those who do not share Mr Debray's views!' – Graham Greene

Not for sale in the U.S.A. or Canada

The Dialectics of Liberation

Edited by David Cooper

The Congress of the Dialectics of Liberation, held in London in 1967, was a unique expression of the politics of modern dissent, in which existential psychiatrists, Marxist intellectuals, anarchists and political leaders met to discuss – and to constitute – the key social issues of the next decade. Amongst others Stokely Carmichael spoke on Black Power, Herbert Marcuse on liberation from the affluent society, R. D. Laing on social pressures and Paul Sweezy on the future of capitalism. In exploring the roots of violence in society the speakers analysed personal alienation, repression and student revolution. They then turned to the problems of liberation – of physical and cultural 'guerrilla warfare' to free man from mystification, from the blind destruction of his environment, and from the inhumanity which he projects onto his opponents in family situations, in wars and in racial conflict. The aim of the congress was to create a genuine revolutionary consciousness by fusing ideology and action on the levels of the individual and of mass society. These speeches clearly indicate the rise of a new, forceful and (to some) ominous style of political activity.

Not for sale in the U.S.A.

Prague Spring

A Report on Czechoslovakia 1968

Z. A. B. Zeman

The dramatic stand of the Czechs in July and August 1968 concentrated the attention of the whole world – West, East, and uncommitted – as no event had done since the Cuban missile crisis in 1962.

The world was able to watch the Russian invasion on its TV screens. But the crucial events which made these scenes almost inevitable had taken place, largely unreported, long before. Dr Zeman travelled widely in Czechoslovakia in spring and summer 1968 and talked to politicians, officials, intellectuals, workers and party men. In this book he tells the dramatic story of the intellectual and economic ferment which opposed, eroded, and finally decisively toppled the Stalinist regime of President Novotný in 1967 and early 1968. He describes how a Stalinist dictatorship with an apathetic and hostile population was transformed in nine months or so into a country in which nothing was closed to discussion, an intense and enthusiastic dialogue between governors and governed was able to develop, and new members from all classes flocked to join the Party.

The story of this transformation is one of the most important in world politics since the beginning of the 1950s. Its excitement is irresistible. Its significance will certainly pervade the next decade.

French Revolution 1968

Patrick Seale and Maureen McConville

In early 1968 rioting students brought one of Europe's
most successful post-war governments to its knees and
galvanized sections of the working class for a spontaneous
Marxist revolution. Weeks later a tidal wave of outraged
propriety had swept the students from the Sorbonne and
drowned the official Left in a crushing pro-government
poll of which even a totalitarian regime could be proud.
What was Paris like, day by day, in those weeks of crisis?
What is the truth about C.R.S. terror-tactics in the vicious
street-battles which shook the capital? Why are students
so hostile to the Communist Party? Do they have a
coherent message for the future? Above all, why should
this revolution occur in a twentieth-century society which
was thought by many to have grown sedate and
respectable?

As correspondents for the *Observer* Patrick Seale and
Maureen McConville observed from the inside the tactics
and strategies on both sides of the barricades. From
conversations and vivid eye-witness reports they have
constructed a trenchant analysis of the roots of the crisis,
its hectic course and its implications for France and
the western world.

Not for sale in the U.S.A.